Keywords for African American Studies

MW00465261

# Keywords for African American Studies

Edited by

Erica R. Edwards, Roderick A. Ferguson, and Jeffrey O. G. Ogbar

NEW YORK UNIVERSITY PRESS  New York

NEW YORK UNIVERSITY PRESS
New York
www.nyupress.org

References to Internet websites (URLs) were accurate at the time of writing. Neither the author nor New York University Press is responsible for URLs that may have expired or changed since the manuscript was prepared.

Library of Congress Cataloging-in-Publication Data
Names: Edwards, Erica R. (Erica Renee), editor. |
Ferguson, Roderick A., editor. | Ogbar, Jeffrey Ogbonna Green, editor.
Title: Keywords for African American studies / edited by
Erica R. Edwards, Roderick A. Ferguson, and Jeffrey O.G. Ogbar.
Description: New York: New York University Press, 2018. |
Includes bibliographical references and index.
Identifiers: LCCN 2018021500| ISBN 9781479852833 (cl: alk. paper) |
ISBN 9781479854899 (pb: alk. paper)
Subjects: LCSH: African Americans—Research. | Sociolinguistics. |
Information retrieval.
Classification: LCC E184.7 .K49 2018 | DDC 306.440896/073—dc23
LC record available at https://lccn.loc.gov/2018021500

New York University Press books are printed on acid-free paper, and their binding materials are chosen for strength and durability. We strive to use environmentally responsible suppliers and materials to the greatest extent possible in publishing our books.

Manufactured in the United States of America

10 9 8 7 6 5 4 3 2 1

Also available as an ebook

# Contents

# Introduction

Erica R. Edwards, Roderick A. Ferguson, and
Jeffrey O. G. Ogbar

When Raymond Williams embarked on his famous *Keywords: A Vocabulary of Culture and Society*, it was to document a major transformation in collective values and interests in the post–World War II world. This was a world in flux, in which the meanings of culture were undergoing a swift change and in which, perhaps more importantly, terms that had circulated almost exclusively in the specialized domains of academic fields were circulating beyond university discourses. *Keywords*, then, was an attempt "to understand several urgent contemporary problems—problems quite literally of understanding [the] contemporary world" (Raymond Williams 1983, 13). What it offered was "not the specialized vocabulary of a specialized discipline . . . but a general vocabulary," a collection of words in everyday circulation, words that were used "to discuss many of the central processes of our common life" (14). In the tradition of Williams's paradigmatic text and the several academic *Keywords* texts that have been issued in recent years by NYU Press, *Keywords for African American Studies* explores the terms, categories, and concepts that delineate the contours of Black studies as an intellectual imaginary and as an experimental project within the U.S. academy. Rather than a definitive or exemplary text defining the boundaries of this scholarly field, this book is evidence of a generative process that we hope will further an ongoing conversation about the potentials and limits of our African American studies vocabulary.

This volume collates the words that have hovered under the surface of our conversations in and about African American studies as well as the terms that have circulated in our classrooms, conference panels, and publications. Cataloguing keywords as an intellectual practice has served as a way of expanding and undoing assumptions about knowledge and power as those categories operate on our everyday lives. And while the keyword as a form of knowledge has become so popular in academic work that it has nearly exhausted its novelty (the American Studies Association hosted a session titled "Kill That Keyword" at its 2014 annual convention, for example), it remains a genre of knowledge production that, in its portability and density, both moves with interdisciplinary fields of knowledge and serves as a record of that movement: *How* do words move? *Whom* do words move? As Meta DuEwa Jones illuminates in her entry on "Poetics" in this volume, if the keyword is traditionally known as a "key to a cipher or code," Black studies turns the keyword into an active process that not only uses words to clarify but also uses words to encode messages of liberation. "Cipher," she writes, "is a verb: actively subversive coding."

The keyword is a form, a genre, of knowledge production that accomplishes at least three relevant tasks. First, it serves as a mode of interrogation, prompting us to take stock of the language we use and the ways it has changed over the decades of this field's formalization.

Second, it makes the work of professional researchers and teachers accessible to laypersons: students, activists, intellectuals, and other individuals and collectivities both within and outside the circle of universities and scholarly publishing. Third, it is a record of change over time; over the more than forty years since the field of African American studies' institutionalization in formal academic units and degree-granting programs, the words here—think, for example, of the word "race" or the word "post-race"—reflect both the nuanced shifts in analysis that result from a long-term evolution of an interdisciplinary scholarly discourse and the speedy erection of a new vocabulary occasioned when our scholarship adapts to dramatic turns in public discourse. This book is an attempt at cataloguing and interrogating that movement of words through time and space.

## Our Approach

This book is an active inquiry into the vocabulary that circulates to describe, and at times circumscribe, Black culture and society in the contemporary world, particularly in the United States. Although African American studies—what Russell Adams refers to as "the intellectual and empathetic treatment of a totality of phenomena" involving Black people (1977, 99)—began to be officially institutionalized in American universities in 1968, its expression in its "off-campus" instantiations dates back at least to the days of the early U.S. republic. It has since then been a project of survival aimed at documenting the vitalities of Black collectivities and cultures, what June Jordan called "Life Studies"; at the same time, it has served as what Christina Sharpe has more recently referred to as wake work: the labor we undertake to "tend to, care for, comfort, and defend the dead, the dying, and those living lives consigned, in the aftermath of legal chattel slavery, to death that is always-imminent and immanent" (J. Jordan 1981, 55; Sharpe 2014, 59–60).

*Keywords for African American Studies* exposes the problem of Black life as a problem for vocabulary. When Du Bois begins his landmark *The Souls of Black Folk*, he exposes keywor*ding* as a problem for a problem people, a problem for living and a problem for study:

> Between me and the other world there is ever an unasked question: unasked by some through feelings of delicacy; by others through the difficulty of rightly framing it. All, nevertheless, flutter round it. They approach me in a half-hesitant sort of way, eye me curiously or compassionately, and then, instead of saying directly, How does it feel to be a problem? they say, I know an excellent colored man in my town; or, I fought at Mechanicsville; or, Do not these Southern outrages make your blood boil? At these I smile, or am interested, or reduce the boiling to a simmer, as the occasion may require. (1903, 2)

If to be Black in America is to provoke the ever-*unasked* question, it is also to live in the silence of the ever-*unanswered* question. Du Bois writes, "To the real question, How does it feel to be a problem? I answer seldom a word" (2). The process of keywording, because of the violence of America—violence our work is implicated in—is both necessary and fraught with its own limits. *Keywords for African American Studies* is, then, both necessary and riddled with the problems of unspeakability. Du Bois turns to these specific problems—the problems that Black living in an age of American imperial expansion presents for Black study—in "Science and Empire," an essay in the 1940 volume *Dusk of Dawn: An Essay toward the Autobiography of a Race Concept*. There Du Bois writes first of his sixteen years as an ambitious sociology professor. Du

Bois's interest in "race contact" clarified his vision of "the whirl of events which swept the world on": Japan's rise through the Chinese and Russian wars, the colonization of Africa by European powers, the U.S.'s annexation of Hawai'i and Puerto Rico, and the construction of the Panama Canal ([1940] 2014, 27). To interpret this swirl of imperialism, Du Bois retreated to "the ivory tower of race" until he was able, following Booker T. Washington's 1895 speech at the Atlanta Cotton Exposition, to synthesize his analyses of race and political economy (28). Importantly, the course of intellectual development was interrupted by the omnipresence, the "red ray," as he describes it, of Black death on display, on the market:

> At the very time when my studies were most successful, there cut across this plan which I had as a scientist, a red ray which could not be ignored. I remember when it first, as it were, startled me to my feet; a poor Negro in central Georgia, Sam Hose, had killed his landlord's wife. I wrote out a careful and reasoned statement concerning the evident facts and started down to the Atlanta Constitution office, carrying in my pocket a letter of introduction to Joel Chandler Harris. I did not get there. On the way news met me; Sam Hose had been lynched, and they said that his knuckles were on exhibition at a grocery store farther down on Mitchell Street, along which I was walking. I turned back to the University. I began to turn aside from my work. (34)

Nahum Chandler describes the lynching of Sam Hose as "the mark for the bearing of a whole era in the life course, not only of a scholar, researcher, thinker, and writer, but of a self-reflexively identified people" (2014, 18n.2). Indeed, we might hear the echo of Du Bois's lament in James Baldwin's *No Name in the Street*, in which he writes, "This book has been much delayed by trials, assassinations, funerals, and despair" (2007, 196), or in Christina Sharpe's *In the Wake: On Blackness and Being*, which opens with a meditation on the relationship between Black death and intellectual labor: "I wasn't there when my sister died. I was in Chicago at the Cultural Studies Association meeting and I was finishing the paper that was my first attempt at the work that became this book" (2016, 1). The press of Black premature death on work—on words—is visible across our vocabulary. Even this volume, an attempt to provide a "snapshot" of that living vocabulary, was delayed by the deaths of friends, family members, and colleagues.

On the other hand, African American studies has flourished in its capacity to generate new terms of existence in the face of conditions of death. Book publications have been vital tools for archiving these terms. Monographs such as Frantz Fanon's *The Wretched of the Earth*, Cedric Robinson's *Black Marxism*, Molefi Asante's *Afrocentricity*, Stokely Carmichael (now Kwame Ture) and Charles V. Hamilton's *Black Power*, Addison Gayle's *The Black Aesthetic*, and Toni Morrison's *Playing in the Dark* have supplied the very words for outlining and debating the political and intellectual priorities of Black studies (Fanon 1963; C. Robinson [1983] 2000; Asante 1988; Ture and Hamilton 2011; Gayle 1971; Morrison 1992). Perhaps to an even greater extent, anthologies and edited critical collections such as Toni Cade Bambara's *The Black Woman*, Gloria Hull, Barbara Smith, and Patricia Bell-Scott's *All the Women Are White, All the Men Are Black, but Some of Us Are Brave: Black Women's Studies*, Mary Helen Washington's *Black-Eyed Susans*, Barbara Smith's *Home Girls*, Beverly Guy-Sheftall's *Words of Fire*, and E. Patrick Johnson and Mae G. Henderson's *Black Queer Studies: A Critical Anthology* have attested to how collaborations among scholars and with activists constantly change the vocabulary of Black life, Black struggle, and Black scholarship (Bambara 1970; Hull, Bell-Scott, and Smith 1982; Mary Washington 1975; B. Smith 1983; Guy-Sheftall 1995; Johnson and Henderson 2005).

## Why *Keywords for African American Studies* Now?

Consider the context against and within which African American studies as both a formal field of study with degree-granting programs and a set of knowledge practices that bear no allegiance to the project of *universitas* unfolds both on and off campus today: the flowering of both local and national social and political movements addressing the evisceration of Black lives by carceral and surveilling apparatuses, the resurgence of overt white supremacy, the decrease in resources devoted to Black studies on many campuses and the opposite (the dramatic increase in resources devoted to programming and hiring in Black studies) on others, the meteoric rise in both the velocity at which knowledge in the field is produced and the sheer number of sites for that knowledge production on the Internet and in public space. These conditions of possibility—or rather, conditions of necessity—for African American studies are the same conditions that mark this moment as an opportune moment for a "snapshot" of our vocabulary. When we began collecting entries for this volume in 2015, people were in the streets throughout the United States attempting a large-scale change in the vocabulary of racial being and violence. What are #BlackLivesMatter or #SayHerName if not eruptions of voice in defiance of the mundane drone of the daily rundown of the black body count? In an era when we, as practitioners of a multisited, heterogeneous field, are being challenged by students and off-campus communities to respond in more intelligent and practical ways to the twenty-first-century challenges of mass incarceration and resurgent white supremacy, the precision with which we interrogate our lingua franca may be a small measure of knowledge production's capacity to both clarify and reflect the world as we know it—as through a mirror, darkly—and turn it upside down.

To say there is nothing exceptional about the disaster unleashed on Black living in the twenty-first century is not to say there is nothing new about its expression or, perhaps more importantly, the vocabulary by which we locate, understand, and expose that assault or the ongoing survival of that assault. As we trade in the knowledge that emerges to expose the ongoing disaster of Black subjection in the New World, in and beyond America, the vocabulary we use to package and present that knowledge is continually changing in its attempts to keep up with and, in its most optimistic moments, defy the ongoing war against Black people.

## Our Process

The process of developing a *Keywords* project requires the assemblage of an interdisciplinary group of scholars with expertise in specific subjects related to African American studies. As editors, we began by identifying terms that function as important, if not essential, in dialogues, discourses, and debates in the field. These words operate as critical nodal expressions of relative ideas and concepts in a specific field of scholarship. While not necessarily unique to African American studies, the keywords in this volume hold specific relevance to the field. Moreover, the elasticity of these terms—their capacity to stretch beyond the field—is not the focus of the entries in this volume. Any elasticity in meaning is explored in the context of African American studies. "Diaspora," for example, has a very different meaning and engagement in this volume than in a general dictionary or encyclopedia, or in other *Keywords* texts.

**INTRODUCTION**     ERICA R. EDWARDS, RODERICK A. FERGUSON, AND JEFFREY O. G. OGBAR

Some of the terms that follow are keywords *in* African American studies—words that have not only circulated in but even structured knowledge in the field: "race," "intersectionality," "blackness." On the other hand, many of these are keywords *for* African American studies, words that have just begun entering our conversations and that are here, in our hands, asking for more airtime. Take "rock," for example. As Daphne A. Brooks uncovers rock as a musical form carved out of Black blues discontent and Black feminist fire, she offers up the word for critique and for claim: "Rock remains in a hard place as long as historians and critics alienate the form from its racially, regional, gendered, and queer roots," she writes. "No popular music genre's name encapsulates its own social and cultural complexities so accurately and so succinctly," she writes. If "rock" is the hard place of thinking race, gender, and sexuality as constitutive of musical sound, Brooks's work here suggests a new vocabulary *for*—rather than describes an existing vocabulary *of*—contemporary Black studies.

The authors included in this volume were tasked with creating entries that accomplish three fundamental things. First, each entry defines a term that circulates in the field and details how the keyword engages lines of thought, research, activist projects, or other critical projects in and beyond the university. Each author explicates the utility of the term, how it circulates, and its current meaning. Second, each entry details how the term has evolved over time. The entries reveal how dynamic certain words, concepts, and points of knowledge are in the wider field. Keywords, like language itself, do not operate in a vacuum but are inextricably tied to a dense fabric of social meanings that change over time. Words such as "religion" or "riot" can mean different things in different places, times, and contexts. In the context of academic inquiry, these words enable and engage very specific phenomena. A term's full meaning

can be properly understood by its proximity and use with other words. Keywords are dependent on concepts, frameworks, and critical genealogies that all function as essential modifiers to those words. It is, therefore, a special task to choose a single word, rather than a broader term, and define it.

Finally, we place each keyword within a specific intellectual genealogy and epistemological context as a node of inquiry. Keywords operate in relation to "particular formations of meaning" (Raymond Williams 1983, 15). They may shift and slowly (or in some cases rapidly) evolve over time. Rarely are words describing various social and cultural phenomena held in interpretive stasis. Inasmuch as our notions of power, gender, and race evolve, the keywords that scholars use to engage these notions adapt and find a degree of malleability in meaning and application. The function, therefore, of these entries is to chart these developments succinctly and substantively in a way not found in either a dictionary definition or an encyclopedic entry. These keywords operate as something more than those helpful reference sources.

The mutability of these words emerges out of a critical engagement among scholars who are in conversation with each other, while simultaneously producing work that refracts the wider world beyond the ivory tower. Just as African American studies was born from a strong relationship between Black communities and academia, the epistemological work remains critically sensitive to the diverse political, social, cultural, and religious phenomena of those communities and their histories.

From spatial, temporal, and topical positionalities through interdisciplinary engagement, interrogation, and theoretical mapping, these entries reflect the dynamic function of both vocabularies and the scholarship therein. The keywords' meanings are not fixed and not always settled in meaning but remain important elements to understanding the field. Since the establishment on college campuses, beginning in the late 1960s, of formal departments devoted to study of Black life, African American studies—a name that we are using as a shorthand to refer to the disparate formations devoted to the study of Black culture and society, such as Black studies, Afro-American studies, African diasporic studies, and so on—has persistently disrupted traditional categories and modes of academic knowledge. As Wahneema Lubiano argues, African American studies scholars intervene in academic discourses in order to "change the world" by "demystifying the relationship of 'knowledge' producers to 'knowledge,' as well as to foreground the connection between 'culture' and Afro-American 'everyday life'" (1996b, 68). In some sense, then, African American studies has served as a decades-long "keywords" project: an experimental, interdisciplinary attempt to document and interrogate "problems of meaning," in Raymond Williams's words, "in the area in which the meanings of culture and society have formed" (1985, 15).

It is important to note how we decided on the terms included in our own title, *Keywords for African American Studies*. As we use "African American" as a shorthand to refer to the diversity of social formations that constitute Black culture and society, we see ourselves exercising one of the central insights of the Black Power era in general and of Ture and Hamilton's *Black Power: The Politics of Liberation in America* in particular. In that book, the authors argue for the central role of self-definition in Black radical politics. As they state, "We shall have to struggle for the right to create our own terms through which to define ourselves and our relationship to the society, and to have these terms recognized" (Ture and Hamilton 2011, 35). Here Ture and Hamilton point to the nomenclatural diversity and dynamism that is part

of Black liberatory struggles, a diversity and dynamism that makes redefinition a way to assess the social and its transformations. Not only has this nomenclatural diversity become a signature feature of African American studies; it has also provided a diversity and dynamism to other fields as well. Consider, for instance, the ways that categories such as "double-consciousness," "intersectionality," and "racial capitalism" have animated discussions across a wide variety of fields and disciplines. This vibrancy can be taken as a sign of Black studies' ability to generate frameworks for a number of histories and social struggles. Ture and Hamilton's passage also points to the inseparability of intellectual and political articulations of Black radicalism.

Redefinition has been a mode of social, self, and cultural reflection all at once in Black intellectual and activist practices. In addition to addressing the need to redefine historical periods such as Reconstruction, slavery, American colonization, civil rights, and segregation, Ture and Hamilton point to the subjective itineraries of redefinition: "There is a growing resentment of the word 'Negro,' for example, because this term is the invention of our oppressor; it is his image of us that he describes. Many blacks are now calling themselves African-Americans, Afro-Americans or black people because that is our image of ourselves" (Ture and Hamilton 2011, 37). Here, the authors promote the multiplicity of terms—"African-American," "Afro-American," "Black"—without the need to establish a signal and universal category. In this way, our use of "African American" in the title of this volume is a reference to this critical assertion—that the "African American" in African American studies is part of a critical nomenclature that includes and expands the category "Black" as a way to radically assess and meet the exigencies of historical periods.

At the same time, we understand the category "African American" as evidence of a problem rather than a resolution. For instance, the category—even as it signals a connection to an African diaspora—announces its own U.S.-centrism. In many ways, we inhabit an academic world in which the "American" part of that diaspora is hegemonic and overwhelms the meanings of Blackness and the understanding of Black social formations. What is lost in that moment is the diasporic capaciousness and antivanguardism promoted in the category "Black." The circumstances of global migration and the increased global visibility of Black communities in Canada, Europe, Latin America, the Caribbean, and Africa necessitates a reconceptualization of Black studies beyond the limited terrain of the U.S.

To some extent, the shifting nomenclature used to describe the discipline reflects the growing attention to Black communities outside the United States. While the first dominant term, "Black studies," of the late 1960s suggested a field of scholarly inquiry unconstrained by national boundaries, "African American studies," which grew in popularity from the 1990s, constricted the implied sites of inquiry. In the twenty-first century, many academic departments and programs have moved toward "African and African American Studies" as a way to explicitly engage both the continent and its descendants in the U.S. Many other programs have adopted "Africana Studies" as an even more inclusive term that captures people of African descent globally. Though not always reflected in the terminology, the field of African American studies has never been solely concerned with what unfolds within one country; the expanding transnational interests, however, are reflected better with the term "Africana." We present the limitations of this volume, therefore, as a provocation for work that transcends those limitations.

If we take seriously enough what the entries in this volume reveal about keywords for African American studies—that they constitute a vocabulary for reimagining the work that we do—we will end up not with a stable definition of African American studies but rather with its explosion. To call this volume *Keywords for African American Studies* is not an attempt to make exceptional our situation in this hemisphere but rather to indict the conditions of our knowledge production in this hemisphere, to mark our own complicity with the neocolonial exercises that make the very idea of America possible, not least the operations of education and linguistic and cultural hegemony. "America" is of course not the horizon or limit or necessary condition for our thought; but, on the other hand, we cannot escape the fact that it does provide a unique set of conditions for *keywording* as a practice of Black thought and Black living. Indeed, the problem of "America" is the very problem that rearranges language itself, perhaps especially the language of scholarship and teaching, keywords and all.

With that tendency toward rearrangement in mind, we offer this volume as a snapshot of our collective present and our collective possibility.

# 1

## Abolition

Sarah Haley

Abolition is most narrowly defined as the end of slavery. But in African American studies, abolition is a keyword that raises a complex set of questions about when, and whether, slavery actually ended. As a concept, then, abolition raises critical questions about black temporality—what shifts in relations of power constitute freedom's beginning and captivity's end? Scholars within African American studies have considered the complexity of abolition as a process; while recognizing the dramatic transformations that emancipation wrought, theorists have challenged its interpretation as grand event, questioned its completeness, and demanded abolition's continued salience for challenging regimes of antiblack captivity. For black studies, abolition means far more than an end but rather a struggle over the terms of the future. From the perspective of the enslaved, abolition meant, at least in part, the reconstitution of relations of property. Abolition is tethered to political and social arrangements outside of regimes of racial and gendered violence and normativity that were inaugurated under slavery. As a site of black studies analysis, abolition offers a rejoinder to linear and triumphant narratives about the history of slavery.

Some analyses of abolition have emphasized its intellectual history; the 1831 inception of William Lloyd Garrison's the *Liberator* looms large in the historiography of abolition as studies have examined distinctions between Garrisonian, evangelical, and political abolitionists;

abolition's role within feminist thought and activism is also particularly significant, as historians have identified antislavery activism as foundational to women's rights organizing and have debated the role of racism in the abolitionist and subsequent suffrage movements (E. DuBois 1978; Kraditor 1981; B. Aptheker 1982; Cott 1987; Yellin 1989; Newman 1999). Importantly, Rosalyn Terborg-Penn demonstrated that "Black women fought racism and sexism simultaneously" in their struggle for abolition and suffrage (1998, 6). Recent work has emphasized a long abolition framework (Sinha 2016, 5), with some scholars emphasizing its centrality to the founding of the American republic, interpreting the Revolutionary War as a revolt to maintain a slave-owning economy that was vigorously challenged by Africans in the colonies (Horne 2014).

There are at least two historical developments that we could consider within the *long abolition* framework, including the movement of free and enslaved black people to define abolition in terms of immediacy rather than gradualism (Quarles 1970; Sinha 2016) and the literary canon of abolitionist essays, poems, and narratives by formerly enslaved men and women, which date from the mid-eighteenth century through the Civil War years; most influential among them are works by Phyllis Wheatley (1773), Olaudah Equiano (1789), Mary Prince (1831), Frederick Douglass (1845), William Wells Brown (1847), Henry Bibb (1849), Sojourner Truth (1850), Solomon Northup (1853), Charles Ball (1858), William Craft

(1860), Harriet Jacobs (1861). Writing against the denunciations and "frightful liabilities" associated with the word "abolitionist" (Douglass [1845] 2009, 98), these narratives collectively provide a foundation for interpreting its meaning, although the words "abolition" and "abolish" appear only sparsely in the texts. Charles T. Davis and Henry Louis Gates surmised that almost half of the black literary canon was produced by enslaved or formerly enslaved authors (1985, xv). This intellectual landscape, along with speeches and post-1865 memoirs and interviews from the formerly enslaved, constituted the abolition movement's most powerful political weapon and continues to generate monumental theorizations of subjectivity, violence, resistance, power, refusal, agency, democracy, capital, objectification, commodification, geography, and performance, grounding scholarship in a range of black studies subfields: political theory, English, history, gender studies, performance studies, and cultural studies.

The field of black studies has emphasized the ways in which the Emancipation Proclamation did not yield the economic and political freedom about which so many captives dreamed. Eric Williams ([1944] 2014) and Cedric Robinson ([1983] 2000) have traced the capitalist interests embedded in abolition. Williams argued that abolition could not simply be read as progress; he asserted that it was also a matter of capitalist expediency, a turning point on which industrial capitalism in the British Empire depended, since "commercial capitalism of the eighteenth century developed the wealth of Europe by means of slavery and monopoly. But in doing so it helped to create the industrial capitalism of the nineteenth century, which turned round and destroyed the power of commercial capitalism, slavery, and all its works" (210). The precise relationship between slavery and capitalism in the U.S. context continues to be historicized and debated (Harris [1982] 1993a; W. Johnson 2013; Baptist 2014; Beckert 2014). As this debate extends to abolition, one historian concludes, "if slavery is capitalism, as the currently fashionable historical interpretation has it, the movement to abolish it is, at the very least, its obverse" (Sinha 2016, 3). Put another way, slavery's grand alchemy—the transformation of persons into property—required both physical and social violence (Smallwood 2007); black abolitionists' ongoing project would be to attack the nexus of violence, extraction, and speculation that gave racial capitalism its form and content.

The economy of slavery was gendered: domestic labor sustained the plantation household and enslaved workers, and black women's capacity to biologically reproduce slave labor was integral to the system (Morgan 2004). Therefore, critical expansive analyses of abolition attend to the significance of gendered racial capitalism as well as the gendered contours of abolitionist practice (A. Davis 1971b; J. Jones 1985; Hine 1994; Hunter 1997; D. White [1985] 1999; Painter 2002; Morgan 2004; Camp 2004; Glymph 2008; Weinbaum 2013; Fuentes 2016; Hartman 2016; Ivy 2016; Owens 2017). W. E. B. Du Bois challenged dominant white historiographic accounts of abolition by centering black male soldiers as heroic agents whose presence in the Union army constituted a decisive "withdrawal and bestowal" of labor that "decided the war" ([1935] 1998, 57). Yet, as Saidiya Hartman asks, "Where does the *impossible domestic* fit into the general strike? What is the text of her insurgency and the genre of her refusal?" (2016, 171). Such questions remain pressing, potentially transforming the meaning of abolition.

Abolitionist struggle has taken place over myriad terrains that exceed the nineteenth-century battlefield and congressional hall and extend to the sites of black women's "war for freedom": the field, the cabin, the street, the rural countryside, the contraband camp. Neither "soldiers nor citizens," enslaved women's "struggle for emancipation—their political history—fits no state narrative, Union or Confederate" (Glymph 2013, 497; McCurry 2010, 9); they became "outlaws and insurrectionists," in order to achieve abolition (Glymph 2013, 490). Under the rubric of black feminist history and theory, then, the abolitionist occupies the position of outlaw, situating law as a production of black unfreedom, striving to dismantle rather than renovate or reclaim the American house of bondage. In the United States and beyond, black women's emancipation acts took the form of deadly encounters in bondage on slave ships; insubordination; surreptitious provision of aid from within the space of the plantation; quotidian work as nurses, cooks, and seamstresses for Union forces; daily labors to dismantle the plantation household as the nucleus of the slave system; and complex labor negotiations to undermine plantation productivity. Yet these forms of resistance, refusal, and sabotage are often underacknowledged (Glymph 2008, 95; Saville 1994; Schwalm 1997; Camp 2004; McCurry 2010; Weinbaum 2013; Bell 2016; Mustakeem 2016). Black women enacted abolition by refusing the gendered racial terror that reproduced the slave system, rendering them sex slaves and breeders. The posting of abolitionist newspapers in slave cabins by enslaved mothers, sisters, and grandmothers counts as abolitionist study and planning; moments, minutes, days, and months of truancy that black women spent in temporary flight from plantation counts as abolitionist time (Camp 2014), as does the "seasonal pattern" of Harriet Tubman's thirteen trips extricating men, women, and children from slavery (Clinton 2004, 86; Clifford Larson 2004). Black women's labor for abolition, like their subsequent domestic work, would be exempted from the protection of law, as military articles shielding black men who enlisted in the Union army did not apply to them (Glymph 2013). Instead, the Militia Act of 1862 prescribed marriage and motherhood as the only path to freedom, effectively erecting an "unequal two-tiered system of emancipation" (Hunter 2017, 172); this disregarded the waged and unwaged labor black women performed for the Union army and instead configured emancipation in terms of gendered dependency. Rendering themselves ungovernable on the plantation, black women were a distinct category of criminal when they fled during war years. As fugitives, they traversed a terrifying landscape of possible injury and execution at every stage of flight during the Civil War. Despite their significant labor for the federal military, the emancipating army extended the vagaries of slavery, subjecting "contraband" black women to sexual assault as well as deleterious discourses about their burdensomeness and licentiousness (D. White [1985] 1999; J. Jones 1985; Schwalm 1997). With black women absconding with their labor power and resisting the forces that continued to terrorize them in the Union, these subtle and extravagant confrontations force scholars to reckon with the gendered meanings of abolition under capitalism and nationalist militarism.

Alongside historical analyses that explore the piracy, strikes, revolts, commons creation (Roane 2017), and marronage (N. Roberts 2015) that constituted abolition's political ground, its temporal terrain remains a critical object of black studies scholarship. Indeed, the field is haunted by the question, to what extent is abolition a matter of the past? How do we grapple with the significance of these grand and mundane black events in the context of both dramatic change and continuity, the "nonevent of emancipation insinuated by the perpetuation of the plantation system and the refiguration of subjection" (Hartman 1997, 116)? The "endings that are not over" (A. Gordon 1997, 139) haunt the afterimage (K. Brown 2015) and "afterlife of slavery" (Hartman 2007) manifesting in the unresolved and unredressable "fundamental familiar violence" and "multiple subjections" that Christina Sharpe calls "monstrous intimacies," "which not only perdure, but are inflicted anew," vexing triumphant progress narratives (Sharpe 2010, 2; Hartman 2002, 758). Abolition mandates a "fully loaded cost accounting" of slavery, its immediate economic afterlife in white-supremacist contract dominion and indebted obligation (Painter 2002, 16; Hartman 1997; Stanley 1998) and black captivity (Daniel 1990; Lichtenstein 1996; Mancini 1996; M. Curtin 2000; K. Gross 2006; Blackmon 2008; Hicks 2010; Perkinson 2010; Childs 2015; LeFlouria 2015; Haley 2016), and the ongoing ravages of racial capitalism, gendered antiblack violence, and captivity. As Hartman argues, "if the ghost of slavery still haunts our present, it is because we are still *looking* for an exit from the prison" (2007, 133, emphasis added).

Abolition's temporality is the present continuous—the tense of a project that is ongoing and incomplete. It is also the subjunctive—the expression of what might be, what could have been, desire. As a concept, abolition addresses the vexing entanglements of past, present, and future; it insists on necessary transformations yet to be actualized. Indeed, both Hartman and Du Bois theorize black futurity through a mode of *looking*. In the chapter of *Black Reconstruction* titled "Looking Forward," which follows "Looking Backward," Du Bois defines abolition democracy as one of "two theories of the future that clashed and bended just after the civil war: the one was abolition-democracy based on freedom, intelligence, and power for all men; the other was industry for private profit directed by an autocracy determined at any price to amass wealth and power" ([1935] 1998, 182). The relationship between the Thirteenth Amendment and abolition was murky from the moment of its passage, as "even the abolitionist movement could not decide whether the Amendment was an end or a beginning" (Foner 1988, 67). Its passage inaugurated a debate within the American Anti-Slavery Society, with Garrison calling for the organization's disbanding in triumph and Douglass and Wendell Phillips successfully insisting that they move forward with suffrage as its goal. The late nineteenth century witnessed continuing black delineations of the meaning of freedom through resistance to violence and monumental assertions of economic, political, and social autonomy (Hunter 1997; Schwalm 1997; Rosen 2009; Hahn 2003).

The ongoing project of abolition is reflected in efforts to dismantle prisons. Angela Davis elaborates abolition's historical limitations to elucidate its future potential; abolition's nineteenth-century incarnation was "primarily a negative process of tearing down" and as such failed to create "an array of social institutions that would begin to solve the problems that set people on the track to prison," creating the condition of possibility for the carceral state (2005, 96). Abolition looks to render obsolete the prison as a structure of racism that enshrines the inequality that capitalism requires (R. Gilmore 2007, 28; R. Gilmore 2015). Analyzing the prison as a savage response to late-capitalist crises of surplus (R. Gilmore 2007), many scholars and activists have come to see abolition as an Afrofuturist alternative. Abolition is employed in black studies as a theory and practice through which to conceptualize the unraveling of material conditions of crisis, abandonment, and dispossession that the prison regime (including its manifestations in surveillance, detention, monitoring, policing) professes to resolve but in fact proliferates. Thus, abolition offers a radical critique of state violence (Berger, Kaba, and Stein 2017), rejecting prevailing notions that the policing and prison systems are merely broken but fixable (Kaba 2015) and proposals to refurbish what is fundamentally a mortal enclosure; to do so would amount to renovating a "fatal machine" that entrenches racial hierarchy (Herzing 2015, 194).

Abolition's twentieth-century theoretical development emerges from within the fatal machine. For the imprisoned intellectual and activist George Jackson (1972), the prison was an enclosure of capital and the repression of dissent. Those who were waging an anti-prison movement from the inside developed a radical prison praxis, situating the prison as a central "constitutive logic" and a practice of domination and control (Rodríguez 2006, 40). Jackson, Angela Y. Davis, Assata Shakur, and Mumia Abu-Jamal are among a host of influential imprisoned and formerly imprisoned intellectuals whose analyses falls within the framework of radical prison praxis and the genre of neoslave/neoabolitionist narrative (Joy James 2005). Although imprisoned and nonimprisoned intellectuals of the civil rights and Black Power movements were more inclined to use the language of revolution than abolition, they nonetheless contended that "America itself was a prison," arguing for an expansive view of the object that needed to be dismantled (Berger 2014, 51).

America's carceral inheritance and inherence belie predominant claims that prisons produce safety. Abolitionist thought elaborates the myriad ways that the prison is a center of imperial tyranny (Rodríguez 2007) and fascism (B. Aptheker 1971). Foundational abolitionist analyses have challenged the proliferation of carceral language and deconstructed carceral categories such as "corrections," "inmate," "safety," "innocence," "guilt," and "criminal," among others; abolition offers a critique of narrow rights and inclusion frameworks exposing the "deadly consequences of making rights contingent on innocence" (Kandaswamy 2016; PREAP [1976] 2005); in the nineteenth century, enslaved women's myriad labors for freedom were part of what made the Civil War a crisis for established gender relations and identities, and contemporary abolitionist analyses seek to throw gender normativity into crisis (Whites 1995).

Abolition incorporates a critique of the heteronormative and white-supremacist notions of gender and sexuality that slavery instantiated and that carceral discourses and modes of policing and containment have reproduced and entrenched (A. Davis 1971b; Spillers 1987); this critique identifies and elaborates the myriad forms of gendered and sexual insurgency that take place in opposition to surveillance and from within jails and prisons (Sudbury 2005; Kunzel 2008; Hicks 2010; Mogul, Ritchie, and Whitlock 2011; Dillon 2012; Richie 2012; Spade, Stanley, and Queer Injustice 2012; Spade 2013; Shabazz 2015; Stanley and Smith 2015; Haley 2016; McDonald and Tinsley 2017).

Abolition as a refusal of racialized gender normativity builds on black feminist analyses of violence and political economy by positing a future beyond gendered racial terror and racial capitalist modes of social reproduction. Davis's 1971 "Reflections on the Black Women's Role in the Community of Slaves" centers the home as a site of slavery's terror and abolitionist insurgency, situating domestic work "as a source of not only individual but also community sustenance and resistance" (Weinbaum 2013, 449), thereby providing a confrontation with the archive and a bold reassessment of the role of both enslaved women's activism and racialized regimes of gendering that is extended in groundbreaking work that followed (Finch 2015; Lightfoot 2015; Millward 2015; Mustakeem 2016; Fuentes 2016; Ivy 2016; Owens 2017).

In the 1970s, movements supporting black women including Dessie Woods and Joan Little, who were criminalized for defending themselves against racial terror, played a "catalytic role" in the development what Emily Thuma calls "anticarceral feminism," placing the elimination of gender violence at the center of historical and contemporary abolition analyses (Thuma 2015, 66; A. Davis 1971b, 1975). This framework is central for twenty-first-century black feminist defense campaigns that seek to free women who have been criminalized for surviving gender violence (Love and Protect / Survived and Punished). This intellectual and activist history shapes the contours of abolition's central project—the eradication of the prison as a necessary facet of societal reordering based on institutions of life sustainment (health, employment, the environment, education, housing) rather than violent enclosures that increasingly exceed U.S. national borders (Meiners 2007, 2016; Loyd, Mitchelson, and Burridge 2012; Schept 2015; Sojoyner 2016). Although prison expansionists increasingly label prisons as service apparatuses for women (Braz 2006), in reality prisons impose gendered forms of harm, diverting resources from child care, health care, housing, and guaranteed income, among other programs. By the end of the twentieth century, U.S. spending on punishment outpaced its allocations for welfare grants by the billions (Kohler-Hausmann 2017, 1).

Incarceration negates these institutions, as funding that would otherwise be used for social programs is allocated toward imprisonment. As Dorothy Roberts contends, the American legal system is rooted in the "monstrous combination of racial and gender domination" that manifested itself in reproductive terror (1997, 23). The policing of black homes, forced carceral labor for social reproduction inside prisons, and discourses of black female deviance represent facets of the prison regime that abolitionist feminism challenges. Late-capitalist law-and-order logics proliferate individualism and privatization as preeminent moral values that rationalize mass imprisonment by criminalizing the precarious.

Integral to abolitionist thought and activism, then, is the theoretical contribution of black feminist history and theory, which has centered reproductive violence, gender violence, and the exploitation of socially reproductive labor as technologies of captivity and argued for the necessity of alternatives. Central to prison abolition is an emphasis on structural over individual causes of societal harm (PREAP [1976] 2005). Black feminist analysis has situated economic dispossession as racialized and gendered violence and has also insisted on alternative modes of accountability for gendered violence (Baker and Cooke 1935; Beale [1970] 2010; A. Davis 1971b; Tillmon 1972; Hunter 1997; D. Roberts 1997; Incite!/Critical Resistance 2014; Nadasen 2005; Orleck 2005; Kornbluh 2007; Gore 2011; Kim 2011–12; Ocen 2012; Willoughby-Herard 2016; Hartman 2016). Such interventions offer a reconceptualization of sociality and forms of community accountability in the face of injury that do not fortify structures of oppression (Bierria, Kim, and Rojas 2011–12). The black feminist black commons, then, is the future toward which abolition looks.

# 2

## Apartheid

Xavier Livermon

The word "apartheid," translated literally from Afrikaans as "apartness," has often existed in a dynamic tension between its ability to describe a particular sociohistorical experience in South Africa and its usefulness as an organizing concept that describes the convergence of settler colonialism and global capital. As a method of inquiry, black studies has been at the forefront of rethinking the notion of apartheid as exceptional, drawing parallels between the formation of racial capitalism in South Africa and elsewhere throughout the African diaspora (Bunche 1992; Vinson 2012; P. Andrews 2014).

Apartheid did not emerge suddenly with the election of the National Party government in South Africa in 1948. Instead, it was a culmination of a number of policies of colonial capitalism that emerged from the very founding of South Africa as a Dutch colonial outpost in 1652. Forms of residential segregation, land expropriation, and labor manipulation were a prominent feature of the colonial project in South Africa that predated the rise of the National Party. Colonial authorities took great pains to destroy independent African political economies, turning African leadership into proxies for colonial authority while expropriating land. With the passage of the Native Lands Act of 1913, only 13 percent of South Africa's land was left in black hands. Over time, black South Africans were reconfigured into an available labor pool for white capital (Bundy 1979).

Population segregation and control of black labor mobility was key to the ideology of apartheid and can be categorized as taking two forms: petty and grand. Petty apartheid typically described the laws of everyday segregation, with every imaginable detail of daily life legislated on the basis of race. Grand apartheid was based on the idea that black South Africans were citizens not of South Africa but instead of the "homelands" artificially created by the National Party government. These homelands corresponded with the 13 percent of land "reserved" for black South Africans by the Native Lands Act of 1913. Grand apartheid ideology officially stripped black South Africans of South African citizenship. As foreign citizens, they were required to possess documentation to prove their right to reside in South Africa—hence the pass laws functioned as a system that managed black migration. Ideally, each homeland (many of which were made up of noncontiguous strips of unproductive and/or overpopulated land) would be granted independence. However, with no political economy independent of South Africa, such independence was primarily symbolic. Instead, the ideology of grand apartheid meant that the apartheid state had no responsibility to provide for its majority black citizenry and that it would effectively determine the terms through which black South Africans could participate in the economy. While the Native Lands Act began the process of creating black South Africans as cheap labor surplus, the policy of grand apartheid took this economic policy to its logical conclusion. Hence, while everyday segregation (petty apartheid) was a key component of apartheid policy, it was in fact secondary to the need to control and manipulate the availability and price and black labor. In order to accommodate the policy of grand apartheid, an estimated three and a half million black South Africans were internally displaced (C. Walker 2008).

Resistance to settler colonialism preexisted the birth of apartheid and took numerous forms, ranging from violent rebellion to political organizing (Mangcu 2012; Odendaal 1984). However, with the increasing violence of colonial law and bureaucracy, a new sense of urgency caused black South Africans to organize in a more united manner, culminating in the formation of the South African Native National Congress (later the African National Congress, or ANC) in 1912. Previous to the formation of the ANC, much of the work of resisting the colonial-apartheid state had been organized locally and along the lines of ethnicity. This newer form of organizing and resistance worked to unify black South Africans across ethnicity and increasingly encouraged the political identity of blackness (A. Marx 1998; Biko 2002). In this sense, Black South Africans began to participate in global black conversations regarding self determination, liberty, and identity. These conversations led black South Africans to identify with and organize around forms of global black consciousness even as they remained attuned to the particularities of their experience in South Africa. Examples of these kinds of cross-Atlantic dialogues included correspondence between W. E. B. Du Bois and Sol Plaatje, a founder of the ANC whose *Native Life in South Africa* was partly influenced by his increasing engagement in Pan-Africanism. Freedom for blacks in South Africa was thus linked to global black freedom movements. As blacks won additional rights in the West, and African and Caribbean countries gained their independence, apartheid stood as the last remaining vestige of a system of legalized racial colonialism for black populations, whose demise was inaugurated by the Haitian Revolution.

Initial political organizing was reformist, seeking to engage colonial authorities and stem against the loss of various privileges (particularly land ownership and voting rights) that the black elites had previously enjoyed.

However, even the most piecemeal reforms were a threat to the system of racial capitalism and were met with systemic violence from the colonial and later apartheid state, along with the erosion of the few political and economic rights black people did possess. The intensification of policies already begun by the colonial state under the guise of National Party apartheid rule called for a more confrontational and radical response politically. In disagreement with the ANC, the PAC (Pan Africanist Congress) was born. Members of the PAC felt that the ANC was too focused on civil rights and integration and co-optation into the existing system. While they defined the idea of the African politically rather than racially, they were also clear that to be African meant accepting African majority rule and control of the political economy.

The Sharpeville Massacre of 1960 represented a watershed moment in resistance to apartheid. In the protest against pass laws organized by the newly formed PAC, thousands of black South Africans had gathered peacefully at the local police station. They were met with extreme violence from the South African police force, resulting in sixty-six deaths. In the political unrest that followed, the National Party government outlawed black political parties (particularly the ANC and PAC), imprisoned (and later assassinated) black political leaders, and drove the rest of black political leadership into exile. The violent response from the National Party government convinced black political leadership that a purely nonviolent response to apartheid was insufficient, and both of the main black liberation parties began to mobilize militarily. The level of violence occurred almost simultaneously with political independence and majority black rule elsewhere on the continent, bringing renewed attention to the injustices of apartheid. South Africa began to be seen as a pariah state, and an international antiapartheid movement, sympathetic to the plight of black South Africans, gained visibility. This international movement drew from and in many ways also overshadowed the critique of apartheid that emerged out of Pan-African, Third World, and civil rights movements operating in the global black world (Nesbitt 2004).

Apartheid itself was not a monolith, and the National Party government was finding it increasingly difficult to navigate the competing interests of various different forms of white capital. On the one hand, extractive and export-focused industries (such as mining), along with racial ideologues, desired an entrenchment of the apartheid policy. On the other hand, internal commercial interests were invested in creating a consuming black middle class. The growth of economic prosperity among black South Africans was simultaneously a threat to and an opportunity for white capital, and the National Party government often implemented the policy of apartheid while simultaneously investing in (unequal and inadequate) urban infrastructure for black South Africans. Contradiction, then, was at the heart of the policy, as the very thing apartheid was designed to prevent (a literate, urban-based black political body) was increasingly visible in the cities of South Africa.

Perhaps in an effort to control and manage competing anxieties about the presence of permanent black urban populations, the National Party regime introduced Afrikaans-only instruction in government schools for the black populace. While this is often cited as the reason for the 1976 Soweto uprisings, Afrikaans education was simply one of several grievances of black South African students. Once again, peaceful demonstration was met with disproportionate violent response by the apartheid regime. In the months that followed, a number of student rebellions around the country began to coalesce in a reinvigorated internal antiapartheid movement. While the international apartheid movement (particularly the work of exiled activists) is often highlighted, internal political movements were key to making the costs of continuing apartheid untenable for the National Party government. The internal battles between competing classes of white hegemony saw neoliberal, pragmatic technocrats within the National Party emerge victorious, and their first order of business was to repair South Africa's international image, demobilize black rebellion, and make South Africa stable for global capital (Bond 2000).

The ANC was tasked as the coalition partner best suited to help the National Party government manage its negotiated settlement and give it international legitimacy. While the ANC did have a great deal of local support, it was also the case that much of its leadership was either jailed or in exile, hence disconnected from everyday struggles in communities. Imposing a top-down approach, the ANC was tasked with demobilizing black insurgency and substituting representative democracy for participatory democracy. The ANC positioned itself as the sole inheritor of the liberation struggle and quickly moved to convert itself from a liberation movement to manager of the South African body politic. The postapartheid state, now led by the black majority government symbolized by the ANC, would be the benevolent patriarch doling out beneficence as well as appropriate punishment to its citizen-children.

The negotiated settlement left much of the economic basis of apartheid intact, now exacerbated under the yoke of neoliberal economic orthodoxy (Desai 2002). Ironically for many black South Africans, they had survived apartheid only to be ushered into new forms of unfreedom, made perhaps all the more insidious by their supposed nonracial nature and the fact of black political control of the state apparatus. Exactly how and to what end black political leadership uses its control of the state is the unanswered question of contemporary

South African politics. Is it that the capture of the state does not matter, or is it that once state capture occurs, the political imagination must be more expansive? Observers have noted that the ANC government has acted less in the interests of the black majority and more as a contemporary form of indirect rule, ensuring that the conditions remain safe for exploitative global capital. In 2012, striking miners in Marikana were met with the single deadliest use of police force on South African civilians since the Sharpeville Massacre. The display of violence shocked the nation and led some critics to suggest that Marikana represented an end to the naivete of South African exceptionalism. In other words, South Africa's problems were not particular to apartheid and its aftermath; instead its problems were symptomatic of the challenges faced by many contemporary capitalist-oriented governments.

If we situate apartheid within a larger conversation of black studies, we can see how it was never the case that South Africa was exceptional. Perhaps the forms of racial capital and bureaucratic excess used to produce and manage South Africa were more extreme, but certainly historical and contemporary examinations suggest important corollaries. The insights of postcolonial studies and indigenous studies are also key in helping to rethink the Americas as settler colonies and to reveal the continuity between colonial administration in South Africa and the rest of the African continent (Mamdani 1996). As a result, it might be useful to think about apartheid both as a specific form of racial capitalism implemented in South Africa and as a general idea that speaks to racialized forms of control and management of subject populations. This general idea has probably had its most controversial application in relationship to Israel, and the term "Israeli apartheid" has been adopted by scholars and activists to describe the contemporary Israeli-Palestinian political economy (U. Davis 1987).

Since 2000, the negotiated settlement of postapartheid South Africa has started to fray. Various different forms of citizen rebellion have emerged, ranging from demands for services to more recent demonstrations by university students against exorbitant fees and insufficient financial aid. While a small black elite enriches themselves, financial control of South Africa remains disproportionately in the hands of white South Africans. For those black South Africans not able to join the new middle classes or the nouveau riche, they find themselves living in a society more economically unequal than during the years of apartheid. As South Africans ask questions about how they arrived at this political juncture and what they should do to end vast economic inequality structured by race, it is worth remembering that racial capitalism and its attendant forms of management are global concerns that plague much of the black world.

# 3

## Black Arts Movement

James Smethurst

If one is going to think about the Black Arts Movement (BAM) as a set of keywords, it is important to consider the component words separately, as well as how they work together in describing the black radical cultural movement of the 1960s and 1970s that was inextricably linked to Black Power. That is not simply a question of defining the denotative meanings of "Black," "Arts," and "Movement" but also of the qualities of those words in how they combine during the Black Power / Black Arts moment.

No doubt "black" is defined elsewhere in this volume and does not need extended treatment here. However, it is worth noting, as John Bracey Jr. does (2014), that when "black" as a term of identification and solidarity was increasingly deployed, largely through the influence of Malcolm X, it was to a considerable extent a gesture of opposition, of rejection, of rebellion, that needed a more elaborated positive content. In other words, what did it mean to be black? One way of looking at the Black Arts Movement is as a sort of investigation of what it meant to be black, of what was the basic cultural, spiritual, and intellectual material of blackness as a move toward freedom and self-determination. It is safe to say that no absolute consensus or definitive conclusion was reached; but the question was asked, and definitions and representations were proposed.

Then there is the word "Arts." What happens to this word when it is brought into conjunction with "Black"? Why is it plural as opposed to the title of the poet,

playwright, critic, and playwright Amiri Baraka's poem "Black Art," which was in many respects a sort of poetic manifesto for the incipient movement? Of course, there is the inverting play on the notion of "black arts" as a timeworn phrase in English denoting evil magic. But it is also proposing a vision of art that is fundamentally at odds with what might be thought canonical notions of European and Euro-American "high art" with hierarchal notions of rigidly separated artistic genres and media, of popular and serious, of middlebrow and avant-garde, with similarly discrete structures of interpretation and valuation (e.g., literary critics, theater critics, music critics, art critics).

Many people proposed the need for a "Black Aesthetic," that is, a fundamentally black system of interpretation and evaluation in which art could be criticized, understood, judged, and, ultimately, created, either in opposition to or outside a dominant white aesthetic system pretending to be universal and designed as a tool of domination. Considerably before Foucault's thought circulated widely in the United States, BAM / Black Power activists understood "aesthetics" as a sort of discourse in the service of power. However, it is also fair to say, as in many other areas of BAM, that there was no real agreement about what a "Black Aesthetic" might entail. Rather, there were a considerable number of possibilities or arguments presented. Probably the fundamental cleavage was between those, particularly many influenced by Maulana Karenga's Kawaida philosophy, who favored what might be thought of as a neo-African avant-garde or vanguard aesthetics, based on some visionary notion of African tradition that rejected both African American popular culture, particularly the blues and various sorts of music influenced by the blues, and much African culture of the colonial and immediate postcolonial eras, and those who saw African American popular culture, especially the blues, R&B, and soul, as part of a long black tradition that would be the bedrock of any revolutionary black culture. In practice, as always with BAM, this divide was complicated and often contradictory. Some of the people most influenced by Karenga, notably Amiri Baraka, were among the strongest proponents of black popular culture, especially music, as an essential part of black identity and any emerging liberated black nation.

However, despite this divide, one thing that united most participants in BAM is an approach to "the arts" that broke down traditional notions of medium and genre. For example, how does one understand the 1967 mural of Chicago's Organization of Black American Culture (OBAC) Visual Arts Workshop, *The Wall of Respect*, in 1967, a work that was key in the growth of the black mural movement of the 1960s and 1970s? One might be tempted simply to consider it in the medium of painting. However, the artists of the workshop included the text of Baraka's poem "SOS," photographs, and more traditionally painted portraits of black political and cultural figures in a variety of styles that also displayed a certain resistance to traditional notions of unity of composition. Certainly, earlier African American visual artists (and non–African American artists) worked with texts. However, *The Wall of Respect* in Chicago was unusual in that it was substantially a visual piece in which the text was at the center of the work. Did the Baraka poem frame the mural and give it its central meaning? Was the mural in many respects a sort of illustration of the poem? Did the mural remind viewers of the visuality of written poetry? Did the poem bring orality into what is not usually thought of as a sonic medium? Again, the answers to these questions, which might be a series of yeses, highlight the challenge to white academic notions of canon and artistic classification that BAM presented.

Furthermore, the creation and reception of *The Wall of Respect* was an intentionally public display of even more varied combinations of media and genres. As the artists worked on the various sections of the mural, there were often performances of poetry, theater, music, and/or dance as the residents of Chicago's South Side watched—and sometimes joined in to one degree or another. The most intense moment of such crossings of media and genres was no doubt the dedication of the mural on August 27, 1967. The dedication featured dance, music, poetry (including a performance by Gwendolyn Brooks and Haki Madhubuti), political speeches, and other sorts of performances. Police sharpshooters were stationed on the rooftops of nearby buildings, heightening the sense of the moment as a sort of theater of the real. The site of the mural continued to be a place for political events, including a large community rally led by the Student Nonviolent Coordinating Committee in 1967, until the destruction of the mural in 1973. In short, *The Wall of Respect* and the other sorts of collaborative work it engendered embodied the sort of crossings that made BAM aesthetics and actual practice in poetry, fiction, theater, music, dance, and visual arts (to the degree that these can be distinguished in BAM) a hybrid of the "Arts" that reached a mass audience and influenced what might be thought of as hip hop aesthetics that famously drew on different genres and media (poetry, popular music, dance, visual art, film and video, and so on) in a way that was eclectic and yet centered in African American expressive culture and experience. In this sense, a direct line could be drawn from *The Wall of Respect* to the video version of Beyoncé's *Lemonade* (2016), among other works.

Finally, there is the word "Movement." In the case of BAM, it has at least a dual meaning. First, there is a notion of a cultural movement in the sense of Romanticism, Surrealism, Dadaism, the Harlem or New Negro Renaissance, the Chicago Renaissance, the Irish Renaissance, the Beats, and so on. Generally, these are groupings of fairly like-minded artists whose networks grew out of social circles, shared aesthetic concerns, geographical proximity, "racial" or "national" identity, and/or sociopolitical interests. There is also the political sense of "movement" as in the abolitionist movement, the March on Washington Movement, the Popular Front, and the civil rights movement that coalesced around a social issue or set of social issues (e.g., the fight against chattel slavery, the struggle again Jim Crow segregation, and the opposition to fascism in the 1930s). Of course, all these political movements had their cultural or artistic component, but in all they were primarily interested in doing political work.

BAM, then, was unusual, especially for the United States, in the sense that it formed a more seamless whole with the Black Power movement than was probably the case with the relationship between any other artistic and political movements in the history of the United States, even the Harlem Renaissance in the 1920s and the black Chicago Renaissance in the 1930s and 1940s, which both had their radical political sides. That is to say that if one wanted to describe the Black Arts Movement as the cultural wing of the Black Power movement, one could just as easily describe the Black Power movement as the political wing of BAM. One thing that characterized Black Power, by and large, was the conviction that culture and the arts were central to both the white domination of black people (and the world) and to the creation of a new revolutionary people/nation. One could not change the political system if one ignored the cultural. Again, it is true that the nature and base of what the emergent revolutionary black nation consisted (or would consist) of was much debated and that to a large degree how one saw the answer to this question shaped one's politics, but culture and the arts were key to most visions of liberation proposed by Black Power. Similarly, BAM activists (who, like

Amiri Baraka, were often among the foremost leaders of Black Power) saw the imperative of engaging the mass of black people (and connecting with masses of people struggling for liberation around the globe) and moving them to change the world. In that sense, BAM was both a popular and vanguard political and a cultural movement at the same time. BAM artists did not simply propose, as did many previous and subsequent bohemias and avant-gardes, to engage a comparatively small number of hip people in coffeehouses, clubs, small galleries, and so on (and, in the age-old contradiction of bohemia, have their work commodified into cool artifacts for wealthy patrons hungry for the newest thing, eventually finding their way into mass celebrity in consumer culture) but to draw black people into revolutionary arts/art practices that, as the New Orleans BAM / Black Power activist Kalamu ya Salaam wrote, "do not necessarily be like / anything you heard before & / yet it will still sound familiar" (1972, 378).

When BAM is thought of in its individual verbal components as well as in their combination, it is a movement and ideological and aesthetic approach. That approach is all about being a material force in the world, changing the world (including the crucial task of how one interprets one's self and one's peers in the world, which is the province of culture and cultural analysis), internationalism, cultural/political self-determination (including, again, judging one's self by one's own standards, not those of the oppressor), pushing the envelope politically and culturally yet in a way that engages rather than alienates the mass of black people, that is popular yet cutting edge or radical at the same time, and that is by the people, for the people, of the people, and (in an important material addendum to the familiar Lincolnesque trio) supported by the people's money and other resources in public arts projects. The notions of a "public sector" of art supported by public funding (as opposed to private patrons), of art that is both radical and popular (as seen in Beyoncé's *Lemonade* and Li'l Wayne's "God Bless Amerika," to give a couple of twenty-first-century examples), that breaks down the barriers between traditional notions of genre and media in "serious" art, may seem like standard operating procedure in the twenty-first century, influencing the sense of what art is, what art is for, what it can and should say about the world, and how it reaches an audience (to whom it belongs, really) of virtually everyone in the United States. However, this was not always the case, certainly not the case before BAM and Black Power. So in the final analysis, the "Black Arts Movement" is a key set of words or a phrase that recalls a particular cultural and political moment, but it is also an enduring, if controversial, legacy and political-cultural sensibility or stance.

# 4

## Black Freedom Movement
Hasan Kwame Jeffries

The Black Freedom Movement is a distinct era in the African American struggle for civil and human rights that began in the mid-1940s with a surge in public protest and ended in the mid-1970s with a shift in emphasis toward electoral politics. It encompasses two of the most unique and enduring periods of black activism. The first is the civil rights movement, which resulted in the elimination of Jim Crow laws in the South and the upending of Jim Crow customs in the North. The second is the Black Power movement, which not only expanded on the gains of the civil rights movement but also elevated African American racial consciousness, forever changing what it meant to be black.

The three words that compose the phrase "Black Freedom Movement" reflect the term's core characteristics. "Black" speaks not only to the racial identity of the vast majority of the Black Freedom Movement's participants—the black masses—but also to the race of its leaders. African American activists, from black preachers to black community organizers, led the Black Freedom Movement by marshaling the energy and resources of the black community. "Freedom," meanwhile, addresses the Black Freedom Movement's wide-ranging goals, which included both civil rights objectives, such as securing the right to vote, and human rights aims, such as access to decent housing. And "Movement" marks that moment as a time when black protest coalesced into a genuine social movement, with generally agreed-on ideological frameworks, strategies, tactics, and aspirations.

For generations, African Americans have described their struggle for justice and equality in language reflective of the Black Freedom Movement's chief characteristics. They have regularly used racial signifiers when naming their organizations. In the 1830s, they routinely included some derivation of "colored" when identifying their political conventions. When they came together in Philadelphia, Pennsylvania, in 1835, for instance, they called their gathering the National Convention of Free People of Colour. They have often identified freedom as their overarching goal. During slavery, black abolitionists such as David Walker argued for a literal freedom from bondage, and enslaved rebels such as Nat Turner took up arms toward this end. And immediately after emancipation, they demanded their freedom rights, insisting on living as free men and women. Indeed, freedom has always been an integral part of African Americans' protest lexicon. During the height of the Black Freedom Movement, for instance, black activists called their protest music "freedom songs," dubbed their parallel educational institutions "freedom schools," and named their independent political organizations "freedom parties." African Americans have also tended to label heightened periods of protest, such as the Back-to-Africa crusade of Marcus Garvey's era, "movements."

In the 1950s, however, black moderates led a decided shift away from using racial signifiers to define and/or describe the struggle. Their influence was far reaching. In 1955, black activists in Montgomery, Alabama, for example, opted to omit racial signifiers when they formed the Montgomery Improvement Association to coordinate the local bus boycott. And a year later, when Dr. Martin Luther King Jr. and his coterie of advisers came together to launch the Southern Christian Leadership Conference, they too adopted the new practice.

Meanwhile, the same contingent of moderate black leaders led a sharp move away from identifying freedom as a primary protest goal. Instead, they framed the struggle exclusively as a fight for civil rights, narrowing the focus of protest to securing only those rights guaranteed by government. In publicly jettisoning freedom as a goal, they obscured and at times ignored long-standing human rights objectives.

These changes were a direct response to Cold War domestic politics. As tensions escalated between the United States and the Soviet Union, federal and state officials began cracking down with increasing ferocity on organizations that challenged the status quo. NAACP leaders Walter White and Roy Wilkins, among many others, feared the political and financial consequences of being red-baited. In response, they rebranded the struggle, reframing it as a civil rights movement, phrasing they believed would be more palatable to whites. Liberal whites latched onto the term, helping it become the dominant descriptor of black protest.

The changes in terminology were never fully embraced by African Americans at the grassroots. Local people continued to invoke freedom when naming their groups. In Mississippi, for example, when voting rights activists formed a statewide umbrella organization to coordinate voter registration efforts, they called it the Mississippi Freedom Democratic Party. At the same time, local people continued to frame their struggle as more than a fight for civil rights. In Lowndes County, Alabama, for instance, when black residents established a countywide movement organization in 1965, they named it the Lowndes County Christian Movement for Human Rights. And by the late 1960s, racial signifiers had returned. Taking a cue from Lowndes County activists, Huey P. Newton and Bobby Seale named their new movement organization the Black Panther Party for Self-Defense. The resurgence of the once familiar practice of incorporating race in movement naming practices was an explicit rejection of Cold War color-blindness and a full embrace of the long history of racial self-identification. And the tendency was not limited to the grassroots. When African American professionals organized, they almost always included "black" in the names of their organizations, such as the National Association of Black Journalists and the National Association of Black Social Workers.

The renaissance of old naming practices and descriptors of black protest did not keep scholars from using the more narrowly constructed catchall phrase "civil rights movement" to describe the work of African American activists. But some scholars, especially those who had taken part in the movement, began pushing back against the vague colorblind nomenclature. In the early 1980s, the historian Clayborne Carson was one of several academics who pointed out the numerous inadequacies of the term "civil rights movement." In an essay titled "Civil Rights Reform and the Black Freedom Struggle" (1986), Carson argued that "use of the term civil rights movement, rather than such alternatives as black freedom struggle, reflects the misleading assumption that the black insurgencies of the 1950s and 1960s were part of a coordinated national campaign . . . rather than a locally-based social movement" (23). "In reality," he said, "these local protest movements involved thousands of protesters, including large numbers of working class blacks, and local organizers who were more concerned with local issues, including employment opportunities and political power, than with achieving national legislation" (23–24). Carson further explained, "Rather than remaining within the ideological confines of the integrationism or King's Christian-Gandhianism, the local movements displayed a wide range of ideologies and proto-ideologies, involving militant racial or class consciousness" (24). For Carson and an increasing number of scholars, historical accuracy required the terms "black" and "freedom" be used to describe 1960s-era black protest.

Since Carson's essay, scholars studying black protest from a black perspective have made the important distinction between a struggle and a movement. For many, "struggle" is an umbrella term that captures the broad contours of the African American fight against white supremacy and for racial justice and equality. It includes the many moments in the African American journey from slavery to freedom when black protest rose to the level of a genuine social movement, such as the abolitionist movement, Back-to-Africa movement, and the Black Power movement. "Movement," on the other hand, refers specifically to those more precise moments of black protest, such as the period from the 1940s through the 1970s, when African American activists came together around a common set of concrete goals, shared a similar approach to change, and organized and mobilized the black masses to challenge the status quo.

By definition, the Black Freedom Struggle is chronologically broad. It stretches from the colonial era, starting with the efforts of the first enslaved Africans to gain their freedom, to the present day, with the Movement for Black Lives. But temporal boundaries are essential to making sense of the start, evolution, and end of social movements. By necessity, then, the Black Freedom Movement is time bound. Pinning its beginning and ending to precise chronological moments connects it to concrete historical forces and developments, such as World War II in the 1940s and the surge in the number of black elected officials in the 1970s. It enables charting the Black Freedom Movement's trajectory and decoding its development. And it makes identifying the factors most responsible for the Black Freedom Movement's demise possible.

Significantly, the chronological specificity central to the Black Freedom Movement in some ways affirms the narrower periodization of the normative civil rights movement framework, which places the movement's beginning in 1954 with the U.S. Supreme Court school-desegregation ruling in *Brown v. Board of Education of Topeka, Kansas* and locates its end in 1965 with the passage of the Voting Rights Act or a few years later, in 1968, with the assassination of Dr. Martin Luther King Jr. But there are critical differences.

First, the Black Freedom Movement does not decontextualize midcentury black activism, pretending as though it was far and away the most important manifestation of black protest. Instead, it locates the activism of the era on the continuum of black protest that stretches both backward and forward in time and constitutes the Black Freedom Struggle. Second, it balances top-down with bottom-up approaches to understanding black protest. Whereas the civil rights movement conceptualization tends to focus on government actors, especially presidents and federal judges, as well as national leaders such as Dr. King, the Black Freedom Movement retrieves everyday people and grassroots activists from the margins of analysis. And third, it treats Black Power protest as a logical extension of earlier forms of black agitation, rather than as an ill-advised break from the past.

The Black Freedom Movement framework also expands understanding of black protest. Ever since civil rights became the dominant lens through which to view 1960s-era black activism, the strategies and tactics used by black activists have been too narrowly configured. Most notably, nonviolence, as both a philosophical approach and a tactic, has been made the standard of black protest, against which all other approaches and activities are measured. While nonviolence enjoyed unprecedented popularity among African American activists during this time—indeed, the unusually high level of interest in nonviolence was a defining characteristic of the era—only a handful of black leaders, Dr. King foremost among them, embraced nonviolence philosophically as a way of life. Many more accepted nonviolent direct action as a useful tactic given the circumstances. But even more than that rejected it wholesale, choosing instead to continue long-standing African American traditions of self-defense and parallel institution building. Rather than focus wholly or substantially on nonviolence, the Black Freedom Movement properly contextualizes nonviolence, putting it alongside and in conversation with the many other forms of black protest.

The Black Freedom Movement framework has gained widespread acceptance among scholars who study black protest from an African American perspective. But its influence has not been limited to them. Its critique of the broad civil rights movement construct has encouraged scholars who have adhered to this mode of analysis to reconsider its underlying suppositions. For the southern historian Jacquelyn Dowd Hall (2005), this meant pushing the starting point of 1960s-era black protest back into the 1930s, to a time when white labor organizers, scattered about the South, found common cause with black workers and activists. It also meant emphasizing the movement's economic objectives.

But Hall's "Long Civil Rights Movement" contradicts the Black Freedom Movement in several important ways. Foremost, it decenters African Americans, giving primacy instead to whites. In the Long Civil Rights Movement, the starting point is essentially the moment when white labor organizers realize that their success is tied directly to, and in many ways wholly dependent on, the success of black activists on the factory floor and beyond. In addition, it credits white labor organizers with injecting an economic agenda into the Black Freedom Struggle, ignoring the black impulse for economic justice that had taken countless forms since emancipation, including the effort by black unions such as the Brotherhood of Sleeping Car Porters to win recognition and collective bargaining rights. At the same time, it posits that the shift away from workplace organizing during the 1950s stemmed from the withdrawal of white labor organizers from the movement, rather than being a pragmatic response to shifting political opportunities brought about by the onset of the Cold War. And finally, it treats the Black Power movement much as civil rights traditionalists have, as a dramatic and unfortunate break from the usual forms of black protest.

The Long Civil Rights Movement has resonated within the academy in large part because it allows scholars whose work intersects only secondarily, or even just tangentially, with the Black Freedom Struggle to claim close association with black protest. But proponents of the Black Freedom Movement have pushed back. The historians Sundiata Keita Cha-Jua and Clarence Lang, for example, offered a biting critique of its shortcomings in "The 'Long Movement' as Vampire: Temporal and Spatial Fallacies in Recent Black Freedom Studies" in the *Journal of African American History* in 2007. And Black Freedom Movement scholars have vociferously pointed out its merits and shortcomings at national conferences, including at the ninety-eighth meeting of the Association for the Study of African American Life and History in 2013.

But the debate surrounding the Long Civil Rights Movement is almost entirely academic, confined to the pages of historical journals and monographs and to roundtables at professional gatherings. Indeed, the public is almost wholly unaware of the disagreements between advocates of the Black Freedom Movement and proponents of the Long Civil Rights Movement. In fact, nonacademics barely know these conceptualizations exist. For most people, the dominant framework for understanding 1960s-era black protest is still the civil rights movement. To be sure, the Black Freedom Movement, as an idea and a term, has made real inroads into the public square, reflected most notably in spaces dedicated to historic preservation, including the Smithsonian Institution's new National Museum of African American History and Culture in Washington, DC. But even spaces that have embraced the Black Freedom Movement fully, such as the National Civil Rights Museum at the Lorraine Motel in Memphis, Tennessee, which centered its five-year, $25 million exhibit redesign and renovation around the Black Freedom Movement, find it hard to shed the civil rights movement moniker.

The inability of the Black Freedom Movement to dislodge the civil rights movement is not simply a function of the latter being deeply ingrained in people's minds. The problem is that the civil rights movement reinforces a set of false assumptions about racial progress in America that many whites find comforting and reassuring. Among other things, they cling to the notion that racial discrimination in the South was the fault of only a handful of southern hayseeds and that racial discrimination in the North was simply an unintended consequence of colorblind public policy. These ideas permit whites to put a great distance between themselves and the past—that was *then* and that was *them*. In this way, they avoid confronting the harsh realities of history. The Black Freedom Movement, on the other hand, draws the past near, rendering plainly visible the ways the past is present. Indeed, while the civil rights movement eases the conscience, the Black Freedom Movement challenges it.

It is highly unlikely that Black Freedom Movement will replace the broader civil rights movement framework anytime soon. The public's attachment to the older way of understanding black protest runs too deep. However, among academicians who study black protest from a black perspective, that shift has already occurred. In fact, the Black Freedom Movement has been the driving force behind the very best scholarship on 1960s-era black protest since the 1990s. Although it may still be a while, all signs indicate that "Black Freedom Movement" will one day roll off the tongues of the public as easily as "civil rights movement" does today.

# 5

## Blackness

Fred Moten

Blackness is enthusiastic social vision, given in (non) performance, as the surrealization of space and time, the inseparability of gravity and matter, fabric's fabrication, field's feel, rub's rub, plain's chant, an endlessly ante-inaugural endlessness of means, an empillowed, haptically ham-boned coinstrumentality of care, in caressive sound and anachoreographic sounding. Anticipating originary correction with self-defensive division and (re)collection, it goes way back, long before the violent norm, as an impure informality to come. Its open and initiatory counterpleasures reveal the internal, public resource of our common sense/s, where flavorful touch is all bound up with falling into the general antagonistic embrace. That autonomous song and dance is our intellectual descent; it neither opposes nor follows from dissent but, rather, gives it a chance. Consent to that submergence is terrible and beautiful. Moreover, the apparent (racial) exclusivity of the (under)privilege of claiming this dis/ability serially impairs—though it can never foreclose—the discovery that the priority of sovereign regulation is false. In order to get the plain sense of this, you have to use your imagination against the world, since in the world—that dream, that nightmare of dominion, overview, and oversight—blackness comes sharply into relief against its negation. On the ground, in the field, in the plain, it doesn't come into relief at all, really, but as a mode of sensuous theoretical practice, it celebrates against predatory and incorporative worldliness, whose primary weapon is the imposition of the desire for worldliness. Blackness, lived both as the denial of and the incapacity for worldliness, is properly understood as constraint when constraint is improperly understood as undesirable, as a radical undesirability in the face of the belligerent fantasy of the freedom of, or of freedom in, the world. Blackness, in and as a kind of fleeting, prior persistence, resists these bad thoughts. It's the good trip before the bad trip that good trips can induce. Blackness is midnight blue as midnight comes again.

If it seems like blackness shows up most clearly against the backdrop of its negation, perhaps this is because affirmations of it—out of the bloody constraint that makes them necessary—are often given as if a claim on property. And yet it is impossible to think it without the making of a claim, though the claim is an effect of a triple dispossession—the giving away of what was never ours, the theft from us of that same thing, and the refusal to take that shit as given. But all this is just to say that same thing is anything but. It's everything but, never the same, must change, and if that imperative implies sameness, it's only because our language, our naming, is inadequate to what is irreducible in the name when the name is irreducible in what is irreducible to the name. Only in a certain profligacy of naming, a terrible and beautiful festival of predication, is something approached—as Ed Roberson (1970) and, then, Aldon Nielsen (1997) show—through the various calligraphies of black chant. Deeper still, the thing we share is not a thing, and though we share it, it is not ours. We share it in our practice of it, which is a plain of commonness in work and play. Constrained to show no restraint, trained in the refusal of training, our interminable refrain is, "I'm serious as a heart attack. I'm just playing."

Our thing, which ain't no thing, which is absolutely nothing, is real, though any isolated instance or aspect of it that is put forward as the real thing ain't. Often thought to be a thing of darkness, it is, more gloriously, more severely, a thing of nothingness. In this regard, being everything in being nothing; it's not a thing, not anything at all but, rather, that shared practice of sharing, that simplest explosion of an absolutely complex simplicity, that we have sometimes thought of under the rubric of the gift, that sometimes we think by way of the concept of the given, but whose materiality is most precisely imagined in giving. On the cusp where generosity and generativity converge, it proffers convergence as a general and inescapable blur. Often thought to be a property of certain bodies or the troublesome property of that troublesome property that stands in, without standing, for the theft of body, as such theft's victim and effect, it is more beautifully, more terribly, an openness of flesh, a monstrosity to be claimed, as Hortense Spillers (1987) proclaims—an animated, animaterial showing, an empathic and emphatic refusal of body and mind, of self in relation to world, all of which have been refused to it as a matter of law and custom, science and philosophy. Blackness is (the improvisational sociology of) quantum sociality. Blackness is the old-new math.

Blackness bears the history of the epidermalization of the alternative. The alternative bears that history in turn, will never not be black, now, whatever else that irreducible and inexhaustible blackness is, or will be. Whenever a cop busts a guy in the head, our busted head is model and precedent. The police were called into being to come get us. Their constantly coming to get us—"Shade! Good God! It's a raid!"—shapes the way we shift our shape. He always be killing us, and we are constrained to survive that (W. Brown [1847] 1970). He's tight grilled. If his situation ain't improvin', he try'n to murder everything movin' (Jay-Z 1998). He imposes improvement on everything that moves. He tries to use everything until it's all used up, but, giving nothing, all he does is (lay) waste, throwing shells everywhere. Part of what we are is the imperative to see him clearly, to look into the argon of his eyes, finally, so we can see that we are not there. The analysis of our murderer, and of our murder, is so we can see we are not murdered. We survive. And then, as we catch a sudden glimpse of ourselves, we shudder. For we are shattered. Nothing survives. The nothingness we share is all that's real. That's what we come out to show. That showing is, or ought to be, our constant study.

# 6

## Body

Jayna Brown

We often take our bodies for granted, as if they were self-evident and as if to think or talk about them was a matter of obvious description. But there is nothing "natural" about the ways we perceive our bodies, and there are many ways to approach the term. What a body means in relation to other bodies and to the world around it has taken shape and shifted meaning through the languages of science, philosophy, politics, and history. Nowhere is this more graphically illustrated than in the ways we understand race, sex, and gender, terms that determine who we are and where we rank in the social structures of the modern world. In African American studies, the term "body" takes on a particular resonance as it is used to draw attention to the visceral nature of racism as well as the physical forms of African Americans' resilience and resistance.

Scientific discourses in the eighteenth and nineteenth centuries were made up of elaborate systems of classification and categorization. Natural scientists such as Johannes Blumenbach and Carl Linneaus drew up detailed hierarchical systems to define and rank the races. These categories, meant to be taken as scientific fact, were descriptions of not only physiognomy but also temperament. Race was considered as much a matter of behavior and intellectual capacity as it was skin color or appearance. In accordance with the hierarchical dichotomy between body and mind, articulated by René Descartes, the European race was associated with the mind and its capabilities, while the African race was associated with the body and its workings. In *Systema Naturae* (first published in 1758), the Swedish natural scientist Carl Linnaeus attributed five races to humankind. He described the *Europeanus* (European) variety as gentle, acute and inventive," while the *Africanus* (African) variety was described as black, phlegmatic, relaxed, . . . crafty, indolent and negligent (Linnaei 1758, 21). In "Geographical Basis of History," the philosopher Georg Hegel claimed that the northern European races shaped history, while the sub-Saharan African was incapable of "realiz[ing] his own being" ([1837] 1899, 93). The white races, from the northern climates, were the creators of civilization, while "the Negro" remained incapable of all historical change.

Race and sex were intertwined as categories used to assess the body. African women were considered hypersexual and excessively fecund. They were used most often as proof that Africans were closer to animals than to humans. In 1774, Edward Long, a British colonial administrator in Jamaica, asserted that there was an "intimate connexion and consanguinity" between blacks and orangutans (370). In 1817, the physician Georges Cuvier wrote his observations of an autopsy conducted on a Khoi Khoi woman named Saartjie Baartman. Like many indigenous peoples, Baartman had been brought to Europe and her body put on display as a living example of the hypersexuality of primitive races. Cuvier's observations of Baartman's genitalia were used as examples of deviant female sexual anatomy. Her brain, genitalia, skeleton, and body cast were kept at the Musée de l'homme in Paris until 2002.

What would come to be called "scientific racism" hardened during the period of nineteenth-century chattel slavery, particularly in the United States. The now-discredited fields of craniology (the study and classification of the skull) and phrenology (the study of the brain) were developed to support the idea of European intellectual superiority. Africans and those of African descent were designated as lower on the evolutionary scale. Prominent men of science argued against Charles Darwin's support of the thesis that all humans were descended from the same species (monogenesis) and insisted that the lower races must have different origins (polygenesis). In popular science, black people were governed by their senses, drives, and appetites, which they were unable to control or restrain. They were therefore incapable of self-government and in need of constant guidance.

After slavery, black people were further criminalized on biological grounds. The Italian criminologist Cesare Lombroso's influential theory of "criminal atavism" reflected the common sentiment of the time. He asserted that criminal tendencies were inherited and that they could be identified by physical traits likened to primitive man. His assessment of the physical features of white prostitutes in *The Prostitute and the Normal Woman* (Lombroso and Ferrero 1893) argued that their criminal proclivities could be identified by their physical likeness to women of primitive races, particularly the Hottentot (Gilman 1985, 226). Black bodies were therefore marked as criminal by biology. They were not capable of being rehabilitated, only contained. The "facts" of race, sex, and class continue to shape the ways black and gendered bodies are perceived and underlie the violent forms of control and punishment black people are still subjected to.

Approaches to how we understand our physical selves have also been proposed by philosophers and theorists. "The body," as an isolated unit of investigation, comes out of poststructuralist theory of the 1980s and 1990s. The proliferation of scholarly work on "the body" established it as a theoretical category. According to poststructuralist theory, systems of knowledge produce their object, and the body is therefore only knowable as a discursive field, historically inscribed by discourses in the natural sciences, medicine, philosophy, and political theory. The French theorist Michel Foucault's influential delineation of the term "biopolitics" showed that political power regulates human life on the level of the biological body (1978, 139). Using seventeenth-century through nineteenth-century France as his archive, he argued that the use of power shifted from that of the sovereign over his subjects to a system in which forms of discipline, surveillance, and control are exerted on the body by institutions including the prison system, medicine, education, and the military. But Foucault's theories, as they do not adequately consider the institutions of slavery and colonialism, are insufficient in their reach to account for the specific forms of biopower exercised on racialized people's bodies. Black people, with bodies that are deemed inherently and biologically deviant, are not subjects that can be disciplined into some sort of obedience. Instead they are to be contained and surveilled, held in a permanent "state of injury," or killed (Mbembe 2003, 21). Angela Davis's work on the prison industrial complex critiques Foucault's ideas of the prison as a reform (1998, 96–106). Foucault (1977, 2003) argued that the system of biopolitics replaced physical punishment, but attention to racialized regimes of power show that systems of violence persisted and continue to circumscribe black lives. The practice of lynching in the nineteenth and twentieth centuries, the sterilization practices that continued into the 1970s, the levels of police brutality experienced by black people in the United States, and the development of the prison industrial complex as an institution meant to contain and control black people show the insufficiency of Foucault's universalist theories of the body.

Studies of the body also took on particular force in feminist theory. Feminist theories challenged the idea of a universal body and critiqued many poststructuralist theories for assuming the European male as a normative subject in their analyses. Feminist theory showed gender to be a product of discursive regimes and that these regimes legitimated the supposed inferiority of women. The American theorist Judith Butler introduced the powerful concept of performativity as a way to understand the production of gender itself. In her influential book *Gender Trouble* (1990), Butler argues that repetitive collective enactments, based in discursive claims, solidify regulatory claims of gender. Butler's concept of performativity has been useful for thinking about the transgressive potential of disobedience to categories of gender. But, like poststructuralist theory, feminist theories do not adequately account for the ways discourses of race shape what the gendered body means or the levels of violence embedded in processes of its racialization (D. Roberts 1997). It also rarely considers that not all bodies are gendered as women in the same way. As Chandra Mohanty argued in "Under Western Eyes" (1984), the category "woman" is also not a universalist category.

With black people's bodies shot through with such long histories of knowledge production, black people would seem unable to escape systems of racial terror. Scholars working in black cultural and political contexts wrestle with these concepts of subject formation, sovereignty, and agency, concepts all linked to the body in theories of race. In *Scenes of Subjection*, Saidiya Hartman asks, "How do the forms, relations, and institutions of power condition the exercise of agency? . . . What exercise of the will, forms of action, or enactment of possibility is available to animate chattel or the socially dead or to the excluded ones?" (1997, 54, 55). In other words, what are the ways black people have been able to set the terms by which they inhabit their bodies under such violent systems of oppression? Scholars continue to explore other ways to understand the body that loosen the hold of racist epistemologies. We can turn to what theorists call "embodied knowledges," that is, ways of perceiving the self and the world grounded in phenomenological ways of knowing. Embodied knowledge challenges Descartes's separation of mind and body, which associated the mind with the higher faculties and the body with animal drives. Instead, the body itself is a site of knowledge production. Theories of embodied knowledge also challenge the idea that the body is a passive recipient of meaning. The body is not an empty vessel, or a tabula rasa, defined by discourse. Nor is it just a medium, channeling the demands of discursive regimes. Such theories of embodied knowledge focus on the collective, rejecting individualism embedded in Western epistemologies, and ground their theories in the idea that the body is always in relation to other beings and the world.

Scholars look to black histories of rebellion, escape, maroonage, and daily acts of resistance for the ways black people use their bodies to refuse the terms by which dominant regimes would mark them. They introduce tropes such as "stealing away" and "fugitivity" as ways to recognize these forms of refusal. As Cedric Robinson ([1983] 2000) shows, insurrections and rebellions were constant during slavery. Political protests are also a form of collective enactment dependent on the body. Organized protests include the silent march organized by the NAACP in 1917 to protest the practice of lynching. As thousands marched silently down Fifth Avenue in New York City, the act protested the exclusion of black people from the democratic protections of the nation, which the public spaces of the city were meant to embody. As Robin Kelley (1994) writes, other forms of disrupting public space include the many unofficial instances of daily resistance on public transportation and on the job, as well as demonstrations against segregation, including the bus boycotts and the sit-in movement begun by students in Greensboro, North Carolina,

in 1960. More recently, to protest the multiple deaths of black men at the hands of police, actions such as "die ins" were organized in the 2010s to disrupt business as usual.

In the twenty-first century, scholarly study of the body has given way to a wider examination of the material world. Thinking of all matter as made of the same elements, organized relationally, decenters the human body, as it questions the liberal humanist model of the possessive individual. Humanity is no longer the pinnacle of an evolutionary ladder. Drawing from the philosopher Gilles Deleuze, scholars have begun to think of the body as an "assemblage of forces, or flows, intensities and passions" (Braidotti 2006, 201). In response to climate change, scholarship has taken a turn to the ecological, and studies of the body have emphasized its connection and enmeshment in wider ecologies. The body becomes aggregate, a combination of cohabiting cells and bacteria, and the boundaries between organic and inorganic, animate and inanimate matter, become porous (J. Bennett 2010). Some scholars challenge the recurrence of the universal body in these theories and pay attention to the vastly different relationship of racialized and indigenous bodies within their environments, from indigenous modes of being within planetary ecologies to the effects of environmental racism (Alaimo 2010).

Many scholars explore expressive cultures as forms through which black people inhabit their bodies on alternate terms. Through music and dance, racialized subjects reclaim their bodies from exploitative systems and violent practices (Kelley 1994). As Achille Mbembe writes, "the slave is able to demonstrate the protean capabilities of the human bond through music and the very body that was supposedly possessed by another" (2003, 22). These performance practices operate in a nonlinguistic register, on a frequency tuned into through feeling and sound. Rather than discourse, we can consider the concept of utterance, which includes tone, pitch, timbre, and nonlinguistic vocalisms, improvisation, and blue notes. Grounded in expressive forms of movement, we can incorporate the knowledge of our physical being with porous boundaries between ourselves, others, and the world. In this way, black cultures and philosophies offer us alternative ways to think about, and live within, our black bodies.

# 7

## Cinema
### Michael Boyce Gillespie

The word "cinema" refers to an art and industrial practice; it names a craft, a business, an enactment of cultural production, and an object of disciplinary study. African American studies is an interdisciplinary and multidisciplinary field devoted to the study of history, philosophic traditions, gender, sexuality, culture, the arts, social life, and political thought as these issues relate to African Americans. The field's appreciation of the idea of race and how this idea is manifest in innumerable facets of American life crucially informs the study of the art of blackness. Therefore, to map out "cinema" as a keyword for African American studies requires us to address several interrelated questions. How might the methodologies and critical tendencies of African American studies inform an understanding of cinema, and subsequently, how might cinema inform an understanding of African American studies? Second, what are the terms of engagement that are most generative for considering cinema and African American studies?

One of the important ways that African American studies has impacted the study of American cinema is through its sustained examination of how cinema, as a part of a larger field of American visual culture, has contributed to, perpetuated, and instantiated a dangerously false conception of visuality as truth or innocuous. This point is especially evident by the reception history of D. W. Griffith's *The Birth of a Nation* (1916). An adaptation of Thomas Dixon Jr.'s *The*

*Clansman* (1905), Griffith's film offered significantly innovative approaches to narrative and editing that became a standard in the development of the language of cinema. Furthermore, the film is a torrid New South text that figures the Confederacy and slavery as noble and heroic gestures. The Civil War is rendered in the rhetoric of Northern aggression, and Reconstruction is pictured as white struggle amid a sea of freed African American savages and duplicitous carpetbaggers. The men of the Ku Klux Klan, in Griffith's Christian rhetoric of love, family, nationhood, are framed as heroes rather than violent terrorists. Cinema studies work in African American studies scholarship has vitally framed *The Birth of a Nation* as a white supremacist text. At the same time, scholarship has detailed African American activist protests against the film, the circulation of the idea of black cinema during the early twentieth century, the growth of black film criticism, and the ways in which African American film spectatorship was a negotiation with turn-of-the-century ideals of black modernity (Everett 2001; Stewart 2005; Field 2015). Yet the critical struggle of disputing egregious tendencies of antiblack visual culture cannot be addressed in strictly the terms of false or *negative* images that must be corrected by authentic or *positive* ones. Instead, African American studies provides ways of understating cinema's place in the broader conceptual field of black visual and expressive culture and, moreover, the ways in which the study of race and cinema might open onto related questions of race and art in other fields of study (e.g., cinema, visual culture, literature, art history, cultural studies, women and gender studies, and queer studies). By enlivening the study of this art and grounding it in questions of race, history, aesthetics, and culture, this approach to reframing the study of cinema widens the aesthetic and formal avenues of inquiry (Guerrero 1993; Massood 2003).

If "cinema" in African American studies refers not just to a discrete set of art objects but to the larger racial-historical context in which the film industry and its products operate, we must consider the structural logic and function of renderings of blackness in film, egregious or otherwise. This kind of interrogation of cinema would follow up on Toni Morrison's call to consider representational systems in less binaristic and unidirectional ways, to, in her terms, "avert the critical gaze from the racial object to the racial subject; from the described and imagined to the describers and imaginers; from the serving to the served" (1992, 90). For the study of cinema, this ultimately means considering the political and aesthetic consequence of various facets that compose the cinematic arts; and it means understanding that the measure of cinema's capacity to render blackness must be understood in terms of particularities over essences. Put simply, to study cinema is never just a question of accuracy, authenticity, or truth. In "'But Compared to What?': Reading Realism, Representation, and Essentialism in *School Daze*, *Do the Right Thing*, and the Spike Lee Discourse," Wahneema Lubiano argues for a greater rigor when considering the idea of race in cinema to avoid engendering it as a natural phenomenon. As she observes, "What is race in the United States if not an attempt to make 'real' a set of social assumptions about biology?" (1996a, 175). Her reading of the reception of Spike Lee's films and the rhetoric of realism is a vital conception of African American studies with attention to gender and to film and media.

Cinema is as an art and critical practice that must be irreconcilable in the sense that it must not be considered exclusively accountable to social categories of race, gender, sexuality, and class. Instead, cinema's generative value to African American studies lies in how it challenges, refashions, and engages with the field's politics and perspectives. This amply provides for a consideration of art as critical and speculative rather than merely a footnote to the lived experience of race. As Stuart Hall notes, "Films are not necessarily good because black people make them. They are not necessarily 'right-on' by virtue of the fact that they deal with the black experience" ([1989] 1996, 445). Hall's succinct disavowal of elementary readings of the idea of black film, ones driven by content and the racial identity of the producers, insists on understanding black visual and expressive culture as a process rather than as an essential product. Just as he calls for an interrogation of how blackness is constructed with his rhetorical query, "What is this 'black' in black popular culture?" scholars must vigilantly consider what is this "black" in black film (1992)?

In the absence of absolute assurances and sanctions in cinema, there is blackness. As Fred Moten writes, blackness "is always a disruptive surprise moving in the rich nonfullness of every term it modifies. Such mediation suspends neither the question of identity nor the question of essence" (2003, 255n1). Moten's qualification of blackness purposefully thrives on its performative quality. For him, blackness operates as a churning and refining force beyond the bounds of identitarian ontologies. It is the potentiality and irreducibility of blackness, an understanding of it as an act and idea, that importantly informs what I term "film blackness." Film blackness marks, enlivens, and amends the idea of black film as an *always disruptive surprise* that might pose new paradigms for genre, narrative, aesthetics, historiography, visuality, and intertextuality. Film blackness entails understanding the ways cinema operates as a visual negotiation, if not tension, between film as art and race as a constitutive, cultural fiction. The conceptual term focuses on the irreducible character of blackness and the radical capacity of black visual and expressive culture, a difference that ceaselessly devises and recasts (M. Gillespie 2016).

As a term that I offer in conversation with "cinema," *film blackness* invites a necessary reckoning with how the idea of black film as an enactment of black visual and expressive culture generates acute and imaginative stagings of the art of blackness and the discursivity of race. If blackness is always already an incitement, question, and process, then the methodological goal of film blackness is not to provide an autopsy of an inanimate system. Rather, film blackness recognizes "cinema" as neither immanent category nor genre nor merely the reflection of the black experience. It insists that cinema's stagings be read for their artistic and epistemological consequence in the sense of understanding how the idea of black film is bound by historiography over history, performativity over essential identity, culture over fantasies of embodied truth. Thus, each film devises something other than an identitarian absolute, and each film tacitly details aesthetic choices that represent *speculations* and *remediations* of history and culture.

Black film offers "cinema" up as a question, not as an answer. This is evident in multiple ways as each film poses a distinct demonstration of how the critical mission and strategies of African American studies can provide for richly complicated and textured understandings of the modalities and nuances that constitute the idea of black film. One such example of film blackness and the critical lens of African American studies as offering strategies for reading and understanding film is Wendell Harris's *Chameleon Street* (1989). It is an independent film based on the real-life exploits of criminal impersonation carried out Douglas Street Jr. starting in 1971. His impersonations include passing himself off as a professional athlete, a reporter for *Time* magazine, a medical student, an exchange student from Martinique, and a lawyer. *Chameleon Street*'s episodic narrative is propelled by the anxious energy of a black genius sociopath bored and inspired by the innumerable privileges and poses that the world has to offer. With each successful impersonation, Street raises the stakes for how one might consider the renegade ways of racial performance. Indeed, the reception history of the film shows how the film challenged the industrial and critical standard of what constituted a black film. The film does not render the life of Street in the immediate terms of a biopic but instead offers several crucial encounters with many facets of black visual and expressive culture. First, the unmoored quality of Street as film character, his ability to circulate with an ethos of convincibility, simultaneously engages with the literature and scholarship on passing and performativity. His movements and poses mark him as an interlocutor and organizer of space and time to such an extent that he is framed as master of many different forms of social privileges and knowledge. Significantly, his performative tactics occur across multiple channels, which include an antidiagnostic dispute, the menace of mimicry, a black modernist measure of intertextuality, and improvisational chaos. Taking these tendencies together as a whole offers us a way of thinking through the critical strategies that African American studies has developed with regard to the considerations of philosophy, black masculinities, literature, and psychoanalysis in contemporary cinema.

The fundamental importance of *Chameleon Street* and other films like it—films that have not been considered in the canon of "black film" or "African American cinema"—cannot be overstated. *Chameleon Street* extensively challenges the conventional (and limited) perceptions of the very idea of black film that circulated at the time of its release and persist today. What followed the film was a critical refusal to understand *Chameleon Street* in the terms of black film, independent film, or art film or to understand it as multivalent and thus engaging all these registers. This critical refusal reveals the deeply antiblack and exclusionary tendencies of categories of knowledge within cinematic practice and knowledge.

Another film to consider as a challenge to and within African American studies is Arthur Jafa's *Dreams Are Colder than Death* (2013). An experimental documentary, *Dreams* focuses on the meaning of Dr. King's "I Have a Dream" speech fifty years later and asks whether the goals and ambitions of the civil rights movement have been achieved: "Does the dream live on? And if so, what has changed?" The query centers on a sustained and prescient consideration of what blackness is, what the history of blackness is, and what the concept means to black people today. During the film's opening sequence, there is a reverse-motion shot of young black men appearing to fly backward from a public swimming pool. Is this a sign of desegregation rolling back? Amid the gymnastics of black bodies cast from the water, the literary critic Hortense Spillers's voice comes on the soundtrack: "I know we are going to lose this gift of black culture unless we are careful, this gift that is given to people who didn't have a prayer." Spillers's "I know" is answered by Dr. King's "I have a dream" on the soundtrack; her comments are ghosted by his famous speech. In this prelude to the title sequence and the introduction of the film's premise, there is the distance between a gift in peril and a prophecy. *Dreams* is an essay film, a nonfiction form of intellectual and artistic innovation whose black stream of consciousness is prefaced by Spillers's concern for the state of black culture.

A visual historiography of black thought on and off campus, *Dreams Are Colder than Death* seethes with a productively agnostic impression of the idea of African American history that is offered in exquisitely visual and mosaic terms. It brings together a group of visual artists, revolutionaries, musicians, academics, filmmakers, activists, and everyday citizens to offer a history of critical resistance, philosophic practice, and expressivity. I would like to briefly focus on Moten's appearance. In the final section of the film, his voice is paired with footage of him walking, and that is coupled with footage from a Trayvon Martin protest rally in Los Angeles. The slow-motion movement of a mass protest devoted to a black boy coded by a hoodie, murdered, and left to die in the rain with no shelter from the storm becomes punctuated by Moten's commentary: "When you say that black people are just an effect of slavery, you raise the question: Can black people be loved? . . . Not desired, not wanted, not acquired, not lusted after. Can black people be loved? Can blackness be loved?"

The question that Moten raises in *Dreams Are Colder than Death* appears in the context of a consideration of blackness and the object of African American studies, a commentary that is interspersed throughout the film. This love signifies a critical devotion to recognize blackness in terms other than horror. Moten suggests that blackness is always already an act of faith within African American studies. This faith speaks to the potentialities of futurity: the immateriality of faith shadows and moderates the affective force of blackness and how blackness as cultural, aesthetic, historiographic, and political praxis is engendered. *Dreams* demonstrates the rigor of black visual and expressive culture as a study of thought, language, and performativity. The film pivots away from the narrative of Dr. King's dream to a dynamic envisioning of black praxis and freedom dreams. *Can blackness be loved?* Moten's question, an exquisite explanation for *Dreams Are Colder than Death*, resounds as a rhetorical call, a devotional affirmation, an act of revolutionary hope. In its devotion to a practice of black intellectual montage, it is a multidimensional and rhythmic configuration of blackness that is significantly informed by ideas that have developed in African American studies.

Rather than an unmediated window on the world, "cinema," in the context of African American studies, signifies this very reconfiguration of blackness. Cinema's relationship to African American studies is fundamentally situated on the premise of art as discursive craft and production rather than as mimetic reflection. As most evident with the idea of black film and the enactments of film blackness, African American studies as a field of critically collaborative plentitude offers vital opportunities for the study of cinema in ways of great benefit to the understanding of art, culture, and history.

# 8

## City

Rashad Shabazz

A city is a geographic region that consists of large numbers of people. Most dictionaries refer to it as a "large town," but cities are more than that. Cities are living organisms. They are not stable; they change over time. The urban planner Lewis Mumford called the city a "theater of social action" ([1937] 2011, 93). And as theaters of social action, cities bring different kinds of bodies into close contact. The feminist geographer Elizabeth Grosz argues that the city is a kind of network that "links otherwise unrelated bodies" (1998, 32). The city is not simply an external thing outside of us; cities "seep into and effect all other elements that go into the constitution of" bodies (Grosz 1998, 35). The French social theorist and spatial thinker Henri Lefebvre described the city as a place where there are "relations of immediacy . . . between people and groups that make up society" (2006, 101). In other words, cities are an "interface" where social groups, institutions, families, and bodies interact and mutually inform one another.

These musings on the city illustrate that cities are not passive landscapes; they are active organisms that produce social life as it produces itself. So what does this mean for Black people? This question is important given the history of redlining, segregation, plantation slavery, forced migration, and mass incarceration. For Black people, the city has been a place where hope, possibility, and virulent racism are linked. If the city is a kind of stage, what dramas have been played out on it vis-à-vis Black people? And how have Black people been informed by the city, and how have they informed it?

For the past century, the city has been the place where Black politics, art, culture, identity, and resistance were played out. The drama has been intense. Riots, anti-Black violence, housing and economic segregation, the birth of new cultural and artistic movements, and identity formations have all happened on the landscape of the city. North American cities, for example, were the places Black southerners fled to in order to escape the terrorism of southern white supremacy and to improve their economic standing. Like Blacks in North America, Blacks in the other European colonies were also pushed and pulled to the European metropolis, escaping colonial racism and poverty. Others made their way to colonies through military and/or university. These push and pull factors radially transformed Black life and the city. The city has been the spatial backdrop that produced a wellspring of Black cultural, artistic, and political movements. It also became the place where the racialization of space and the fight against it were most intense.

For most of the discipline's existence, geography and geographers were not concerned with Black people. The discipline did not find Black people suitable subjects of study until the 1960s, which has made Black geographic knowledge marginal in the discipline. Black sociologists and artists were the first to examine Black people in the city. W. E. B. Du Bois's *The Philadelphia Negro* (1899) was the first study of Black life in a major city, and it set the stage for future studies. James Weldon Johnson's *Black Manhattan* (1930) charted Black migration from the U.S. South and the Caribbean to New York from the early twentieth century until the 1930s. St. Clair Drake and Horace Cayton's pathbreaking book *Black Metropolis* (1945) examined Black life in Chicago (which was the site of the largest section of migrants in the nation) from the first leg of the Great Black Migration (1917) until the early 1940s. All three of these texts are socio-logical. Nevertheless, each engaged the question of how the geography of the city transformed Black life and how in turn Black people transformed the city. All three studies demonstrated that economic, political, family, and cultural life of Black people were drastically altered by cities. For them, the city was not simply a different place were Black peopled lived but a new arena for the evolution of Black life that presented new opportunities and new challenges.

Black artistic expression and Black life flourished in cities. Twentieth- and early-twenty-first-century Black arts have essentially been urban arts movements. The Harlem Renaissance, jazz, and hip-hop are artistic movements that are rooted in city space. The same goes for fashion, dance, filmmaking, and painting. Again, this is not a North American phenomenon. Diasporic forms of dance, music, and performance have also emerged from Black city life.

Many Black writers have made the city their canvas. Richard Wright used the city to craft his most well-known character—Bigger Thomas in his novel *Native Son* (1940). James Baldwin saw the city as a complex space of gender, racial, and sexual fluidity in works such as *Go Tell It on the Mountain* (1953), *Giovanni's Room* (1956), and *Another Country* (1962), while for Anne Petry's novel *The Street* (1946), the city was the space of patriarchy and racism. Frank London Brown's novel *Trumbull Park* (1959) and Lorainne Hansberry's play *A Raisin in the Sun* (1958) both show the intensity of Chicago's racial segregation and Black people's steadfast opposition to it.

No Black art form has acknowledged the centrality of the city more than music. The city has been ever present in the lyrics, tempo, harmonies, and syncopation of Black music. We see this in jazz, rhythm and blues, blues, hip-hop, reggae, and house. It can be heard in the frenetic pace of Dizzy Gillespie's "Groovin' High" (1947) or Charlie Parker's "Thriving on a Riff" (1957). Stevie Wonder's "Living for the City" (1973) charts the Black migration narrative, Marvin Gaye's "Inner City Blues" (1973) captures the despair of poverty and political violence, and Prince's "Uptown" (1980) sees the city as a space of racial and sexual fluidity and cultural freedom. Rap music has made the city the cornerstone of its lyrical and musical expression, as well. Rappers are never decoupled from the cities that influence their idiosyncratic style. And they use their music to pay homage to the places that birthed their style. Boogie Down Production's "South Bronx" (1987), N.W.A.'s "Straight Outta Compton" (1988), Tupac Shakur and Dr. Dre's "California Love" (1996), Jay-Z's "Empire State of Mind" (2009), Common's "Southside" (2007), Jermaine Dupri's "Welcome to Atlanta" (2002), and E-40's "Tell Me When to Go" (2006) are just a few of the songs that acknowledge the city in the creation of rap music's sonic force.

While art and culture have been profoundly shaped by urban landscapes, forms of constraint, immobilization, and containment have also been a hallmark of Black life in the city. As I have written elsewhere (Shabazz 2015), Black people in cities have faced and continue to face the legacy of carceral containment that is built into the landscape and architecture of their communities. Be it policing, housing, urban planning, or security practices, Black people in cities such as Chicago have faced punitive geographies that made some parts of the city prison-like. The impact of these practices has created implications that go beyond high incarceration rates and immobility. These practices have affected performances of Black masculinity, mobility, and the general health of the community.

But containment has only been one facet of the urban racial struggle. Segregation, economic underdevelopment, environmental racism, and police violence are the social forces that have given rise to many modern antiracist movements. Black nationalism was an urban movement. Started in the early twentieth century, Black nationalism grew in Black cities such as New York, Philadelphia, Detroit, Chicago, and Los Angeles. The concentration of Black people in those cities and the philosophy that championed economic and political control, as well as cultural renewal, influenced many Black city dwellers and their communities. Harlem and the South Side of Chicago, for example, were the centers of Black nationalism, and Black nationalism had significant impact on the politics expressed in these cites.

Black political organizing was also rooted in the racial geography of the city. The Black Panther Party for Self-Defense was started in Oakland, California, in 1968. Focused on defending Black communities from police violence, the Black Panthers were influenced by Black nationalism, but they were also informed by the politics of class struggle and anticolonialism. More than simply self-defense, the Panthers provided a number of programs for the urban poor. Free breakfast, shoes, medical care, and trips to visit incarcerated loved ones were essential programs for Oakland's Black community.

These political movements were not limited to North America. The antiapartheid movement was centered in Johannesburg, as was the Black Power movement in London. As in the U.S., the intensity of racism in these cities and the large numbers of Black people who were being subject to it gave rise to challenges.

Why does the space in which Black life is performed and constituted matter? It matters because Black matters are spatial matters. And the places where Black people express their identities and struggle for recognition influence the tone and terror of their lives. Space and where we are in it determine in large part our identity and future mobility in the world. Space is not just an empty container; it is a dynamic social and geographic sphere where the spatial makeup of place influences and is influenced by the people who inhabit it.

Another reason the city is so important is because space is central to subject formation. Space influences how subjects are formed. More than an empty signifier, space helps to inform the forms of mobility and immobility, access and denial; it produces the "instrumentalities through which individuals express themselves" (Wright 1940, xxvi). In other words, space creates the context for the production of subjects. Moreover, if the environment is "warped or tranquil the mode and manner of behavior will be affected" (Wright 1940, xxvi). Before human geographers explored the relationship between people and place, Richard Wright was examining how the small, cramped and confining domiciles on Chicago's South Side were impacting identify formation of Black migrants from the South. What he discovered is that while geography is not destiny, it does inform the production of subjects.

The city also changed Black life because of the nature of the environment. Despite being places that bring different people together, cities have been where racial segregation was most intense. Through laws, urban planning, architecture, and violence, Black people were *spatialized* in cities. It was the possibility of differently racialized people coming into contact, particularly Blacks with whites, that produced the architecture of confinement that created Black geographies. This is why segregation efforts have been so intense in cities. The threat of Blacks and whites in close proximity, for example, spurred efforts to intensify racial segregation. In this meshing but yet deeply divided geography, Black people lived with what Richard Wright called a "taunting sense of possible achievement" (1940, xxvi). They were spatially close to whites and the economic structures they controlled, while being segregated from them and cut off from their economic benefits. This has been the dominant pattern of racial organization in the city for the past century.

Black people have not only shaped the city but also been shaped by it. The intense racial segregation of the city informs Black people's mobility within in it. The city informs performances of gender and the health of the community. It shaped the kinds of foods Black people eat, the sports they play, the clothes they where. The city informs whom they develop relationships with, their sexual options, and their political persuasions.

As cities around the world become the places that capital flies to and where the poor and working class are pushed out, Black people's relationship to them is sure to change. The rising cost of housing in North American and most western European cities will force Blacks throughout the diaspora to move to new places. Whether these new places will be cities remains to be seen. But what is for certain is that once again the geographies on which Black life is constituted will be struggled over.

# 9

## Civil Rights
Quincy T. Mills

The civil rights movement looms large in twentieth-century African American studies. Regardless of one's politics or the dearth of course material on race in American primary schools, the struggle for integration, Rosa Parks, Martin Luther King Jr., and the March on Washington (sans the "for Jobs and Freedom" part of the march's title) have come to stand in for civil rights. The heroic icons and damning imagery naturalizes civil rights as a corrective to American democracy. Yet "civil rights" is a rather vague term. Do noncitizens have civil rights? If not, where can they turn for protection? Do political actors decide the boundaries of civil rights? And does the "civil" in "civil rights" account for the exigencies of humanity or the demands of everyday human existence?

"Civil rights" defines the protected rights and privileges of citizens. As a keyword used to articulate the quest for equality, it tends to rest on two major strivings: inclusion and protection. The numerous civil rights acts since the end of the Civil War and congressional amendments marked the legislative struggles to codify citizenship for Black people and hold the federal government accountable for protecting those rights and privileges. As such, the field of civil rights has historically fallen into the realm of enumeration—a listing of positive and, later, negative rights endowed to citizens, also called birthright citizenship. The act of enumeration can obscure the essence of being. Where does the right to live fit into the enumerated list of protected rights, which would be assumed under Thomas Jefferson's poetic rendition of protest ensconced in the beginning of the Declaration of Independence—"life, liberty, and pursuit of happiness"? "Civil rights" is a malleable term that intersects with equal rights and, most radically, with human rights. In fact, Black people who fought for civil rights and scholars of African American studies use this keyword interchangeably with "freedom struggle" or "struggle for racial equality" (Sugrue 2008). This keyword is as essential to the foundations of the United States as freedom, democracy, and equality, and it is contested through keywords such as "equity" and "humanity."

Civil rights come with the expectations of freedom. In the eighteenth century, at the time of the American Revolutionary War, free Black citizens articulated claims on citizenship. While they did not use the term "civil rights," they based their demands on the rights accorded free men. In 1787, Rev. Prince Hall, born in Barbados, a Revolutionary War veteran, and the founder of Black freemasonry in colonial America, was among the petitioners to urge the Massachusetts State Legislature to grant Black citizens access to common education because they had "the right to enjoy the privileges of free men." The petitioners based their claim on having "never been backward in paying [their] proportionate part of the burdens under which [other free men] have, or may labor under" (H. Aptheker 1951, 19–20). Hall and the other petitioners emphasized that they deserved access to education because they paid taxes as free men. This petition said nothing of their enslaved counterparts. In the nineteenth century, Alexis de Tocqueville made similar observations about the fruits of a tax-paying Black citizenry. He noted in his travels through Pennsylvania that even among the Quakers, "freed Blacks are not allowed to exercise civil rights. They pay the taxes; is it not fair that they should have a vote?" (1841, 282). These free Black citizens and Tocqueville pointed to specific expectations of freedom and citizenship: education and the franchise. These observations prefigure the battles over civil rights in the antebellum North, similar battles that hinged on access to education and suffrage.

Until the end of the Civil War, civil rights as a keyword bounced around northern states, where Black citizens struggled to define their freedom and citizenship in the national shadows of slavery. The end of the Civil War might have settled the physical conflict between the North and South, but freedom remained contested terrain, which means "civil rights" emerged as a keyword in the reconstruction of the union. From 1865 to 1896, states defined and redefined Black citizenship but also what rights and privileges they should enjoy. To be sure, states responded to the push and pull of Black assertiveness and white resistance. African Americans did not need the state to define civil rights for them, as enslaved or freed people. No longer bound to a master, they decided when they would work despite being bound to an employer. African Americans of Edisto Island, South Carolina, petitioned President Andrew Johnson that they had a right to keep and purchase land they had worked, land that had been ceded to them through Field Order Number 15 and then stripped from them and returned to former Confederates at Johnson's order. African Americans set up small schools. They reconstituted families that had been torn asunder during slavery. They organized political conventions as a collective forum to discuss the direction of Black men's votes. They did not articulate the reconstitution of their lives as a quest toward civil rights but rather as an exercise of freedom. When African Americans were denied those freedoms, such as when the Black Codes emerged in what seemed like mere moments after the fall of Appomattox, they entered "rights" talk: the expectations and entitlements of citizenship.

CIVIL RIGHTS   QUINCY T. MILLS

Facing these kinds of restrictions on public life, African Americans were undaunted, forcing the federal government to legally define civil rights through legislative acts, most notably the Civil Rights Acts of 1866 and 1875, the latter of which the Supreme Court rendered unconstitutional in the *Civil Rights Cases* of 1883. The 1866 act—"An Act to Protect All Persons in the United States in Their Civil Rights, and Furnish the Means of Their Vindication"—defined national citizens as all persons born in the United States (except Indians). The 1866 act served as an act of inclusion, which held white citizenship as the standard that Blacks should be brought up to. It outlined the rights that citizens, regardless of race, would enjoy, including "to make and enforce contracts, to sue, be parties, and give evidence, to inherit, purchase, lease, sell, hold, and convey real and personal property, and to full and equal benefit of all laws and proceedings for the security of person and property, *as is enjoyed by white citizens*" (Civil Rights Act 1866). Considering the devastating decision in *Dred Scott v. Sandford* (1857), Radical Republicans helped to pass the Fourteenth Amendment to overturn *Dred Scott* and solidify Black citizenship. Yet citizenship did not necessarily open the doors to civil rights.

The Civil Rights Act of 1875 expanded the definition of civil rights beyond individual market transactions and juridical access, to include equal enjoyment of the public sphere, or an unfettered mobility to live freely. African Americans wasted no time testing the new act. Within days of its passage, they sought admission in theaters, hotels, and restaurants. In an uncanny twist of fate, they even tested the act against their own brethren. Black barbers operated their commercial barbershops exclusively for white patrons. Black activists ironically drew on the Civil Rights Act in their protests to suggest that open access should not be contingent on the race of the proprietor. Private property and whiteness, or the

will of white patrons, curtailed Black men's mobility in the public sphere (Q. Mills 2013). These acts, and questions of their constitutionality, emerged because Black citizens sought to live their lives freely and to make choices. Because they were denied access to these rights, the state provided legal definitions that would serve as recourse in the courts if those rights were denied. But Blacks had to file suit to be heard; however, courts seldom lent a listening ear.

In the immediate years after the end of Reconstruction, the Supreme Court gave southern states a sign that the federal government would allow the states to define civil rights. Whiteness equaled property, and if its public face were challenged, the state would protect it by deeming it private and outside the list of "protected rights." In the *Civil Rights Cases* of 1883, the Court held that Congress, in the Civil Rights Act of 1875, had overstepped its powers under the Fourteenth Amendment in trying to regulate private discrimination. The Court interpreted the Fourteenth Amendment to prohibit discriminatory state action "such as the enactment of laws that denied equal protection," as opposed to the acts of private property owners exercising their property rights (Tushnet 1996, 75). So, as long as the state did not require discriminatory action, private parties could exclude anyone.

At the turn of the twentieth century, race-based and colorblind policies emerged in tandem and shaped the contours of civil rights as a keyword. The *Civil Rights Cases* proved to be the pallet that *Plessy v. Ferguson* (1896) rested on. When the Supreme Court upheld Louisiana's separate-but-equal train-car policy, it paved the way for segregation laws in other areas of society. In turn, Black activists mounted their civil rights struggles against this behemoth of de jure racial ordering. Yet alongside these explicitly race-based policies were state-enacted colorblind policies that said nothing of race but targeted

African Americans. At the turn of the twentieth century, southern states rewrote their state constitutions and effectively disenfranchised their Black citizens. Among the criteria for voting, states required a poll tax and literacy tests. While these requirements applied to all potential voters, Black citizens were denied access in nefarious ways.

The claims of private property and states' rights won out in the wrangling over the civil rights debates in the late nineteenth century. Yet the struggles for freedom extended far beyond hotel rooms, theater seats, barbershop chairs, classroom seats, and the ballot box. Was it a civil right to be protected from lynching? These were private acts, though sanctioned by state actors (police, jail clerks). The Enforcement ("Ku Klux Klan") Act of 1871 came close to providing such protections by prohibiting terrorist organizations, such as the Klan, from violently or otherwise preventing Black voting, jury service, or office-holding (Bardolph 1970, 52–54).

Black activists refused to stand by while Black men and women were lynched for suspicion, for false allegation, or simply for being. For example, Ida B. Wells was a pioneer in investigative journalism. Wells declared lynching an act of terror. "Thomas Moss, Calvin McDowell, and Lee Stewart had been lynched in Memphis," she noted in her autobiography, "one of the leading cities of the South, in which no lynching had taken place before, with just as much brutality as other victims of the mob; and they had committed no crime against white women. This is what opened my eyes to what lynching really was. An excuse to get rid of Negroes who were acquiring wealth and property and thus keep the race terrorized" (Wells-Barnett 1970, 64). With a keen methodological approach, she produced three pamphlets—*Lynch Law in All Its Phases*, *A Red Record*, and *Mob Rule in New Orleans*—debunking the myth of black hypersexuality as a factor in lynching cases. She embarked on a national and international campaign not simply to "change the law" but to "tell the truth freely" to alter the public discourse (J. Royster 1996, 40; Bay 2009). While Wells did not frame her antilynching crusade as a call for civil rights, lynching and extralegal racial violence largely proved such an overwhelming stain on American democracy and the contours of citizenship that, thanks to Wells, Black activists increasingly looked to the federal government for protection.

The National Association for the Advancement of Colored People (NAACP) carried on Wells's antilynching crusade. While the civil rights organization is most known for dismantling de jure segregation in public education, particularly through *Brown v. Board of Education* (1954), its initial campaigns included increasing public awareness of racial violence and lobbying for an antilynching bill. The organization's turn toward litigation and desegregating education stemmed from its successful mob-rule case, *Moore v. Dempsey* (1923), which ruled the defendants were denied due process when white mobs loomed in the shadows of their trials, thus intimidating them and the jurors. Megan Francis notes that two decades of antilynching activism put the NAACP on the radar of the Garland Fund, which eventually provided funding to focus on desegregating public schools (M. Francis 2014; Tushnet 1987).

In the post–World War II period, racial violence continued to inform understandings of civil rights. Black activists found a listening ear from President Harry Truman's administration in the immediate aftermath of the war and an emerging Cold War political moment. In the wake of postwar racial violence in Columbia, Tennessee, Georgia, and Louisiana, a coalition of organizations such as the NAACP, Urban League, and the new National Emergency Committee Against Mob Violence pressured Truman's administration to act. Truman, urged by an aide and the attorney general, favored a national civil rights committee to address racial violence; and with an executive order, he established the President's Committee on Civil Rights. Truman charged the committee to "make recommendations with respect to adoption or establishment by legislation or otherwise of more adequate means and procedures for protection of civil rights of the people of the United States" (Lawson 2004, 14). Racial violence was considered under the umbrella of civil rights atrocities. The historian Steven Lawson notes, "Truman used the terms *civil rights* and *civil liberties* interchangeably with racial discrimination and religious bigotry" (2004, 21). Strikingly, the Committee on Civil Rights did not centralize the keyword "civil rights." Phileo Nash, an aide to Truman, noted, "The use of the word 'civil rights' . . . came about in the course of our staff studies. We thought it advisable to find a term that was slightly fresh, and the word civil rights was not used for this function at that time" (Lawson 2004, 21). The committee brought together the "rights essential to the citizen in a free society" mentioned in the Declaration of Independence, the Bill of Rights, and Franklin Roosevelt's Four Freedoms to highlight the "four basic rights . . . essential to the well-being of the individual and to the progress of society": the right to safety and security of the person; the right to citizenship and its privileges; the right to freedom of conscience and expression; and the right to equality of opportunity (Lawson 2004, 51). In fact, the title of the final report, *To Secure These Rights*, was pulled directly from the Declaration of Independence (C. Wilson 1947). They were not the only ones questioning the keyword "civil rights."

Historically, this framework of civil rights (inclusion and protection) has been insufficient to realize Black freedom; however, in the 1960s, many activists outside of radical leftist circles began to voice this concern. Just four days after Senate Democrats launched a filibuster of the civil rights bill on March 30, 1964, Malcolm X delivered a speech, titled "The Ballot or the Bullet," to a mostly Black audience in Cleveland, Ohio. In part, he urged African Americans to "expand the civil-rights struggle to the level of human rights" in order to "take the case of the black man in this country before the nations in the UN" (Malcolm X [1964] 1994, 34). He reasoned that anyone who deprived African Americans of something, such as rights, that belong to them were criminals. For Malcolm, it seemed futile to appeal to the very criminals who were responsible for denying basic rights and protections. "Civil rights keeps you under his restrictions, under his jurisdiction," he argued. "Civil rights keeps you in his pocket. Civil rights means you're asking Uncle Sam to treat you right. Human rights are your God-given rights. Human rights are the rights that are recognized by all nations of this earth. And any time any one violates your human rights, you can take them to the world court" (Malcolm X [1964] 1994, 35). In July, Malcolm presented a petition to independent African heads of state at the Organization of African Unity (OAU) meeting to urge them to initiate an investigation through the UN Commission on Human Rights, an act he could not initiate as an individual. He was unable to sway his African colleagues.

Martin Luther King also came to realize that "civil rights" as a keyword was limited, but it took the fire of a rebellion for him to see it. African Americans in Los Angeles and other major cities across the country grew increasingly frustrated with a lack of decent and affordable housing, limited access to jobs that paid a living wage, and the constant violence from police brutality. The Los Angeles uprisings in August 1965, just a year after the Civil Rights Act of 1964 had passed and five days after the Voting Rights Act had been signed, jolted King and other southern activists fighting for civil rights to rethink this keyword. "The flames of Watts illuminated more than the western sky," he argued; "they cast light on the imperfections in the civil rights movement and the tragic shallowness of white racial policy in the explosive ghettos" (King [1965] 1991, 189). He came to realize that a restructuring of American democracy, not legislative reform, could repair economic dislocation and restore human dignity. Bayard Rustin also recognized that economic dislocation demonstrated that "at issue, after all, is not *civil rights*, strictly speaking, but social and economic conditions" (1965, 26).

These men said what women had articulated already. When the student sit-in movement swept the South, Ella Baker urged critics and supporters not to be fooled into thinking those young people were fighting for the right to purchase a hamburger or the right to sit next to white consumers in a diner. She argued that students were "seeking to rid America of the scourge of racial segregation and discrimination—not only at lunch counters, but in every aspect of life" (E. Baker 1960, 4). Like Baker, Fannie Lou Hamer understood and projected the ways traditional civil rights discussions needed to touch every aspect of life. Hamer, from Ruleville, Mississippi, was fired from her job as a sharecropper and kicked off the land for attempting to register to vote. Hamer connected disenfranchisement, a privilege of citizenship, and economic reprisals and dislocation in her fight for civil rights. In 1964, she helped organize the Mississippi Freedom Democratic Party and ran for a Mississippi seat in the U.S. Congress. The "poverty of segregation" was inextricably bound with access to the ballot. Black patients received substandard health care compared to white patients. "Poverty and poor health," she ascertained in a *Memphis World* article, "form an unbreakable circle, one which need attention from the people who are suppose to represent us" (Hamer 1964, 8).

There was nothing exceptionally masculine about "civil rights" as a keyword; however, men often assumed it was their role to lead the pubic charge in fighting for it, which often resulted in its heterosexual and masculine framing. As a member of President John Kennedy's Commission on the Status of Women Committee on Civil and Political Rights, the activist Pauli Murray fought to include protections against sex-based discrimination as a civil right. She took the "Big Six" male civil rights leaders to task for not including women in the meeting with President Kennedy after the March on Washington for Jobs and Freedom in August 1963. The men hoped to convince Kennedy to help get the Civil Rights Bill passed, which President Lyndon Johnson ushered through Congress after Kennedy's assassination. The act was meant to replace the 1875 Civil Rights Act, which had been struck down in 1883. When Senator Everett Dirksen announced in April 1964 that he would consider removing the word "sex" from Title VII of the Civil Rights Bill, Murray was asked to prepare a memo to Congress, since, she recalled, she could "act freely" and was a "victim of both race and sex discrimination" (1987, 356). Murray described her memo as a "strongly worded document, pointing to the historical interrelatedness of the movements for civil rights and women's rights and the tragic consequences in United States history of ignoring the interrelatedness of human rights." She pointed out, "A strong argument can be made for the proposition that Title VII without the 'sex' amendment would benefit Negro males primarily and thus offer genuine equality of opportunity to only *half* of the potential Negro work force" (1987, 356–57). The "sex" amendment remained. Murray believed that Black women had to be in the room to ensure a more universal framing of civil rights. With Murray's work, sex was included in Title VII of the 1964 act.

If historical subjects have contested the boundaries of civil rights, scholars of African American studies have also questioned this keyword. Few scholars define the meanings of civil rights; however, many debate its conceptual, temporal, and geographical boundaries. The scholarly framing of the keyword "civil rights" centers on its connection to the Black Power movement. The temporal markers of the civil rights movement traditionally move from the Montgomery Bus Boycott (1955–56) to either the Voting Rights Act of 1965 or Martin Luther King's assassination in 1968. Jeanne Theoharis, Komozi Woodard, and Jacqueline Dowd Hall suggest that the modern civil rights movement began in the 1930s and extended beyond 1968. This reperiodization is tied to a reframing of civil rights to account for economic issues (workers rights, welfare rights), southern exceptionalism, and the continuities with the Black Power movement (Theoharis and Woodard 2003; J. Hall 2005). In arguing the limits of the traditional civil rights narrative, scholars have increasingly used the term "Black Freedom Movement." Sundiata Cha-Jua and Clarence Lang (2007) argue that the "Long Movement Thesis" flattens the distinctions between civil rights and Black Power as distinct waves of black activism and political worldviews.

The line between the temporal and conceptual uses of civil rights are still at play in the usage of "post–civil rights." Some Black activists celebrated the legislative gains and marked a new phase of struggle, while others were disillusioned that civil rights gains were limited in scope and marked the inadequacies of a civil rights framework to address the structural challenges to Black freedom. Yet when scholars reference the post–civil rights era, it is more for the temporal marker than the contestations of the keyword "civil rights." The very term "post–civil rights" suggests civil rights have been obtained; however, colorblind politics and the ambiguities of the keyword "civil rights" dangerously suggests freedom and equal opportunity has been obtained. For example, with the proliferation of mass incarceration and the prison industrial complex, Black activists and African American studies scholars have turned their attention to the infrastructures of justice and denial of humanity to Black people. The Black Lives Matter (BLM) movement emerged in 2013 when George Zimmerman was acquitted in the killing of the Black youth Trayvon Martin. Frustrated that justice had not been served, Black queer activists Alicia Garza, Patrisse Cullors, and Opal Tometi started a Twitter hashtag that grew into a larger movement against state violence toward Black people. While some people have referred to this moment as a resurgence of civil rights, is Black Lives Matter a manifestation of civil rights or human rights? At the core of BLM protests are the shootings of unarmed Black people. Only the lack of scale keeps police shootings far from the line of genocide. The right to live reminds all that civil and human rights are not mutually exclusive.

# 10

## Coalition

Samantha Pinto

"Coalition" is a critical keyword in modern political organizing, denoting the practice of connecting various political groups of differing cultural, social, and/or ideological identities through a common goal or struggle. In the U.S. and internationally, coalition work is now a staple tactic for rallying institutions—and sometimes electorates—for specific policy changes whose interests cut across various economic, cultural, and political lines. In the academy, organization theory, or social organization theory—a branch of sociology and sometimes psychology—became increasingly interested in coalition organizing as a dominant mode of politics in the wake of civil rights and feminist organizing in the 1960s and '70s U.S., as well as global student, anticolonial / Third Worldist, and antiwar movements in the same time period. Coalition's key historical emergence as what we might think of as a social justice practice was then born of and around the time that African American studies—as well as Chicano/a studies and the formation known as ethnic studies in the academy by the 1980s—emerged as an institutional critique of higher education's politics around race and ethnicity.

Coalition as a political strategy in African American politics, of course, dates further back: from antislavery and women's rights collaborations in the nineteenth century—from Ida B. Wells and Anna Julia Cooper and other black feminist activists calling for political affiliations between what we might term early or first-wave civil rights movements (postabolition in the Reconstruction era) and the suffrage movement that was assumed to largely involve white women—to work between the SCLC and SNCC and any number of organized efforts in the second wave of civil rights in the 1960s, spreading into the 1970s Black Power movement. All of these coalitions sought some strategic solidarity with intersecting marginalized groups for certain events and issues. But it is on the heels of the masculinizing narrative of Black Power and Black nationalism and the whitewashing of the feminist revolution of the 1960s and 1970s in the U.S. that black feminist thought emerged to theorize both itself and coalition as central to African American studies and politics. "Coalition" is then a word and a concept in African American studies that issued in no small part from the active erasure of black women as subjects of and actors in dominant feminist and African American political discourse in the United States.

Coalition stands somewhere in the middle of "solidarity" and "intersectionality" as an activist practice and a theoretical tool of working across certain identitarian boundaries. Black feminist theorists defined and refined the word in the key texts of their fields, most notably as collected in the revolutionary 1983 edited volume *Home Girls: A Black Feminist Anthology* (B. Smith). There one can find both the Combahee River Collective's 1977 foundational statement of black feminism and the necessity of coalition and Bernice Johnson Reagon's transcribed 1981 speech on coalition from the West Coast Women's Music Festival. Contemporary scholarship in the field seeks to place this work alongside that of Audre Lorde (another contributor to *Home Girls*), Patricia Hill Collins, and other black feminist intellectuals of that and the following generation as the historical authors of coalition politics, as African American studies has come to know them. This brief essay traces those lines and situates "coalition" as a keyword that has come to redefine feminist and antiracist thought today, as well as the political movements in African America that follow this moment in black feminism.

In Reagon's manifesto on coalition as both necessary and risky political practice, the black feminist theorist and musicologist uses this scene as a way to imagine coalitional work through the metaphor of everyday life—that, literally, one can live in a house or "a little barred room," as she calls it, for only so long, as "there is no hiding place" from difference (2000, 356). She also tells us up front in her essay that coalition work is "the most dangerous work you can do" (356). This is the starting point for understanding the significance of theories and practices of coalition to African American studies, as coalition primarily emerges as a complex methodology—and political goal—of black feminist thought. Coalition work is a paradox for Reagon—that which threatens one's existence but is also the only way one can "figure out" how to keep existing. I emphasize Reagon's reasoning at length to ground coalition in a history of black feminist thought that is deeply reflective and pragmatic about both the need for organizing around particular intersectional identities and also the crucial need for issue-based coalition work. Both are "dangerous," both are inescapable, both are articulated here in Reagon's 1981 work. Coalition, then, is not a word that negates what, in shorthand, has become the term "identity" (organizing around a set of social and cultural markers) but one that exists, necessarily, in simultaneity with those strategic designations.

Reagon's words on the danger but also the call to survival that coalition work entails follow on the heels of the Combahee River Collective's powerful 1977 stance (also included in both *Home Girls* and *This Bridge Called My Back: Writings by Radical Women of Color*, edited by Cherríe Moraga and Gloria Anzaldúa and first published

in 1981). The collective articulates the foundational presence of black feminist thought in social movements even as it calls out disillusionment with those politics, foregrounding the need for coalitional politics built on both antiracism and antisexism. If the Combahee River Collective lays out the historical conditions that undergird the need for coalitional politics, Barbara Smith lays out the ways that creating black feminist theory around multiple sites of oppression has led, in fact, to more and not less of a desire for coalitional work: "Approaching politics with a comprehension of the simultaneity of oppressions has helped to create a political atmosphere particularly conducive to coalition building. . . . A commitment to principled coalitions, based not upon expediency, but upon our actual need for each other is a second major contribution of black feminist struggle" (2000, xxxiv–xxxv). Here, Smith echoes the sentiments of the frequently cited Audre Lorde on the significance of organizing around difference when she explains that this model of coalitions is particularly suited toward the political positions of Third World women.

Historians, philosophers, and sociologists have also turned to the history of black feminist organizations as a way not just to uncover the work that black women did in and under the umbrella of feminism but to recast contemporary feminist history itself as a narrative of coalition—some obvious successes, some "failures" in the way we traditionally conceive of politics (found in the work of Stephanie Gilmore [2008], Sandra Harding [2009], Kimberly Springer [2005], Myra Marx Ferree, Beth Hess, and Patricia Yancey Martin [Ferree and Hess 2000; Ferree and Martin 1995], just to name a few scholars in the fields). Alongside the work of Patricia Hill Collins (2013), Maria Lugones (2003), Benita Roth (2004), Nira Yuval-Davis (2011), and bell hooks (2015), this scholarship has become a model of thinking through social movement organization and its temporalities—how and why groups might come together across a range of specific, timely issues or even syllabi (see also R. Lee 2000) and how we might see those crossings as generative even if they "end," and end in failure. In a 1994 interview, Angela Davis cites Lorde and others in her bid for coalitional thought and political action: "There are more options than sameness, opposition, or hierarchical relations," she asserts, later suggesting that "we need to be more reflective, more critical and more explicit about our concepts of community" across difference (Davis and Martinez 1994). Davis's words are, in fact, foundational to the historians and social movement organizational theorists. She makes the case that the history of black feminist organization and thought is, by definition, coalitional—with all of the nuances of temporality, "success," and "leadership" that entails. She sets coalitional politics apart from the normative prescription of American politics to assume a universal standpoint for its citizens but also from the imperative of a homogenized minority position for any given social movement.

This turn to recognize the enduring depth of black feminist contributions to contemporary political life and thought is remarkable in at least two ways of anticipating future directions of African American and feminist studies: First, it works to undo African American political and cultural imperatives for a single great leader or leaders—a model debunked by Erica R. Edwards in her 2012 *Charisma and the Fictions of Black Leadership* and one that has gained popular attention in the Black Lives Matter movement. It does this by claiming the significance of group political action as the history of black feminism, not just its new direction. Second, it foregrounds the primacy not just of the practice but of theories of coalition as the ground for contemporary, post–civil rights feminist thought—and of black feminists as the intellectual authors of this galvanizing force

in the field of social justice. In backdating the history of coalition—as a concept and as practice and as the primary narrative of the foundation of African American studies and feminist studies—it clarifies the radical work that, yes, scholars such as Angela Davis, Audre Lorde, and others have done but also the work of collective praxis, thought, and intellectual articulation as central to the field. This can be traced through the iconic Combahee River Collective Statement to the *Home Girls* anthology (and also *This Bridge Called My Back* and *All the Women Are White, All the Blacks Are Men, but Some of Us Are Brave* [Hull, Bell-Scott, and Smith 1982], which paved the way for the transnational and multicultural feminist boom of anthological production of the late 1990s and early 2000s) to the myriad organizations that not only worked on everyday issues in their communities but also sought out various definitions of coalition—from temporary to enduring ones—to tackle intersectional issues.

These anthologies, in their multiracial, interdisciplinary makeup, stand as published enactments of coalition politics; in their use in ethnic and feminist studies classrooms, they insist on strategic alliances but also historical narratives of difference and difficulty as the basis for contemporary political thought. It is these instantiations of coalition politics that also make the word "coalition" so central to the thinking and doing of African American studies today and that look to the vibrant future of political thought across intersectional and interdisciplinary academic fields.

# 11

## Colonialism

Shona N. Jackson

"Colonialism" shares its roots with the Latin terms *colōnia* and *colonus*. *Colōnia* is a colony or settlement of conquered or annexed lands by Roman citizens. *Colonus* designates someone who settles, cultivates, or farms land (Glare [1982] 2000). The terms refer, respectively, to a reorganization of space and to its peopling with foreigners, whose political loyalties remain external to the colonized space (Kohn 2014). Neither term, however, distinguishes among types of colonialism such as settler, administrative, or extractive. They elide the accompanying violence, administrative apparatuses, and displacements of the original inhabitants of colonized territories. Later definitions of "colony" encapsulate early Latin meanings when denoting a "settlement in a new country" or "a body of people who settle in a new locality" (*Oxford English Dictionary*, n.d.-a). In a feeble attempt to account for the extant occupants of colonized space, a genealogical definition of the term, which dates its first use to an 1853 lady's travel journal, designates it as "the colonial system or principle. Now freq. used in the derogatory sense of an alleged policy of exploitation of backward or weak peoples by a larger power" (ibid.).

Contemporary literary and cultural definitions restore the power relations obscured by colonialism's roots, making a distinction among the type and scale of Greco-Roman empires, later ones—for example the Mongol, Ottoman, and Aztec empires—and the forms of "modern colonialism" initiated by Europe in the fifteenth century (Loomba [1998] 2005). These definitions elucidate colonialism as a form of domination *and* settlement in which one country politically dominates another (Childers and Hentzi 1995). Comprehensive meanings consider colonialism a form of cultural domination that is either limited to its geographic and political dimensions (Palmisano 2001) or exceeds them as the hegemonic expression of a colonizing European modernity (Ashcroft 2012). Bernard S. Cohn (1996) labels it an enabling system of knowledge production about the peoples and spaces being conquered. Cohn follows Edward Said—whose *Orientalism* marks the advent of postcolonial studies in academe—in looking beyond the administrative apparatuses of colonialism at its violent intellectual project within which the production of knowledge about colonized space is substituted for the space itself (Said 1979; Baudrillard 1988; Mudimbe 1988).

The cultural and epistemological turn in iterating colonialism's mechanisms of subordination links to emphasis on the psychological aspects of domination in which the colonized is perceived as the product of an imbibed, negative self-image that is "the result of a series of aberrations of affect" (Fanon [1967] 2008, xii; see also Bhabha 1994; R. Young 1995; Dangarembga 1988; Morrison [1970] 2007; Ellison [1947] 1995). Frantz Fanon first introduced the principle of "sociogeny" to capture the antagonistic remaking of the colonized subject's culturally specific biological self within the socioeconomic terrain of the colony and the cultural image of the colonizer (Fanon [1967] 2008). For Fanon's former teacher Aimé Césaire, in this remaking there is "no human contact," only "relations of domination and submission" that transform *both* colonized and colonizer and make the entire colonial system a process of "thingification," the re-production of all humans as objects (Césaire [1972] 2000, 42).

Philosophical considerations build on Fanon and Césaire to argue that colonialism's effects are not only material or psychological but ontological. Sylvia Wynter claims that European colonialism initiated new "genres of the human" (McKittrick 2015, 9) in which the Judeo-Christian concept of Man that was dominant in the fifteenth century was eventually secularized and overrepresented as though it were the totality of what it meant to be human across all cultures and societies (Wynter 1991; see also Wynter 1995). This secular, biological, and economic version of Man is the outcome of the modes of production (capitalism) and thought (Renaissance and Enlightenment) that developed with Europe's modern, colonial project. It is the dominant mode of being that continuously produces "the *niggers*, the *non-whites*, the *natives*" as "*poor* and *jobless, homeless, relatively lowly skilled*, and *under-developed*" (Wynter 1991, 274) in relation to the fully sovereign, "transparent" (Silva 2007) subject of Western, European Man (see also Dussel [1985] 2003). From the fifteenth to the late twentieth century, European colonialism and its invention of race, as the primary distillation of its principles and means of portability of its logic, is inextricable from secular humanism and rational capital. These perspectives are underscored by claims that colonialism is indispensable to capitalism and that the Enlightenment is rife with colonialist, racialist thinking that is constitutive, not aberrant (Loomba [1998] 2005; K. Marx 1853; Hegel [1837] 1899; Judy 1991; Eze 1997; Silva 2007; Buck-Morss 2000; Sebastiani 2013). Some societies escaped direct, western European control, yet most live the outcome of colonialism through its globalization of markets and of the dominant culture and mode of being human that drives those markets. What the African American poet Langston Hughes saw as the lack of a "house in the world" for black selfhood is, broadly, the unhousing of nonwhites that colonialism has wrought in its denial of "ontological sovereignty" (Hughes [1931] 1995; David Scott 2000). Together, these collective and contemporaneous accounts of colonialism redefine it as political, economic, cultural, discursive, cognitive, philosophical, and pernicious. It outstrips the control of lands and peoples considered subordinate within the worldview of Europe and its modern philosophical projects of self-determination, as they are secured by its global politico-economic institutions.

Modern, European colonialism is broken into two "waves": a first from the fifteenth to mid-nineteenth century and a second commencing in the late nineteenth century through the late twentieth century (Palmisano 2001). The first wave turned sub-Saharan African peoples into immutable subordinates of modernity. It began in 1415 with the Portuguese conquest of Cueta, which remains in European control, impacting even the current Syrian civil war (Russell-Wood 1995; Dearden 2016). Successful capture of Muslim Cueta gave the Portuguese a strategic advantage. In 1434, they were the first to navigate around the westernmost tip of Africa, Cape Bojador, opening a sea route to southern Africa (Russell-Wood 1995). Chronicles of those voyages reveal the Christian worldview under which discovered peoples and lands fell. The expeditions were undertaken because "up to that time no one knew . . . what there might be beyond this cape" and "to increase the holy faith in Our Lord Jesus Christ" (Azurara 1936, 130). The suffering of sub-Saharan blacks who died because of these first discoveries is thus tempered by the fact that when they died, "they died Christians" (ibid.).

This theocentric worldview guided the principles of natural slavery, just war, natural law, and later the law of nations, which governed European explorations and wealth accumulation (Wynter 1991, 1995; Robert Williams 1990; Kohn 2014; Pagden 1982; Russell-Wood 1978). Within it, the peoples and lands of sub-Saharan

Africa were beyond God's grace and subordinate to Christian, European Man (Wynter 1991). This fallen status derived from the Aristotelian view of the Earth as the "centre of the turning spheres," all "subordinate to the ultimate sphere of immutability, where God resides" (Scruton [1981] 1995, 13). This Christian cosmogony was transposed onto the physical Earth and the "effective division of the world's population into Christians and heathens" (Russell-Wood 1978, 27). The temperate zone (containing the heart of Christian Europe) was likened to the higher spheres and thus redeemed, while the torrid zone (which includes the racialist, European, geographic construction of sub-Saharan Africa and the southernmost tip of India) reflected the fallen spheres needing redemption. This division governed Christian Europe's social structure's elevation of the nobility and clergy above lay peoples (Wynter 1991). The subordinate status of African peoples below Bojador, as "enemies of the faith," affirmed an extant worldview, which, if challenged, would be chaotic for the Judeo-Christian social order (Azurara 1936; Wynter 1991).

The Portuguese voyages did not lead, initially, to wide-scale African colonization. They resulted in the capture of small numbers of blacks, transported to Europe for nonchattel slavery and servitude (Azurara 1936). The end of the fifteenth century saw an established trade in goods and black slaves, with posts and "strong houses," such as that at São Jorge da Mina (Elmina) in 1482, on the coast of present-day Ghana (Russell-Wood 1978, 1995). Early slaves labored on sugar plantations and in domestic, skilled and semiskilled work (Russell-Wood 1978; Saunders 1982). An outgrowth of imperialism, this first type of colonization does not involve large-scale European settlement. It is often referred to as "extractive" or "franchise" colonialism, in which colonizers largely function as administrators who oversee Indigenous labor in the extraction of resources for the primary benefit of the imperial metropole (Kauanui and Wolfe 2012). It does not require actual colonies but is a mechanism of control through which colonies are produced (Loomba [1998] 2005).

Columbus's 1492 arrival in present-day Bahamas expanded a phase of early Greco-Roman colonization: settlement. In the Western Hemisphere, it resulted in the formation of what are today the United States and Canada, still-colonized Greenland, thirty-five independent Caribbean and Latin American countries, and roughly a dozen nonindependent Caribbean territories (OHCHR, n.d.). Domination of the Americas is the first, modern settler-colonial project. Under its auspices, Africans were transported to achieve the transformation of Indigenous space into *colônias*. Indigenous peoples throughout the Americas were enslaved, forcibly removed from their lands, and in the United States, reduced to 567 federally recognized tribes and numerous nations that do not qualify for recognition (U.S. Bureau of Indian Affairs, n.d.). In 1510, modern, chattel slavery commenced with the first shipment of blacks to the Americas under Charles V, leading to the transportation of 24.7 million blacks across the globe, with 10.7 million to the Americas (Saunders 1982; Nellis 2013). Chattel slavery depopulated portions of the sub-Saharan region, negatively impacting African societies that would later be colonized (Inikori 1983). Black enslavement, first under existing concepts of slavery in Christendom and later as chattel, was an essential component of this first wave of European colonialism, concurrent with the colonization of India and the beginnings of a limited settler colonialism on the African continent.

The nineteenth century saw the end of the slave trade, the end of slavery, and the commencement of the second wave of modern, European colonialism, in which the colonization of Africa proper began and the U.S. increased its territorial expansion onto Indigenous lands through the doctrine of Manifest Destiny. By the early twentieth century, nearly 75 percent of the globe had been colonized by Europe, including Africa, the Americas, the Caribbean, South Asia, Southeast Asia, Hong Kong, and Australia. The limited territorial foothold of Europe in Africa ended when Belgian King Leopold II saw the continent as a means to increase Belgium's size and wealth (Bate 2003; Stanard 2011). Leopold's reconceptualization of Africa as a "magnificent cake," which he secured with the Berlin Conference in 1884–85, resulted in a colonial project in which Africa's extant, Indigenous territorial borders were redrawn, giving Europeans control of 90 percent of the continent (Hochschild 1998; Ward, Prothero, and Leathes 1912).

Out of this colonization emerged contemporary, independent African countries marred by continuing economic exploitation, foreign intervention, political-ethnic conflicts, and forms of violence that are direct legacies of European colonialism and its institutions, including the Biafran war (Nigeria), apartheid (South Africa), the Tutsi genocide (Rwanda), and the Darfur genocide (southern Sudan) (F. Cooper 2002; Freund [1984] 2016; Schmidt 2013; Mamdani 1996). Colonialism relegated Indigenous Africans to positions like that of Native Americans, where different rights adhere in what is considered native versus state space (Mamdani 2001; Bruyneel 2007). The primary goal of this colonization was extractive—rubber, precious minerals, oil—and led to the formation of a mix of both extractive and settler colonies on the continent. Europe conceptualized this continental colonization as a civilizing mission for which the church was essential in the subordination of African social and political structures, religious systems, and languages (Achebe 1991; Wa Thiong'o 1986; Farred 2008). Though Leopold II initiated this mass colonization whereby Belgians used rape, kidnapping, and bodily mutilation to force Africans to produce rubber (Bate 2003), the civilizing narrative was so strong that when the Democratic Republic of Congo was at the point of a hard-fought independence in 1960, the then Belgian leader, King Baudouin I, affirmed that their independence was "the crowning of the work conceived by the genius of King Leopold II" (*Guardian* 1960). With the exception of Liberia, which began as an overseas colony of U.S. special interests, of the fifty-four countries in present-day Africa, only Ethiopia, which suffered a brief Italian occupation and the deposition of Emperor Haile Selassie I, is considered not to have been a true colony of Europe.

The exit from colonial rule also had two waves: a violent, revolutionary one in the eighteenth and nineteenth centuries that resulted in the United States, Haiti, and the Latin American states and a second in the late twentieth century that began with Egypt in 1922 and India in 1947 and culminated in a mass exit of countries from the control of a Europe weakened by World War II. Inaugurated by Said but congealing largely in the late 1980s, postcolonial studies emerged to examine colonialism's afterlives through the critical optics of Marxism and poststructuralism (Gandhi 1998). The field has been overrun by efforts to critique its limits, including its Eurocentrism, its privileging of time over the various forms of continuous and contiguous colonial power (neocolonialism and neoimperialism), and its hegemonic status within Western academe (Appiah 1991; Shohat 1992; McClintock 1992, 1995, Spivak 1999; Mishra and Hodge 2005; Chibber 2013; Dirlik 1994).

In the wake of the melancholia (Gilroy 2005) and self-eating, postcolonial studies poorly addresses three enduring colonial realities that plague blacks. First, the waves of independence did not result in economic stability or prosperity. Independent black states colonized by Europe face economic dependence and underdevelopment (Kincaid 1988; Black 2001; Henwood 2000).

**COLONIALISM** SHONA N. JACKSON

Haiti is the poorest country in the Western Hemisphere, and Guyana (now majority Indian) in 2014 had a GDP nine hundred times less than that of its former colonizer (Britain) and five thousand times less than the United States (World Bank, n.d.). Most of the twenty-five poorest countries in the world are African (Tasch 2015). In the United States, "white households are worth roughly 20 times as much as black households" (Coates 2014). From the capture and sale of peoples living south of the Sahara in the fifteenth century, blacks entered modernity as laborers. With the end of slavery, the achievements of independence and civil rights, black lives still represent not the accumulation of wealth but enduring poverty.

Second, postcolonial studies fails to properly account for slavery and its aftermaths. If slavery was concomitant with European colonization of the Americas, the precursor to the colonization of Africa, and a vehicle in the rise of capital (Eric Williams [1944] 2014; Inikori 2002), then should it not be considered a form of colonization in which the target of domination is not space but the body? The study of African enslavement and the transportation of millions across the globe is often bracketed off from European colonization of continental Africa and the colonization of the Americas, in which slavery was inaugurated with Indigenous peoples (Reséndez 2016). Chattel slavery is a contradiction within and formative element of the republican principles that emerged, especially in North American society (Patterson 1991). Yet it often remains outside considerations of the hemispheric, American colonial project, especially when that project is seen as a largely settler-colonial one, in terms of the control of space and its extant populations. Malcolm X's exclamation that African Americans "didn't land on Plymouth rock, the rock was landed on us" expresses the inversion of colonialism on the black body, where black flesh is the figurative space

of the American colonial achievement on Indigenous lands (Malcolm X 1964). Focus on the administrative ends of normative types of colonialism ignores that the postcolonial status that the United States achieved in its separation from Britain did not extend to blacks, who remained colonized through the administration of institutions such as slavery, Reconstruction, and Jim Crow. The Civil Rights Act of 1964 and the Voting Rights Act of 1965 did not end the permissive "internal colonization" of black bodies through the mechanisms of structural racism (Carmichael and Hamilton [1967] 2003; Kazanjian 2014). This reinterpretation of the black American situation as colonial entered wider debate with an interrogative 1969 issue of the *Black Scholar*, "Black Cities: Colonies or City States?" The issue reflects arguments of those such as Aimé Césaire and Leopold Senghor, who viewed the African American situation as fundamentally colonial (Césaire et al. 1956; Dworkin 2018). In the colonization of the black body, the prison industrial complex as the neoexpression of Jim Crow laws is one regulatory mechanism designed to maintain black colonized status through forms of structural racism and violent legal discipline and death (Michelle Alexander 2012; Wolfers, Leonhardt, and Quealy 2015). Political movements such as Black Lives Matter highlight this ongoing colonization of African Americans through state-sponsored violence (K. Taylor 2016).

The third limit of postcolonial studies emerged in the late 1990s with attempts to understand not colonization as a whole but the formation of particular types of settler societies such as North America, Canada, Latin America, and South Africa, among others. The term "settler colonialism" encapsulates the broader meanings of colonialism and also returns us to the Greco-Roman origins of settlement: the large-scale settling of inhabited lands by outsiders (Stasiulis and Yuval-Davis 1995; Wolfe 1999; Elkins and Pederson 2005; Farred 2008; Kazanjian 2014).

Within modern settler colonialism, Indigenous inhabitants of a territory are produced as displaceable subjects whose function is to be eliminated and "replaced" by the settler (Fanon 1963; Wolfe 2006; Veracini 2015). Indigenous studies further shifts the focus from the colonizer and the colonized to the settler and the native, giving primacy to the domination of land and space as an usurpation of Indigenous sovereignty and to native "survivance," the survival and resistance of Indigenous peoples (Fanon 1963; Vizenor 1999; Rifkin 2009). Indigenous studies critiques the structures of knowledge used in both postcolonial and settler-colonial studies (L. Smith 1999; Byrd 2011; Kauanui 2016). Settler-colonial and Indigenous studies recast slavery as an instrument of white, settler colonization in which enslaved blacks significantly influenced hemispheric settler projects as "conscripts" of colonialism who either take the place of the white settler or advocate white settler logics (Warren 2016; Weaver 2014; Bushnell 2009; Loomba [1998] 2005; David Scott 2004).

The situation in which blacks emerge as involuntary settlers is especially evident in the Caribbean and the United States. In the Caribbean, blacks and South Asians, rather than the whites who first oppressed them, hold the dominant political positions (Knight 1990; Kale 1998; C. Singh 1988). Though pawns of Europe's extractive colonial processes, the descendants of the formerly enslaved and indentured articulated nationalisms against their colonizers, turning them into willing colonials with regard to extant Indigenous groups wherever they pitted Indigenous a priori land claims against rights earned through plantation-based labor (S. Jackson 2012). These new Creole indigeneities articulate the death of Indigenous peoples as formative and continue to usurp Indigenous rights (Forte 2004–5; S. Jackson 2012). In the U.S., blacks' struggle for full citizenship after slavery and in the civil rights era reinforced

their contributions to America as a settler-colonial project, making them subordinates within and "complicit" with forms of white, settler power (Byrd 2011; V. Deloria 2003). Calls for reparations stemming from the failed promise of forty acres and a mule (Coates 2014; N'COBRA 2004) ignore that the land comes from someone. In the late nineteenth and early twentieth centuries, American blacks in Africa also functioned as aspirant colonials aided by American imperialism, which they hoped to subvert (Dworkin 2017). The "Back-to-Africa" movements that began in the early nineteenth century, articulated by whites such as Benjamin Coates, and religious-financial concerns such as the American Colonization Society congealed into a colonial project that resulted in the creation of independent Liberia in 1847 and the displacement there of Indigenous Africans (Lapsansky-Werner and Bacon 2005; Garvey 2004; Magness and Page 2011). The African emigration schemes and advocacy for leadership in Africa by diasporic blacks in the late nineteenth century and first half of the twentieth century, such as by the African American George Washington Williams and the Jamaican-born Marcus Garvey, respectively, led in particular to a sense of a broad, politically informed cultural citizenship or Pan-African belonging for blacks (Dworkin 2017). This "diasporic citizenship," however, does not mitigate the fact that African Americans seek belonging and nativity in the wedge between the fullness of white settler power and its modes of citizenship, on the one hand, and the limits of its enactment on native lands and bodies, on the other (Laguerre 1998; Ben-zvi 2018).

Colonialism is a practice and logic that organizes the modern world through the uneven distribution of resources and subordination of black and brown bodies. It emerged within the ongoing philosophical project of Europe and its hyperrational, politico-economic expression in capitalism, with its a priori subordination of difference. It has no terminus for those who are within "the binary opposition of the *genetically redeemed* and the (supposedly) *genetically condemned* (Dubois's *Color Line*)," which "encodes the criterion of our contemporary model of *Man*" (Wynter 1991, 275; Du Bois 1903). It acquires new dimensions for populations that attained at least political independence and those that, barring that, live with the liberal expressions of colonialism within putatively democratic states.

# 12

## Criminal
Dylan Rodríguez

The figure of "the criminal" permeates the symbolic, ideological, and militarized racial-economic foundations of the U.S. nation-building project. Gendered racial notions of criminality permeate the foundations of U.S. modernity, structuring the primary power relations of chattel enslavement, (conquest and settler) colonialism, global imperialism, and variations of domestic warfare (from Manifest Destiny to the War on Drugs).

While religious and (proto)juridical discourses of crime and the criminal can be traced to multiple points of civilizational origin, the U.S.—and hemispheric "American"—case furnishes a paradigmatic example of the structural interdependence between two methods of conceptualizing/inventing the criminal that guide its deployment across geographies and moments. First, the legal-cultural creation of the criminal as an *abstracted category* of human social deviancy contextualizes the overlapping, interdisciplinary emergence of criminology, early-twentieth-century eugenics, and contemporary "racial profiling" (as both de facto forensic practice and police tactic). In this sense, historically specific conceptions of the criminal rely on changing, though always *generalized*, classifications of specific behaviors, traits, movements, and physiological comportments (including gender presentation, racial signification, and disability) as pathological, dangerous, antisocial, and/or violent. Second, the creation of these abstract, generalized notions of criminality enables a focused, period-specific *militarized imagination* of the criminal that mobilizes normalized regimes of state violence: surveillance, legally sanctioned bodily punishment, incarceration, and war. The constant and creative production (encompassing both the cultural imagination and official description) of the criminal bridges (a) the cultural differentiation, identification, and interpretation of gendered racial bodies with (b) the state-sanctioned disciplining and policing of human bodies and movements within and against normative place, time, affect, and institutional location (from school, office, and playground to prison, stage, and automobile). It is thus necessary to conceptualize the criminal as a primary *discursive position* against which a Euro-American and Western civilizational imperative consistently defines itself as an orchestration of vindicated, state-legitimated, ritual (national, racial, heteropatriarchal) violence.

Among the earliest circulated texts purporting to serve as a guide for defining, profiling, and investigating criminals was *The Malleus Maleficarum* (Witches' hammer), published in 1486 as a witch hunters' tool during the Spanish Inquisition. The European roots of the criminological conception are entangled in the targeting, torture, and killing of women, and this form of gendered sexual dominance multiplies in force and sophistication with the advent of the Conquest era and the emergence of the transatlantic chattel relation. A somewhat more recent and durable European formulation of criminality persists with remarkable force in the Italian physician Cesare Lombroso's protoeugenicist book *The Criminal Man*, published in 1876. Lombroso utilized demographic and physiological data gleaned from 383 incarcerated people to construct a tripartite typology of criminals: born criminals (those of "degenerate" and "lower evolutionary" biological character), insane criminals, and "criminaloids" (those with mental and emotional features conducive to criminal behaviors

under triggering external circumstances). Lombroso elaborated this schema by formulating a criminal anthropological metric based on eighteen physical (racial) characteristics ("asymmetry of the face," "lips fleshy, swollen, and protruding," "chin receding, or excessively long, or short and flat, as in apes," "excessive length of arms," etc.). According to this early form of criminological science, a person possessing five or more such phenotypic traits was likely a "born criminal." Crucially, the contemporary practice of criminological profiling remains tied to these and other foundational texts, as "the scientific community has yet to abandon the spirit of Lombroso's three essential criminal classifications. Both modern criminologists and the modern scientific community of forensic neurologists, psychiatrists, and psychologists continue to look for the 'mark of Cain'" (Turvey 2002, 2–7).

These and other authoritative conceptions of criminality and the criminal precede, parallel, and constitute the emergence of modern ideological and cultural discourses of "race." It is within the complex process of instituting modern forms of (state) power that critical examination of the creative and coercive legal-cultural work of *criminalization* demystifies the primary role of the criminal figure in the narrative scripts of Manifest Destiny, racial chattel enslavement, American apartheid, law and order, zero tolerance, and the systemic asymmetries of latter-twentieth-century and early-twenty-first-century domestic-to-global carceral warfare. (A focus on the historical modalities of criminalization also helpfully refutes the post-racialist liberal mobilizations of the term "mass incarceration," which fail to account for the gendered racial specificity of the "mass" criminal figure.)

Criminalization entails the dynamic classification of particular human acts and human beings as actual and anticipated offenses against a juridical-civilizational order. The radical criminologist Nils Christie succinctly states, "Acts are not, they *become*. So also with crime. Crime does not exist. Crime is created. First there are acts. Then follows a long process of giving meaning to these acts" (2000, 22). Following Christie, the creation of "the criminal" as such is a creative, dynamic, and fundamentally *political* project undertaken by an ensemble of state institutions (judges, districts attorney, legislatures, sheriff's departments, etc.) and cultural-discursive systems (corporate/mass media, social media, Hollywood film, etc.).

*There is no such thing as an objective, apolitical, or transhistorical conception of "crime" or "criminals" that is not formed and deformed by the material-historical conditions of its construction.* Stuart Hall et al.'s classic study of "mugging" in 1970s Great Britain explicates how "crime both touches the material conditions in which life is lived, and is appropriated in the ideological representations of that life" (1978, 150). Drawing from Antonio Gramsci's (1971) theorization of "common sense" and Stanley Cohen's (2002) explication of "moral panic," the study clarifies how particular historical conjunctures are characterized by a "general race-relations crisis" taking on the "particular form of a confrontation between the Black community and the police" (Hall et al. 1978, 280) Such crises unfold through political and electoral shifts in the state apparatus, generalized ideological and pragmatic symbiosis between police and media regimes, and complex rearticulations of class contradictions and antagonisms in a manner that resonates with racialized "law-and-order" campaigns. Hall et al.'s critical work provides a symptomatic entry into a longer historical archive of gendered racial criminalization within the rise of the modern social and national forms.

Contrary to being a scandalous excess of the racial/racist state in the Conquest, racial chattel, U.S. apartheid, and/or "post–civil rights" (or "post-racial")

periods, *racial* criminalization is a primary, indispensable, and dynamically structuring modality of what the Black radical social theorists Frantz Fanon and Sylvia Wynter name as "sociogeny" (Fanon [1967] 2008; David Scott 2000; Wynter 2003): the complex, changing processes through which external sociocultural "codes" produce notions of life, (human) being, identity/self, and historicity, within which "difference is psychically lived, fantasized, [and] contested" (Marriott 2011, 79). Criminalization—and, by extension, hegemonic criminological practices—composes a form of normalized warfare against those (human) beings that embody the symbolic orders of death, pathology, and unassimilability into the order of Civilization, which itself thrives in the long historical disordering, immobilization, and/or (attempted) destruction of other human socialities.

The Native American historian Luana Ross considers the extended, comprehensive colonial fabrication of Indigenous peoples and life practices as incorrigible violations of formative U.S. criminal jurisprudence, drawing from a vast historical archive to argue that "the values that ordered Native worlds were naturally in conflict with Euro-American legal codes." Citing various examples of the U.S. state's brutally efficient criminalization of traditional tribal codes within the cultural and legal processes of colonial conquest, Ross's historical account enables a reading of U.S. criminal law as complicit in cultural genocide, particularly in the vast criminalization of "usual, everyday behaviors of Natives as [criminal] 'offenses'" (1998, 16). From the creation of the Bureau of Indian Affairs and the congressional passing of the 1825 "Assimilative Crimes Act" to the notorious 1887 Dawes Act and the mid-twentieth-century legal process of termination (tantamount to forced assimilation, evaporation of tribal sovereignty, and legally enforced cultural genocide), the condition of Indigeneity in the

U.S. instance is fundamental to the settler-colonial nation's criminal justice regime.

The formation and geographic metastasizing of gendered racial criminalization is both permeated and actively shaped by the dynamic, systemic forces of anti-Black criminalization. To invoke common notions of the criminal is to draw on a historically vast, supple, and dynamic reservoir of materially accessible images/imaginations of already-profiled and implicitly *Black and Afro-descended* "criminals." In fact, African Indigeneity was a focal point for the genesis of modern hemispheric criminal justice and criminological apparatuses and is traceable to the transatlantic slave trade (Marcus Rediker writes that the slave vessel was "a mobile, sea-going prison at a time when the modern prison had not yet been established on land"; 2007, 45) as well as the earliest stages of the diasporic African presence in North America. This is to suggest that the long historical criminalization of Black people in the United States is best understood within the genealogy of the global criminalization of Black life, Black cosmologies, and Black geographies (McKittrick and Woods 2007).

Lerone Bennett Jr. describes in the classic text *Before the Mayflower* how "African[s] brought [their] mind and [their] ethos to America with [them]. . . . The first generation of African-Americans were carriers of an African world view" (1984, 42). This collective embodiment and practice of diasporic life continuity was central to the earliest iterations of racial criminalization: "In 1680 the Virginia Assembly said that 'the frequent meetings of considerable numbers of Negroe slaves under pretence of feasts and burials is judged of dangerous consequence'" (43). In continuity with the Virginia founders, the American physician Samuel Cartwright infamously crystallized the link between the racial chattel institution and the precursors of criminological (hence social) science in his 1851 coining of the medical diagnosis "drapetomania" to describe "the disease of mind" that "induces the negro to run away from service" (707). According to Cartwright, this criminal act could be corrected through modest improvements to the housing, clothing, and nutrition of the enslaved. He emphasizes, however, that if such white benevolence fails to quell the enslaved's inclination "to raise their heads to a level with their master," then "humanity and their own good require they should be punished until they fall into that submissive state which it was intended for them to occupy in all after time" (709; see also Franklin and Schweninger 1999, 274–75). It is useful to consider this academic invention of drapetomania as an anticipation of what would soon become a conceptually inextricable, complexly institutionalized connection between the racialized figure of the criminal, gendered anti-Black criminalization, and the rise of a modern white civil society consistently cohered through criminological/social science, criminal law, and physiologically directed racist state violence.

Writing in 1895 amid the southern renaissance of lynching that unfolded over a full half century, the antilynching activist Ida B. Wells-Barnett deepens the critical archive on gendered racist criminalization by illuminating the *racist sociality* produced in the creation of a paradigmatic criminal figure: the Black (cisgender) male rapist/sexual predator of white women. She writes, "Humanity abhors the assailant of womanhood, and this charge upon the Negro at once placed him beyond the pale of human sympathy. . . . The world has accepted the story that the Negro is a monster" ([1892] 2002, 60). Wells-Barnett's work frames a crucial facet of the long historical production of the criminal: the complex entanglement of criminalization with the layered, state-sanctioned and white-supremacist civility of gendered racist, colonial, and anti-Black dominance—in their varying scales and forms—compose a *criminological social totality* in which extralegal (and fatal) violence against criminalized beings is sanctioned by the state, systemically condoned by a racist heteropatriarchal juridical order, and valorized by a national-cultural order that thrills in the waging of domestic/continental and global warfare. Wells-Barnett's renowned study of lynching demonstrates that it is frequently the case that not even the threshold of "the least evidence" is required for either criminal conviction or state-sanctioned (extralegal) punishment of Black people under the cultural reign of U.S. white supremacy and its proliferations of violence (Wells-Barnett [1892] 2002, 87).

Dorothy Roberts, echoing the work of Angela Y. Davis, Hortense Spillers, Saidiya Hartman, and a longer genealogy of Black feminists, builds on Wells-Barnett's era-specific work by offering a historical analysis of the unique criminalization of Black (cisgender) women and girls. Working from the well-documented fact that "America has always viewed unregulated Black reproduction as dangerous," Roberts locates Black motherhood and Black women's biological capacity to bear Black children at the nexus of the U.S. criminal justice regime, from the chattel period onward (1997, 8). Roberts identifies the biological nexus of racist dominance that not only provides a framework for gendered human differentiation but also enacts a logic of *transgenerational* and *immutable* criminalization that preys on notions of genetic as well as cultural heredity.

Sarah Haley's (2016) close examination of multiple penological and criminological archives in the U.S. South spurs a critical elaboration of this gendered racist technology, illustrating how the policing and incarceration of Black women not only is central to the formation of an apartheid "Jim Crow Modernity" but also structures the postemancipation construction of the U.S. criminal law apparatus in and of itself. Black women—which is to say Black people—are projected into law and national culture as subjects of gender-racial deviance (criminal, sexual, and otherwise) in the process of cohering a modern infrastructure of jurisprudence and everyday cultural intercourse. To echo the two-part schema suggested at the beginning of this entry, Haley's study illuminates how Black women are criminalized through the fabrication of abstracted categories of gendered racial pathology as well as a militarized social imaginary that marshals state violence toward their generalized, institutional vulnerability and subjection. In fact, the historical archive reflects how this complex process of criminalization and gendered racist state violence forms a primary discursive and legal foundation for U.S. modernity, insofar as it rests on the capacity to conceptualize and institutionalize human difference, criminality, citizenship, and U.S. civil society as such.

These and other gendered racist forms of criminalization suggest that a logic of social neutralization, racial terror, and potential liquidation (via law enforcement, state-condoned extralegal violence, and civil/social death through incarceration) animates the modern criminological enterprise, which encompasses academic, legal, and hegemonic cultural institutions. The figure of the criminal is *originated, structured, and dynamically reproduced in relations of racial and civilizational dominance.*

Notions of criminality and criminal threat are deeply cultural-political productions: they are generated in and across multiple discursive layers, including *visual signifiers* of incorrigible Black sexual endangerment of white civil society (e.g., the prominent, notorious exploitation of Willie Horton's mug shot in George H. W. Bush's 1988 presidential campaign), *populist rhetorics* of indecency and criminal social deviance (Barry Goldwater's 1964 "law-and-order" campaign against the Black and domestic U.S. Third World and anticolonial rebellions and freedom movements; Hillary Clinton's 1996 coining of "superpredators" as a catchphrase reference to since-debunked imaginaries of spreading Black youth criminal behavior), and *popular cultural forms* (including video games, television and film entertainment, social media, corporate news programs, and politically themed radio shows and podcasts). Thus, when Hillary Clinton authoritatively states that superpredators possess "no conscience, no empathy," she is accomplishing more than an ephemeral condemnation (and rhetorical dehumanization) of an entire generation of Black children. She is also prefiguring and configuring a disciplinary, punitive, and militarized *national narrative and institutional mobilization* that draws on the racial chattel archive: Clinton continues, "we can talk about why they ended up that way, but first we have to bring them to heel" (Gearan and Phillip 2016).

"The criminal" prompts, signifies, and preemptively valorizes legitimated state and state-condoned racist violence, mobilizing the power of jurisprudence, policing, and (gendered racial) common sense to produce, fortify, and/or militarize the geographic containment and (collective) subjection of targeted human groups. At the crux of the historical criminological and protocriminological enterprise is a differentiation between what Wynter identifies as the Renaissance-era distinction between the "saved" and the "cursed," the Enlightenment and Scientific-era distinction between the "selected" and the "dysselected," and the fatal racial and racial-colonial distinction between bourgeois Man and a global field of "natives" and "niggers" (David Scott 2000, 136).

Critical examination of the peculiar racial-colonial criminological regimes of the United States provides a globally instructive case study of the constitutive and socially productive presence of anti-Black racism within the dynamic symbiosis of modern nation-building, the statecraft of domestic militarization and de facto warfare, gendered racialization, and civil/social death. While different historical and geographic contexts will require both subtle and significant translations of this analytical framework, the U.S. example nonetheless enables a genealogy of criminalization as a *civilizational* power relation and paradigmatic feature of modern societies structured in dominance (S. Hall 1980).

A groundswell of mobilized urgency and activated political emergency is responding to the gravity of this long historical condition. A spectrum of protests and rebellions against gendered racist police violence has spread across the U.S. during the 2010s and is characterized by a complex and often internally contradictory continuum of liberal-reformist to radical-abolitionist challenges to white-supremacist, anti-Black, and settler-colonialist policing strategies, from Ferguson, Missouri, and Standing Rock, North Dakota, to Newark, New Jersey, and Pelican Bay State Prison, California. Activist groups, foundation-funded organizations, historically policed-and-profiled communities, and various organic collectives of ordinary people (many of whom have not previously identified as "activists") are militantly exposing and challenging the everyday implications of policing *as racist state violence and warfare* in a manner that both invokes and critically rearticulates prior periods of insurgency and liberationist movement.

Yet, in response to this climate of protest and uprising, a statecraft of *racial policing reform* is emerging that attempts to quell public criticism while relegitimating and even strengthening police authority and prestige. The racial/racist state and its vast pedagogical extensions, from the nonprofit industrial complex (Rodríguez 2009) and policy think tanks to the corporate media and school administrators (Sojoyner 2016; Wun 2016), are reconfiguring their cultural, material, and political investments in a cultural form and institutional structuring of policing state power that pivots on the constant winning of hearts and minds (including among those inhabiting racially profiled geographies) and that strives to produce a climate of generalized consent among both the racially criminalized and those who live under the entitlements of presumed innocence. In this sense, the activist and potentially transformative scholarly labors of critical conceptualization, theorized collective movement, and historicized reflection are—as always—well positioned to engage and disarticulate the figure and social position of the gendered racial criminal as a sustained, necessary precondition of its undoing, hence its abolition as such.

## 13

## Diaspora
Shana L. Redmond

"Diaspora" is a contested term. The African diaspora is, like the nation, an "imagined community" (B. Anderson [1983] 2006) conceived of and performed based on imperfect memories, evidence, and agendas. As the historian Colin Palmer asserts, "In many respects, diasporas are not actual but imaginary and symbolic communities and political constructs; it is we who often call them into being" (2000, 29). Within Black studies literatures, diaspora is mobilized as a method in pursuit of collectives whose histories and cultures were/are otherwise hidden or forcibly taken as part of the development of Western epistemes (formal and informal) and the violences of chattel slavery and colonialism. Variously referred to as "Black," "African" or a series of national monikers prefixed by a version of "Afro-," the actors who called for the African diaspora are loosely tied together by a recognition of indigenous Africa as origin as well as a relation to Blackness as sociocultural identity. No more stable than "diaspora," "Black(ness)" too is a contested term. The literary scholar Michelle Wright argues that "from the start, Black identity has been produced in contradiction" (2004, 1), noting the irregularity of the category and appellation as well as the fact that Blackness as production—*becoming*—and as material experience only exists relative to a series of additional constructions and world systems that produce "differences and disagreements among black populations on a number of registers" (B. Edwards 2003, 7). The word "diaspora," then, invites experimentation within the categories of identity—citizenship, race, ethnicity, gender, sexuality, class, and ability—that the theorist Stuart Hall argued are "never complete, always in progress" (1990, 222). Diaspora as performance and practice is contested and (re)made over and over again, revealing its complexity and dynamism, which stems from the constant agitation among its subjects as well as the movements that disperse those persons around the globe. As such, the African diaspora is a people, process, encounter, ambition, and project.

More than a constellation of individuals, the African diaspora proves to be a political project of affiliation and camaraderie that unites members through historical condition as well as deliberate choice. Indeed, diaspora has been a formative element in the construction of modern Black identity. The language of an "African diaspora" rose to popularity in scholastic discourse in the 1950s and early 1960s in large part through the work of historians of Africa who brought grounding to the term through studies of anticolonial struggle in Ghana and other African nations. The popular birth of the term from and in continued reference to resistance movements necessarily makes the African diaspora a politically charged formulation designed to be read in contradistinction to structures of power. According to Lisa Brock, "if we rid ourselves of race and nation hierarchies, which were/are largely constructed at 'the top' by elites, important comparative paradigms might evolve and analytical lessons be drawn from isolating specific processes of oppression and the experiences of those below on 'the bottom'" (1996, 11). Investment in scholastic inquiry "from below" is a hallmark of much of the work in the African diaspora, including that of the historian Robin D. G. Kelley, who has theorized new frames for Black resistance, arguing that "we have to step into the complicated maze of experience that renders 'ordinary' folks so extraordinarily multifaceted, diverse, and complicated. Most importantly, we need to break away from traditional notions of politics" (1994, 4). The "translocal" politics described by Frank Guridy (2010) between poets in Havana and Harlem is one example of the ways in which scholars have shown the intimacies of diaspora and how those microrelationships became a defining element of influence and change on multiple scales. This revision to our understanding of politics, which is not held captive to formal organization, mass mobilizations, or charismatic leadership, opens up opportunities for examining how transnational cultures of thought and action function at the ground level and reveal the density and impact of diasporic contact.

Regularly used as a synonym for "African diaspora," the term "Black Atlantic" (Gilroy 1993) brings with it a series of provocations detailing the fluidity of identities across the expanse of difference. Like Peter Linebaugh and Marcus Rediker (2000), the literary scholar Omise'eke Tinsley details the intimacies that structured the transatlantic slave trade and intervenes in narratives of its formation by arguing that the "black Atlantic has always been the queer Atlantic" (2008, 191). Deep engagements with eroticism, desire, consumption, and masculinity widen the scope of global Blackness in consideration of how nonnormative bodies produce counterpoints to narratives of the family, respectability, and labor (J. Allen 2011; Carrington 2010; Ferguson 2004; Thomas 2011; Tinsley 2010; Erica Williams 2013). The intellectual investment in the Black Atlantic—no less the Black Pacific and Black Mediterranean—suggests that the buoyancy of Black cultures and identities have been built in between spaces and are supported by myriad strategies, including the creation of new knowledges. The ocean's edge is a location of critical inquiry in diaspora studies and a location where feminist geographies become "demonic" (McKittrick 2006), manifesting the crossing and "interrupt[ion] of inherited boundaries" (M. Jacqui Alexander 2005, 6) that show again how diaspora refuses containment, producing instead new constitutions and ways of living.

The African diaspora's relation to the three "classic" diasporas (Jewish, Greek, and Armenian) was marked in the language of the First African Diaspora Studies Institute, which convened in 1979 at Howard University and offered this definition of the African diaspora: "the voluntary and forced dispersion of Africans at different periods in history and in several directions; the emergence of a cultural identity abroad without losing the African base, either spiritually or physically; the psychological or physical return to the homeland, Africa. Thus viewed, the African diaspora assumes the character of a dynamic, ongoing and complex phenomenon stretching across time and geography" (Harris [1982] 1993b, 5). This dynamism has been displayed in multiple forms, from the techniques of agricultural innovation carried by enslaved Senegalese women and men to the rice fields of the hemispheric Americas to the efforts by the African Union—the cooperative continental governing organization—in the late aughts of the new millennium to prioritize diaspora as a strategy of socioeconomic advance for Africa. These relations, in addition to many others forged through radicalisms and performance, index the coherence of the term, even when it is unevenly experienced or accessed. The "voluntary" aspect of the diaspora is witnessed through the multiple movements of Black peoples throughout the world due to ongoing independence struggles, crises in labor, and genocide that, following the forced dispersals of slavery and imperialism, extend diaspora's teleology well into the future. Along with the dispersal of African-descended subjects, Hazel Carby and Tina Campt encourage scholars

of the African diaspora to reckon with the inter- and intranational "settling" of these populations, which requires investigation on different registers of Black existence. Similarly, the cultural theorist Paul Gilroy (1993) famously suggested a focus on "routes" rather than "roots" in the African diaspora in order to trouble both the unidirectionality and racial essentialisms that impair diaspora study.

Africa holds a compelling and urgent location with the diaspora as a site of the "originary displacement," as Nahum Chandler (2000) names it, tradition, and, in some cases, repatriation. As a sociocultural project, diaspora is reliant on the traditions and movements stemming from Africa, which stands as "a site of struggle and imagination but also as the progenitor of a flexible set of transferable knowledges of technique and performance" (Redmond 2014, 6). Yet, in spite of Africa's centrality, it remains vulnerable to caricature, fancy, and/or outright dismissal in literatures of Blackness. The theorist Achille Mbembe argues that within Western discourse and scholarship, Africa—"a great, soft, fantastic body"—is an "object of experimentation" requiring constant supervision and intervention (2001, 8, 2). The mischaracterization and/or disarticulation of Africa from the wider African world haunts the field, leading diaspora scholars to imagine alternatives. Instead of "African diaspora," the anthropologist Xavier Livermon (2018) proposes the language of "Afrodiasporic," which he argues mitigates against the scholastic and discursive erasure of Africa.

Africa's representation as an entry to diaspora functions on at least two different registers: it is an opening into the long histories of culture, exploitation, and violence as well as a metaport or site of *re*entry. The traditional diasporic fixation with return to a homeland has rightly come under scrutiny in post–civil rights African diaspora literatures. Unlike Greek, Armenian, and Jewish diasporas, there is no singular "home" or nation of origin for the African descended, making "return" more of a philosophical exercise than a practical aim or movement objective. That is not to say, however, that it has been pure fantasy. The influential diaspora theorist and movement icon Marcus Garvey is perhaps the most lionized advocate for Black repatriation in the postemancipation moment. His mantra of "Africa for Africans" and investment in a return to Africa was tied to gains in political power for global African peoples—power that, due to colonialism and Western hegemony, could only take root on the continent. As he argued after World War I, in the cause of colonial expansion "white propagandists have been printing tons of literature to impress scattered Ethiopia, especially that portion within their civilization, with the idea that Africa is a despised place . . . where no human being should go, especially black civilized human beings" (2004, 93). Though he never traveled to Africa and was only able to encourage the passage of a minimal number of members from the Universal Negro Improvement Association, return to Africa was a significant organizing strategy within diaspora, if not a tangible end, and carried weight well beyond the height of Garveyism in the 1920s. In a study of African American expatriates in postindependence Ghana, the historian Kevin Gaines documents a diverse group of activists and intellectuals whose various investments in Pan-Africanism and Black nationalism led them to practice "a transnational culture of opposition to Western culture seeking the preservation of colonial and neocolonial dominance over the majority of the world's peoples" (2006, 12–13). These legacies also encourage contemporary members of diaspora to chance their fate at "home" with mixed yet profound results, demonstrating again how Africa is imagined as a terrain of struggle that welcomes participation from its

children near and far, even if those children initially are referred to as "stranger" (Hartman 2007).

Explorations of the multiple, intersectional identities in diaspora are a constituent part of its epistemological and political work. According to Brent Hayes Edwards African diaspora is a sign "formulated expressly through an attempt to come to terms with diverse and cross-fertilized black traditions of resistance and anticolonialism" (2001, 53). This critical offensive in the literature highlighted a multicentury diasporic assembly now theorized as the Black Radical Tradition and in so doing exposed submerged histories and performances of identity formation while also contending with Western thought, culture, and the very notion of "civilization." Canonical Western epistemes were read as terrain for critical disruption and dismantling; as the social theorist Cedric Robinson argues, "Solon, Aristophanes, Plato, Isocrates, and Aristotle . . . all could not entirely conceal or effectively dismiss the moral challenges of the poor (*demos*), slaves, and women" ([1983] 2000, xxvii). These subjects indeed surfaced, leaving a "record of resistance, for four centuries or more, from Nueva España to Nyasaland, [that] leaves in no doubt the specifically African character of those struggles" (5). The shared concerns and qualities of these critiques and mobilizations indicate a corresponding labor from a coordinated body. Histories of radical organizing and movement building in the African world (Bush 1999; Gore 2011; Horne 1997, 2014; Kelley [1990] 2015, 2002; Makalani 2011; Von Eschen 1997) have built on these synergies and demonstrate how Black subjects' "defiant citizenship . . . gave way to diaspora through an identification with blackness as a condition of affinity and camaraderie beyond knowable signs and signals such as homeland, language, and appearance" (Redmond 2014, 127).

Elucidating the scenarios and circumstances that give rise to the African diaspora exposes how race is imagined, constructed, and repeated and why diaspora developed as "a means to theorize both culture and politics at the transnational level" (B. Edwards 2001, 55). That culture and politics are twinned in this description is not a coincidence. Culture is a formative element of political study in the African diaspora and has provided new idioms and methodologies in its study. Visual art and aesthetics (Brody 2008; K. Brown 2015; Copeland 2013; Fleetwood 2011, 2015; K. Jones 2011; McMillan 2015; Mercer 1994), dance (Cox 2015; DeFrantz 2001; Gottschild 2003; F. Griffin 2013), literature (Carby 1999; E. Edwards 2012; Goyal 2010; Moten 2003; Nwankwo 2005; David Scott 2004; Stephens 2005), and other artistic forms (and their breaks) materialize the continuities and disjunctures that constitute the African world. Due to music's accessibility, ample supply, and demand in the global Commons and marketplace, it is perhaps the most resonant art form within diaspora. According to Samuel Floyd (1995), it is precisely the hearing and maintenance of African traditions throughout the long, global genealogies of Black music that constitutes its power. Black music is a hybrid tradition of diasporic exchange that exhibits a series of techniques and performances over time/space that according to the musicologist Olly Wilson are "not basically quantitative but qualitative" (1983, 2). In working against neat, determinate outcomes, engagements with Blackness as/in/through sound necessarily evince the sometimes messy and ephemeral nature of diaspora by exposing the significance of encounter, spontaneity, and rehearsal to its practice. Recent theoretical interventions in the study of the African diaspora, including "soundtexts," "anthemic event," and "stereomodernism," variously articulate the ways in which musical productions have mediated and challenged the exclusions of access and citizenship faced by subjects throughout the African world (E. Hill 2013; Redmond 2014; Jaji 2014).

As a flexible and dynamic "way of life," culture and its performance also have inspired some observers to invent or entrench diasporic essentialisms (Raymond Williams 1983). While recognizing that continuity "in the work of Afro-Americanists and Afro-Caribbeanists is in part the measure of the sympathetically affirmative character of the anthropology of peoples of African descent in the New World," David Scott has critiqued anthropological uses of "Africa" and "slavery" as synonyms for the "authentic past" of diasporic subjects (1991, 263). While genealogies of diaspora may begin with the continent and/or enslavement, they are not the only openings to its examination, nor are either static phenomena. As scholars have amply documented, enslavement was not a uniform institution, nor was it totalizing in the lives of its captives (Blassingame [1972] 1979; V. Brown 2008; Diouf 2014; Finch 2015; Gomez 1998; Morgan 2004; Roediger 2014; Smallwood 2007; D. White [1985] 1999). Similarly, the richness of African histories and cultures begs for a continuation of material readings that evade easy overtures to universalism and consensus while still being mindful of and holding onto the symbiotic approaches to life and living that occur globally (Higginson 2014; Kelley 2012; Pierre 2012; Ray 2015; Rodney [1972] 1981; Soyinka 2012).

Presently caught between physical and state violence and (the violence of) neoliberal incorporation, the African descended worldwide are facing economic and political conditions that very well may widen the difference gap between their various communities. With African-descended people having lived slavery and abolition in the U.S. and Britain and across the Caribbean and Latin America, colonialism and war in the clash of nations during World War I and II, and the genocide and imperialism that continue to outline the shape of global capital, one can know that the form and function of the African diaspora has not reached its end, perhaps not even its zenith. If we believe, as Cedric Robinson has written, that "the peoples of African and the African diaspora had endured an integrating experience that left them not only with a common task but a shared vision" ([1983] 2000, 166), then we are left not with a tomb of dead practices but a canvas of invention that will hold the futures expressed and impressed on it, whatever they may be.

# 14

## Diversity
Nick Mitchell

To speak of diversity today is to enter the traffic clustered around what has come, over the past four decades, to serve as one of our most powerful and pervasive languages of social betterment. Diversity, it would seem, has strayed well afield of its etymological vintage in Old French. In the twelfth century, *diversité* referred not so much to difference understood as a neutral fact of life but to difference decked out in suspect connotations: "oddness, wickedness, perversity." In the contemporary United States, "diversity," in its transits through the hegemonic lexicon—that is, the institutionalized languages by which power both solicits consent and fashions itself as such—no longer carries the sense of a difference that is threatening, dangerous, strange, or fearsome. Quite the contrary, we might say: in the dominant imaginary, diversity has come to enjoy a taken-for-granted equivalence with the concept of the good. To be or to become diverse is to be good, and what is good cannot retain its goodness for too long without putting its embrace of diversity on conspicuous display.

In this more contemporary sense, the goodness that diversity appears to offer derives from the myriad values it promises to social actors. Diversity typically refers to a wide-ranging and often contradictory set of legally regulated and organizationally mediated efforts to reform public and private institutions and organizations, with the avowed or implicit intention to undo or interrupt historically sedimented, socially entrenched, and culturally normalized practices of discrimination and exclusion. At diversity's heart, though, is a popular and problematic fantasy about difference—specifically the idea of progress thought to result from the harnessing of difference toward higher ends—common well-being, social cooperativity, and unity of purpose. Diversity, then, is about difference but also about its overcoming—the promise that difference, properly conditioned, either will make *no difference* or, better yet, will transform difference into an asset primed for accumulation. Diversification—understood here as the processes involved in the production, distribution, circulation, and enactment of diversity discourses—tends to be taken up by institutions and organizations that are built on hierarchies of concentrated prestige, privilege, and power (or the mechanisms of social mobility and the access to pools of cultural capital that enable their attainment). Elite and middle-class places of work and learning, popular cultural visibility, and the symbols of achievement—these mark the most conspicuous grounds where struggles over the value and legitimacy of diversity tend most visibly to be waged.

Diversity's ascent to the status of a social good has been both stalled and propelled by contestation over the nature of racism and over the proper response to its recognition, by state and nonstate actors, as a central feature of U.S. life. The occasion and the urgency of such a recognition came in the latter half of the twentieth century, set into motion by the simultaneous pressure exerted, directly, by the legal and direct-action arms of the civil rights movement as well as, less directly but insistently, the institutional and ideological demands on U.S. statecraft presented by the Cold War. The latter case involved U.S. officialdom's understanding that international legitimacy would require conspicuous effort to demonstrate that American prosperity did not discriminate on the basis of race or gender (see Melamed 2011; Dudziak 2000; Borstelmann 2001). "Affirmative action,"

a term hailing from New Deal public policy, was given a new lease on life in 1961 by the black activist lawyer (and insurance-industry millionaire) Hobart T. Taylor, in what would become President John F. Kennedy's Executive Order 10925, staked out federal-government and federal-government-contracted employment as the site to implement and elaborate the principles of nondiscrimination. Following on the heels of several years of protracted and often lethal mass-movement-fueled struggle, the passage of the 1964 Civil Rights Act transformed the spirit of Kennedy's executive order into comprehensive legislation, codifying and, at least in theory, lending constitutional authority to its enforcement.

In spite of the Civil Rights Act's demand for nondiscrimination—and owing much to dense anxieties about what social relations the end of formal legal segregation would call for—the law prescribed remarkably little about the *forms* that nondiscrimination should take or about the affirmative action necessary to achieve it. But it pointed to a key need in writing the accumulated historical effects of racism: to fight "not only overt discrimination but also practices that are fair in form but discriminatory in practice." Civil rights activists sought to participate in its shaping by amplifying the pressure to alter hiring and admissions practices by deploying (or threatening to deploy) a range of tactics that included boycotts, occupations, and sit-ins, which the expansion of television as a major force in U.S. mass culture made all the more newsworthy. Meanwhile, businesses and institutions dependent on (or solicitous of) federal funds scrambled to preempt further government regulation by defining nondiscrimination on their own terms. Perhaps nowhere did this struggle over the definition of the affirmative action needed to achieve nondiscrimination play out more spectacularly than in historically white colleges and universities. Institutional leaders who sought to develop affirmative admissions programs variously clashed and collaborated with minority student activists who sought to challenge, direct, and intervene in determining the definition and scope of affirmative action. As Martha Biondi (2012) shows, black student activists at San Francisco State College, for instance, sought to challenge universities to rethink the objective basis of who qualified for higher education, fighting "to extend [the college's Educational Opportunity Program] to students who had the talent to succeed in college but who had been deprived of an adequate secondary education" (52).

Many of these same activists, furthermore, elaborated the nondiscriminatory principles that affirmative action was, in theory, a mechanism of achieving, in order to press universities to institutionalize its commitment to nondiscrimination in the form of programmatic and curricular reform. Black studies (Rooks 2006; Rojas 2007; Biondi 2012; I. Rogers 2012) and soon ethnic studies (Okihiro 2016) and women's studies (Boxer 1998): the late-1960s and early-1970s struggles to establish these knowledge formations had their institutional genesis in the efforts to transform affirmative action from solely a discourse of accumulation—the need for universities to admit *more* minoritized students in order to conform to federal mandates—to a discourse of qualitative transformation, one that called for a *different* institution. The university, for many of these students, needed not only to admit but to recruit and to fund the retention of minorities; moreover, it needed to confront its own role in supporting and sustaining imperialist war, neocolonial exploitation, and epistemologies of domination (see, for example, Ladner [1973] 1998).

Though these efforts were still in their infancy, by the close of the 1960s, they had cumulatively transformed affirmative action such that it no longer registered primarily in the negative sense—that is, in efforts to achieve compliance through the demonstrated *absence*

of discrimination in the hiring and treatment of employees. Rather, it had come to refer to a positive project as well—one that sought to affirm the operations of antiracism not only in the absence of discrimination but in the *presence* of minoritized subjects. The minoritized body in general, and the black body specifically, thereby became a key corroborative feature in the discourse of affirmative action: the visible presence of minorities would be necessary evidence of *active* assent to nondiscrimination in principle and practice.

But to say that affirmative action took as its object the practices of the overwhelmingly white and male places of work and learning is to miss a key part of the story. Affirmative action was not simply an institution-making project but a subject-making one; in other words, it achieved much more than the reform of a range of social locations to incorporate minorities into areas of work, education, and experience to which they had been effectively, if not always legally, barred. It was also, and crucially, a project of constructing pathways of upward social mobility as a countermeasure to broad-based social rebellion. Affirmative action found its way to social imperative in a moment when the country was aflame and when the traditional means of quelling or preempting black uprising faced, in the wake of international scrutiny, a crisis of legitimacy—perhaps best exemplified by the urban uprisings that responded to the assassination of Dr. Martin Luther King Jr. in April 1968. The support and funding for the ramping up of increasingly militarized "law and order" policing and the increased activity of clandestine state-led counterinsurgency through COINTELPRO in targeting black radical organizations are the well-known responses of the U.S.'s repressive state apparatus to black rebellion on a mass scale. But the tendency to regard affirmative action straightforwardly as a civil rights movement victory may be the result of underestimation of the degree to which affirmative action functioned as the U.S. state's *ideological* complement to the repressive campaign or, relatedly, of ignoring the extent to which the abstract ideas espoused by the movement became concrete through its coalition with corporate liberalism (R. Allen 1969; A. Reed 1979; Fergus 2009).

Such a view emphasizes the degree to which the expansion of affirmative action in the late 1960s and early '70s owed to the need to develop a form of crisis management sufficiently keyed to the project of formalizing an *absorptive* version of antiracism in the U.S. state and civil society. Systematic abandonment—state-sponsored white flight and the increasing automation of industry—had decimated tax bases and driven up poverty and unemployment in U.S. cities, where black populations increasingly resided. Because affirmative action was a mode of provisioning access to a range of social pathways to the "American Dream" and, more to the point, because capitalism, the material basis of that dream, requires inequality, affirmative action offered an ideological strategy to encourage a narrow interpretation of the racial foundations of inequality. It thus facilitates the displacement of "the causes of capitalism's structural unevenness onto naturalized fictions of human differences" (Melamed 2014, 85)—hence the overwhelming focus on racism as borne out in individual and institutional practices of discrimination.

The narrow interpretation of racism-as-individualized-discrimination—and the liberal individualist understanding of freedom that it left in place—that was required in order to prescribe affirmative action as a fitting solution also made it vulnerable. The problem here lay in the fact that affirmative action *required* discrimination: its implicit theory of antiracism consisted in the idea that active and targeted recruitment, hiring, admission, promotion, and retention of minorities provided a way not only to counter the effects of past discrimination but also to prevent those practices from continuing into the future, a continuation likely, proponents reasoned, because discrimination had normalized the exclusion of minorities from wide swaths of U.S. society. Affirmative action, by this line of reasoning, *required* discrimination *in favor* of minorities as a counterbalance against the social inertia that had made regularized discrimination, conscious and not, a fact of life. Critics of affirmative action insisted that it constituted a state-sanctioned form of "reverse discrimination" or, more damningly, "reverse racism," in a way that was potentially in contravention of the Fourteenth Amendment's Equal Protection Clause. In so doing, affirmative action critics argued that the only fair and constitutional way to enact antiracism was to turn a blind eye to the compounded effects of racisms past and present. Advocates of "colorblindness" conveniently ignored an over-century-long history of the use of purportedly race-neutral policy in order to legitimize the suppression of black political participation, arguing that the only constitutionally fitting path to an antiracist society would be found by discounting the accumulated historical effects of racism in order to act as if race did not matter at all.

Attacks on affirmative action intensified through the 1970s, building steam with the emergence of the burgeoning neoconservative movement, which sought to drive a wedge in the civil rights organizational coalition by appealing to minoritized groups that, they claimed, would be unduly harmed by affirmative action, culminating with the 1978 Supreme Court verdict in *Regents of the University of California v. Bakke*. The *Bakke* ruling struck down the University of California at Davis medical school's affirmative action program, which, the Court found, constructed an illegal "quota system" in order to facilitate minority admissions. Importantly, though, the Court did so without producing a consensus that colorblind admissions constituted the only constitutional alternative. Rather, the Supreme Court justice and erstwhile corporate strategist Lewis Powell, a Harvard Law School graduate, had been moved by an amicus brief filed by his alma mater with several other elite universities signing on in support of UC Davis's affirmative action efforts. The brief described Harvard's affirmative action approach as one that avoided minority admission quotas and instead considered the particular value of race alongside other criteria with the aim of producing a "heterogeneous student body" that fulfilled the compelling interest in exposing the nation's future leaders to people of backgrounds different from their own. Thus, while Powell's opinion maintained that "racial and ethnic considerations are inherently suspect," it conceded that "the goal of achieving a diverse student body is sufficiently compelling to justify consideration of race in admissions decisions under some circumstances" (*Bakke*, 438 U.S. at 267).

Enshrined in the Powell opinion, diversity would partly supplant nondiscrimination as the *positive* goal of affirmative action. Diversity, for Powell, was attractive because it corresponded to the state's interest of enhancing its capacity for governance (by familiarizing future leaders with representatives of the future led) while allowing for wide administrative discretion on what constituted diversity. The UC Davis medical school special admissions program "totally excluded" applicants who were not "Negro, Asian, or Chicano," no matter how strong their qualifications, "including their own potential for contribution to educational diversity" (*Bakke*, 438 U.S. at 319). To deny whites their *own* claim to diversify, by Powell's logic, was both to infringe on the individual rights guaranteed them by the Fourteenth Amendment *and* to hamper the discretion of university officials to decide what differences matter most in order for the institution best to extract the value

of diversity. No longer anchored to criteria of historical exclusion or systematic oppression, diversity preserved affirmative action by tying it to the *deregulation* of difference, freeing managers, at least in theory, from being restrictively bound to civil rights definitions of the differences that mattered and tying diversity management to the recognition and production of difference (Kelly and Dobbin 1998).

Ironically, today we often use "diversity" interchangeably with "affirmative action." But it was an *attack* on affirmative action that made the hegemony of the language of diversity possible and necessary. If liberal understandings of racial justice—however narrow in their conceptualization—had breathed life into affirmative action, those understandings would prove inessential to diversity, which secured its tenure as a discourse on the extractability of value from properly managed difference and the entitlement of whiteness to the production and consumption of the value extracted. That whiteness could claim the capacity both to diversify *and* to be injured by diversification would present a central paradox in the decades to come. Stoked to a significant extent by U.S. imperialist wars, the end of the Cold War, and the rise of neoliberal capitalism, transnational migration began to raise the specter of a majority nonwhite U.S. population. White revanchism, seeking to regain material and symbolic ground perceived to have been lost to the civil rights and Black Power movements, gained counterinsurgent ground with Reagan's election in 1980. Its groundswell effectively spelled the end of federal affirmative action enforcement; in the following decade, conservative get-out-the-white-vote referendums in California (Proposition 209; 1996) and Washington State (Initiative 200; 1998) eliminated it at the state level.

But diversity had been built to outlast these attacks on affirmative action. In the same two-decade span that witnessed this assault on affirmative action, diversity management became professionalized in human resources departments around the country. Diversity management helped to teach corporations not only that perceived discrimination threatened the bottom line but also that in the increasingly competitive environment of neoliberal globalization, the diversification of professional and managerial staff could offer corporations the capacity to expand into or gain advantage in emerging consumer markets. Diversity's prestige, as Christopher Newfield (2008) argues, bolstered "the claim that for businesses competing in overwhelmingly nonwhite global markets and for armed forces fighting with 40 percent minority personnel, diversity *worked*" (116). Diversity promised to corporations a route to the accumulation of legitimacy, if not also of capital itself.

The accumulation-driven diversity imperative is not limited to private corporations. Recently, in fact, public universities have learned that their commitment to diversity can work to their benefit in times of austerity. The University of Illinois at Urbana-Champaign (UIUC), for instance, touts its diversity as an institutional achievement and has continued to do so even as its African American and Native American students dwindle in number. Arguably, these dwindling numbers do not bring diversity to crisis precisely because the logic of diversification have developed such that diversity has been defined through the kind of deregulation that Powell's opinion called for, deregulation that aligns the definition of diversity with the interests of those who wield institutional and social power. In other words, the exclusion of members of these groups from the definition of diversity is not incidental but rather operates by design. At UIUC, increasing numbers of students, nominally "of color," who hail from transnational bourgeoisies augment the university's global diversity profile while bringing in the added cash flows of out-of-state student tuition dollars. These students figure quite literally as "assets" to the university, aiding the development of the university's comparative advantage in serving international student populations and thereby promising the magnetism of future capital to it.

Increasingly, scholarly accounts of diversity tend to relate critically to the concept. Sara Ahmed's (2012) remarks on the persistence of institutional racism in spite of the institution's conspicuous lauding of the virtues of diversity is a case in point. Ahmed's account, drawing as it does from interviews with university diversity practitioners in the United Kingdom and Australia, also documents the increasing emergence of diversity discourses in the management of race in postimperial and settler-colonial contexts outside the United States. Ellen Berrey, whose 2015 historical institutionalist study *The Enigma of Diversity* is probably our most thoroughgoing investigation of diversity discourses as they migrate and consolidate in and through various social milieux, argues that diversity is "a mechanism of containing and co-opting racial justice, as it largely leaves untouched persistent racial inequalities and the gulf between rich and poor" (9). For Walter Benn Michaels (2006), diversity, with its ideological obfuscation of the sources of inequality, represents neoliberalism in its most concrete manifestations. In sum, the emerging critical literature on diversity helps to significantly trouble any straightforward association of diversity with social justice, even though these works diverge significantly in their diagnoses of the foundations of social inequality.

Diversity figures prominently in the institutional life of contemporary African American studies but less as a keyword per se than as a concept that simultaneously animates and regulates the field's institutional life. Unlike other fields, and in fact oftentimes so as to ease the burden that other fields might be made to bear, African

American studies programs and departments are regularly cited by universities as evidence of institutional diversity and as a mechanism for its production. In this way, the field figures prominently in the university's institutional epistemology: with African American studies in place, the university is better able to *know* itself as diverse and to know more confidently that its claims to diversity are not just skin deep—rather, they register in the form of knowledge. Avowing a formal commitment to African American studies, then, the university substantiates the claim that that diversity is manifest in intellectual substance, not just surface. In the absence of a critical engagement with the on-the-ground institutional politics of diversity, African American studies remains bound in significant degree to a crisis-management function. To interrupt diversity's claim to social justice—or, more pointedly, the entitlement of its relation to the concept of the good—might thus also be to throw the field's contemporary conditions of possibility into crisis.

There are good reasons to do so. In 2014, the tech entrepreneurial company Priceonomics published on its website a ranking of "The Most and Least Diverse Cities in America." Atop the list of least diverse cities was Detroit, Michigan, which with 80.7 percent African American residents squeaked just ahead of El Paso, Texas's 79.7 Hispanic/Latino population. Unencumbered by even the most minimal considerations of history, structure, and power, this conceptualization of diversity neither answers to nor accounts for histories of discrimination or public policy, much less the overall architecture of white supremacy they were fashioned to uphold. In fact, in such representations, a black numerical majority is arguably presented as evidence of black *dominance*, a dominance presented as a problem that diversification can solve. (The reliably Democrat-voting Detroit, whose 42.3 percent poverty rate ranked it highest among large cities in the U.S., was at the time of the Priceonomics article's publication under the control of a non-democratically-appointed city manager, installed by Michigan's Republican Governor Rick Snyder.) Within the ideological parameters of our most prominent social justice imaginary, such a deployment of diversity might appear as a *misuse* of the concept. My point, however, is that to regard Priceonomics' representation of Detroit as nondiverse as mistaken is to look past just how much of diversity discourse, past and present, supplied its conditions of possibility. In this model, diversification and white gentrification are part of the same logical process: in fact, Priceonomics itself provides business models that seek to rationalize and streamline the very forms of hipster entrepreneurship that regard low-income-low-rent cities such as Detroit as a frontier-like opportunity for investment and profit extraction.

Diversification here offers a progressive patina to the political and economic forces driving the displacement of poor and working-class black Detroiters. Foreclosed homes, the shutting off of water to tens of thousands of residents, pension cuts for city workers, human rights violations—the signs of class war waged against the black poor are also the signs that herald the city's diversification. With this in mind, if diversity is to be a keyword for African American studies, it should not allow us to remain locked within the confines of the now hegemonic common sense that diversity does or should exist to do some measure of justice by black folks. But in this task, shrouding the term in suspicion will do us little analytic service. Rather than taking refuge in the negative connotations available from its twelfth-century vintage, embracing diversity's *critical value* would mean emphasizing its usefulness as a lens for training attention on racial capitalism in its material and ideological transits.

# 15

## Double-Consciousness

Reiland Rabaka

With roots in nineteenth-century psychological and philosophical discourse, the concept of double-consciousness was primarily popularized by W. E. B. Du Bois in his classic work *The Souls of Black Folk* (1903). He brought the term into twentieth-century social, political, racial and cultural thought and innovatively used it to capture and convey African Americans' feelings of dissonance and dividedness between their distant African ancestral homeland and their present American environment. Du Bois first used the term in an 1897 *Atlantic Monthly* article titled "Strivings of the Negro People." It was subsequently revised and republished under the title "Of Our Spiritual Strivings" in 1903 in *The Souls of Black Folk*. Several of Du Bois's key contributions to African American studies, if not American studies more generally speaking, arising out of *The Souls of Black Folk,* revolve around the dilemmas and dualities or, rather, the conundrums and complexities of what it means to be black in a white-dominated world.

In *The Souls of Black Folk*, Du Bois created several seminal concepts of race and critiques of racism to complement his earlier efforts to establish the social scientific study of race in the interest of emancipating the oppressed or, rather, in Du Bois's own words, the "earthly damned" (1903, 227). Many of the concepts of racial lived experience that Du Bois articulated in *The Souls of Black Folk* are intellectually interconnected and endlessly intersect. Ultimately, these concepts offer several of his most enduring contributions to critical race studies in general and African American studies in particular. Undoubtedly his interconnected concepts of "double-consciousness" and the "color-line" are incredibly significant. However, it is also important to observe that his theory of blacks' "Veiled" visibility and invisibility, as well as his emphasis on blacks' unique "second-sight" in and "gifts" to the white-dominated world are equally relevant with regard to critical race studies and African American studies. That being said, "double-consciousness" serves as a primary point of departure for critically comprehending the major recurring themes and concepts of *The Souls of Black Folk*, if not Du Bois's iconic contributions to African American studies, American studies, and critical race studies more broadly speaking.

The conceptual culmination of Du Bois's insurgent efforts to make both blacks and whites aware of the physical and psychological damage that life within the Veil and life along the color-line had on the "souls of black folk" was, of course, his intellectual history-making discourse on double-consciousness and its corollary concept of second-sight. He revealingly wrote, in perhaps the most widely commented on passage in *The Souls of Black Folk*,

> After the Egyptian and Indian, the Greek and
> Roman, the Teuton and Mongolian, the Negro is
> a sort of seventh son, born with a veil, and gifted
> with second-sight in this American world,—a world
> which yields him no true self-consciousness, but
> only lets him see himself through the revelation
> of the other world. It is a peculiar sensation,
> this double-consciousness, this sense of always
> looking at one's self through the eyes of others, of
> measuring one's soul by the tape of a world that
> looks on in amused contempt and pity. One ever

feels his two-ness,—an American, a Negro; two souls, two thoughts, two unreconciled strivings; two warring ideals in one dark body, whose dogged strength alone keeps it from being torn asunder.

The history of the American Negro is the history of this strife,—this longing to attain self-conscious manhood, to merge his double self into a better and truer self. In this merging he wishes neither of the older selves to be lost. He would not Africanize America, for America has too much to teach the world and Africa. He would not bleach his Negro soul in a flood of white Americanism, for he knows that Negro blood has a message for the world. He simply wishes to make it possible for a man to be both a Negro and an American, without being cursed and spit upon by his fellows, without having the doors of Opportunity closed roughly in his face. (1903, 3–4)

It was here, with these hallowed words, that Du Bois indelibly etched his name into the annals of African American studies in specific and American literary and cultural history in general. Although the Veil and the color-line are central tropes in *The Souls of Black Folk*, Du Bois's concept of double-consciousness and its corollary concept of second-sight are simultaneously essential to understanding *The Souls of Black Folk* and vital to critically comprehending the conundrums and contradictions of racial colonization and racial segregation in a nation, the United States, that often pretentiously prides itself on its cultural liberalism and long-standing commitment to democracy. Observe that Du Bois's doubling discourse connected the Veil with second-sight ("the Negro is a sort of seventh son, born with a veil, and gifted with second-sight in this American world"), and America (i.e., the United States), representing the white capitalist-colonialist world in

deep-seated denial, was to those "born with a veil" "a world which yield[ed] [them] no true self-consciousness, but only lets [them] see [themselves] through the revelation of the other world."

Then, as if faithfully harking back to his stated intention at *The Souls of Black Folk*'s opening—that is to say, to candidly explore the "strange meaning of being black here in the dawning of the Twentieth Century" (1903, vii)—Du Bois articulated his own homespun *ontology* of black life-worlds and black life-struggles in a white capitalist-colonialist world: "It is a peculiar sensation, this double-consciousness, this sense of always looking at one's self through the eyes of others." Indeed, Du Bois's concept of double-consciousness also seems to have profound implications for a *social psychology* of black life-worlds and black life-struggles in a white capitalist-colonialist world. For example, it might be useful to quickly list some of the psychological concepts and conditions that Du Bois's conception of double-consciousness appears to be conceptually connected to, if not during his day, then certainly in the twenty-first century: schizophrenia, paranoia, dysmorphophobia, inferiority complex, and anxiety disorder, among others.

Black life-worlds, Du Bois correctly assumed, would be "strange" and "peculiar" to whites because of the ideology of black invisibility, the diabolical dialectic of white superiority and black inferiority, and antiblack racist (mis)conceptions of blacks and blackness. The concept of double-consciousness asserts that the very color-line that racially divides the white world from the black world simultaneously creates a tortured "two-ness" in blacks' souls (and psyches). In fact, the racial ruptures of the color-line ultimately drive blacks to constantly question whether they are Africans or Americans (and even whether they are human) to such a doggedly excruciating degree that their souls become doubled and divided like the loveless racially colonized world that they are forced to live in or, rather, endure. Du Bois's concept of double-consciousness, then, is also a discursive doppelgänger, textually representing the consequences of blacks' racial colonization and the ways in which the color-line not only racially divides society but, even more, black souls and black selves.

Du Bois distressingly wrote of "two souls, two thoughts, two unreconciled strivings; two warring ideals in one dark body, whose dogged strength alone keeps it from being torn asunder." But a question begs: where do blacks get the "dogged strength" that keeps their souls and bodies "from being torn asunder"? After painting such a bleak picture of the "souls of black folk" and their trials and tribulations in the white capitalist-colonialist world, this seems like a fair question, and indeed, it is a query that Du Bois ingeniously answered with his saga of blacks' second-sight. Second-sight symbolizes blacks' ability, even in the face of adversity (i.e., holocaust, enslavement, colonization, segregation, and neoapartheid), to see both Africa (the black world) and America's (the white world's) strengths and weaknesses and the ways in which these two worlds could and should learn from and, even more, aid each other.

Here emphasis is placed on the epic aspects of Du Bois's theory of second-sight by referring to it as the "saga of second-sight" in an effort to accent the fact that, first, if indeed a saga is a "story of heroic achievement" and, second, as David Levering Lewis observes in W. E. B. Du Bois: Biography of a Race, 1868–1919 (1994), if Du Bois's writings, especially his memoirs, utilized the "language of the saga," then it is important for us to make a connection between Du Bois's autobiography and his African and African American historiography (19). In other words, Du Bois's "saga of second-sight" demonstrates not only that his soul is bound up with those of the "souls of black folk" but also that he boldly believed

that just as he was able to arrive at the critical black consciousness (as opposed to double-consciousness) of second-sight, so too could and would his beloved black folk break free from the gruesome grasp of double-consciousness. In order to wrench themselves free from the clutches of double-consciousness, as Du Bois had, black folk would have to systematically and critically study continental and diasporan African history, culture, and struggle on their own terms—that is to say, consciously countering the "ideological hegemony" of antiblack racist capitalism and colonialism, among other ills.

Du Bois described African Americans in the passage quoted earlier as being "gifted with second-sight," and it is their experiences in and visions of the "two worlds within and without the Veil" that ultimately distinguish their special contributions to American and world culture and civilization (1903, vii). In essence, whereas the majority of whites suffer from *white blindness to blackness*, blacks have been blessed (or "gifted," as it were) with second-sight as an ironic consequence of their having endured racial colonization and other forms of racial oppression at the hands of whites. But blacks, it should solemnly be said, should never take their giftedness for granted, as it is neither automatic nor axiomatic: because double-consciousness, truth be told, constantly makes second-sight dangerously double-edged and always and ever enervating on account of both the intensity and depth of blacks' internalization of *antiblack racist (mis)conceptions of blacks and blackness* and the paradoxes of the trajectory and transmutations of American and global apartheid. Bearing this in mind, we can conclude that double-consciousness is at its conceptual core about *double or divided selves in the process of spiritually, psychologically, and socially evolving out of tortured "two-ness" into "self-conscious manhood"*—which is to say, *self-conscious humanhood*. However, it must be emphasized, the only way to achieve *self-conscious humanhood* is through ongoing insurgent antiracist and radical prohumanist struggle or, as Du Bois put it, unceasing "striving."

The discourse on double-consciousness has developed considerably since Du Bois's day. In fact, the interdisciplinary influence of the concept can be detected in its ongoing critical engagement and utilization by historians, philosophers, literary theorists, political scientists, and sociologists, among others. For instance, Gerald Early's important edited volume *Lure and Loathing: Essays on Race, Identity, and the Ambivalence of Assimilation* (1993) took Du Bois's conception of double-consciousness as its primary point of departure and featured reflective essays by Darlene Clark Hine, Henry Louis Gates Jr., Toni Cade Bambara, Molefi Kete Asante, Nikki Giovanni, and Wilson Jeremiah Moses, among others. Paul Gilroy's *The Black Atlantic: Modernity and Double Consciousness* (1993), Anne Rawls's "'Race' as an Interaction Order Phenomenon: W. E. B. Du Bois's 'Double-Consciousness' Thesis Revisited" (2000), and Paul Mocombe's *The Soulless Souls of Black Folk: A Sociological Reconsideration of Black Consciousness as Du Boisian Double-Consciousness* (2008) collectively demonstrated the sociological significance of the concept of double-consciousness. Denise Heinze's *The Dilemma of "Double-Consciousness": Toni Morrison's Novels* (1993), Sandra Adell's *Double-Consciousness / Double Bind: Theoretical Issues in Twentieth-Century Black Literature* (1994), Henry Louis Gates Jr.'s "The Black Letters on the Sign: W. E. B. Du Bois and the Canon," and Danny Sexton's "Lifting the Veil: Revision and Double-Consciousness in Rita Dove's *The Darker Face of the Earth*" (2008) illustrated the ways double-consciousness proved to be a recurring theme in African American literature. Finally, the political scientists Adolph Reed in *W. E. B. Du Bois and*

*American Political Thought: Fabianism and the Color-Line* (1997), Robert Gooding-Williams in *In the Shadow of Du Bois: Afro-Modern Political Thought in America* (2009), and Lawrie Balfour in *Democracy's Reconstruction: Thinking Politically with W. E. B. Du Bois* (2011) each emphasized the continuing political importance of double-consciousness.

Consequently, for more than a century, *The Souls of Black Folk* has been praised and criticized, interpreted and sometimes misinterpreted, by so many scholars from so many different disciplines that there can be little doubt of its hallowed place in intellectual history. One of the key attractions of the volume undoubtedly centers on Du Bois's articulation of the concept of double-consciousness and its related concepts (e.g., the "color-line," the "Veil," "second-sight," and the "gift theory"). Scholars working in diverse disciplines, such as history, philosophy, political science, psychology, anthropology, economics, education, literature, and religion, among others, have drawn from and, in turn, contributed to the evolving discourse on double-consciousness. Moreover, *The Souls of Black Folk* and the key concept of double-consciousness have been particularly well received in a number of *interdisciplinary disciplines* that emerged between the middle of the twentieth century and the early decades of the twenty-first century. For instance, *The Souls of Black Folk* is widely considered a foundational text, and the discourse on double-consciousness a major discursive point of departure, not only in African American studies but also in related interdisciplinary disciplines such as American studies, ethnic studies, cultural studies, critical race studies, subaltern studies, decolonial studies, and postcolonial studies. Obviously, the concept of double-consciousness continues to capture and convey the "two-ness" and "strange meaning" of the souls of black folk in the twenty-first century.

# 16

## Empire

Fanon Che Wilkins

W. E. B. Du Bois famously declared that "the problem of the Twentieth Century is the problem of the color-line" (1903, vii). Du Bois's words have been quoted extensively, and it would be hard to find a more cited passage in African American letters. Yet the proverbial problem, as it has been often cited from *The Souls of Black Folk*, has been routinely deployed as a prophetic observation principally concerned with the domestic plight of African Americans. Hard on the heels of the failures of Reconstruction, the persistence of white supremacy, and the legal codification of Jim Crow, "the color-line" has remained an opening salvo for grappling with the conundrum of race and racial oppression on U.S. soil.

Yet, if one continues to read the adjoining words that follow Du Bois's most famous utterance, one will note that his declaration extended far beyond the domestic confines of the United States. Indeed, the color-line was "in the relation of the darker to the lighter races of men in Asia, in America and the islands of the sea" (1903, 13). The color-line was global and crisscrossed oceans, continents, nations, and empires.

African life in the Western Hemisphere always sat at the vortex of Euro-American empire as it evolved over four tumultuous centuries. The writer Toni Morrison (1992) has astutely observed that the transatlantic slave trade stamped African bodies as the first objectified subjects of the modern world. Without question, slavery made modernity possible, and the expansion of European empires paved the way for the colonization of the Americas, Asia, and Africa.

It is within this context that the field of African American studies (and its disciplinary corollaries: Africana studies, African diaspora studies, Caribbean studies, slavery studies, etc.) has been forced to wrestle with Euro-American empire from its inception. This essay, however, focuses on the mid-nineteenth century up through the twentieth and thematically considers how African Americans confronted and resisted empire at home and abroad.

Although Du Bois published *The Souls of Black Folks* in 1903, his global conception of "the color-line" was in direct response to imperial expansion in both hemispheres. Across the Atlantic, Germany's Chancellor Otto von Bismarck organized the Berlin Conference of 1884–85 and formally ushered in the infamous "Scramble for Africa." Fourteen European nations and the United States sent representatives to Berlin. In the wake of the conference, Germany, Belgium, Britain, France, Portugal, Spain, and Italy succeeded in dividing the continent into various spheres of colonial control.

The United States did not emerge with its own African spoils; however, it had expanded its imperial reach much closer to home. Indeed, U.S. colonialism began on its own shores. Armed with an Anglo-Saxon drive for new territory and an unquenchable thirst for fossil fuels and precious metals, and buoyed by the philosophical justification of Manifest Destiny, U.S. empire took shape through the genocidal wars against indigenous peoples, considered collateral damage in the service of *progress*. As the U.S. Calvary pushed West, it also turned its barrels south and instigated a war with Mexico in 1846 under the pretense that the Rio Grande marked the true boundary between the two nations. Within two years, Mexico was defeated and forced to cede two-thirds of its land to the United States.

After successive internal wars to subdue the indigenous peoples of North America and codify the settler-colonial edifice of empire, the United States intervened in the Cuban War of Independence in 1898 and emerged a victor in full control of Spain's colonial possessions. By seizing Cuba and annexing Hawaii, Puerto Rico, the Philippines, and Guam, the late nineteenth century signaled a new day in U.S. empire.

Thus, the "the relation of the darker to the lighter races of men in Asia, in America and the islands of the sea," which Du Bois so eloquently addressed in the opening passages of his classic text, were structured by a new imperial cartography of U.S. empire building. The historian Michael Krenn has noted that U.S. expansion in the nineteenth century grew out of a range of factors including economic depressions in the 1870s, 1880s, and 1890s as a result of overproduction, glutted domestic markets, strained labor relations, and populist resistance to it all. Moreover, U.S. "military strategists, most notably Capt. Alfred Thayer Mahan, argued that a large navy was the key to power in the modern world" (2006, 36). U.S. naval prowess found justification in ideas of "survival of fittest," popularized by Charles Darwin's 1859 study *On the Origin of Species*. The pseudoscientific application of Darwinism only reinforced long-standing racist practices that facilitated the devaluation and dehumanization of large swaths of humanity, a precursor to Euro-American colonization.

African Americans, along with their counterparts throughout the African diaspora, resisted these practices. This resistance found formal expression through organizations as varied as the National Association for the Advancement of Colored People (NAACP), the Urban League, the African Blood Brotherhood (ABB), and the Universal Negro Improvement Association (UNIA). As the U.S. Navy patrolled the Pacific and the southern Atlantic in search of new resources and markets, African Americans continued to endure the racist backlash of Reconstruction's failures. Thus, U.S. imperial expansion abroad coincided with a renewed regime of racial terror at home, and nothing embodied this crisis more poignantly than the rise of lynching.

At the turn of the century, African American activists devoted significant organizational effort to combatting lynching. No figure embodied this fight more than the activist Ida B. Wells. Wells's crusade for justice took her across the United States, yet, like the abolitionists before her, she traveled to England to educate and appeal to the moral conscience of the British public, some of whom found lynching reprehensible.

Wells made her first trip to England in 1893 under the invitation of English Quakers. After failing to raise money to support her activism on that trip, she returned to England in 1894 as an international correspondent for the *Daily Inter-Ocean*, a Chicago-based Republican newspaper opposed to lynching. Wells's public speaking and incisive journalism moved British audiences and catalyzed some people to create antilynching organizations in England and beyond. Like abolitionists had decades earlier, Wells moved between an older empire (Britain) and an emerging one (United States), making the fight against lynching a global issue and placing the grievances of African Americans at the center a new geopolitical order that saw the United States emerging as a global superpower with colonial bounty scattered across the hemisphere.

Yet as U.S. empire expanded, others crumbled in the aftermath of World War I. By 1918, the German, Austrian-Hungarian, Ottoman, and Russian empires were no more. Against the backdrop of this massive geopolitical shift, black folk around the world continued to resist racial capitalism, white supremacy, and colonial domination. Drawing on older traditions of resistance rooted in Ethiopianism and Christian Revivalism,

African people around the world found political refuge in redemptionist visions of Africa grounded in providential sensibilities that crisscrossed the black world.

It was within this context that the Jamaican migrant Marcus Mosiah Garvey established the headquarters for the UNIA in Harlem, New York, in 1916. Garvey's arrival coincided with the first wave of the Great Migration that saw black southerners and Caribbean migrants pouring into northern cities in search of jobs, opportunity, and reprieve from Jim Crow and colonialism. Garvey's Pan-African vision and unprecedented organizational acumen resonated with the hopes and desires of a determined people committed to principles of self-organization and self-reliance. Indeed, the *Negro World*, the UNIA's newspaper and primary organizational tool, circulated globally through the hands of black sailors and railroad workers both formally and informally.

The UNIA was monumental in the fight against Euro-American empire that gripped and constrained black life in every corner of the globe. It would be a mistake, however, to measure its power and transformative gravitas by its organizational growth and decline or the life of Garvey himself. As Garveyism became localized, its presence could be felt in trade unions, religious organizations, and cultural celebrations that edified and reified black pride and dignity. As one scholar has noted, the global organizing efforts of black folk during the interwar years might be best understood as "the age of Garvey" (Ewing 2014).

Garveyism invigorated grassroots organizational activity among black working peoples around the world. During the World War II, the U.S. black press used its pages to link the African American fight for democracy to larger anticolonial struggles in Africa, Asia, and the Americas. Black writers, activists, and intellectuals engaged in solidarity initiatives rooted in the common experiences of aggrieved communities directly shaped

by slavery, racial capitalism, and colonial domination. Thus, the African American freedom struggle's universalism grew out of a recognition of the inextricable linkages between Jim Crow, anticolonialism, and the global fight against Euro-American colonialism as it recalibrated during World War II.

World War II was unquestionably a watershed period in the history of African Americans' quest for full citizenship in the United States. Once the U.S. entered the war following Japan's attack on Pearl Harbor on December 7, 1941, the *Pittsburgh Courier*, the nation's largest black newspaper, inaugurated its "Double V Campaign," taking aim at ending fascism abroad and racism at home. In addition, fighting in the Pacific theater proved to be more complicated for black combatants in the U.S. Army. Unlike their white counterparts, African Americans had a long-standing affinity for the Japanese that stretched back to the Russo-Japanese War of 1905, in which Russia was defeated by a nation of color.

African American literature is replete with narratives of sympathy and adoration for Japan. In rereading these narratives, the literary scholar Etsuko Taketani suggests that we might conceptualize black participation in World War II as part of the "black Pacific," which projected "a community imagined contrapuntally to [the] regional order in the making, in which a sense of belonging is manufactured by the performance of black narratives that invent history, one that African Americans imagine they share with the colored peoples of the Pacific Rim, especially Asia" (2014, 6–7).

With Europe in shambles and Japan decimated by the atomic bomb, the United States ascended to world supremacy. African American journalists were careful to note that following the war, the United States began to extend its imperial reach into the Caribbean and South America. New military bases were established in Trinidad and Jamaica. The Jamaican Bauxite Company, a subsidiary of the Aluminum Company of America, garnered greater market share on the island. U.S. military presence in the region only reinforced the power and might of huge conglomerates such as United Fruit Company in such places as Surinam, where they had had a hold on national economies for decades.

For much of the rest of the century, African Americans resisted U.S. empire and called into question the ways in which U.S. foreign policy and militarism reinforced racism and bigotry at home. African American activism has remained critical to challenging American exceptionalism and underscoring the shortcomings of the professed virtues of American democracy.

# 17

# Family
Candice M. Jenkins

Scholars of black life and culture have taken an interest in the notion of "family" from at least the turn of the twentieth century; W. E. B. Du Bois's groundbreaking sociological study *The Philadelphia Negro* (1899) devoted a chapter to "the Negro Family," which explored everything from typical urban family size (significantly smaller than families in rural areas), variations in family income and expenditures across classes, and details of family life, including various types of cohabitation and child rearing. Notes Du Bois, "The home was destroyed by slavery, struggled up after emancipation, and is again not exactly threatened, but neglected in the life of city Negroes" ([1899] 1996, 196). This emphasis on the deleterious consequences of slavery and plantation life for the black family forms a through line from Du Bois to later sociological and historical studies, perhaps most famously E. Franklin Frazier's comprehensive *The Negro Family in the United States* (1939), which argued that black family life had been deeply affected by slavery's abuses and that the resultant fracturing of the nuclear family structure continued to reverberate in the black community of the early twentieth century.

Twenty-five years later, the sociologist, senator, and assistant secretary of labor Daniel Patrick Moynihan relied heavily on Frazier's work when drawing up the report, commissioned by President Lyndon B. Johnson, that became *The Negro Family: The Case for National Action* (1965). Moynihan's report, which detailed what he called the "tangle of pathology" of black family life, argued that African American communities "ha[ve] been forced into a matriarchal structure which, because it is so out of line with the rest of the American society, seriously retards the progress of the group as a whole" (29). Moynihan's report generated significant controversy not simply because of this claim about black matriarchy, which echoed the work of Frazier and other black sociologists and pundits writing in the 1960s, such as Kenneth Clark and Whitney Young, but because his work appeared to emphasize not structural racism and socioeconomic disadvantage as the cause of these issues within the black family but rather something dysfunctional inherent to black culture itself. Feminist critics of the report and of the controversy surrounding it have since pointed out the masculinist emphasis of much of the critique of Moynihan; most of Moynihan's critics agreed with his assessment of black women as overly dominant within black households, as well as his argument that black families "reversed [the] roles of husband and wife" and thereby emasculated the black man (30). Where such critics disagreed with Moynihan was on causes of and solutions to this issue: Moynihan's work was repeatedly interpreted, precisely because of its emphasis on the "tangle of pathology," as victim blaming (see, for instance, William J. Ryan's 1971 response to Moynihan, *Blaming the Victim*) and as insufficiently attentive to the importance of jobs and other structural changes in potentially transforming black family life.

The Moynihan report's continued influence in the latter years of the twentieth century, and even into the twenty-first, is undeniable; the trope of black family "pathology" popularized by Moynihan continues to circulate in the United States, particularly in political commentary about black families from both ends of the political spectrum. If such commentary, divorced even from Moynihan's research into the causes of such assumed "pathology," rarely looked to the slave past to justify present-day black struggles, research on the antebellum period that emerged in the years immediately following the civil rights era, including John W. Blassingame's *The Slave Community* (1972), Eugene Genovese's *Roll, Jordan, Roll: The World the Slaves Made* (1974), and Herbert G. Gutman's *The Black Family in Slavery and Freedom* (1977), actually questioned conventional wisdom about the fractured and fragile black family structure under slavery, instead emphasizing the way that enslaved blacks had formed crucial bonds on the plantation. These studies—along with work such as Angela Davis's "Reflections on the Black Woman's Role in the Community of Slaves" (1972), which explicitly countered the lingering belief in black "matriarchy" under conditions of enslavement, instead focusing on black women's forced equality with their male counterparts, as well as their insurgent resistance—opened a critical space for scholars of African American history and culture to attend to different forms of "family" and kinship structure than the heteropatriarchal *nuclear* family. The anthropologist Carol Stack's *All Our Kin* (1974) is a notable example of this sort of critical reframing of notions of "family" and attention to how impoverished blacks nonetheless found ways to share resources and create lasting kinship bonds even under difficult material circumstances.

The nuclear "family," which, as the feminist literary scholar Hortense Spillers famously argued in her groundbreaking 1987 essay "Mama's Baby, Papa's Maybe: An American Grammar Book," is a discursive and ideological institution deeply implicated by histories of white supremacy and racist violence, has also and as a result been a central means by which captive black bodies had been excluded from "Western" conceptions of gender and culture: "It seems clear, however, that 'Family,' as we practice and understand it 'in the West'—the *vertical* transfer of a bloodline, of a patronymic, of titles and entitlements . . .—becomes the mythically revered privilege of a free and freed community" (74). Spillers's work spoke back to and paved the way for other black women's writing on "family" that highlighted the institution's fraught history and the ways that the word "family," particularly in its narrowest senses, has operated as a disciplinary term—with those who are disciplined *by* the concept overwhelmingly black women, the mothers, sisters, daughters, and wives whose behavior within the embattled black family unit has so often been scrutinized and found wanting. A great deal of this writing has taken place not in the sphere of scholarship and analysis but in that of fiction.

Published in the same year as Spillers's essay, Toni Morrison's Pulitzer Prize–winning novel *Beloved* (1987) explores both the traumatic mechanics of slavery's decimation of black patriarchal "family"—husbands and wives, parents and children separated; intrafamilial violence; the haunting presence of those who are lost—as well as the less conventional "family" bonds that the enslaved nonetheless forged and the ways that such bonds sustained and fortified slavery's victims and survivors. Other critically acclaimed works by black women, such as Alice Walker's *The Color Purple* (1982), also a Pulitzer Prize–winning novel, Ntozake Shange's *For Colored Girls Who Have Considered Suicide / When the Rainbow Is Enuf* (1975), and Gloria Naylor's *The Women of Brewster Place* (1982), not only questioned the restrictive definitions of "family" that continued to be applied to black Americans, portraying a number of alternative forms of kinship and familial connection, including same-gender relationships, but also examined the ways that domestic violence and other intimate abuses by African American men disrupted the black heteropatriarchal "family" from within.

The hostile response to these works by some black male reviewers and critics—see, for instance, the sociologist Robert Staples's "The Myth of the Black Macho: A Response to Angry Black Feminists" (1979)—led the scholar Deborah McDowell to pen the essay "Reading Family Matters" (1989), in which she calls such figures' critical reliance on a "totalizing fiction" of African American community wholeness, a story of "the Black Family cum Black Community headed by the Black Male who does battle with an oppressive White world," a black "family romance" (78). In the world of media, this black family romance found expression in television via a number of popular series depicting African American family life, including *Good Times* (1974–79), *The Jeffersons* (1975–85), *227* (1985–90), *Family Matters* (1989–98), *Roc* (1991–94), and, perhaps best known and most influential, *The Cosby Show*, which ran from 1984 to 1992 and depicted a wealthy professional black couple and their five children. Experts disagree about the ultimate value of the "positive image" of the black family that Cosby portrayed, with the sociologist Herman Gray arguing in 1995, for instance, that despite the show's groundbreaking exploration of diversity *within* blackness, with its specific focus on the black upper middle class, the show "seemed unable, or unwilling, to negotiate its universal appeals to family, the middle class, mobility, and individualism on the one hand and the particularities of black social, cultural, political, and economic realities on the other" (81–82). Yet the show's meaning and legacy as a powerful cultural image of "family" has perhaps been troubled most by the long list of sexual-assault allegations leveled against an aging Bill Cosby, which ultimately challenge the show's validity as an idealized black household that purportedly was based on Cosby's own equally ideal family life.

McDowell's work on the family romance highlights another common but contested use of the word "family" in African American communities, as a marker of *racial* belonging; understanding the larger black community as a "family" has been signaled, historically, by linguistic and discursive gestures such as the "brothers and sisters" of the civil rights and Black Power movements, a form of address that grows out of similar language common to the black church. And while the more inclusive term "sibling" is growing in popularity as African Americans who identify as transgender become more visible and vocal about the ways that words such as "brothers" and "sisters" can be exclusionary, the very language of "family" as a metaphor for black community has also been questioned in some quarters, most notably by the black British scholar Paul Gilroy. Gilroy, in his 1991 essay "'It's a Family Affair': Black Culture and the Trope of Kinship," critiqued the way that the metaphor of "family" reduced "the crisis of black politics and social life" to "a crisis of black masculinity alone" (204) and predicted that "disastrous consequences follow when the family supplies the only symbols of political agency we can find in the culture and the only object upon which that agency can be seen to operate" (207). Ultimately a critique of U.S.-centric racial politics, Gilroy's analysis emphasized that alternative forms of community building, such as those found in transnational or global diasporic contexts, might prove a more fruitful and inclusive way of conceptualizing community.

The word "family" as a signal of membership has also circulated within black queer and LGBT (lesbian, gay, bisexual, and transgender) communities, as a means of recognizing and embracing those who are open or closeted members. The sociologist Mignon Moore is one of few scholars who have examined how conventional notions of "family" are embraced and also contested by black LGBT subjects; her book *Invisible Families: Gay Identities, Relationships, and Motherhood among Black Women* (2011) argues that "the family life of gay women of color has for many years been largely invisible to African Americans" (2) and uses ethnography to explore "how Black lesbians' participation in and enactment of their intersecting identities as Black, as women, and as gay people influence family formation, mate selection, expectations for partners in intimate relationships, and other aspects of family life" (3). Notably, with the landmark 2015 U.S. Supreme Court ruling *Obergefell v. Hodges*, same-sex marriage became legal in all fifty states, making it possible for existing LGBT families to seek legal protections from the state that had previously been denied.

While stereotypes about the brokenness or pathology of the black family continue to circulate in the twenty-first century, recent scholarship continues to refute such perceptions; a Centers for Disease Control and Prevention (CDC) report from 2013 for instance, details how black fathers are actually as involved, if not more involved, with child rearing as white or Latino fathers in similar living situations, debunking the persistent myth of the "absent" black father (Jones and Mosher 2013). That this myth persists—alongside other oft-repeated narratives about the black family in "crisis"—may explain why African American families continue to face higher levels of scrutiny from the state. One result is that black children are overrepresented in foster care, despite statistics that indicate that "children of all races are equally as likely to suffer from abuse and neglect" (see the U.S. Government Accountability Office's 2007 report, *African American Children in Foster Care*). As African American studies continues its work in the twenty-first century, "family" is sure to continue as a complex and contested term, with an array of meanings that are shaped by, but strive to move beyond, black history in the U.S. and around the globe.

# 18

## Feminism

Michelle M. Wright

While variously understood, "feminism," in its Western contexts, usually means a belief that all human beings should enjoy the same political, economic, and social rights. As a "keyword," feminism is a concept often misunderstood as signifying a genealogy solely of women's rights and social, political, and economic advancement. This brief essay lays out the distortions that often attend initial or superficial engagements with feminism, specifically in African American studies, enabling a definition of feminism that ably skirts and negotiates those false avatars that seek to contain feminism to its least accurate meaning: a movement wholly about and for women.

Like all other ideologies and movement, the history of feminism is most often structured and analyzed as a linear progress narrative; in the white Western context, twentieth-century white feminist history has been organized as a series of generations, defined as "waves" (we are currently in "third wave" feminism). White U.S. feminism often points to its origins in the mid- to late nineteenth century with the rise of the suffragette movement, then marks its points of advancement through salient figures such as Elizabeth Cady Stanton, Susan B. Anthony, Betty Friedan, Barbara Gittings, Bella Abzug, and Gloria Steinem and events such as the passage of the Nineteenth Amendment in 1920. U.S. Black feminism takes a much more complex route, as some of the earliest abolitionists were also Black feminists who showed how the failure to honor human rights rendered enslaved Black women the most striking and cogent symbols of this oppression, where legally sanctioned rape and forced breeding not only rendered the Black female body into a grotesque machine for reproduction but denigrated her offspring, relegating children to the status of products, not humans. As this essay will show, at each crucial stage in African American history, Black feminists were often the ones looking at questions of justice and equality more deeply and broadly than were many of their counterparts.

In the late nineteenth century, the antilynching and human-suffrage advocates Mary Church Terrell, Frances W. Harper, and Ida B. Wells (among others) laid out blueprints for an equitable society that located Black women as the foundation and even bellwethers for this equality. After all, they reasoned, to what degree could a Black woman truly be free, much less teach others about equality and justice, if she were forced to obey men (whether father, son, husband, or male guardian) in all things, as the laws at the time dictated? From the outset, Black feminism not only enjoined us to look outward, at racist oppression, but also forced us to look at our own communities, where patriarchal norms are often held up as desirable goals and where asymmetries of power are presented as "natural" and/or "moral."

While these advocates' work is known to most Black feminists today, most traditional and dominant narratives of U.S. Black history foreground and focus on icons such as Frederick Douglass, W. E. B. Du Bois, Martin Luther King Jr., and Malcolm X, celebrating them (and justifiably so) as inspirational and successful leaders of "the race" whose work has led to significant sociopolitical gains for African Americans. Yet these mainstream histories and biographies fail to tell the whole story: they ignore or remain ignorant of a remarkable and almost unique history of Black female writings and activism in the early fight for abolition and then socioeconomic power. Rather than (as is often assumed or claimed) playing marginal roles primarily focused on the rights and plights of women, Sojourner Truth, Maria Stewart, Harriet Tubman, and Mary Ann Shadd Cary were central and essential shaping forces (Margaret Washington, n.d.), whether through their activism, their organizing, their mentoring, or their intellectual contributions that provided canny analyses of bigotry at the individual and state levels accompanied by forceful arguments and strategies to secure human suffrage.

For example, at the end of the Civil War, while W. E. B. Du Bois laid out a blueprint for socioeconomic and political parity in the now classic *The Souls of Black Folk* (1903), Black women activists, journalists, and writers such as Ida B. Wells-Barnett, Maria Stewart, Frances W. Harper, and Pauline Hopkins laid out far more inclusive projects for a Black future in which men and women worked together to secure human suffrage—while *Souls*, as Hazel Carby has pointed out in *Race Men* (1998), imagines Black men as the heroes that would either rescue the Black female damsels in distress or else resist their Jezebel charms. This is not to say that these Black female intellectuals were perfect: Wells tended to ignore the Black women who were murdered in her internationally famous antilynching crusade (e.g., *On Lynchings* and *Southern Horrors*, both published in 1892), focusing only on the men. And although Frances W. Harper should be celebrated for her ability to depict a complex and diverse Black collective emerging from the Civil War, both enslaved and free, novels such as *Iola Leroy* (1892) are uneven in their depiction of former slaves (although, to be fair, as Rod Ferguson notes in his landmark book *Aberrations in Black* [2004], a majority of the Black cognoscenti also indulged in ugly stereotypes about the effect slavery had had on moral and cognitive intelligence).

Following a few decades later, the Harlem and Chicago Renaissance is still broadly understood as the first "modern" moment in which Black artists and activists debated their place in the modern world, most especially within the United States, in view of their recent enslaved past. While Black feminist writers such as Zora Neale Hurston, Jessie Fauset, and Nella Larsen are typically accorded credit for bringing women into these questions, they were asked far more difficult, broader questions than many of their male counterparts were simply because they *did* focus on, rather than ignore or marginalize, gender difference and, in doing so, supplied more lasting and universal solutions. While Langston Hughes's poems and plays provide a brilliantly smooth and blended synthesis between "Negro" folk art and the Western modern in his imagery, cadence, and philosophies, Hurston's *Of Mules and Men* (1935), *Their Eyes Were Watching God* (1937), and *Dust Tracks on a Road* (1942) underscore an endlessly reproductive tension between the folk and the modern, one in which aspects of each can be found in the other. The result, especially in *Their Eyes*, is a Blackness that, unlike most depictions in Harlem Renaissance writing, is untethered from a history of whiteness, much less the ultimately white-dominated yardstick of modernity and civilization. Larsen also provides a multidimensional Blackness that speaks beyond its time, especially in her novella *Passing* (1929), in which the destabilization of race, the lack of a clear dividing line between Black and white, reveals the unstable and constructed nature of gender, sexual, and class identities as well. In other words, racial hierarchies and intraracial heteropatriarchies seek to order and control "inferior" races, genders, classes, and sexualities all at once, neatly laying bare the lie that socioeconomic and political equalities can be secured one marginalized collective at a time. Similarly, Larsen's *Quicksand* (1928) shows how Black women are so easily left behind even as Black collectives flourish through the growth of Black colleges and universities, Black intellectual society, and the Black church, thus connecting gender rights to social institutions. Modeled on heteropatriarchal logic, social institutions offer limited power for women.

Unfortunately, the talent and achievements of these nineteenth- and early-twentieth-century Black female artists and activists were largely bypassed in the wake of the civil rights and Black Power movements. While some figures, such as Bayard Rustin, and some legal gains, such as the Civil Rights Act, did in fact partially address gender parity, the concerns of Black feminists were at best marginalized and at worst aggressively rejected. One of the most memorable points in U.S. Black history in which Black women found themselves excluded and denigrated is during Black nationalism of the 1960s and 1970s, which correlated to the foundation of the Combahee River Collective and especially the rise of Audre Lorde, a global feminist par excellence who made explicit and frequent connections between Black women from the United States and the Caribbean and the working classes, gender relations, labor relations, colonialism, Black Europeans, queer politics, parenting, interracial relations, nonexclusionary female coalitions, industrialization, climate change, environmentalism, and agricultural, as well as racism and misogyny in white Western health care. It is difficult, if not impossible, to think of a single male theorist whose work and vision intersect with so many topics, challenges, and crises informing our media, syllabi, and research projects today—and yet, while well-known, Audre Lorde is most often taught or cited in relation to Black women rather than the vast collectives and topics she influenced. Indeed, the viewpoints and politics of Combahee was so far ahead of its time that contemporary Black feminist thinkers, such as Brittney Cooper, Keeanga-Yamahtta Taylor, and Erica Edwards, have revisited these writings and applied them to contemporary concerns—Taylor most explicitly with her edited volume *How We Get Free: Black Feminism and the Combahee River Collective* (2017).

Even in African American feminism's disagreements, it has shed light on different views and practices across the African diaspora that more mainstream discourses on diasporic alliances and connections have ignored. The debate between "womanism" and "Black feminism" takes us into complicated territory, because Black women from African nations often have a different set of goals and ideals for achieving gender parity. These differences have led to vibrant, productive debates on the diverse beliefs, cultures, ideologies, and practices enjoyed by Black women from across the globe, and while they were born out of debates on feminism versus womanism, they are relevant to all those who define themselves as members of Black community. In other words, even in debate, Black feminism engenders a rich array of important concepts and arguments on the very nature of Blackness and its meaning in the world.

The concept of Black feminism as multidimensional has in fact been a central topic of conversation for the past twenty years—at least through Kimberlé Crenshaw's concept of "intersectionality," as found in her article "Demarginalizing the Intersection of Race and Sex" (1989). A foundational and still-leading scholar of critical race studies, Crenshaw argues that the simultaneous oppressions faced by women of color through their marginalized racial and gender identities render them twice as invisible, including, ironically, in discourses on anti-Black racism or sexism/misogyny. Yet even as the idea of intersectionality has illuminated and brought to the fore specific oppressions, it has also generated a great deal of dispute over its efficacy as an agent of change, much less of social, political, and economic justice.

As Jennifer Nash has shown in "Intersectionality and Its Discontents" (2017), some of this debate may be misplaced, given that Crenshaw's focus is on domestic violence against women and court proceedings in which Black women are the defendants. In other words, one cannot take intersectionality out of context and expect it to still work. Indeed, intersectionality has been used to conflate the *epistemological representations* of Black women with their *ontology*, that is, how they are seen (and treated) by others versus how they understand and perceive themselves. As a result, rather than seeking the corrective that Crenshaw pursues, "intersectionality" has often been misapplied to assert that due to Black women's status as "Other of the Other," as Michele Wallace put it some four decades ago in *Black Macho and the Myth of the Superwoman* (1979), they are well and truly merely marginal players in this great game of history.

It seems, then, that a disturbing pattern emerges when we look at the fate of those discourses that have attempted to critique the marginalization of Black women in the U.S., from Michele Wallace to Kimberlé Crenshaw. Protesting the marginalization of Black women becomes a war of attrition, in which misguided allies of Black feminist thinkers outdo themselves in (re)presenting the ontology of Black women as next to nothing at all.

Hortense Spillers's move toward Black female embodiment as a site of resistance and correction, beginning with the now-canonical "Mama's Baby, Papa's Maybe: An American Grammar Book" (1987), may well become the most viable strategy in this depressing war. I would argue, however, that we also need to keep our focus on how Black feminists and writings and activities are represented in scholarly and pedagogical media. At the very least, underscoring the central epistemic heft of Black feminism might counter the rather rigid belief both within and without the academy that Black women and their concerns are, at best, a footnote in Western and global intellectual, political, and economic histories.

The education scholar Cynthia Dillard pursues this tack in "The Substance of Things Hoped For, the Evidence of Things Not Seen" (2000). Dillard opines that an "endarkened feminist epistemology," one in which the goal is inclusivity and diversity (rather than the "great man" approach that girds most white Western bodies of knowledge), would not only increase the qualitative value of resulting epistemologies but positively impact minority students who are normally expected to imbibe a narrative in which bodies are simply objects on which historical agents and events act (662).

In contemporary Black studies, two central moves have been made that have a negative impact on Black feminism. In one, Black feminism is redefined as fully in lockstep with, rather than critical of, Black discourses that imagine the struggle for equal rights through Black male bodies alone. In the second, dubbed "anti-Blackness," any serious analysis of gender and sexual difference is rejected in favor of arguing that all Black peoples are all equally disenfranchised because of racism—regardless of their individual social, economic, and political privileges. Put together, the effect has been a near silencing of the ways in which sexism and homophobia impact Black women's lives and bodies, so that "Black feminist" discourse is reduced to critiquing anti-Black racism to the exclusion of all other bigotries, acts of violence, and power asymmetries sanctioned either by the state or within African American communities themselves.

There are, of course, many scholars today who practice and advocate a U.S. Black feminism that works to engage all relevant bodies and identities equally. These scholars and works should be brought front and center into our syllabi, our scholarship, our speaking invitations, and our collective publications. They are not "simply" feminist; as Mae G. Henderson has shown us in "Speaking in Tongues: Dialogics, Dialectics, and the Black Woman Writer's Literary Tradition" (1993), Black feminism is one of the least simple things of all.

# 19

## Gender

C. Riley Snorton

Derived from the Latin word *genus*, which refers to a race, class, or kind of something, "gender" shares its root word with concepts such as "genre," "genealogy," "genetics," and "genius," among others. Its etymology provides a partial context for how the term is frequently deployed to describe a finite system of types that are indexical of a bipartite model of sex to confer either a masculine or feminine designation. Among humans, and with an implied binaristic model of gender intact, gender is conceptualized as the product of a patriarchal ordering of difference invested in maintaining a relation of male dominance to female subordination. Although gender is colloquially used to refer to a generalizable typology to designate species into "men," "women," and sometimes "transgender" or nonbinary categories, such usage for black and blackened people is, at best, imprecise and, at worst, obscurant given gender's arrangement with race and other modalities of difference.

Gender's structures of meaning and attendant incoherences are particularly legible when situated alongside violent forces of racialization, which have indelibly shaped gender as a system of signification. The production of gender as a naturalized category calcified at the height of the European colonial era, and each node of the slave trade produced a critical environment for the numerous ways gender was articulated, disarticulated, and lived. As Hortense Spillers explains in her noted essay "Mama's Baby, Papa's Maybe: An American Grammar Book" in reference to the ordering of the New World, a project that would require both the theft of land and the theft of body, "Under these conditions, we lose at least gender difference in the outcome, and the female body and the male body become a territory of cultural and political maneuver, not at all gender-related, gender specific" (1987, 67). Spillers notes, "in th[is] historic outline of dominance, the respective subject-positions of 'female' and 'male' adhere to no symbolic integrity" (66). Rather, gender and what are often linked as cognate concepts, namely, the body and sexuality, are disarticulated for black and indigenous people in an American grammar produced by settler colonialism and chattel slavery.

As particular historical conditions constitute the grounds for the "ungendering" of blackness within a dominant symbolic order, Sylvia Wynter and others have gestured toward different semiotic arrangements that more accurately describe the particular expressivities of racialized gender. In an afterword to a collection of essays written by Caribbean women critics, Wynter uses William Shakespeare's *The Tempest* to provide one explanation for how forces of racialization, in their colonial manifestations, alter orders of difference such that "*sex-gender attributes* are no longer the primary index of 'deferent' difference, and in which the discourse that erects itself is no longer primarily 'patriarchal,' but rather 'monarchal' in its Western-European, essentially post-Christian, post-religious definition" (1990, 358, emphasis in original). For Wynter, colonization and the establishment of a symbolic ordering to articulate colonial rule shifts "the primacy of the *anatomical* model of sexual difference . . . to that of the *physiognomic* model of racial/cultural difference," such that encounters between different genders in this context are as much, or perhaps more, marked by the colonial rubric of racial domination as mere sexual (anatomical) difference (ibid.). Suggesting monarchal logic, expressed as the relationship of ruler over servants, gestures toward an alternative logic for how gender is assigned, as Wynter offers a rearrangement of the patriarchal formulation of the father over household to address how gender shifts according to its racial and sociohistorical contexts.

In matters of production and reproduction, race assembles the body, such that it proliferates gender (see, e.g., Morgan 2004; Hartman 1996; Haley 2016). In "Seduction and the Ruses of Power," for example, Saidiya Hartman argues for the "divergent production of the category woman," as she focuses on the legal and cultural responses to rape of enslaved women in the United States (1996, 556). For Hartman, gender, as it is produced through forced sex between slavers and the enslaved, constructed a female subject position, in which the "erasure or disavowal of sexual violence engendered black femaleness as a condition of unredressed injury, which only intensified bonds of captivity and the deadening objectification of chattel status" (556). While Hartman is careful not to produce a false equivalence between violence and gender, her argument underscores the psychic dimensions of gender with regard to injury, as it also reiterates how the meanings of gender are multiplied in light of the sexual violence that constituted chattel slavery.

Within the realms of lived experience, gender provides an aperture into modes of survival and personal or collective experiences of vitality (or lack thereof). Womanist and black feminist scholarship and activism have provided numerous rubrics for understanding how gender shapes one's experiences of blackness, emphasizing the importance of self-determination and self-definition (see, e.g., Lorde 1984; A. Walker 1983; Combahee River Collective 1978). Attention to gender's analytic utility within black communities has produced, for example, meaningful critiques of male chauvinism within black liberation movements or careful documentation of how sexism privileges nontransgender men within some iterations of a black studies canon (see, e.g., E. Edwards 2012; Carby 1998; Bambara 1981). Black masculinity studies has also brought focused attention to the gendering of African American and African-descended males and to the interrelatedness of black masculine gendering and black politics across the long twentieth century and has made use of textual, psychoanalytic, and spatial analyses to draw links between masculinity and blackness, as a lived category and as a potent vehicle for racial representation (see, e.g., M. Ross 2004; P. Harper 1996; Richardson 2007; Marriott 2000). Within the field, concepts such as "hypermasculinity," which describes a racist projection onto black males in which black men are reduced to their genitalia, which is itself magnified—and retroactive responses to that projection—have come to explain how black masculinities are experienced and represented as hyperbolically masculine and therefore in excess to dominant codes of masculinity (see, e.g., Poulson-Bryant 2005; Fanon [1967] 2008). Furthermore, scholarship on the related concepts "the culture of dissemblance," "the politics of respectability," and "the salvific wish" highlight how black women practiced and espoused distinctly gendered modes of self-protection and policing in reaction to or to guard against antiblack racism and violence (see, e.g., Hine 1989; E. Higginbotham 1993; E. White 2001; Jenkins 2007).

Lived experiences of gender have also received considerable focus in scholarship within black queer and transgender studies, in which many scholars have attended to the performative dimensions of gender in order to highlight its contingent and situational production. For example, Marlon Bailey's study of contemporary ballroom culture, defined as "a community and network of Black and Latina/o women, men, and transgender women and men who are lesbian, gay, bisexual, straight, and queer," describes a five-part "gender system" that structures how members are adjudicated in ballroom competitions across North America (2011, 367). The black trans studies scholars Enoch Page and Matt Richardson, moreover, have brought attention to transubjectivity as a concept to examine how gender remains a possible terrain to examine how black people have negotiated oppression (2010, 62–63). The possible connections between black studies and transgender studies are manifold in light of this discussion so far. Namely, as scholarship on black genders has frequently expressed how black genders are figured outside the traditional symbolics of "male" and "female," black studies functions as a generative site for exploring how gender nonconformity and transness are imagined and experienced.

In the preface to *Feminist Studies'* "Race and Transgender Studies: A Special Issue," Matt Richardson and Leisa Meyer make explicit a critique of the limitations "of a predominantly white referent for transgender subjectivity as currently represented in critical theory" (2011, 247). Taking queer of color critique as a referent, "trans of color critique," as a field of inquiry, has emerged as a scholarly articulation of the necessity of reading imbrications of racial formations and trans/gendered practices simultaneously. Like its scholarly forebear, trans of color critique is less a response to the perceived whiteness of transgender studies than a field constituted by an insistence on thinking racial and transgender concerns alongside and in light of other modes of difference (see, e.g., Page and Richardson 2010; Snorton and Haritaworn 2013; Wallace and Green 2013; Green and Ellison 2014; Cotten 2011; Snorton 2017). Writings by trans activists and intellectuals, such as CeCe McDonald (2015), for example, draw attention to the ways prisons and carceral logics express the personal vulnerabilities and political stakes of practices of black and trans self-determination.

In the broadest sense, gender, in all of its manifestations, is another metric of black self-invention. Relatedly, gender as an analytic becomes a critical mode to examine how blackness is lived and experienced. Whether gender is explored in relation to the frequently violent ways it has been given and enforced or in light of the ways it has been (strategically) deployed and redefined, scholarship on gender highlights a terrain of black life. Thus, gender might be understood as a testament to the unruly, monstrous, and marvelous ways blackness persists in the midst of ongoing forms of violence and violation. Put simply, scholarship on black genders reveals how gender (and sexuality) is as multiplicative as power is diffuse.

# 20

## Hip-Hop

Damon Chandru Sajnani

The word "hip-hop" has various uses and overlapping meanings. People who most identify with hip-hop recognize it as a *culture*, and this meaning was developed and is advocated in explicit contrast with the more mainstream understanding of the term as a musical *genre*. When understood as a genre, it is most often thought to be synonymous with "rap music." The term is also used to reference a dance style, and—in my experience—this is the word's primary association for those who are least familiar with it. Related to its historical association with Blackness and social critique, hip-hop is also sometimes characterized as a cultural or social *movement*. As KRS-ONE rhymes, hip-hop is "more than music, hip is the knowledge, hop is the movement" (2007).

The term began as a wordless vocable in scat singing that interspersed the rhymes of early rappers in the late 1970s. Keith Cowboy is credited with originating the term, Luvbug Starski popularized it in his live performances, and it was most famously appropriated on rap's first hit, "Rapper's Delight" (Sugarhill Gang 1979). Afrika Bambaataa, hip-hop's first theorist, applied the term to the culture by 1982 and announced its foundational values as "peace, unity, love, and having fun" (Bambaataa 1984). While these values sound deceptively generic, they represent a strategic rejection of the conditions of violence, disunity, hatred, and misery brought about by the oppression of working- and sub-working-class Black and Brown people in the postindustrial Bronx (Sajnani 2015).

The capitalization and spacing of the word varies by source. Usually "hip" and "hop" are separated by a space or hyphenated. The Temple of Hip Hop originally advocated spelling it as one word to signify maturity into a proper noun and, later, in *The Gospel of HipHop*, assigned specific meanings to various common spellings. Accordingly, "hip-hop" is "our creative force in the World. It is our lifestyle and collective consciousness," while "Hip Hop" refers to "our culture and artistic elements," and "hip-hop" is "Rap music product and its mainstream activities" (KRS-ONE 2009, 63, 80).

The most common and complex entanglement of meaning is between the uses of hip-hop as culture and genre. In both everyday conversation and scholarship, even when hip-hop is affirmed as a culture, it is not uncommon for discursive slippage to occur between this and the more mainstream usage. Further, the meaning of hip-hop *as a culture* is interpreted in various ways. The most surface version follows from the most historically recent usage of the word "culture": as related to the expressive arts. From this vantage, hip-hop is more than a music genre because it comprises the "four elements" of DJing, breaking (break dancing), emceeing (MCing, rapping), and bombing (graffiti writing). The more robust version draws on the meaning of "culture" as a particular way of life (which is rooted in eighteenth-century critiques of European domination and presumptions of superiority; Raymond Williams 1983, 89) and an emphasis on what many hip-hoppers refer to as "the fifth element": knowledge. Most often, the distinction between culture and genre is discussed as if both are singular, with the music having multiple *sub*genres. However, some writers have proposed a dichotomy of the culture as well (e.g., Sajnani 2014), and others conceive the culture as comprising several generations and the music as comprising many distinct genres (e.g., Iton 2008).

Hip-hop originated in the postindustrial 1970s Bronx largely populated by poor and working-class Black and Latinx people. Through the development and convergence of street arts, young people reappropriated and re-created their social and physical environments. The musical expression of this culture proved most commodifiable, and within a decade from the release of the first rap hit in 1979, the music went from being perceived as a novelty to establishing a firm foothold in the mainstream—even as it was defined in opposition to it. This early period was hip-hop's "golden age," characterized by a diversity of styles, content, and themes, including the prominence of Afrocentricity and social consciousness. While rap entered the mainstream in the 1980s, it *became* mainstream in the 1990s, and the early part of this decade saw the shift to the gangsta era.

Not only did gangsta rap offer less social criticism in this period, but it became the dominant form of major label rap music, sharply narrowing hip-hop's representations. Although this shift is widely acknowledged in the literature, there is yet to be a sustained evidenced-based account of how and why it happened. In the first decades of the new millennium, aspects of hip-hop aesthetics have not just penetrated but arguably come to dominate U.S. popular culture. Further, this postgangsta period has seen a rediversification of images and themes, including a handful of prominent artists reprising the role of rapper as social critic and, perhaps, some broadening of the space for representations of gender and sexuality.

Scholarship has widely discussed the "core four" elements, but the particular character of hip-hop "knowledge" has received less attention. The term sometimes references general knowledgeability or specific knowledge about hip-hop culture and its arts. However, it can also connote a greater sociopolitical specificity. Analysis

of hip-hop's ubiquitous allusions to "street knowledge," "game," and, most definitively, "knowledge of self" reveal at least two broad features of hip-hop knowledge. First, it exists in contrast to mainstream ideas, which are understood to have been shaped by dominant interests. Second, it is invested and pragmatic in offering mental and material liberation to the oppressed. These broad common denominators reveal the fifth element as a counterhegemonic body of knowledge.

Hip-hop's discursive use of "knowledge" is grounded in countercultural Black theory and systems of thought, most directly from the Nation of Gods and Earths, the Nation of Islam, and the Black Panther Party. "Knowledge of self," in these traditions, includes revelation of hidden truths about Black history (and, more broadly, the history of people of color) that, once revealed, empower the oppressed to see their oppressors as they truly are and combat their oppression effectively. "Knowledge of self" is also connected with self-definition and self-determination, which are the core concepts of Black nationalism and indicate hip-hop's continuity with Black Power ideology (Rose 1994; Perry 2004; Ogbar 2007).

Various scholars studying hip-hop around the world argue for a dissociation of hip-hop from Blackness or African American culture (A. Bennett 2000; T. Mitchell 2003; Sarkar 2008). These arguments are motivated by a drive to affirm the legitimacy of their respective hip-hop scenes against versions of authenticity grounded in problematically essentialist notions of racial Blackness. Yet, while denying the Blackness of hip-hop, they universally assert the culture's significance as a voice of youth expression and social critique, particularly for locally marginalized peoples. What these arguments fail to consider is that hip-hop's Blackness may reside not in a requirement that all adherents be Black but in the way the culture's constitutive counterhegemony derives from its association with the Black Freedom Struggle in the United States.

Another challenge emanating from scholars outside the U.S. is a critique of hip-hop's "Bronx origin myth" (Androutsopoulos 2009; Pennycook and Mitchell 2009; Omoniyi 2009). For Tope Omoniyi, "the mainstream narrative that assigns the birth of Hip Hop to the Bronx" undermines Nigerian hip-hop artists' quest for a "legitimate nonsubordinate" hip-hop identity (2008, 114). Thus, Omoniyi prefers the alternative origin myth that represents hip-hop as a precolonial oral tradition "transplanted to North America through the Middle Passage" (116–17). This narrative enables continental Africans to "reclaim" hip-hop from its previous appropriation by African Americans (118). Unfortunately, this pits "continental Africans against African Americans in a zero-sum contest for Hip Hop legitimacy" (Sajnani 2013). By contrast, many continental Africans conceptualize themselves and African Americans as sharing a global Black identity grounded more in contemporary struggles against racism and neocolonialism than reified notions of precolonial culture. Through this diasporic sensibility, they pay homage to hip-hop's Bronx pioneers without subordinating Africans on either side of the Atlantic to American nationalism (for instance, see Kangam Squad 2013).

Another difficulty concerns the best way for scholars to engage hip-hop language and concepts that seek to delimit and define the scope and character of hip-hop. Hip-hop is replete with dichotomous typologies—with overlapping and often contradictory criteria—that seek to categorize and bound it. For example, conscious versus commercial, underground versus mainstream, hip-hop versus rap, and, perhaps most fundamentally, real versus fake. On the one hand, scholars must be critical of cultural circumscription (S. Hall 1992). On the other hand, when scholars too easily gloss or dismiss these distinctions without recognizing them as theoretical tools developed by hip-hop adherents and practitioners, they disregard the obligations of *hiphopography*, which James Spady, H. Samy Alim, and Samir Meghelli define as the need for scholars "to engage the cultural agents of the Hip Hop Culture-World directly, revealing rappers as critical interpreters of their own culture" (quoted in Alim 2009, 18–19).

Another widespread use of the word "hip-hop" is to describe "a generation." In the late 1990s, Bakari Kitwana—lead editor of the *Source* magazine—and his colleagues began referring to "the Hip-Hop Generation" as an alternative to discussing hip-hop as a genre or as "the hip-hop nation." Kitwana specified the hip-hop generation as African Americans born between 1965 and 1984 (2002, xiii). Jeff Chang criticized this definition as too narrow, suggesting instead that the hip-hop generation includes "anyone who is down" and ends when "the next generation tells us it's over." He noted that generations are powerful fictions that "allow claims to be staked around ideas" (2005, 1–2), and this might explain why the term spread so widely through U.S. literature and beyond. Many important questions can be raised about the way these uses enable certain narratives while foreclosing on others. For instance, while Chang's articulation allows for greater inclusivity, it also reduces the ability of the hip-hop generation to articulate the concerns of the people Kitwana intended it for. Further, even the expanded version of "generation" forecloses on the possibility of hip-hop as a culture in the multigenerational sense of "a way of life" passed down from one generation to another.

The generational trope might also elide hip-hop's more radical politics. For instance, it underlies another broad claim in the scholarship that frames hip-hoppers' critiques of contemporary leadership by Black civil rights–era establishment figures as "generational"

(Kitwana 2002). What this frame overlooks is how these conflicts might, at least in some cases, involve a critique of civil rights ideology and establishment politics from the vantage of a more radical Black Power sensibility that scholars have recognized as foundational to hip-hop (Rose 1994; Ogbar 2007). Thus, for example, what Chang interprets as Public Enemy's generational critique might better be understood as a critique of the failures of civil rights ideology and a call for a more radical politics (Chang 2005, 252, 269, 278). Further, Chang's deracialized and dehistoricized use of the generation analytic has the consequence of grounding oppositional politics in the "time-immemorial" trope of youth rebellion against parents (Chang 2005, 125). When the theorization is diluted to this degree, it is fair to ask if it is too shallow to ground Chang's implicit claims that hip-hop fundamentally offers a challenge to contemporary structures of race and class domination.

Hip-hop is also very commonly described— sometimes defined—as a "youth culture." Interesting questions are generated by comparing this usage with the generation idea. While Kitwana proposed "the hip-hop generation" as synonymous with "Black youth culture" in 2002 (xiii), the generation paradigm forces this question: does hip-hop still belong to members of the hip-hop generation Kitwana specified (who are no longer youths), or do they forfeit it to today's youngsters? The historical association of hip-hop with youth leads many people to argue that hip-hop is, and should remain, a lively domain for youth expression and innovation. Others, such as Chuck D, argue that the continued depiction of hip-hop as exclusively a youth culture reflects the United States' enduring treatment of Black culture—and Black people—as disposable. Thus, while white rock becomes classic as it ages and superstars pack stadiums as octogenarians, 50 Cent ridicules Jay-Z on social media for trying to "be the best rapper at 47" when the game belongs to youngsters (*Daily News* 2017).

Similarly, the predominance of the generational analytic may result in insufficiently nuanced readings when conflicts over the meaning of hip-hop arise between younger and older people—or even when someone criticizes someone else of the same age by invoking hip-hop criteria established over the culture's near-five-decade history. Thus, when Ice-T critiqued Soulja Boy for killing hip-hop with weak lyrical content and skill, Kanye West defended the young artist by emphasizing his stylistic innovation and resonance with youth. Debates such as these are often framed as the application of "old" criteria of hip-hop that should instead "let hip-hop evolve." Like other hip-hop debates outlined here, this discussion is happening around the world: in Senegal in 2013, I interviewed several rappers concerned that newer artists were less committed to hip-hop's mission of social critique. However, the veteran rapper Books remarked that even if this is true, "evolution is inevitable."

Critiques that bemoan "hip-hop today" are sometimes just nostalgic complaints about "kids these days." Other times, they are rooted in fundamental concerns about co-optation and representation that are perennial to Black culture and history. Chuck D makes this point by rapping, "I ain't mad at evolution, but I stand for revolution" (Public Enemy 2012). Further, these debates play out differently depending on interlocutors' sense of the word "hip-hop," for instance, whether it is principally perceived as a genre or a culture (and which sense of "culture") and whether its Black working-class connections are considered relevant. When people engage these debates, the issues are layered and intersecting as, for example, in David Banner's remark that "whites are getting more lyrical and we're mumbling" (BET.com 2015). To different people, different aspects of these competing claims appear subjective, while others seem obviously factual. However, all definitions are interest laden, and the question of "who gets to name" is always a question of power. The truths that seem most self-evident may appear that way precisely because they contain the deepest levels of ideology.

Of course, hip-hop innovation and continuity are not inherently contradictory: consider J-Cole's ode to Nas, Janelle Monáe's time-traveling rebel alliance with Erykah Badu, and Kendrick Lamar's subtle invocations of Public Enemy during his 2016 Grammy performance. These examples illustrate how some of the most acclaimed cutting-edge contemporary artists are both innovating on and paying homage to the elders.

# 21

# Incarceration

Damien M. Sojoyner

The term "incarceration" often conjures up a familiar motif. Popular television and digital media programming such as *Oz*, *Prison Break*, and *Orange Is the New Black* rely on a commonsense understanding of prison as being a place that holds the vile and immoral. According to narratives drawn from these shows, prison is not a place that is violent because people are locked in cages for more hours than they are not, denied basic human rights, and forcibly removed from their communities; rather, the programs reinforce the notion that people housed within prison are some of the most violent creatures on the planet and thus create an environment of extreme violence. While the entertainment version of incarceration is filled with drama and a clear sense of hero and villain, the reality of incarceration is quite the opposite: mundane and layered in nuance that very often blurs the distinctions between right and wrong.

Similar to entertainment, the discussion of incarceration has become very popular within academia. While there has been a long history of rigorous academic engagement with prisons in contemporary capitalism (most notably the 1998 "Critical Resistance" conference in Berkeley, California), unfortunately, too much of the current discussion pertaining to incarceration within academia falls prey to the same pitfalls of entertainment: an oversimplistic argument that draws a crowd but is very weak with regard to substantive argumentation. The simplicity of the analysis can be traced back to a failure to grapple with incarceration as a Black studies project. The lack of theorization and engagement with Blackness leads to very simplistic narratives and catchphrases that are problematic.

As an example, one of these phrases is the term "mass incarceration." As argued by Dylan Rodríguez (2015), there is no such thing as mass incarceration; rather, there has been and continues to be a targeting of Black people in the United States. The statistics bear out that Black people carry the tremendous effect of incarceration on their communities. If you remove Black people from the proverbial equation of incarceration statistics, we are no longer discussing "mass incarceration." The term is thus dangerous in that it leads to an analytic method and, correspondingly, a solution set that ignore the centrality of Blackness within the discussion of incarceration. The current system of incarceration was designed with a particular focus on Black populations across the United States. The manner in which these structures developed was drastically different from state to state; however, the intent was quite clear. Remove such logic from any type of analysis, as in the case of "mass incarceration," and the results produce the worst type of multicultural reform-based policies that solve absolutely nothing.

Importantly, as we think through incarceration, we have to think through how it is articulated through the political, economic, social, and cultural facts of Blackness. That is, incarceration is something much more than just the physical walls of the prison; rather, incarceration is integral to a U.S. state process that has rendered Black people what Ruth Wilson Gilmore (2007) labels as *unfree.* A central part of U.S. imperialist ideology since the late nineteenth century, incarceration has become the primary expression of racial, political, and social difference that has designated Black people as permanently unfree subjects.

A politics that coalesced within the bowels of capitalist formation, the difference-making enterprise is predicated on the invention and reinvention of racial categories. As argued by Cedric Robinson, "The tendency of European civilization through capitalism was thus not to homogenize but to differentiate—to exaggerate regional, subcultural, and dialectical differences into 'racial' ones" ([1983] 2000, 26). Through continuous internal and external power struggles, a key tension within Western civilization has been the attempted incorporation of people, culture, and land into hierarchical narratives of difference. Such a process has required the violent erasure of history and place to make difference appear natural. Not at all a simple task, it has become central to the Western empire tradition to develop and implement ideological and physical models that forge difference into a precarious state of being. It is here, within the genealogical tradition of Western imperialist social visions, that we locate incarceration as a central cog within the difference-making machine. Recognizing that the roots of incarceration span back several centuries, the focus of this discussion is on the utilization of the incarceration model as central to the modern development of Western expansion.

While incarceration has taken shape and form across the world and throughout the African diaspora, as a model, it is of grave importance that we understand its implementation within the United States. Given that the rates of incarceration within the United States stand in contradistinction to other countries, it is equally vital that we parse through the nuanced and often uneven development of incarceration in the United States. Such analysis gives life to the methods and intentions of incarceration as a difference-making project, while also breaking with oversimplistic interpretations of incarceration as being in a linear conversation with other models such as slavery, sharecropping, or rapid abandonment. Much of the scholarship within Black studies has been attuned to the mechanizations and particularities of each of these moments and the ties that bind them across time and place. However, there is also careful attention paid to the manner in which each model is vastly different from its antecedent or proceeding form. For example, while commonsense rhetorical invocations link slavery with modern form of prisons, it has been critical work within Black studies on incarceration that has pushed back against such a problematic assertion. While connections surely exist among models of racial exploitation, the seductive desire to provide intimate relationships across epochs is counter to the historical record, is misleading in terms of analysis, and as a result is an abysmal failure as a generative source of solutions.

While the birth of prison dates back to the late eighteenth century, the seeds of incarceration as commonly discussed in current parlance were planted during the post-Reconstruction period of the United States. Rocked by the uprising of the formerly enslaved to free themselves from the clutches of racial bondage, northern industrialists, coupled with their plantation-bloc brethren, entered into a desperate alliance to maintain the existence of the United States (W. Du Bois [1935] 1998). Black people were living in autonomous enclaves throughout the southern U.S., and the infamous Hayes Compromise and subsequent fall of Reconstruction drove them back under the thumb of the recently defeated plantation bloc. Dispossessed from their land, Black people were reconstituted into a new labor regime that demanded the rebuilding of the South to fit into the industrial model set forth by northern financial interests. The central mechanism within that rebuilding process was the incarceration of Black men and women throughout the U.S. South. However, rather than being shackled within the confines of jails or prisons, Black

southerners were funneled into a convict lease labor system that saw the formerly enslaved forced into the clutches of work camps that functioned to remake the southern economy (Haley 2016; LeFlouria 2015). From dredging swamps to mining coal to building roads, the infrastructure of the U.S. South was made by the hands of Black men and women.

Central to the southern financial and material economy, incarceration proved vital to the U.S. imperialist project. In the aftermath of Reconstruction, the fragility of race as a socially constructed relationship of power was quite evident (C. Robinson 2007). In order for the industrial model to thrive and expansion to move forward, the ideological imperative of race as "real" had to remain a salient part of the white imagination. Given the wide scope of white poverty throughout the U.S. South and the socialist tendencies of particular sects of European immigrants in the North, it was critical that race function as a unifying bond to counter white angst toward the inequities inherent within capitalist modes of operation. To this end, Blackness functioned as the backdrop to galvanize whiteness, and incarceration became the model by which the fictive was made real. In the South, while labor was of the utmost concern, incarceration functioned in the capacity to reimagine race through forms of gendered difference. Sarah Haley, in a masterful account of convict leasing in the U.S. South, argues that "southern punishment was a technology of gender construction, reconstituting and reinforcing ideologies of absolute racial difference through black female abjection. . . . Gender regulation was necessary for the development of racial regimes of carceral capitalist development" (2016, 251). In particular, Haley's insights bring to the fore that Black women's labor and bodies within the convict lease system were used to reimagine white womanhood within a patriarchal gaze. Serving a dual purpose, the incarceration of Black women ensconced white women back into the U.S. imperialist project while also providing a seductive path for poor white men to forgo their potential class interests with Black people under the guise of protectors of vulnerable white women. Building within a rich canon, Haley's insights are in concert with critical Black studies approaches to discipline, such as work by Beth Richie (1996, 2012), Angela Y. Davis (2003), Ruth Wilson Gilmore (2007), Maisha T. Winn (2011), Dorothy E. Roberts (2012), Simone Browne (2015), and Christina Sharpe (2016), who argue for a much more nuanced understanding of the relationship among Blackness, gender, sexuality, class, and forms of discipline.

While the South was in the midst of massive economic, ,political and social change, urban centers in the North were attempting to repair the many racial seams that had been torn asunder following the Civil War and Reconstruction. With massive migration into northern seaports from Europe and the U.S. South, the constructions of race that had been established during formal slavery were on shaky ground. In whites' attempt to regain power, two models were utilized to reestablish racial order: film and criminalization. As meticulously argued by Cedric Robinson (2007), at the turn of the twentieth century, film became the dominant medium with which to reestablish fictive myths of race and racial difference in the popular psyche. The rapid growth of film (as a medium) and the film industry (as an economic and political force) was accompanied by the intense criminalization and subsequent incarceration of northern Blacks.

A coordinated process of the highest order, the criminalization of Black people in northern locales was ushered in by several state actors (politicians, police, philanthropic agencies), but perhaps none had as lasting an effect as did members of the esteemed U.S. academy who used their positions to craft legislation, effect public policy, and frame the conversation to connect Black people and criminality. Khalil Muhammad insightfully points out that a primary means to make the Black criminal argument "real" was to create a Black subject that stood in sharp contrast to the European immigrant. Writing about intimate connection between black criminality and the establishment of the social sciences in the U.S., Muhammad states, "Charles R. Henderson, a pioneering University of Chicago social scientist, declared that 'that evil [of immigrant crime] is not so great as statistics carelessly interpreted might prove.' . . . But where the 'Negro factor' is concerned, Henderson continued, 'racial inheritance, physical and mental inferiority, barbarian and slave ancestry and culture,' were among the 'most serious factors in crime statistics'" (2011, 7). Even after the famed anthropologist Franz Boas ushered in the turn within the social sciences that shifted the focus away from biological imperatives of racial difference, academics engraved criminality onto the cultural norms of Black people while whitewashing immigrant culture into a homogeneous fixed category.

Incarceration during the late nineteenth and early twentieth centuries in the United States was designed to construct difference with the intent to reify specific political, racial, economic, and gendered norms during a time of immense upheaval following Reconstruction. Yet, while incarceration has persisted to be a dominant difference-making model of U.S. racial politics, the social contexts of given time periods are of extreme importance. The forms of incarceration that followed during the later half of the twentieth century and into the twenty-first century were, and continue to be, much different than those of the earlier epoch. While much of the earlier forms of incarceration were about explicit forms of forced labor, incarceration that has dominated the current landscape is largely absent of such forces.

Due to the tireless agitation, fight, and provocation on the part of Black civil and human rights groups, the convict leasing system has been eradicated, and the transformation of the lease system into a state-run bureaucracy, such as the case with the Parchman Farm in Mississippi, has been abandoned. Yet, in the wake of those victories, the United States as a nation-building enterprise did not cease to develop new forms of exploitation. The general neoliberal turn that was marked by massive state and private capital disinvestment during the late 1960s through the 1980s had a profound impact on Black rural and urban communities alike (Kelley 1998; Woods 2000). Many of the living-wage, working-class jobs that were vital to the stabilization of Black communities were uprooted either to newly formed suburbs or to sites of low wage labor in countries that had either formed nefarious ties with the United States or been run amok by the U.S. military governance project (Lernoux 1980; W. Robinson 1992; Vasquez 1993; Peña 1997; M. Davis 1990). Additionally, government programs that had become the backbone of many communities were stripped of funding and left in shambles.

The common refrain in light of these events is that with the passage of nonviolent drug laws, prisons were built in order to put unemployed Black people back to work in the prisons. Harking back to a forgone era, the rhetoric invokes the notion that private prisons have become the new form of forced labor akin to the lease system, and Black people have once again been forced back to slave-like conditions of extracted labor. Yet the reality of the latest iteration of incarceration could not be further from the commonsense understanding of the intent and purpose of prisons. While private prisons do exist in the U.S., they do not assist in understanding the function and intent of incarceration. Ruth Wilson Gilmore in her brilliant tome on the development of prisons in California writes, "Although the absolute

number of private prisons has indeed grown, the fact is that 95 percent of all prisons and jails are publicly owned and operated. So, the argument that more people are in prison due to the lobbying efforts of private prison firms doesn't stand up to scrutiny. The firms are not insignificant, especially in some jurisdictions, but they're not the driving force, either. Despite boosterish claims by stock analysts, private prison firms consistently hover on the brink of disaster, while public sector unions fight against losing jobs with good pay and benefits" (2007, 21–22). Further, within these public race facilities, prison labor is not being extracted to provide a free source for private or state-run capital interests. Gilmore further explains that the free-labor explanation contradicts the fact that small businesses have lobbied both state and federal governments to protect against the extraction of prison labor as a means by which large corporations can monopolize particular markets. As a result, at a very basic level, the notion of free labor extraction from prisoners goes against the fundamental edicts of contemporary capitalism and thus is a very problematic analytical stance to understand the intent of incarceration.

This leads to a very important discussion about how incarceration functions as a difference-making model in the current context. That is, when the terms "prison" and "incarceration" are invoked, the immediate tendency is to reflect on people physically locked up behind cages. While the encaging of people is a very important part of incarceration, what is often glossed over is the vast number of people who are still a part of the system but are living unfree within the clutches of the probation and parole systems. While these people are no longer constrained by the physical barrier of iron bars, there are severe limitations with regard to a lack of freedom of movement (i.e., out of the city, county, and state), an inability to attain housing and employment, and being at the complete mercy of the police (i.e., not having any rights with regard to search and seizure within a domicile or having to respond during any moment of the day or night or face retribution in the form of a return back to prison).

It is important to note that Black studies approaches to incarceration focus less on the particularities of the physical site of prison and provide much more substantive analysis on the intent, rationale, and multiplicity of ways by which attempts are made to subsume Black communities within a racial capitalist state that is governed by the logics of incarceration. At the crux of the matter, Black studies approaches to incarceration are not looking to produce a more culturally responsive police force or a more humane prison or to develop strategies that reform "criminal" Black men to become rightful heirs to their households. Rather, the primary tropes that emanate from Black studies scholarship on incarceration are immersed within a politics of abolishing both the police and all of the mechanizations that are a part of the carceral state, casting aside gendered norms associated with criminality and violence and focusing on the creation of a world that is free from modalities of difference.

As pointed out by several scholars including Beth Richie, Ruth Wilson Gilmore, and Dylan Rodríguez, the United States is governed by the internal logics of incarceration (Rodríguez 2006; R. Gilmore 2007; Richie 2012). As teachers, activists, students, artists, parents, and children, it is our duty to reveal the underbelly of such a heinous model of social organizing and be steadfast in our demands for alternative social visions that disavow difference-making projects and embrace principles of community and love.

# 22

## Intersectionality
Lisa B. Thompson

The term "intersectionality" has come to stand for a body of feminist racial analyses, a set of organizing strategies, and a political-ethical standpoint for activists, articles, and intellectuals. The critical race theorist and black feminist legal scholar Kimberlé Crenshaw first wrote on intersectionality in her essay on workplace discrimination, "Demarginalizing the Intersection of Race and Sex: A Black Feminist Critique of Antidiscrimination Doctrine, Feminist Theory and Antiracist Politics" (1989). First presented as a talk at and then subsequently published by the *University of Chicago Legal Forum*, Crenshaw coined and introduced the term "intersectionality" as both an experience and an analytic. For Crenshaw, intersectionality is a revision of theories of discrimination and subordination in law, race, labor, and gender studies and a naming of black women's embodied knowledge, historical positioning, and exploited labor. While originating from and foundational to the fields of critical race theory and the revision of legal theory by scholars such as Derrick Bell, Mari Matsuda, Charles Lawrence, Patricia Williams, and Richard Delgado, Crenshaw's theory of intersectionality shares much with both literary/feminist theory and radical politics in action. Intersectionality aligns with Hortense Spillers's use of "imbrication" (2003), Cherríe Moraga's foundational woman of color critique of "the ranking of oppression" and call for racialized feminist analyses of the "specificity of oppression" (Moraga and Anzaldúa 2015, 24; see also Moraga [1983] 2000), Patricia

Hill Collins's black feminist theory (1990), Hazel Carby's "societies structured in dominance" by "race, gender and class" (1999, 97), and Michele Wallace's sense of black female incommensurability and radical negation (1990). And it has as its genealogical foundation the pathbreaking black feminist writings of Paula Giddings (1984), Barbara Smith (1983), Akasha Gloria T. Hull, Patricia Bell-Scott, and Barbara Smith (1982), Mary Helen Washington (1975, 1980), Toni Cade Bambara (1970), Barbara Christian (1985), and Frances M. Beal ([1970] 2010). Interventions by feminists of color have been taken up in academia, in organizing collectives such as Black Lives Matter and the undocuqueer movement, and, in general, as a political and ethical perspective.

Intersectionality has become a keyword for classrooms, meetings, and households, used to battle against racist, sexist, classist, and homophobic ideologies and policies. It is essential to situate intersectionality within black feminist knowledge production prior to and since the term's emergence. The roots of this notion can be traced to the abolitionist Sojourner Truth when she queried "ar'nt I a woman" while delivering a speech at the Women's Rights Convention in Akron, Ohio, on May 29, 1851. Truth skewers both the racist leanings of the suffrage movement and the deeply embedded sexist culture that gave rise to it. In remarks attributed to her, Truth illustrates the intersection of race, gender, and class by insisting that the punishing labor and brutal violence she endured as a formerly enslaved black woman did not disqualify her from womanhood (D. White [1985] 1999).

As black feminists such as Angela Davis (1981), June Jordan (1985), and Alice Walker (1983) articulated earlier, Crenshaw's 1989 essay invokes the complex legacy of black female insurgency from abolition onward by citing not only Truth but Anna Julia Cooper and Pauli Murray. This propels intersectionality beyond legal theory, antidiscrimination discourse, and case study into the fields of feminist theory, antiracist strategies, and public policy. The term "intersectionality" gained traction due to the advent of the blogosphere and web-based activism but, at bedrock, because of its usefulness for succinctly naming structural and systemic inequality. The theory of intersectionality provides a lens through which to understand how identities operate in the U.S.

Crenshaw returns to and broadens the concept of intersectionality in a later essay on domestic violence, "Mapping the Margins: Intersectionality, Identity Politics, and Violence against Women of Color" (1991), published in the Stanford Law Review. While the earlier essay worked primarily through and against the racial binaries black/white and the gender binaries man/woman, the later work expands to address women of color, echoing a decade or more of the feminist of color print and political movements. Still rooted in black feminist theory, the theory of intersectionality argues for a more complex understanding of identity and "the identity politics of African Americans, other people of color, gays and lesbians" (Crenshaw 1991, 1242). The concept of difference, integral to the theorizations of subjectivity, political movements, and emancipatory visions of feminist thinkers such as Audre Lorde and Chela Sandoval, is highlighted throughout. Crenshaw cautions that "intersectionality is not being offered here as some new, totalizing theory of identity" and proceeds to distinguish and define structural intersectionality as "the location of women of color at the intersection of race and gender" (1244-45). "Political intersectionality" is discursive for Crenshaw and is the result of how both feminist and antiracist politics have, paradoxically, often helped to marginalize the issue of violence against women of color. And, in keeping with her original impulse, she uses intersectionality as both a descriptor of experience and a theoretical vantage point, or what she names here as an "approach within the broader scope of contemporary identity politics" (1245).

Intersectionality has moved from a vanguard theory in the emergent field of critical race studies to ingrained parlance across the humanities and social sciences. Shortly after the publication of Crenshaw's landmark essay, a cluster of groundbreaking texts in the 1990s made explicit use of the term and theory of intersectionality, including Toni Morrison's anthologies *Race-ing Justice, En-gendering Power: Essays on Anita Hill, Clarence Thomas, and the Construction of Social Reality* (1992) and *Birth of a Nation'hood: Gaze, Script, and Spectacle in the O. J. Simpson Case* (coedited with Claudia Brodsky Lacour, 1997) (both include a Crenshaw essay), as well as Valerie Smith's *Not Just Race, Not Just Gender: Black Feminist Readings* (1998). Scholars working in a disparate range of disciplines and fields from literature to politics have used the term and theory to articulate the ways multiple components of identity operate within power structures.

Crenshaw's use of the traffic metaphor to analyze power and domination and her sophisticated theorization of race-gender in the context of jurisprudence have proven applicable and usefully expansive for groups and genealogies not originally included within the frame of the theory of intersectionality. The concept of intersectionality is currently at the matrix of trans theorizing and organizing and much feminist and antiracist writing of the contemporary blogosphere, on sites such as *Crunk Feminist Collective, Feministing, Very Smart Brothas, The Angry Black Woman,* and *New South Negress,* which combine theories emerging from university classrooms and publications, vernaculars of urban and rural black life, and popular millennial media platforms and attitudes. The expansion of intersectional theory is possible largely due to Crenshaw's astute mobilization of, as Bim Adewunmi asserts, an "everyday metaphor" that "anyone could use" to demonstrate "how different power structures interact in the lives of minorities, specifically black women" (2014). While many scholars and activists find "intersectionality" generative at our current cultural and historical moment, the term does have critics, including scholars such as Nikol Alexander-Floyd (2012), Jennifer Nash (2008), and Jasbir Puar (2013). Furthermore, some organizers are skeptical of its applicability to contexts beyond U.S. identity politics of the late twentieth and early twenty-first centuries, while others are concerned by the emphasis on representation over materialist analyses. Despite the critiques, "intersectionality" continues to hold much sway and remains a useful term.

# 23

## Jazz
### Eric Porter

"Jazz" and early variants "jaz" and "jas" have uncertain and contested roots. The term may or may not have origins in Chicago, New Orleans, Africa, baseball, or sex, although all would make sense given subsequent associations. We do know that the word "jazz" was, during the 1910s, increasingly used to describe a musical orientation (if not quite a genre) being developed by composers, solo pianists, and ensembles of various size. This music was hybrid, incorporating elements of African American blues and religious song, Caribbean dance genres, U.S. popular dance and folk music, marching band music, European classical music, ragtime piano, and the transplanted, modified West African rhythms that shaped some of these and other constituent forms. The music's hybridity plotted its emergence at a particular set of coordinates in Black diasporic time and space. It sounded a contradictory postemancipation experience defined by movement across regions, from country to city and sometimes to metropolis, as it simultaneously reflected increased access to education, the encounters with different kinds of labor, and the thrill of new forms of sociability and intimacy. This early music also expressed—by virtue of where it could be played and how it was interpreted—the limits of all of these things. Jazz may thus be understood alongside other, sometimes mutually influential, diasporic expressions—*son cubano*, for example—that articulated the pulse of Black modernity in the early twentieth century.

Jazz soon began to anchor a complicated and contested discursive formation. It swept up in its wake meanings associated with its distinct rhythmic and tonal characteristics, its roots in Afro-diasporic culture and society, its emergence in the United States, its popularity across the globe, its performance locations (cities, neighborhoods, nightclubs, brothels, living rooms), its modes of transmission (radio, record, live encounters with breath, muscle, and vibration), and other elements. Jazz quickly became viewed as a symbol of, and a vehicle for conversation about, the United States, Africa, African American social and political aspiration, embodied Blackness, sexuality, changing gender roles, modernity, the city, and much more. Commentators often heard opposite things in elements of the music, to which they responded both positively and negatively. For example, early critics both praised and condemned jazz for evincing a modern sensibility in its rhythmic conception, while others loved and despised those same rhythmic elements for being "primitive."

Given these complex meanings, jazz presented a range of opportunities and challenges to Black thinkers and others invested in making Black lives better or simply matter. Some quickly looked to jazz as an instrument for Black artistic and political advancement. In 1919, James Reese Europe, after a successful stint as a military bandleader, said that he had "come back from France more firmly convinced than ever that negroes should write negro music": "We won France by playing music which was ours and not a pale imitation of others, and if we are to develop in America we must develop along our own lines" (Vernon [1919] 2014, 12). The *Chicago Defender* that year said that because of Europe's favorable impression on "white people," "[he] and his band are worth more to our Race than a thousand speeches from so-called Race orators and uplifters" ([1919] 1998, 15). As both comments indicate, jazz's Black-affirming meaning and function were often linked dialectically to its broader visibility and consumption, for better and for worse. Langston Hughes described jazz in 1926 as "one of the inherent expressions of Negro life in America; the eternal tom-tom beating in the Negro soul—the tom-tom of revolt against weariness in a white world, a world of subway, and work, work, work; the tom-tom of joy and laughter, and pain swallowed in a smile" ([1926] 1998, 56), but it did not take long for him to lament that his blues were "taken" and "gone" ([1940] 1959, 190).

In the 1925 essay "Jazz at Home," the Afrocentric historian Joel A. Rogers called jazz "a marvel of paradox: too fundamentally human, at least as modern humanity goes, to be typically racial, too international to be characteristically national, too much abroad in the world to have a special home." Yet even as he acknowledged the music's cosmopolitan reach and function, he maintained a Black proprietary investment: "But somebody had to have it first: that was the Negro" ([1925] 1977, 216). Rogers thus referenced perhaps the fundamental challenge informing Black studies engagements with jazz over time: how does one balance a recognition of the Afro-diasporic origins of jazz, the legacies of Black accomplishment in the art form, and its African American communal function with an acknowledgment of, and a critical perspective on, the music's complex social and political life, occasioned by its use by non–African American musicians, consumers, critics, intellectuals, and capitalists, in the United States and elsewhere.

The collective Harlem Renaissance assessment of jazz was mixed indeed. Some elite intellectuals paid very little attention to it. Others embraced the music as a reflection of Black spirit, experience, emotion, and/or biology while being compelled to address its appropriation, popularization, primitivization, and denigration. Jazz could signify Black distinctiveness, but it was often that distinctiveness that made jazz controversial—except

when its Black roots were being denied. Harlem Renaissance debates about jazz were, as such debates often are today, a pointed commentary about the place of Black people as well as about the liberating and constraining aspects of racial thinking in a society structured by racism. Such challenges were not lost among musicians, some of whom had (as many do today) vexed relationships with the term "jazz" because they felt it did not do justice to the breadth of their artistic projects and because of the ways it signified the economic, discursive, and social limitations under which they labored. Indeed, Duke Ellington often suggested he was trying to transcend the parameters of the genre. "I am not playing jazz," he said in 1930. "I am trying to play the natural feelings of a people" (Tucker 1995, 45).

Early commentary about jazz was constrained by its androcentrism and heteronormativity. It still is. The Black jazz community mirrored gender and sexual inequalities in the broader society, the labor force, and the arts in general. This is not to say that the early jazz community was uniformly male and misogynist or heteronormative or homophobic. Female and queer musicians and their allies shaped the music as instrumentalists, singers, bandleaders, and producers; helped to create queer performance spaces and networks in urban black communities; and offered a critical perspective on gender relations in the lyrics of blues and jazz songs. But such interventions did not fundamentally alter the marginalization of women and queer folk in musicians' circles and the cultivation of the idea that one's artistry was linked to one's manhood. Moreover, as jazz was taken up by critics and intellectuals invested in using the music to gauge Black life, their assessments often reproduced the masculinism of contemporaneous African American uplift and Black nationalist ideologies as well as dominant, stereotypical fantasies about Black male power, sexuality, and style. Not only did intellectual practice help fetishize the music as a heteromasculine accomplishment—which continues to shape understandings of jazz today—but it also has limited collective understandings as what counts as jazz, as putatively "feminized" musical components or movements (flutes and violin, all-women's bands, male bands playing "sweet" jazz, and so on) have been relegated to the margins of the conversation.

The conversation about jazz shifted in significant ways during the New Deal and Popular Front era, with significant ramifications for its status as an object of Black studies. Although the music business and jazz writing were still shaped by significant inequality and racist expression, jazz was often praised as an expression of African Americans, and of the "common man" more generally, that articulated the ideals of a potentially more egalitarian, democratic U.S. society. In other words, jazz was at this moment less an object of controversy than in the previous decade and more likely to be celebrated on its own terms. And when Popular Front culture opened up more possibilities to make and hear music as a form of protest, the prospect of making or hearing an explicit politics in jazz increased with it. Billie Holiday's performances of the union activist Abel Meeropol's antilynching song "Strange Fruit" (1939) played a critical role in this politicization.

Also profoundly shaping the perceived politics of jazz was bebop, an emergent jazz genre that hit the public imagination in the mid-1940s as ascendant civil rights and anticolonial movements were calling into question the global racial order. It would be a mistake to assume too neat a connection among the music, the intent of its practitioners, and the social and political movements that defined the moment. Commentators such as Anatole Broyard and Ralph Ellison called into question bebop's roots in and efficacy as politics. But it was clear to many practitioners that there was some connection between music and social context. As the drummer Kenny Clarke put it in retrospect, "There was a message to our music. . . . Whatever you go into, go into it *intelligently.* . . . The idea was to wake up, look around you, there's something to do" (Gillespie with Fraser 1979, 142). Regardless of musicians' intent, others heard, marketed, and consumed bebop as a dissident and sometimes militant cultural expression. Related to its presumed militancy was its "avant-garde" aesthetic orientation. That jazz could be both a subversive, antiestablishment cultural expression *and* a serious artistic movement profoundly influenced how Black studies subsequently interpreted the music.

Jazz's associations with avant-gardism and politics became more and differently pronounced in the late 1950s and 1960s as musicians engaged in greater levels of experimentation in the music, commented more frequently on social and political issues in lyrics and composition titles, and increasingly took on the role of activists by speaking out about broader social issues and seeking to improve the conditions under which they labored. Again, we cannot assume that radical musical expression correlated neatly with radical politics, although sometimes they did. Figures such as Charles Mingus, Abbey Lincoln, Max Roach, members of the Association for the Advancement of Creative Musicians, and a good deal of others were inspired by the contemporaneous Black Freedom Movement and ascendant cultural nationalist ideologies. Activist musicians were also, after the early 1960s, often forced to address the declining fortunes of the jazz business and the music's shrinking younger audience because of competition from rock, soul, and other forms of popular music. Thus, jazz's unprecedented capital as high modernist art and black political expression came precisely at the moment when many people feared for its survival. The contemporaneous critical conversation about the music was therefore heated. As some Black musicians and writers emphasized the vanguard elements of jazz, offered critiques of its political economy, and insisted that they had a kind of proprietary relationship to it, many liberal white critics pushed back, with their colorblind ideology and privileged position as arbiters of musical and discursive taste under threat and with significant worry that politicizing the music would hurt the jazz business even more.

Jazz thus presented inspiration as well as some challenges to Black studies at the moment of the field's consolidation and incorporation into the university. It was an affirmatively political and artistically legitimate art form that was being written about with increasing frequency by Black intellectuals—Ralph Ellison, Albert Murray, Amiri Baraka, and Jayne Cortez, to name a few—across the ideological and stylistic spectrum. Jazz was thus an object of interest itself as well as a theme, device, inspiration, vehicle for debate, and so on that could be addressed by scholars and critics more interested in Black literary and intellectual culture. But jazz still presented its contradictions to those who sought to write about it. Baraka's celebrated 1966 essay "The Changing Same: R&B and the New Black Music" (L. Jones 1967), for example, struggled to reconcile the importance of the socially and spiritually redeeming aspects of avant-garde jazz with the fact that this style had relatively limited popularity with Black audiences. A similar theme was taken up by Cortez in her 1969 poem "How Long Has Trane Been Gone." The saxophonist John Coltrane might be, like Malcolm X, the "true image of black masculinity," but too few Black people knew his music—a phenomenon that Cortez explained as a function both of the music industry's division of the music into separate genres *and* of a more general lack of historical and cultural awareness among the people themselves ([1969] 1997, 1957–59). Ellison and Murray provided

counterpoint as they suggested that the attention to the music's political resonance and socioeconomic circumstance was preventing us from fully understanding its aesthetic and ritualistic function as a universal art form. Another challenge occurred when jazz was taken up by Black studies in the form of musicians themselves. As Black studies programs came on line during the late 1960s and 1970s, some hired jazz musicians as faculty. The University of Massachusetts was a notable site, with Reggie Workman, Archie Shepp, and Max Roach serving on its faculty. Although such appointments could bring a degree of professional stability and the ability to focus intensely on developing one's compositions, performance practice, and research, some observers lamented the institutionalization of the art form and the distancing of it from its communal roots.

Commenting in the early 1970s about the range of musical styles and approaches described as jazz, Ellington wondered, "I don't know how such great extremes as now exist can be contained under the one heading" ([1973] 1976, 453). One might say something similar about the wide array of meanings inscribed in the keyword "jazz" in the wake of the jazz renaissance of the 1980s and beyond. This music, despite its relatively small market share of downloads, CD sales, and radio play, has continued to resonate widely in the culture as an avatar of hip sophistication, Black historical memory, romance, masculine accomplishment, and much, much more. The New Jazz Studies academic movement that emerged as an inter- and cross-disciplinary scholarly conversation around 1990 has taken on the project of exploring such meanings in both past and present. We now have a much better perspective on critical debates about the music and on the ways jazz and its practitioners have been represented in other art forms. Concomitantly, we know more about the complex ways that jazz has been a vehicle for identity formation and self-actualization for members of disparate cultural communities. Perhaps most important, in light of previous exclusions, is work that illuminates the place of women in jazz and the function of jazz as a gendered and sexualized creative, discursive, and institutional practice. Another valuable growth area is scholarship that considers how such issues of power and identity have played out in places other than the United States. Although this work often pushes back on Black studies' (and Black intellectuals') proprietary relationship to the art form—and sometimes reasonably so given the ways jazz has served U.S. nationalist and imperialist projects—the term "jazz" continues to function quite interestingly in these conversations as a "marvel of paradox," as Rogers would have it, with Black studies' intellectuals, who play a significant role in the New Jazz Studies movement, continuing to insist on jazz's "Negro" past and present.

# 24

## Linked Fate
### Shayla C. Nunnally

Historically, Black racial-group members experienced racial discrimination, regardless of their social status or class. Thus, their historical political orientations centered on advancing the entire racial group, often irrespective of subgroups' (e.g., class, gender, sexuality) political preferences and self-interest (McAdam 1982; K. Tate 1993; and Dawson 1994). Whether racial-group interests or class interests structure Black Americans' contemporary political preferences is a critical debate in the political science literature. As this debate has been premised on mostly a "racial" identity, political scientists have expanded this research query to question whether Black Americans' racial interests (as racial-group members) supersede their class interests (as individuals) and whether other intersecting identities such as gender, sexuality, and ethnicity also play a role in Blacks' political consciousness, policy preferences, and political behavior.

The political scientists Katherine Tate (1993) and Michael Dawson (1994) offer seminal studies on Black Americans' political behavior in the late twentieth century. They document Black Americans' contemporary social, economic, and political circumstances and research their policy preferences to illustrate the relevance of group-based, political activism, beyond the social movement politics of the civil rights era, toward electoral politics that address issues disproportionately affecting the racial group. Recent statistics indicate continuing disproportionate trends in Black Americans' unemployment, poverty, homeownership, generational wealth, and overincarceration in comparison to whites' (U.S. Census Bureau 2010a, 2010b; Michelle Alexander 2012). Blacks often see these contemporary issues as solidarizing and important for their political consciousness and activism on behalf of the Black racial group (Miller et al. 1981; Shingles 1981).

Dawson (1994) finds that most Blacks continue to perceive their economic conditions relative to those of whites. Group-based, psychological processing of economic conditions challenges conventional economic theories that ignore race and focus on individualized self-interest. More commonly, class interests purportedly serve as the foundation for people's political preferences; yet class politics has differed for ethnic versus racial groups in the United States.

Ethnic-politics models that examined the political development of European immigrants in the early twentieth century were based on the assimilation experiences of such groups, which formed lower-status, communal enclaves and participated as ethnic voting blocs in American politics. Acquiring more affluence and socioeconomic diversity (including being acknowledged as racially "white"), European immigrants' political interests shifted from ethnic-group politics to interests premised on their socioeconomic statuses (Dahl 1961). This led to these groups shedding their ethnic-based political interests in favor of their more divergent and personalized, class-based interests. Such a process of assimilation was not applicable to the experiences of Black Americans, who continued to face racism, regardless of their socioeconomic advancements, and who experienced a different structuring of the middle class than white Americans did (Patillo-McCoy 1999).

Some scholars question the solidarizing effect of racism among Blacks in the post–civil rights era. The sociologist William Julius Wilson argued in his book *The Declining Significance of Race* (1980) that social cleavages and divergent class interests evolved among Blacks because racial discrimination became less salient, as more affluent Blacks advanced socioeconomically, after the gains of the civil rights movement, leaving poor Blacks behind. Just as European immigrants shed their ethnic solidarity in political interests, once Blacks became more socioeconomically diverse, their economic diversity increased their potential for political polarization and decreased retention of racially homogeneous political interests. In Wilson's view, disproportionate economic advancements for poor Blacks warranted specific political redress that a focus solely on racial issues would not afford. Civil rights policies often addressed issues not specific to the Black poor's interests. Seeking to discern whether Black Americans determine their political preferences on the basis of race or class interests, Michael C. Dawson (1994) introduced "Black linked fate" to the political science literature, in order to understand the significance of race in contemporary Black political behavior.

According to Dawson in the canonical book *Behind the Mule: Race and Class in African-American Politics* (2004), race informs Black Americans' behavior more than class does. This is because of the continuing societal influences of race in the United States, whether through continuing racial discrimination or Black institutions and social networks that reinforce the salience of Black racial solidarity through the lens of a racialized political economy that distinguishes, yet amalgamates, Black people across class lines. As Dawson and others note, the Black middle class is economically vulnerable and closely connected to the lived experiences of Black Americans of dissimilar, and often lower, socioeconomic statuses (Patillo-McCoy 1999). Dawson submits "Black linked fate" to describe the way that race primarily functions in Black Americans' psychological processing of American politics.

Dawson (1994) theorizes that historical experiences of racial discrimination and contemporary social networks reinforce the significance of race as a psychologically "linking" force in Black Americans' lives. Black linked fate leads Blacks to supplant their self-interest for solidarized, racial-group-oriented political interests. Race serves as a psychological shortcut, or heuristic, for determining individualized political interests, and the "Black utility heuristic" determines the functionality of race in Blacks' political perceptions.

Using 1984 and 1988 National Black Election Studies public-opinion data, Dawson (1994) finds that as much as 64 percent (in 1988) of Black Americans in the surveys (63 percent in 1984) report the affirmative in response to the survey question, "Do you think what happens generally to women in this country will have something to do with your life?" Additionally, respondents who answer in the affirmative are asked, "Will it affect you a lot, some, not much, or not very much?" Even in more recent surveys, an overwhelming percentage of Black respondents continue to affirm this statement (Nunnally 2010; Simien 2005).

Dawson determined that higher socioeconomic status does not detract from this perceived linkage. Black Americans with more education and status are more expressive of perceptions about the relatively lower economic position of Blacks compared to whites, and perceiving that Black Americans are economically subordinate to whites is a greater predictor of subscription to Black linked fate. Class variables are not predictive of Black linked fate, other than the indirect effect of education increasing the perception of Blacks' economic subordination compared to whites' economic status.

A major critique of Black linked fate is that it does not address the multiple ways that Blacks identify,

experience, and politicize being Black in America. Ethnicity, gender, and sexuality are intersecting identities (Crenshaw 1991) that reduce monolithic constructions of race and enhance the likelihood for diverse political preferences. Black racial-group members, who experience discrimination other than that based on race, become "secondarily marginalized" within their racial group, when "consensus issues" purport, yet fail, to represent all Black racial-group members' political interests (C. Cohen 1999).

Dawson premises his theory on the specific, historical racial discrimination experiences of African Americans as an ethnic group. It does not account for these histories on the basis of ethnicity, gender, and sexuality. As the Black American population becomes more ethnically diverse with Black immigrants from around the world (U.S. Census Bureau 2011; Assensoh 2000; R. Rogers 2006), Black linked fate less accurately defines Blacks' psychological connections, social networks, and racial histories across Afro-Caribbeans, Africans, and African Americans in the United States (Nunnally 2010; Greer 2013; C. Smith 2014). However, evidence suggests that race remains a centralized component in Black immigrants' self-image and identification, especially as Black immigrants become more generations removed from immigration and report greater frequency of racial discrimination experiences (C. Smith 2014).

Scholars also acknowledge that Black linked fate may be limited in its ability to account for the "doubly bound" oppression of racial discrimination and sexism experiences of Black women (Gay and Tate 1998; Simien 2005, 2006). To quote Evelyn Simien, "To ignore the simultaneous effects of race and gender is to obscure the complexity of multiple-group identity, cross pressures, and the hierarchy of interests within the Black community" (2005, 546). Evidence suggests that Black linked fate and gender linked fate (with other women, regardless of race) are positively correlated and, perhaps, mutually constitutive for Black women (Simien 2005). For Black women, racial identification also has a more consistent effect on policy preferences than gender identification does (Gay and Tate 1998).

Cathy Cohen (1999) examines the tensions and divergences in Black political organizing during the emergence of HIV/AIDS politics in the 1980s and 1990s. Whereas the historical Black church played an important leadership role in Blacks' liberation throughout America's racial history, the institution was much less vocal and participatory in organizing the Black community to address the disproportionate rates of contraction of the disease among Black Americans during this time. Cohen points to the fissures within the church over embracing political issues that affected Black group members whose behaviors (homosexuality and illicit drug use) were perceived as anathema to the values of the church. Thus, often poor and gay Black Americans, who were more disproportionately affected by HIV/AIDS, were secondarily marginalized by other Black group members.

Black linked fate tends to be a concept studied mostly within the political science discipline. Since its inception, not only have scholars expanded the concept to consider Black intersectionality, but also scholars of other racial and ethnic groups' politics have explored whether the concept describes the political psychology of these groups (Lien, Conway, and Wong 2004; Sanchez and Masuoka 2010) and subgroups within these populations (Gay, Hochschild, and White 2014).

# 25

## Mixed Race
### Habiba Ibrahim

"Mixed race" is an outcome of racial formation that has been variously defined in relation to blackness throughout the course of U.S. history. The development of slavery in the U.S. and elsewhere accounts for how mixed race has routinely been absorbed within the category of blackness. As reliance on indentured and slave labor grew in the colonies and states from the seventeenth to the nineteenth centuries, the definition of blackness—a social classification to which slaves were relegated—expanded to absorb larger numbers of laboring, captive bodies. The rule of "hypodescent," which is the basis for what is colloquially termed the "one-drop" rule, refers to the means by which this expansion occurred.

In 1662, the colonial assembly in Virginia enacted a statute that deviated from English doctrine, which determined that children follow a patrilineal line of descent. According to Act XII of the statute, "Children got by a Englishman upon a Negro woman shall be bond or free according to the condition of the mother" (A. Higginbotham 1980, 43). Since white men outnumbered white women in the colonies, the implied circumstance for the legislation was the higher likelihood that interracial sex occurred between white men and black women (Moran 2001, 21). The shift to matrilineal descent for the children of black women set a colonial and national legal standard that protected the interests of white men. As Deborah Gray White explains, racial formation augmented a gender hierarchy: "Half-white children told a story of a white man's infidelity, a slave woman's helplessness . . . and a white woman's inability to defy the social and legal constraints that kept her bound to her husband regardless of his transgressions" ([1985] 1999, 40).

The "one-drop" rule, which originated in the South and eventually applied to the rest of the U.S., categorized "all persons with any known black ancestry" as black, regardless of mixedness or physical appearance (F. Davis 1991, 11). Although the condition of being a slave was eventually granted only to those who were deemed to be black, and the growth of an enslaved labor force happened through excluding subjects "known" to be of mixed race from the legal and social privileges of whiteness, mixed race existed as its own social category in various places. During the nineteenth century, Charleston, South Carolina, and New Orleans, Louisiana, had populations composed of free, mixed-raced persons who occupied a social status that was distinguishable from either blackness or whiteness.

"Mulatto," the imprecise term used to classify people of black and white ancestry, was included on the U.S. Census for the first time in 1850 to count both free and enslaved mixed-raced people. "Mulatto" has a Spanish- and Portuguese-originating meaning that refers to both a "person of mixed race" and a "mule," an interspecies hybrid. The animalistic quality attributed to persons of mixed race—biological hybridity and subsequent inferiority—was intrinsic to debates of the day about whether black people belonged to a human species that was distinctive from that of white people. The impetus for a "mulatto" category was to test the racial scientific theory that the offspring of interracial "amalgamation" were inferior and would ultimately be eradicated (M. Anderson 2015, 46). The 1890 census included additional subcategories of mixed race, "quadroon" and "octoroon." By 1930, all categories of black/white mixed

race disappeared from the census. This reflected the rise of the Jim Crow era after the 1896 Supreme Court decision *Plessy v. Ferguson*, which deemed a "separate but equal" organization of blackness and whiteness as the law of the land (Nobles 2000, 64). With the color line—the hierarchical schema of black/white racial classification—firmly in place, mixed-raced people not only shared the dispossession of black people. They were black. "Passing" narratives published during the first two decades of the twentieth century—with James Weldon Johnson's *Autobiography of an Ex-Colored Man* (1912) and Nella Larsen's *Passing* (1929) among the most notable examples—explored the mixed-racial condition of running up against a stringent color line. Although the cultural trope of the "tragic mulatto/a" existed prior to the 1920s, the problem it expresses—the social impossibility of being "neither black nor white, yet both" (Sollors 1997) intensified during the first decades of the century.

By the mid-twentieth century, the social practice of racial passing gave way with the emergence of the civil rights era and collective black pride (Wald 2000). By the end of the era, the Supreme Court decision in *Loving v. Virginia* (1967) struck down remaining state-level anti-miscegenation laws, deeming them unconstitutional. The decision was a watershed moment for the recognition of mixed-racial families and the precursor to what would become a multiracial movement: not only were straight, interracial couples allowed to legally marry in all states, but also the children of mixed-racial unions would have birthright legitimacy—which includes inheritance rights—conferred by both parents.

Just two years prior to the *Loving* ruling, in 1965, Daniel Patrick Moynihan's government policy paper, *The Negro Family: The Case for National Action*, commonly known as "The Moynihan Report," had been published. According to the report, the rise of black single mothers revealed a troubling aberrance from the (white) cultural norm of patriarchal families. To consider the *Loving* decision in relationship to "The Moynihan Report" and subsequent discussions about the "breakdown" of the black family is to see a divergence of black and mixed-racial political ends waged through the category of "family" (Ibrahim 2012). The manner in which "family" acts as a conduit between personal matters (private intimacy and care) and political matters (public policies on the distribution of wealth, public funding for the "welfare state," racialized perceptions of responsible parenting) had intensified significance for both black and mixed-racial communities from the 1960s onward.

Almost thirty years after *Loving* in the 1990s, the emergence of "mixed race studies"—or, as it has become known, "critical mixed race studies"—coincided with the boom of a cultural movement that promoted the recognition of mixed race as a separate social category. Just as U.S. black cultural studies of the 1980s and '90s challenged homogenizing historiographies and social scripts, so too did scholarship on multiracialism complicate preconceptions about how subjects inhabited "race" as a social category. Collections such as Maria P. P. Root's 1992 and 1996 volumes, *Racial Mixed People in America* and *The Multiracial Experience*, respectively, along with Naomi Zack's 1993 monograph and 1995 volume, *Race and Mixed Race* and *American Mixed Race*, mark an earnest inauguration of mixed race studies as a distinctive interdisciplinary subfield of American studies.

During this era, the single most pressing issue for multiracial advocates and organizations was setting up a way to classify racial and ethnic mixedness on the 2000 census. Ultimately, political collaboration with congressional leaders led to the current "mark one or more" policy that officially allows individuals to self-identify by choosing all ethnic and racial categories that apply (K. Williams 2006). The collective push toward multiracial

classification began in the 1970s. In 1979, Interracial and Intercultural Pride, more recently known as iPride, became the first mixed-race organization in the country. It began with a group of parents who prompted area public schools to develop ways to classify their mixed-racial children on school forms. By the 1990s, both parents and mixed-racial adults wanted the state to recognize officially how they understood the complications and nuances of race for themselves and across their families.

While many proponents of classifying mixed race advanced the notion that mixed racialism makes up a particular identity, the historical mutability between mixed race and blackness seemed to have been forgotten: historically, "blackness" had been constituted as a mixed-race category. Thus, tacit antiblackness, or a renunciation of black identity along with its historical diversity, seemed to be operative in the cultural and political push to classify and publicly claim mixed racialism (J. Sexton 2008). In an era when race- and gender-conscious policies—or affirmative action—were routinely challenged and repealed, mixed racialism became a convenient alibi for a growing disregard for racial equality. Newt Gingrich was Speaker of the House in 1997 when he declared before a subcommittee that a multiracial category on the census would "be an important step toward transcending racial division and reflecting the melting pot which is America" (quoted in K. Williams 2006, 55). The rise of neoliberalism as a political-economy philosophy during that last three decades of the twentieth century wrought an indifference to race that positioned "biracialism as postracialism" (R. Martin 2011, 267) or as a feather-light and transcendent form of race that compared favorably to historically heavy blackness.

It was sometimes unclear, even to proponents of mixed-racial recognition, whether multiracial people and their families constituted a particular community that shared a set of political and social interests, and the first-person narrative became the multiracial movement's primary genre. During the 1990s and the first decade of the new millennium, a slew of collected stories and essays that captured first-person accounts of the mixed-racial experience were published. Such accounts lined up with concerns about the nuclear family that multiracial advocates addressed through work in organizations such as Biracial Family Network (BFN), Project Reclassify All Children Equally (RACE), and Association of MultiEthnic Americans (AMEA). Thus, "family" and the "individual" are two concepts that were essential to the development of multiracial cultural politics.

As the outcomes of the same historical processes, both "blackness" and "mixed race" are inherently diverse, intersecting, and related like family. If mixed race matters today, it is because of its potential to explicate how race continues to be instrumental to current political reasoning that organizes national governance and social life. As public conversations about former president Barack Obama's mixed/black identity have illustrated, mixed race contradictorily serves as an alibi for postracialism and evidence that racial hierarchies remain. Mixed racialism has signified both the end of racial history and the ongoing afterlife of race.

# 26

## Nadir

Michele Mitchell

"Nadir" can be a specific medical term that indicates the "minimum value of a fluctuating quantity" or an astronomical term that describes either "a point on the celestial sphere diametrically opposite some other point" or "the point on the celestial sphere diametrically opposite to the zenith and directly below the observer" (*Oxford Universal Dictionary* 1955). Yet "nadir" is perhaps most frequently used as an antonym for the more general sense of "zenith," or "high point." Put another way, "nadir" indicates the lowest point possible for a person or collective; it can identify the very worst moment of a particular era or situation as well. The English historian Henry Hallam (1777–1859) used the term "nadir" during the early nineteenth century to refer to what he considered a particularly abysmal period in human history. In the first volume of *Introduction to the Literature of Europe, in the Fifteenth, Sixteenth, and Seventeenth Centuries*, Hallam bluntly referred to the "seventh century [as] . . . the *nadir* of the human mind in Europe" ([1837] 1876, 4). Hallam might have drawn from a 1793 definition of "nadir" as "the place or time of greatest depression or degradation" in making such an assertion (*Oxford University Dictionary* 1955).

Over one hundred years after Hallam published his argument, the eminent African American historian Rayford W. Logan (1897–1982) would deem the period from the end of Reconstruction through World War I (1877–1918) as the nadir of Afro-American history ([1954]

1965). African-descended Americans were under siege during this era when the federal government withdrew U.S. troops from the South and U.S. imperialist forays simultaneously drew on early-nineteenth-century racialist logic and generated new theories about race. As Logan saw it, sectional and political fissures created by the Civil War were mended by the turn of the century, once "both parties had decided that American principles of justice, liberty and democracy did not have to be applied . . . to Negroes. The United States had emerged as a 'world power,' but at home it was faithless to its own basic principles as far as nine million black citizens were concerned" ([1954] 1965, 96). If Logan was perhaps aware of Hallam's work, Logan himself used the term as it was defined during the 1790s, a time when chattel slavery became entrenched in the fledgling American republic due to the Haitian Revolution *and* the contemporaneous invention of Eli Whitney's "cotton gin" (Rothman 2004, 33–34).

It is perhaps ironic that Logan did not consider enslavement as constituting the lowest point for people of African descent in the United States (Foner 1997, xiv). If the Reconstruction era (1863–77), in which black Americans' civil rights were expanded, could be considered a mixed success at best (Foner 1988; L. Edwards 1997; Stanley 1998; Hahn 2003; Schwalm 2009; Masur 2010; Downs 2011), the decades immediately following the U.S. Civil War witnessed the very freedom for which enslaved people, freed blacks, and abolitionists had fought and died (e.g., Blight 2001). Still, the sheer level of racism, violence, disfranchisement, discrimination, exclusion, peonage, and forced dependency that many black Americans endured during the late nineteenth and early twentieth centuries perhaps seemed all the worse for Logan because such depths occurred *after* the legal end of slavery. Moreover, because he wrote and then revised *The Negro in American Life and Thought: The Nadir,*

*1877–1901* (later *The Betrayal of the Negro from Rutherford B. Hayes to Woodrow Wilson*) during the height of the modern civil rights movement, Logan was arguably influenced by the violence and deaths that marked his own era, a time of activism, achievement, and backlash that can rightly be seen as a "Second Reconstruction" in U.S. history (Franklin 1986, 16; Marable 1984).

Other major historians writing during the modern civil rights movement shared Logan's bleak assessment of the late nineteenth and early twentieth centuries. In 1961, John Hope Franklin contended that the years from 1877 to 1923 constituted one "long dark night" for U.S. blacks (quoted in Logan [1954] 1965, 11). August Meier pointedly argued two years later that "the development of American industrial capitalism" came "at the expense of the Negroes" because national unity between 1880 and 1915 was literally predicated on black "subordination" (1963, 24–25). Whereas Logan, Franklin, and Meier all offered different periodizations of the nadir, each powerfully analyzed a particular era when African-descended Americans attempted to negotiate a difficult, if not altogether treacherous, sociopolitical landscape of "redemption" for the South and "reunion" of the nation (Woodward 1966). Regardless of the terminology used, many African Americanists—whether Logan's cohort, in the recent past, or presently—have put a distinct spin on what Americanists refer to more broadly as the Gilded Age and Progressive era. In other words, a period that witnessed a "search for order" as well as "fierce discontent" was a time when African Americans trod "a highway through the wilderness of post-Reconstruction" (Wiebe 1967; McGerr 2003; C. Tate 1992, 3–22).

The late nineteenth and early twentieth centuries in the United States witnessed successive waves of economic depression, considerable labor unrest, severe restrictions on immigration from Asia, nativism sparked by large waves of immigration from southern and eastern Europe, and massive dispossession for American Indians. These decades were, without question, filled with a mixture of uncertainty, anxiety, and hope for black women, men, and children. To begin, mainstream discourse was suffused with contentions that African-descended Americans were so unfit for the rigors of free labor and citizenship due to indolence and inherent inferiority that racial extinction was a real possibility. African American discourse during this period was therefore dominated by concerns about racial destiny, about whether to emigrate or instead focus on intraracial reform in order to ensure a robust collective future. But communities of African descent also became more diverse after emancipation, and such diversity complicated the very notion of a united black collectivity. African Americans moved within the South, westward, and to cities across the nation; workers branched into fields other than agriculture; education enabled the expansion of a professional class; immigration at once generated and underscored ethnic variation. As a people no longer divided into "slave" and "free," black Americans increasingly found themselves divided into distinctions based on educational attainment, occupation, behavior, and social life instead. Some educators, activists, and reformers even wrote and published advice literature in which they provided academic and civic instruction as they advised members of the race on etiquette, respectable leisure activity, morals, and personal behavior. Both class distinctions and intraracial tensions became more evident as African Americans debated which strategies would best suit their collective struggle for civil rights (e.g., M. Mitchell 2004).

During the 1880s and 1890s, for example, a vigorous debate emerged regarding what sort of education was best suited to the needs and prospects of African American youth. Many southern whites viewed black education with skepticism and hostility because they linked it to black assertions about the right to vote. Bennet Puryear, a onetime slaveholder and educator, opposed both public education in general and black suffrage in principle. Puryear additionally maintained that an educated black person was unsuited for his or her destiny as a manual laborer, as he contended that "to invite the negro from those pursuits which require firm muscles and little intelligence . . . is to invite . . . his sure extermination" (1877, 11, 17, 24–27; see also Litwack 1998, 96). Some African Americans even questioned the usefulness of a liberal arts (or "classical") curriculum for the race and instead advocated vocational (or "industrial") education. One cohort of African American educators, notably Booker T. Washington, believed that systematic vocational education was essential for a race barely removed from slavery. Critics of vocational education, such as W. E. B. Du Bois, felt that such an approach merely palliated anxious whites who were against political, economic, and sexual "social equality"—not to mention intellectual attainments, scientific investigation, or artistic aspirations—for African-descended Americans (e.g., J. Anderson 1988).

Indeed, whereas some blacks were convinced that vocational education was the race's most pressing need, other African Americans viewed education as important preparation for professions (Bair 2000, 312). One reason why this debate between Washington and Du Bois was so "bitter" is that both men represented "two camps" of race educators and activists who competed for the "allegiance of a very small sphere of black youth who attended normal schools, secondary schools, and colleges" (J. Anderson 1988, 105). If enslaved people found ways to become literate and legions of former bondspeople were largely self-taught during the initial decade of freedom (H. Williams 2005), the formal attainment of literacy and knowledge was such a critical sphere of activity during the nadir because educational opportunity of any sort had been long denied to the vast majority of African Americans.

Successful and well-educated African Americans were viewed as especially problematic in that their very existence gave lie to persistent claims that black people were innately inferior. Yet people of African descent contended with debates over education as they endured deepening racial segregation. To compound matters, black men faced steady disfranchisement, and lynching took drastic tolls on black communities throughout this era. Not only were segregation, disfranchisement, and lynching interconnected, but lynching also became all the more common as black men lost the right to vote during the 1880s and 1890s; these decades witnessed the veritable "rout" of black Americans from party politics, whether mainstream or third party (Gaines 1996, 20). Above and beyond recognizing the political nature of lynching, the race journalists Alexander Manly and Ida B. Wells recognized that charges about rape used to justify lynching denied the consensual nature of sexual liaisons between black men and white women. Wells even stressed that many lynchings were, in fact, the barbaric murders of African Americans who were successful, prosperous, or "'sassy'" (Bederman 1995; G. Gilmore 1996; Gunning 1995; Prather 1998; Wells-Barnett [1892] 1996, 60). The majority of lynching victims were black, yet Asians, Mexican Americans, American Indians, immigrants, and native-born whites were lynched as well. Significantly, however, the targeted use of lynching as a means to terrorize and control African Americans en masse began during the early 1890s and lasted well into the next century.

Black people remained politicized and found common cause all the same. The late nineteenth and early twentieth centuries witnessed unprecedented institution building among African-descended Americans in the creation of a vibrant black press as well as a notable range of reform and benevolent institutions. Black people acquired various forms of property and established diverse businesses as their ever-growing attainment of literacy facilitated various intraracial initiatives, including explicitly politicized activity in churches. African American writers were notably prolific during the nadir. Indeed, what was a time of peril was indeed an era of promise and progress, too (e.g., W. Simmons 1887; Majors 1893; Kletzing and Crogman 1898; Bruce 1989; E. Higginbotham 1993; Terborg-Penn 1998).

Still, the decades immediately preceding and following the turn of the twentieth century seemed nothing less than "a virtual abyss" in that African-descended Americans became "the butt of [a] . . . national joke" through popular culture—not to mention scientific racialist and sociopolitical discourse—that demeaned, dehumanized, and grossly caricatured black people (Lemons 1977, 104, 106; Logan [1954] 1965; Gossett [1963] 1989, 253–86; P. Morton 1991, 17–53; Goings 1994). To be sure, African Americans produced their own discursive, visual, and material counterarchives to combat their debasement in U.S. culture (e.g., Meier 1963; Carby 1987; Moses 1978; Bruce 1989; Gaines 1996; Library of Congress, Lewis, and Willis 2003; S. Smith 2004; M. Mitchell 2004; McCaskill and Gebhard 2006). Yet the ways in which African-descended Americans were ridiculed in print and material culture proved especially powerful in that technological advances facilitated wide-scale production of "everyday items that depicted African-Americans as . . . objects worthy of torment and torture" (Lemons 1977, 103; Goings 1994, 14). And as much as both mainstream uses of photography and Afro-American counterarchives combined portraiture with a "'scientific' catalogue of facial types" (S. Smith 1999, 3), it was also the case that images collected by scholars such W. E. B. Du Bois at once combatted and

**NADIR**   MICHELE MITCHELL

entrenched racialist, ethnographic usages of photography meant to catalogue, differentiate, and discriminate between ostensible "race types" (S. Smith 2004; M. Mitchell 2004). In other words, the ways that popular culture, material culture, photography, social science, and science portrayed African-descended Americans during the nadir were highly fraught—so much so that black Americans found it difficult to overturn racist depictions of themselves.

The nadir was more than a low point for black people in general. The late nineteenth and early twentieth centuries actually witnessed an erosion of black women's sociopolitical power in comparison to the immediate postemancipation period. During the late 1860s and the 1870s, women—and, for that matter, children—actively participated in mass political meetings and viewed black men's franchise as collective property. The nadir thus witnessed a diminution of black women's sociopolitical power in that women experienced "not a new authority but rather a lost authority, one they now often sought to justify on a distinctively female basis" by the 1890s (E. Brown 1994, 108). African-descended women's formation of the National Association of Colored Women in 1896 signified a flourish of sociopolitical activity that lasted well into the twentieth century. Clubwoman or not, black women initiated some of the most important reform efforts launched by African Americans; their remit included agitation for woman suffrage and against lynching. Elsa Barkley Brown's compelling argument that "the black public sphere" was contentious and "more fractured . . . at the end of the nineteenth century" (1994, 111) therefore underscores how women's history and feminist studies scholarship has simultaneously enriched and challenged conventional understandings of what the nadir entailed for African Americans (Terborg-Penn 1998; Martha Jones 2007; Materson 2009; Zackodnik 2011; Hendricks 2013).

So, too, does work by literary studies scholars, sexuality studies scholars, and historians of sexuality. Critically, fin-de-siècle American culture featured an "emphasis on the surveillance of bodies that was embedded in expert discourses such as sexology" that resulted in a "profound reorganization of vision and knowledge" that lasted until the 1920s (Somerville 2000, 10). More specifically, sexology introduced more rigid classifications of sexual behavior at a time when the African-descended "octoroon" Homer Plessy was the plaintiff in the Supreme Court case *Plessy v. Ferguson*, which resulted in the entrenchment of racial segregation in the United States. During an era when black men were increasingly seen as possessing a bestial sexuality and black women were deemed intrinsically lascivious, distinct categories such as "invert" and "heterosexual" informed an emerging discourse about homosexuality. Therefore, the insistence that "questions of race . . . must be understood as a crucial part of the history and representation of sexual formations" (Somerville 2000, 5) complements literature that interrogates the sexualized underpinnings of forms of racial terrorism during the postemancipation era (e.g., Rosen 2009). Scholarship about race (Wiegman 1995; Somerville 2000; Duggan 2000; Findlay 2000; M. Ross 2004; Freedman 2013) that considers gender and sexuality in tandem—including discourses about "whiteness"—therefore suggests that African Americanists' conceptualization of the nadir will continue to be revised by thoroughgoing scholarly analyses of sexuality as well as work that examines how "race" has been constructed through law (e.g., A. Gross 2008; Pascoe 2009).

Overall, thinking in terms of a nadir is at once productive and problematic because the years from the postbellum period through World War I (1865–1918) witnessed both horrific backlash and tremendous gains for African Americans. If we think of how African-descended

Americans created social movements, built institutions, and gained literacy, the era does not appear to be such a low point. When we examine the nuanced discursive, visual, and material culture that black Americans produced during the fin-de-siècle and early twentieth century (McCaskill and Gebhard 2006), the period also does not seem to be the "low, rugged plateau" identified by Logan ([1954] 1965, 11, 341–58). To be sure, as early as 1963, when August Meier published *Negro Thought in America, 1880–1915*, scholars have realized that Logan's argument looked somewhat different once African Americans' own voices were inserted into the narrative in a more fulsome manner. For example, the nadir arguably contained part of what has been dubbed a "golden age of black nationalism" (Moses 1978). Logan's conceptualization of the era has nonetheless retained such staying power because he cogently demonstrated just how thoroughly politicians abandoned the protection of African Americans' civil rights after Reconstruction's end. "Nadir" has remained meaningful as a keyword, too, because Logan examined how black people were portrayed in print culture in such a salient fashion. Still, subsequent scholarship complicates Logan's portrayal of the era on multiple fronts.

As a keyword, "nadir" is destabilized by analyses of class, region, migration, immigration, empire, gender, sexuality, ethnicity, crime, and ostensible deviance that complicate our understandings of African-descended Americans as a collective (Grossman 1989; Gatewood 1990; Watkins-Owens 1996; W. James 1998; Guridy 2010; Hunter 1997; M. Mitchell 2004; Summers 2004; K. Gross 2006; Hicks 2010). This is not to say that scholarship produced during the past thirty years has necessarily overturned Logan. Rather, thinking about mobility, difference, intraracial tensions, or specific cohorts within African-descended communities turns our optic in directions that do not necessarily privilege Logan's perspective, which ultimately focused on the integration of black Americans into the U.S. body politic and the nation's political economy.

Conventional African Americanist invocations and usages of "nadir" might well be based on what are now outmoded approaches to understanding the workings of "race" in American history. There are perhaps ways in which Logan's—not to mention subsequent—discussion of the nadir is largely predicated on a mid-twentieth-century "race relations" paradigm that privileges the black/white binary. Scholars rightly explore African-descended Americans' quest for the full perquisites of U.S. citizenship, for full integration into sundry aspects of society following the abolition of slavery. Moreover, critical literature that either implicitly invokes or expressly uses "nadir" as a concept has productively assessed intraracial dynamics and/or resistance throughout the postemancipation era. Such scholarship has profoundly deepened our understanding of this period.

All the same, the specific angle of vision offered by such work can limit our appreciation of how the late nineteenth and early twentieth centuries were devastating for various populations living in the United States—not to mention territories the U.S. gained through imperialist expansion and sovereign nations that experienced U.S. colonialism during this period. The concept of a nadir of African American history could possibly cohere less, given that African Americanists are rigorously engaging work that analyzes the late-nineteenth- and early-twentieth-century histories of other collectivities, including immigrants from southern and eastern Europe. Scholarship by scholars in allied fields already pushes us to think more broadly about the nadir in that the period witnessed the markedly violent dispossession of indigenous populations and purposeful exclusion or surveillance of immigrants from

Asia as well as wide-ranging debates about race, ethnicity, and citizenship (Rafael 1993; Jacoby 2008; Guidotti-Hernández 2011; Leong 2001; Glenn 2002; E. Lee 2003; Lui 2005; Cahill 2011; Sohi 2011; Lew-Williams 2014; Kramer 2015; Jacobson 1998; MacLean 2000; Shah 2001; P. Mitchell 2005; Molina 2006; M. Jacobs 2009; P. Deloria 2015). Such scholarship therefore encourages African Americanists to consider the nadir in an ever more capacious manner that assesses how this era was either abysmal or uniquely challenging for a range of racialized and "othered" populations. Whether another keyword displaces "nadir" in African American studies remains to be seen, however.

# 27

## Nationalism
Yohuru Williams

In the field of African American studies, the term "nationalism" is far more evocative than "advocacy or support for" the nation. Instead, it encompasses a rich history of Black political thought and resistance. Such nationalism focuses on the acquisition of a territorial homeland—a nation—but also Pan-Africanism, a continental vision of African unity and Black consciousness. It has inspired a social, political, spiritual, and cultural identification with Blackness situated in a now largely discredited theory of racialism that genetically connected all Black peoples.

As long as nation-states exist, "nationalism" as a keyword will have sociopolitical meaning. Until the dismantlement of imperial and colonial structures and until people can point to a distinct cultural heritage, the term will also have cultural currency. Debates, over Jerusalem and the occupied territory in the Middle East and the Baltic republics and Armenia and Azerbaijan in the former Soviet Union, for example, will always have meaning as contested borders due to the legacy of imperialism. The same pall hangs over every continent touched by imperialism and colonialism, wherever present conflicts over territories linked to national identity remain fresh.

Black nationalism, however, is unique in its relationship to imperialism due to the African slave trade. Peoples from diverse regions in West Africa, enslaved and transported to the Americas, were robbed of their national and ethnic identities. The very prerequisite for classical nationalism—identification with a specific place tied to a distinct history and culture—was already in that sense absent from Black nationalism. This history led its proponents, from Queen Mother Moore to Malcolm X, to imagine and construct alternative forms of binding and to focus on nation-building through social, cultural, and political affinities, not solely defined by connection to a narrowly specified homeland or culture.

Over the centuries, efforts to identify these affinities resulted in various cultural and political Black nationalist movements seeking to establish a cultural unity based on race that incorporates the millions of people of African descent throughout Africa and its diaspora. While the strength of these ideas ebbed and flowed over the period of what the historian Wilson Jeremiah Moses (1978) has termed the "Golden Age of Black Nationalism" from 1850 to 1925, encompassing the founding principles articulated by Martin Delany to the Pan-Africanism espoused by W. E. B. Du Bois, they coalesced around a set of basic issues succinctly defined by Marcus Garvey as slavery, peonage, and alien economic and political control (2004, 85). The literary and intellectual output of the various proponents of Black nationalism have augmented the meaning and power of the term at various points in history, while the unique history of the leaders and movements that have claimed it have sufficiently marked the term to give it a unique history all its own, from which it continues to derive a real but fluid and contested meaning.

Generally speaking, discussions of Black nationalism incorporate everything from efforts by nineteenth-century abolitionists to secure a colony for the emigration of former slaves to Marcus Garvey's celebrated back-to-Africa movement, which remains one of the most heavily identified political movements with Black nationalism. No discussion of Black nationalism would be complete without examining other social, cultural, and political movements and expressions, such as the religious Black nationalism practiced by the Moorish Science Temple and the Nation of Islam or movements such as the Black Power and Black Arts movements of the late 1960s that built on the philosophies of leaders such as Delany and Garvey, incorporating elements of Black nationalist thought into their own programs and ideologies. Rather than focusing on a return to Africa, these movements employed other means of connecting people of African descent through religion, art, music, and culture with an eye toward building Black political and cultural unity. This has been a bone of contention for some critics of the concept. They argue deviation from the core aim of securing and occupying an autonomous Black nation-state negates the fundamental appeal to classical nationalism—which gave birth to the modern nation-state and on which the theory of classical nationalism is built. As James Turner observed in 1970, "without control over land, resources and production, there can be no self-determination for a people" (quoted in Draper and Foner 1970, 6).

To account for this problem in the 1960s at least, the historian Theodore Draper noted the propensity of some Black nationalists in the United States to embrace what he described as a "quasi-nationalism." They introduced "substitutes for sovereignty, such as separate, autonomous, all-black Black Studies programs and departments" over the preferred nation state. In the quest to understand and differentiate strains of nationalist thought, theorists deployed descriptors such as "religious Black nationalism" and "cultural nationalism" as stand-ins for the state (Draper and Foner 1970, 6). Nevertheless, these categories still coalesce around a drive for Black solidarity. They were also not exclusive. Cultural Black nationalists who embraced cultural expression as a form of nation-building were often still proponents of classical nationalism.

Draper's critique notwithstanding, more recent scholarship has been much more expansive in defining Black nationalism, allowing for the inclusion of other forms of Black political, social, and cultural autonomy. In 2001, for instance, Dean Robinson expanded the definition "to include both those who favored separate statehood, as well as, self-help identified 'nationalists' who supported the more modest goal of Black administration of vital private and public institutions" (2001, 4). Such broader conceptions of Black nationalism illuminate some of the challenges that continue to plague its contemporary use.

In much of the popular as well as scholarly discourse on Black nationalism, for instance, the emphasis remains on platforms for political unity, characteristically situated around what Tommie Shelby has termed the "always contested, conception of 'blackness,'" which he further characterizes as "unsound or impractical for contemporary African American politics" (2005, 25).

In an age when conversations around ideas such as globalization and post-racialism have become common, classical Black nationalism appears anachronistic, even as elements of its core, such as unified Black political participation, remain vibrant. Many people still speak of a unified Black community around issues such as police brutality and voting rights. This is in contrast to the work of the historian Sterling Stuckey (1987), who argued that this common legacy of racial oppression was actually embedded in a shared African American culture that he located as one of the primary building blocks of Black nationalism dating back before the period of classical Black nationalism identified by Wilson Jeremiah Moses and rooted in the shared experience of different African peoples forcibly brought to the Americas, who, in spite of oppression, intermingled during the nineteenth century to realize a common culture—which they continued to nurture and retain after emancipation.

These cultural foundations, coupled with the persistence of African rituals and customs, formed the nucleus around which African Americans fashioned themselves into a people—providing fertile ground for nationalist views such as those espoused by Garvey and Delany. Thus, while Dean Robinson notes, "Neither Garvey nor the black nationalists who preceded him had any intention of reclaiming African culture, as some 1960s 'modern' nationalist would" (2001, 9), the philosophy and ideologies they forwarded included a need to recover a shared Black history and culture that created the space for a later reclamation and veneration of the same.

More recently, scholars have proposed a shift away from embracing a problematic classical Black nationalism to a more pragmatic Black nationalism. While Delany constructed a definition of classical Black nationalism to rival the racialist thinking of his day, he more often employed a pragmatic Black nationalism, largely defensive in posture and constructed around a shared legacy of racial oppression, as opposed to a shared culture or ancestral homeland.

Other scholars have suggested that Delany's conceptualization of African migration and Black nationalism was more tactical, evinced by his rejection of categorical separation. As he explained in a letter to the abolitionist William Garrison in 1852, "I am not in favor of caste, nor a separation of the brotherhood of mankind, and would as willingly live among white men as black, if I had an equal possession and enjoyment of privileges" (quoted in Cone 2003, 405). When these rights were denied, Delany promoted emigration until the midst of the Civil War; he championed the cause of the Union in hopes that a Northern victory might result in emancipation and legal equality. With such hopes dashed by the Republican Party's abandonment of Reconstruction and the continued denial of equality, Delany continued to imagine a place that could serve as an African homeland and shield from racial oppression.

Contemporary debates over Black nationalism still largely pivot around these issues. It is the essence of pragmatic Black nationalism, for instance, that is evident in part of the program of the contemporary Black Lives Matter movement. As the founders note in their 2016 statement of beliefs, "We are unapologetically Black in our positioning. In affirming that Black Lives Matter, we need not qualify our position. To love and desire freedom and justice for ourselves is a prerequisite for wanting the same for others" (Black Lives Matter, n.d.-b).

While "Black nationalism" remains problematic as a keyword and political construct in its relation to classical nationalism, it developed, due in large part to Black history and cultural production, a meaning of its own divorced from its classical counterpart. While early adherents sought to link their conceptions to Western notions of hegemony, later strains always evinced this tension. In this regard, a more pragmatic concept of Black nationalism broadly construed can inform contemporary efforts to recover its roots beyond, until recently, the exclusive pantheon of its most well-known, primarily male and heteronormative leaders.

Moving beyond heteronormative constructs of Black nationalism provided Black feminist activists opportunities to understand and imagine other possibilities for addressing racial and nonracial forms of inequality. As Third World Women's Alliance's Myrna Hill observed in her 1971 essay "Feminism and Black Nationalism," "the issues that most concern Black women, low wages, community-controlled medical care—are the Black struggle! . . . It is male supremacy," she concluded, "that undermines the Black liberation struggle by holding back half our fighters and helping out our oppressors" (1971).

In the 1950s and 1960s, efforts at decolonization sparked nationalist movements across Africa. While it is important to explore these efforts at self-determination and unification, Black nationalism, at its core, always depended on Black political imagination. After spearheading the fight to win Ghanaian independence, Kwame Nkrumah, for instance, developed a political blueprint derived from Pan-Africanism, which aimed to free the continent from alien political rule and economic subjugation, as first articulated by Marcus Garvey. This concept of the "imagined community," proposed by Benedict Anderson ([1983] 2006) in his groundbreaking study of decolonization in Indonesia, is a useful construct for understanding American Black nationalism, which shared an emphasis on race rather than the nation-state as a central unifying force.

While employing this lens might yield more interesting pathways to uncover what continues to give the term its cultural currency, scholars such as Kwame Anthony Appiah have found ample grounds from which to critique Black nationalism, including its questionable moral appeal to Black separatism. Others have pushed back against this view, pointing to those elements of Black nationalist thought that continue to resonate with a powerful form of identity politics that sees such separation as essential to fostering Black unity as the bedrock of political and cultural alignment among people of African descent.

Modern Black social justice movements have sought to avoid this dilemma by framing contemporary Black liberation struggles with a more pragmatic form of Black nationalism that focuses on the persistence of racism in all of its forms. This strategy has allowed a widening of the tent by concentrating on the treatment of Black peoples while jettisoning appeals to an imagined homogeneous Black community and to classical nationalist platform with heteronormative and sexist paradigms of leadership and structure. In this vein, the Black Lives Matter movement explicitly states as part of its "herstory," for instance, "As a network, we have always recognized the need to center the leadership of women and queer and trans people. To maximize our movement muscle, and to be intentional about not replicating harmful practices that excluded so many in past movements for liberation, we made a commitment to placing those at the margins closer to the center" (Black Lives Matter, n.d.-a).

Perhaps few would identify Black Lives Matter as a Black nationalist organization. However, embedded in its DNA are critical elements of the pragmatic Black nationalist thought that sought to find space for unity, self-defense, and social and cultural affirmation in the face of racial terror and oppression.

# 28

## New Negro Renaissance
Erin D. Chapman

Formerly known as the "Harlem Renaissance," the New Negro Renaissance was an era of cultural and political foment, exhilaration, and self-generated "opportunity" among people of African descent as they gathered, through immigration and migration, in the world's metropoles—New York City, Chicago, Los Angeles, Washington, DC, London, Paris, even Tokyo—in the decades leading up to and following World War I and continuing through World War II. The generation of African Americans and Afro-Caribbean immigrants who came of age in this period proudly branded themselves "New Negroes," signaling their modern, self-determined distinction from the docility and dependence on white benefactors they saw in their parents' and grandparents' generations.

Concentrating on the period's literary production, which occurred in the U.S.'s new publishing center of New York City, and locating the inspiration for that production in the black enclaves that African American migrants and West Indian immigrants made for themselves in the northeastern portion of the island of Manhattan, scholars such as David Levering Lewis, Cheryl Wall, and Nathan Huggins used the term "Harlem Renaissance" to capture the urban, modern sophistication of younger black writers in the period between the world wars. The term was always inadequate, however, as it tended to prioritize the literary over other, equally significant artistic genres, such as film, dance, and music, and divorced the realm of artistic production from its complex sociopolitical contexts, especially the varied political activism and cultural foment burgeoning among newly urban and industrializing black working classes. In the most basic sense, furthermore, the term "Harlem Renaissance" is deeply misleading as it negates the broad sweep of the era's cultural foment, including the active alliances and collaborations that the New Negroes formed across multiple urban spaces, political movements, and racialized, colonial geographies.

The poet laureate of the Renaissance, Langston Hughes, for example, was born in 1902 in Missouri; graduated high school in 1920 in Cleveland, Ohio; lived in Mexico City, New York City, and Washington, DC; attended Columbia University; gained a wealth of experience about the African diaspora and world politics while sailing the Atlantic working as a ship's steward; sojourned in Paris, Tokyo, Haiti, and Moscow; graduated from Lincoln University in Pennsylvania; served as a correspondent during the Spanish Civil War; and published two books of poetry, a novel, and a book of short stories, all before the advent of World War II. The term "Harlem Renaissance" hardly encompasses the travels, influences, alliances, or cultural production of this one man, let alone his generational sisters and brothers of African descent across the United States and around the globe.

Seeking to recover and to emphasize these many layers of complexity, a new set of scholars of black America and the black Atlantic in the interwar period have "escaped from New York" along with historians Davarian Baldwin and Minkah Makalani (2007). These scholars have renamed the period's racialized cultural production the "New Negro Renaissance" in recognition of the New Negro generation's commitment to self-determination in various guises, the deep connections between the generation's cultural expression and its diverse political activism, and the geographical multiplicity of the generation's connections, collaborations, and ongoing migrations.

In contemplating the significance of the New Negro Renaissance to the interdisciplinary field of African American studies, it is useful first to break the term down to its constituent elements. First, the heart of the term: "Negro." Quite simply, if directly translated from the Spanish or the Portuguese, "Negro" equals "black." "Negro" signifies the first formation of our current racial regime through the Hispanophone and Lusophone origins of the Atlantic slave trade. In this word, "Negro," we find the root of particular, peculiar New World processes of racialization with all they continue to signify. Here is the original formation of blackness and its dichotomous relationship to whiteness and also the formation of British North American configurations of sex and class—the creation of the "white" (as opposed to "English" or "Christian") planter (elite) and indentured (working) classes.

Here, too, is the rise of white-supremacist patriarchy—the legal, social, and economic means of securing the dominance of white male elites and of providing at least the chimera of a route toward elite status for all white males. Through the institution of a matrilineal inheritance of slave status and the imposition of penalties that effectively stripped white women who engaged in interracial sex of their white privilege, the unity of white men across class lines held the line against "amalgamation" while also asserting white patriarchal privilege over black bodies and denying black men the privileges and responsibilities of patriarchy.

Socially as well as linguistically, across English, Spanish, and Portuguese, "Negro," unless qualified by "woman" or some other descriptor, equaled "black male." Black patriarchal aspiration emerges again and again in the New Negro Renaissance. The New Negroes wanted to claim patriarchal privilege for black men, to finally win "manhood rights" for black men and for the race. They wanted to untangle that legacy of slavery and be reborn as real men.

Explicitly or implicitly recognizing the centrality of masculinity to the assertion of New Negro identities and politics, a range of scholars of the New Negro Renaissance have illustrated the new racialization and revitalized black masculinity of the period through analysis of the boxer Jack Johnson's triumph over the white favorite Jim Jeffries and the recitation of Johnson's infamous exploits with a series of white wives and girlfriends. For the theater critic David Krasner (2002), Jack Johnson's movements in the boxing ring were emblematic of New Negroes' new performances of race and bold challenges to white supremacy. The historian Kevin Mumford (1997) uses Johnson's flouting of sexual-racial boundaries and his apparent enjoyment of the social turmoil his behavior excited as an enactment of the "interzones" forged according to the interdependent racial and sexual discourses shaping early-twentieth-century urban space. For Davarian Baldwin (2007), Jack Johnson is an unequivocal hero, the embodiment of New Negro masculine self-determination and defiance of the racial status quo. The era's suffusion in the glory of bold masculinity and commitment to the realization of black patriarchal aspiration is further demonstrated in Melinda Chateauvert's (1998) analysis of the determination of the members of the Brotherhood of Sleeping Car Porters, the first inarguably successful all-black labor union, to win "manhood rights" on behalf of themselves as workers and on behalf of the race as a beleaguered population. Likewise, New Negroes as diverse as the filmmaker Oscar Micheaux, the sociologist and *Opportunity* editor Charles S. Johnson, and the would-be emperor Marcus Garvey advocated the black man's right and responsibility to lead his family and the race as a patriarch with the necessary earning power,

freedom, and respect to provide for and protect his wife, children, and community.

"New" equals modern, remade. This word "new" was utilized in a range of ways around the turn of the century and through the Great Depression to signify the emergence of a perceived modernity, until World War II remade the world yet again. In this early-twentieth-century, "modern" era, there were a New Negro, a New Woman, and a New South. In this new era, the United States shook off the last vestiges of its Civil War pallor and flexed its newfound imperial might, exerting itself to conquer the Philippines, Cuba, Puerto Rico, and Haiti and then extending its reach to fulfill its share of the "white man's burden" through economic and political influence over the whole of the Americas.

Within the United States, middle-class, white, Protestant Progressives sought to infuse a white-supremacist, heteropatriarchal moral order into a civilization they saw as decaying and overrun by Catholic, Jewish, and racially and ethnically tainted immigrant and migrant populations. North and South, white Progressives imposed de facto and de jure racial segregation and passed laws establishing the "one-drop rule" and laws against "miscegenation"—again holding the line for white-supremacist patriarchal privilege. They incited a "white slavery scare" in their endeavor to "rescue" white girls and women from the moral evil of prostitution; made the sale and consumption of alcoholic beverages illegal; utilized the new "science" of eugenics to restrict reproduction among poor, mentally ill, criminal, and non-white populations; and criminalized the political "machines" that many urban immigrant populations had built to facilitate their sociopolitical and economic empowerment. This new white-supremacist, heteropatriarchal moral order filled the void left by the elimination of slavery as a system of socioeconomic hierarchy that had generated the discursive logic assigning meaning to blackness and whiteness, man and wife, lady and gentleman, citizen, slave, human, and savage.

Thus, the early decades of the twentieth century saw the rise of a new racial regime, a new set of language, laws, and logics that abhorred slavery as the unfortunate outgrowth of a misguided past but that nevertheless reasserted the racial, sexual, gendered, and economic hierarchies that slavery had established. And within this remade racial regime, a new generation of black people came of age and asserted for themselves a new sociopolitical role.

By the thousands, they founded and joined labor unions, civil rights organizations, all-black sororities and fraternities, political clubs, and religious societies. They supported the Atlantic-wide, multilingual, black nationalist project of Marcus Garvey's Universal Negro Improvement Association, marched against lynching at the behest of the National Association for the Advancement of Colored People, and also eagerly thumbed the latest editions of the National Urban League's *Opportunity* magazine. They were elected to federal offices for the first time since Reconstruction, demanded women's suffrage, created a million-dollar beauty industry, and advocated socialist revolution in the ranks of the Communist Party of the USA. In urban centers across the United States and around the world, New Negroes worked long hours in backbreaking jobs—many of them performing much the same old work that their enslaved great grandparents had—in order to afford the novel experience of draping themselves in glamorous suits and gorgeous dresses cut in the latest fashions. They did not surmount or transcend the racial regime encircling them, but they refused the old accommodations. One way or another, they would define "a new day begun."

And, finally, "Renaissance" equals rebirth, revitalization, a new emergence, a cultural transformation, a reimagining, a reconceptualization, renewal. In some ways, then, "New Negro Renaissance" is a repetitive statement—a renewed rebirth, a revitalization of a remade racialization.

As a generation, the New Negroes were the grandchildren of the freedpeople. They were the children of the Reconstruction generation, the generation that had witnessed their parents' emancipation and then the slow, deliberate, federally sanctioned renunciation of freedom, the reracialization of the U.S. polity. The New Negroes grew up in the midst of their parents' realization that the U.S. would never relinquish the blackness that remained necessary as a guarantor of white freedom. And so the New Negroes took that racialization in their own hands, molded and maximized it as they pleased. Finding race unavoidable and indelible, they sought to reconstruct it to serve their own interests.

And so Marcus Garvey's Universal Negro Improvement Association declared, "The New Negro Has No Fear" (on a placard at a UNIA parade in 1924), while investing blackness with a unique and inviolable distinction, a royal history, and an imperial future. New Negro artists, performers, and writers, such as Josephine Baker, J. Rosamond Johnson, Bessie Smith, and Claude McKay, made their names trading on racial representations on the page, stage, and screen. In the popular, segregated cabarets in northern cities, Duke Ellington, Fredi Washington, Ethel Waters, Lena Horne, and other New Negro musicians and dancers simultaneously proffered the exotic, jazzy eroticism that white audiences eagerly anticipated and also intriguingly refused the revelation of their inner selves. They were modern in the manipulation of the primitive brush with which white-supremacist modernity painted them.

It is noteworthy that the New Negro Renaissance or some aspect of the era, its cultural productions, socioeconomic transformations, migrations, political mobilizations, and newly wrought racial-sexual identifications, is taught in virtually all the disciplines constituting African American studies curricula. The New Negro era sits between the other two readily recognizable, "known" periods of black and American sociopolitical, racial reconstruction: slavery/emancipation and civil rights. The New Negro era and its major figures and artifacts occupy the historical and ideological space between Frederick Douglass and Martin Luther King Jr., between the slave narrative and the Black Arts poem. It is the northern interlude between the two moments of grand southern revolution and southern black revelation. It is the passage from a U.S. history that shames us to a U.S. history that inspires us. The New Negro era is the gateway, the bridge, the ambiguity, the link between two known subjectivities—bound/free, oppressed/empowered, slave/citizen. But the falsity of the dichotomies bedevils us. For, in so many ways, blacks remain in that liminal space—still bound but nominally free; continually oppressed but, through the success of global celebrities such as Oprah, Jay-Z, Beyoncé, and Obama, seemingly empowered; still enslaved yet continuously forced to assert and reaffirm our citizenship, our humanity, our right to life itself.

Since emancipation, each successive generation of African Americans has thought itself somehow more racially progressive, more "free," more sophisticated and savvy about race politics than the preceding one. The identifier "Negro" may have gone out of fashion, but the "newness" of the "New Negro" never has. Each successive generation of black people seeks to refashion race, to reconstruct racial formations and racial identity after its own proclivities. We are no different, as we still struggle to navigate the zeniths and nadirs of those dichotomies. Along the way, we do well to be mindful of the machinations and missteps, the twisted routes laid by the original New Negroes.

# 29

## Pan-Africanism
Tsitsi Jaji

"Pan-Africanism" denotes a variety of political and cultural movements that advocate solidarity among people of African descent. The term "pan-African" was coined at the turn of the twentieth century and may designate, variously, alliances between all African countries, all people native to Africa, or all people of African heritage across the globe. Each strand has its own distinctive history, and the term's relevance today lies in its potential to analyze the impasses in these histories and/or reanimate their goals in contemporary contexts. According to Google's N-gram tool, the use of the term peaked in the 1960s, coinciding with struggles for liberation and civil rights among people of African heritage and the establishment of formal structures to facilitate cooperation among newly independent African states. However, the term was first used among diasporic Africans, and its relevance for African American studies in an era of globalization is indicated by the resurgence of the term since the 1990s.

What exactly "pan-Africanism" designates has long been debated, and one might argue that contentions over its meaning and purpose are, in fact, the most representative referents of the word. In other words, to see Pan-Africanism *in action* we must look at moments when people of African descent have struggled over naming a recurrent desire to advance a common purpose. A 1962 essay by the historian George Shepperson, published in one of the foundational journals of African

American studies, *Phylon*, began with alarm at how the term was being "bandied about with disturbing inaccuracy" (346)—a clear example of how "pan-Africanism" has also generated heated scholarly debate. The essay distinguishes between a discrete set of political gatherings associated with a central figure, W. E. B. Du Bois (who happened to be the editor of *Phylon*), designated with the proper noun "Pan-Africanism" and a collection of often ephemeral, predominantly cultural movements designated with the common noun "pan-Africanism." Shepperson included the Pan-African Congresses held in 1919 (Paris), 1921 (London), 1923 (Lisbon), 1927 (New York), and 1945 (Manchester), although a subsequent 1974 congress hosted by Julius Nyerere in Tanzania claimed the mantle of continuing this tradition. These congresses constitute the most stable canon of Pan-Africanism, and as such, they generate little controversy as exemplars. However, Shepperson's distinction remains influential and productive, not only as an analytic tool but as a starting point for revision, and this essay offers a survey of some of the more fraught uses of "pan-Africanism."

The belief in shared destinies among diverse communities of African descent predates our term. "Pan-Africanism" usefully designates the survival strategies developed in the face of the depredations of the transatlantic slave trade. Because the mass deportation of Africans to the Americas often threw together members of different African ethnicities who shared neither language nor religion, diasporic Africans developed new spiritual practices, fraternal societies, and political resistance movements adapting African cosmologies to a new context. Syncretic religions such as Haitian Vodoun, Cuban Santería, Jamaican Kumina, and Brazilian Candomblé drew on multiple sources and sometimes facilitated organized uprisings, most spectacularly in the Haitian Revolution of 1791–1804. Similarly, American Protestants who foregrounded a continental heritage, such as the African Methodist Episcopal Church (a denomination that was founded in Philadelphia and spread to the Caribbean and West and Southern Africa by the end of the nineteenth century) and congregations such as the First African Baptist Church (in Savannah, Georgia), built long-lasting traditions of education and political activism.

Arguably, an early discourse of pan-Africanism emerged through another abolitionist motivated by religious convictions: David Walker's 1829 *Appeal . . . to the Coloured Citizens of the World* addressed the problem of slavery in the United States as one of world-historical consequence. However, his objections to the American Colonization Society's proposal to transport free New World blacks to Liberia were at odds with another, more widely recognized foundational figure for pan-Africanism, Edward Wilmot Blyden. Blyden, born in St. Thomas, emigrated to Liberia in 1850 and became an influential voice in education, politics, and publishing. As an early advocate of Ethiopianism, he built on popular interpretations of scriptures prophesying renewal in Africa, especially Psalm 28:11, which states, "Princes shall come out of Egypt, Ethiopia shall soon stretch out her hands unto God" (KJV). Blyden suggested that the Back-to-Africa movement was an African parallel to Zionism; however, Liberia's tortured history, as fraught as Palestine's, suggests that the philosophies also advanced gravely problematic settler-colonial logics. Blyden's newspaper columns and early articulations of Ethiopianism influenced future forms of pan-Africanism, and his embrace of Islam late in life presages its role in the pan-Africanist turn of figures such as Malik el-Shabbaz (Malcolm X). Such narratives complicate the term's histories, particularly since many of the most prominent twentieth-century pan-Africanists embraced leftist philosophies skeptical of religion.

The term enters the printed record through advertisements for a conference held in 1900 in London. The first Pan-African Conference was organized by the Trinidadian barrister H. Sylvester Williams along with members of the African Association he had formed in 1897. The shift in nomenclature from "African" to "Pan-African" mirrored contemporaneous currents of nationalism, such as pan-Slavism and the unification movements of Italy and Germany in the late nineteenth century. The Pan-African Conference proposed to discuss what was known as the "Native Races" question. Representatives of African descent from all parts of the British Empire, the United States of America, Abyssinia, Liberia, and Haiti were invited, as were a number of allies of other races (primarily white Brits). The closing address (by a committee led by Du Bois) introduced one of the most familiar diagnoses of race relations, that "the problem of the twentieth century is the colour line." Along with imperialism, lynching, and other matters, deep concern was raised over the labor conditions in South Africa and Rhodesia. This demonstrates a key function of such public Pan-Africanist events—gathering information from advocates (in this case, a report from Mrs. A. V. Kinloch, a South African woman married to a mining manager) to mobilize global support for local struggles. Although the conference did not yield lasting organizational structures, it built on earlier gatherings such as the 1893 Chicago Conference on Africa that were pan-Africanist in spirit if not in name and presaged future projects that grounded antiracist and anti-imperialist work in a global African community.

One important strategy that emerged was *print pan-Africanism*. Across the globe, the black press already closely followed international events, but soon explicitly pan-African publications such as the *African Times and Orient Review*, founded by the Egyptian entrepreneur and actor Muhammed Dusé Ali in 1912, arose.

Newspapers were also important as the official voices of specific organizations, and one of the most rancorous splits between advocates of pan-Africanism—the long-running feud between Du Bois and the Jamaican-born Marcus Garvey—can be traced in the pages of their respective publications, the *Crisis* (the official organ of the NAACP) and *Negro World* (associated with the Universal Negro Improvement Association and published in three languages). Indeed, while Garvey's call for black people in the diaspora to move "back to Africa"—with Garvey himself as the continent's provisional president—and his fiscal problems troubled other black leaders, the sheer number of people who at one time subscribed to his ideas is the strongest evidence of his pan-Africanist influence. The international convention he led in 1920 offered a spectacle that drew thousands to witness the event in Harlem, and the UNIA boasted subscribing members not only across the U.S. but also in the Caribbean and Africa. Such a widespread membership would not have been possible without *Negro World*.

The prominent place of journals such as *Légitime défense*, *L'étudiant noir*, and *Tropiques* in forging ties among Francophone students and artists of diverse African descent offers another example of print pan-Africanism. Indeed, such publications fostered the rise of *négritude*, a literary movement that began in Paris, where students from across the French Empire met and exchanged political and aesthetic visions. First coined by the Martinican Aimé Césaire as a tactic to recuperate the derogatory valences of the French term for black person, *nègre*, *négritude* became a cultural principle whose meanings evolved and diverged in the hands of Césaire's friends Léopold Senghor of Senegal and Léon Damas of French Guyana. Ironically, *négritude* eventually became a site of contestation, but the most heated debates unfolded in contexts that could be considered pan-Africanist, such as the First World Festival of Negro

Arts, held in Dakar in 1966. While rarely explicitly political, print pan-Africanism can be traced in the international coverage of magazines such as *Ebony, Negro Digest, Drum,* and *Bingo* and in an analogous body of scholarly publications such as *Phylon, Présence Africaine, Transition,* and *Callaloo,* all of which encompass a broad range of material by and about work by people of African descent.

Such lists reveal one of the limitations of pan-Africanism as an anthologizing tool: the immense African presence in Latin America (not only in Brazil but also in the Spanish-speaking world) is rarely adequately represented. Another limitation of approaches that foreground global black experience is the exclusion of North Africans in pan-Africanism, a problem all the more ironic considering Dusé Ali's role and the prominence in Black Power and black consciousness discourses of the Martinican psychiatrist Frantz Fanon's theorizations of Algerian colonization. Some attempts at reconciling this tension include the Pan-African Festival of Art and Culture held in Algiers in 1969 and the aesthetics of jazz musicians such as Randy Weston (drawing extensively from Moroccan music) and Sun Ra (whose fascination with Egypt influenced his Arkestra's performance style and led to concerts there in the 1970s and '80s).

On the African continent, pan-Africanism has often designated state-based projects, and in the main, the rhetoric of cooperation has often exceeded concrete diplomatic or economic union. The Organization of African Unity (OAU), which was founded in 1963, grappled with one of the central tensions within pan-Africanism. On the one hand, pan-Africanism works toward collective liberation of people of African descent fighting domination. On the other hand, such liberation requires dismantling local forms of oppression and securing sovereignty and thus is potentially at odds with suprastate policies. Indeed, the OAU was formed only after a dispute between the Casablanca bloc (Ghana, Algeria, Morocco, Egypt, Mali, and Libya), which advocated moving rapidly toward political federation, and the Monrovian bloc (Senegal and most other former French colonies, Nigeria, Liberia, and Ethiopia), which pressed for economic cooperation. The dispute was resolved at a conference in Addis Ababa, headquarters for the OAU and its successor, the African Union (AU). Since 2007, the AU has included the diaspora as the sixth official region.

Ethiopia's role is fitting, given the symbolic weight that Ethiopia has carried in diaspora imaginaries. The long history of one of the few African kingdoms that did not fall to European imperialism was a source of pride well beyond Ethiopia's borders and beyond the nineteenth-century Ethiopianism described earlier. When Mussolini invaded what was then known as Abyssinia in 1935, Africans on the continent and in the diaspora rallied in support, and events were covered extensively in the global black press. Among the most enduring organic intellectual traditions to emerge from Ethiopianism is Rastafarianism. A spiritual tradition that reveres the last Ethiopian emperor, Haile Selassie, as divine, Rastafarianism has influenced the philosophies of many reggae musicians, including the most explicitly pan-African, Bob Marley, whose song "Africa, Unite!" (1979) still captures the aspirations of a rich panoply of movements.

What can pan-Africanism do for African American studies today? It might account for the influence of Caribbean intellectuals such as Sylvia Wynter and C. L. R. James on the field in the U.S. It could analyze the Black Arts Movement's embrace of African symbols. It could uncover legacies of the solidarity work that supported liberation struggles in Southern Africa. Pan-Africanism could broaden movements for racial justice in the U.S.

Recent initiatives such as #BlackLivesMatter could trace links between racialized policing in the U.S. and stringent European policies toward migrants crossing the Mediterranean from North Africa or the treatment of favela residents in the lead-up to the World Cup and Olympics. And campaigns against mass incarceration would offer a different account of disproportionate sentences for drug offenses if the circuits of trafficking through the Caribbean, Latin America, and West Africa were part of our analysis. These are but a few examples of why "pan-Africanism" continues to speak to the field.

# 30

## Passing
Allyson Hobbs

"Passing" is a word that has historically denoted a clandestine and hidden process, designed to leave no trace. Conventional wisdom is that few sources exist because those who passed carefully covered their tracks and left no record of their transgression. The term "passing" suggests a type of instability, a "moving through," or the lack of a stable home or place. Passing was equated both with opportunity (access to white-collar employment, better neighborhoods, a host of social courtesies) and with death (a forever severing from one's family, friends, and communities).

It is likely that the word "passing" first appeared in print in advertisements for runaway slaves. Slave masters panicked about the possibility that some enslaved people might be able to "pass themselves off" as white and escape to freedom. Advertisements described enslaved people in exhaustive detail, sometimes noting that a particular slave could "sing a good song" or could speak a language other than English or was last seen wearing a particular garment. Most urgently, these notices warned readers to look carefully: an enslaved man or woman might "pass for a free person." In the antebellum period, white skin functioned as a cloak and could mask one's slave status, disrupting the racial certainties of the slave regime.

Racial passing can be a type of self-imposed exile. Between the late eighteenth and the mid-twentieth centuries, countless African Americans passed as white, leaving behind families, friends, and communities, often without any available avenue for return. Lives were lost only to be remembered in family stories. To pass as white was to make an anxious decision to leave one racial identity and to claim to belong to another. It was risky business. In today's multiracial society, the decision to pass may seem foolish, frivolous, or disloyal. Once one circumvented the law, deceived neighbors, tricked friends, and sometimes duped spouses, there were enormous costs to pay. In each historical period, those who passed experienced personal and familial losses differently. Their experiences open a window onto the enduring problem of race in American society and onto the intimate meanings of race and racial identity for African Americans. In the antebellum period, enslaved men and women lived with a looming threat of loss, knowing that they could be bought, sold, and forever separated from their families if their master lost a card game. To pass as white during this period was to escape—not necessarily from blackness but from slavery—with the intention of recovering precious relationships and living under the more secure conditions of freedom. After emancipation, to pass as white was considered by many African Americans (and most famously by James Weldon Johnson in the 1912 novel *The Autobiography of an Ex-Colored Man*) to be "[choosing] the lesser part" and "sell[ing] one's birthright for a mess of pottage" ([1912] 1995, 100). In the short-lived but hopeful moment of Reconstruction and, later, during the long years of Jim Crow, passing meant striking out on one's own and leaving behind a family and a people. Without a doubt, benefits accrued to these new white identities. But a more complete understanding of this practice requires a reckoning with the loss, alienation, and isolation that accompanied, and often outweighed, its rewards. As early as the 1940s and through the 1960s, personal testimonies began to declare that the losses were simply too much to bear; it was time to give up and "come home."

The history of passing offers multiple ways of looking at the color line. Passing reveals the bankruptcy of the idea of race. Passing uncovers that the essence of identity is found in the ways that one recognizes oneself and is recognized as kindred. These forms of recognition may begin with superficial markers such as skin color, speech, and dress, but these are only indicators of associative relations, ways of being in the world, and an imagined sharing of a common origin and iconic experiences. Passing works as a prism: it refracts different aspects of what we commonly think of as racial identity and reveals what is left once the veil of an ascribed status is stripped away. Behind that veil, what we know as "race" is simply the lived experience of a people, expressed perhaps as an ache for family and interconnections or sometimes as a longing for music, humor, and food. Thus, passing unmasks race as conventionally understood, revealing the intimate and personal meanings of a putative racial identity.

For many family members and friends of those who passed, racial identity came to mean much more than an individual's rejection of the race. It meant no longer belonging as a family member and no longer sharing experiences, stories, and memories of times past. To be sure, the experiences of African Americans who decided to pass as white varied widely and cannot be collapsed into a singular narrative. Family relationships were not always easy or harmonious, but the loss of kinship that resulted was equally acute for troubled or dysfunctional families as it was for stable ones.

Racial passing in the American context must be acknowledged as a subset of a much larger phenomenon. The poor passed as the rich, women passed as men, Jews passed as Gentiles, gay men and women passed as straight, and whites sometimes passed as black. Of course, the reverse of each of these dyads was plausible given specific conditions and circumstances. In societies with relatively open and fluid social orders, the permutations on passing were endless. In our contemporary moment, the term "passing" is often used to describe the experiences of transgender people who may pass as women or men and undocumented people who may pass as citizens.

Passing is not exclusively an American enterprise. Passing has a complex history around the world and especially in nations with similar racial compositions as the United States, such as Jamaica, South Africa, and Brazil. Perhaps the most celebrated cases of passing have occurred in the United States because of the stark binary between black and white. Within the United States, there was never been an official category like *branquinha* (whitish) in Brazil, "colored" in South Africa, or "Jamaica white" in Jamaica (a term that describes people who appear white enough to pass, yet "everyone" knows that they are mixed race). "Mulatto" appeared on the U.S. census between 1850 and 1930, but it never gained the same traction in American politics and society as the intermediate categories in other nations. The distinctiveness of the bipolar American racial regime—the persistence of the "one-drop rule"; the lack of official categories for multiracial people; the social and economic distance between blacks and whites and the illegality of interracial marriage until the *Loving v. Virginia* case in 1967; and the history of the United States as a white-majority, black-minority nation until increased immigration led to massive demographic changes in the mid-twentieth century—creates conditions ripe for the singular and spectacular nature of racial passing in the United States.

Race is socially constructed and performative. From a passer's point of view, race was neither strictly a social construction nor a biological fact. The line between black and white was by no means imaginary; crossing it had profound, life-changing consequences. Race was quite real to those who lived with it, not because of skin color or essentialist notions about biology but because it was social and experiential, because it involved one's closest relationships and one's most intimate communities (Michaels 1997, 137). Scholars may view race as a social construction, but this concept does not always correspond to the ways that race operates in everyday life. Echoing the social constructionist argument, W. E. B. Du Bois famously wrote that a black man is "a person who must ride 'Jim Crow' in Georgia" ([1940] 2014, 77; quoted in S. Andrews 2007, 146). Du Bois's statement raises the question, what would a black man be without Jim Crow in Georgia? Is it possible to remove all of the structures that separated blacks from whites? If such structures were dismantled, what would be done with the recollections, the impressions, and the stories passed down? For these reasons, a black man would still be a black man even without Jim Crow—not because of skin color or blood or any other factor inhering in biology but because of the memories that bind him and social forces that surround him. It is possible to pass for something without becoming what it is that you pass for. The core issue of black-to-white passing is not becoming what you pass for but losing what you pass away from.

# 31

## Performance

Stephanie Leigh Batiste

A staged public piece of theatrics or music comes immediately to mind when one thinks of the noun "performance"—or perhaps, in everyday use, an exaggerated or fake show of oneself for others. In African American studies, the word has developed broader resonance to incorporate not only creative display, for better or worse, but also a complex way of knowing Black experience and ways of being. From disciplines such as theater and anthropology, "performance" comes into African American studies through attention to practice, to cultural resonances through time and communities, to transformation, and to Black creative virtuosity. The word "performance" and its uses announce African American studies' concern with community, storytelling, memory (and its loss), action and activity, and experiences of Blackness. In this way, the term "performance," in Black performance studies, offers the body, memory, and practice as bearer and keeper of knowledge, thus challenging the primacy of text. Performance fundamentally contests the importance of written texts and documents as having primary or original meaning as the bearer of knowledge for all cultures. In scholarship, an overemphasis on text as a bearer of history and as evidence of civilization has allowed those who have controlled text and object archives, often European colonists, to define consciousness, identity, and society. Performance as a lens into culture restructures claims to and lineages of knowledge. This is especially important for Black populations in the West, whose access to literacy and thus the creation and preservation of text was violently outlawed, with broad consequences.

The canonical work of the anthropologist, novelist, playwright, and performer Zora Neale Hurston provides a creative template to think through how the word has moved and developed resonance in a long history of Black scholarship and creativity. This combination of reflection and culture making illustrates the way the word has moved through research, literature, theater, social patterns, music, storytelling, and philosophy. Hurston studied, recorded, memorized, wrote about, fancied, and participated in Black cultures in a way that was rigorous and playful. (Both rigor and play are characteristics that performance offers to scholarship.) In a remarkable passage from her novel *Jonah's Gourd Vine* (1934), Hurston uses charismatic and musical language to link the dances and music at a Black harvest party to an African past: "They called for the instrument that they had brought to America in their skins—the drum—and they played upon it. . . . The great drum that is made by priests and sits in majesty in the juju house . . . and speaks to gods as a man and to men as God. Then they beat upon the drum and danced" ([1934] 1995, 29). Here, the embodied memory of collective music making and movement with the holy instrument of vitality, the noble body, distills performance as a bearer of Black knowledge and being. By dramatizing a community celebration through performance in literature, Hurston in turn celebrates narrative, movement, the inheritance of expression, expression of the body, and rhythmic histories in the Black diaspora through text. In this way, a celebration of performance in her writing reorients the canon and the routes through which we trace Black cultures and identity. It also affirms and celebrates Black transnational roots and identifications. Hurston poses such performances within private cultural spaces as central to Black culture and consequently to Black studies.

Rich in vibrant community, divine connection, and genealogical sensibility, this moment of transcendence in the novel takes place at a Black American cultural event set in the early twentieth century. Hurston's *Jonah's Gourd Vine* stretches in many directions to invoke slavery, folk culture, gender divides, religion, family, love, and Black modernism. Hurston's complex engagement with performance traditions subtends this reach. This scene and others like it in Hurston's oeuvre place repertoires of Black embodied knowledges in service of newly articulating histories and investigating the present of Black cultures. Performance takes on diverse vectors for making meaning. It appears as embodied display and social ritual, verbal play and memory, public showing and private communication. It links hemispheric and African Black cultures in the constitution of diaspora. This early-twentieth-century reference to African influences slow-cooked across space and time helped to forge a concept of diaspora that diagnosed from whence Black performance traditions evolved.

"Performance" emerges in African American studies as subject, method, practice, and mode of being. In work such as Hurston's, creativity, criticism, theatricality, and self-conscious performance of oneself and Blackness model how "performance" resonates through African American studies. The study of Black performance continues to bear the marks of its formal and critical foundations to mark and explore Black ingenuity. In "How It Feels to Be Colored Me," Hurston states, "I am a dark rock surged upon, and overswept but through it all, I remain myself. When covered by the waters, I am; and the ebb but reveals me again" ([1928] 2004, 1031). In this essay's form, Hurston submits play and irony as a mechanism, or method, for exploring Blackness. In contrast, however, Hurston offers a moment that is sure, solid, and god-like in its transcendence and immovability. She persists despite the washing of the water flowing like time or, more theatrically, a heavy curtain overtaking and revealing the subject. Between comma and semicolon, the "I am" stands alone, an echo of the divine declaration "I am that I am." The confident insistence, "The ebb but reveals me again," delicious in its assonance and concision, presents also a seething defiance and wet love of self. Blackness as internal certainty and external envisioning is given and taken like the wave, while the dark rock remains unmoved. Thus slipping between fixities, Hurston counters her "fast brown—warranted not to rub or run"—as assigned by whiteness a few lines previous, with her own assured stability ([1928] 2004, 1031). She feels her race unassailed by surges and tempests that would annihilate her. The gritted teeth of her brown growl in the repeated *r*'s of "rub" and "run" gives way to the open sounds of a prayer. Through language play and irony, movement and stability, Hurston models changeability as form in the performance of a yet resilient Black identity.

Blackness, then, increases the capacity of performance to encompass display, practice, and complex ways of being. The word "performance" offers a consideration of what Black people do, what Black people make, what Black people *are*, that is, rather, *how we do being*. Black performance reverses the way the performance studies scholar Richard Schechner defines performance on a scale of "being, doing, and showing doing." Schechner explains that "'showing doing' is performing: pointing to, underlining, and displaying doing" (2002, 22). Showing doing bears the character of making known to another. Blackness collapses this scale. "Being" as grand existence is not separate from or prior to performance. Blackness makes things known to another without the intentionality of the doer or be-er. That is, Blackness overperforms; it does extra work, performing itself. At the same time, Blackness calls up a performance of the self that makes one audience to one's own selfhood. The position of oneself in witnessing this performance has been the subject of Black philosophies of selfhood, consciousness, and identity. In studies of Blackness, performance renders the making of identity and meaning a mobile, shifting, and blending state and enterprise. Performance renders Blackness both an experiential and an epistemological mode. The performance of oneself and the awareness of oneself in performing Blackness and implicated in the performance of Blackness constitutes an autoperformativity that can be both internally and externally motivated. In W. E. B. Du Bois and Frantz Fanon, autoperformativity is embodied in "double-consciousness" (Du Bois 1903) and a "third-person . . . racial epidermal schema" (Fanon [1967] 2008, 90–95). To oversimplify these Black structures of being, being seen, looking at, and doing the self, Du Bois describes a seeing oneself through the eyes of others; Fanon, a condition of having to know or reckon with the self in terms of the color of one's skin as connected to definitions of race. These structures of being as related to looking, to seeing, to doing, and to audience situate performance at the foundation of twentieth-century Western philosophies of Blackness, philosophies that continue to resonate in research in African American studies. The Veil, second-sight, and doubled and externalized self-awareness articulate Black ways of performing Blackness and Blackness performing wherein the perpetrator of each action and state shifts in position and activity—or occupies more than one at a time. Further, Du Bois and Fanon consider how one becomes audience and witness to the impacts of one's Blackness on one's environment. Often, intentional forms of creative display play in the spaces between versions of self and the environment.

Embodiment and materiality remain central in theories of performance because of its focus on doing. By "materiality," I mean the physical existence of matter and substance as significant. These include the presence and personhood of the performer as an entity and not only an idea. As practice, performance is also intellectual and spiritual. Performance practice as a creative mode is critical and theoretical, like the scholarship that attends to it. Even the existential disembodied self, not material at all, becomes a point of play. The body as memory, as display, as receptor, as creator, as bonded, as free exists with impact on culture and knowledge. Black performers are always creating. Black performers create. The present tense in motion and in place both play here, marking continuity and intervention. Consciousness, selfhood, and embodiment are merely linked. The position of the self in its awareness is neither static nor forgone, neither set nor necessary. She or he is necessarily neither resistant nor complicit. That is, performance, itself, though invoked in contemplations of existence and ontology, does not predetermine the character of the subject or subjectivity. It tends to allow embodiment in its proliferating forms to posit meaning.

The breath, muscle, sometimes voicing, conventions, and rhythms of the stage inflect musical performance, and vice versa. Music is often understood through composition, sound, and feeling. Musicians' performance and their rendering of the music itself fall at and between these conventional measures of writing and reception. The musicians' making of the music, rendering of the music, relationship to their instruments, and display in play offer embodied layers of music as performance and performance of music—Hurston's drum playing and played upon. Musicians demonstrate masterful physical and sonic methods of receding into their music and/or standing out in front of it, making musical performance complex in relation to sound. Their

PERFORMANCE STEPHANIE LEIGH BATISTE

impact is at once embedded and explicit, emotional and sonic, resonant and displayed in an infinite spectrum of registers. Black musicians' capacity to both disappear into the music, deemphasizing their own presence, and emerge out of it in myriad ways mirrors the playing of identity in the simultaneous presence of multiple creative productions seen and unseen, perceived and below consciousness. The "style" and theatricality of musical performance varies significantly according to performer and genre. These performance choices also constitute genre so powerfully as to define modes of Black being and eras of Black life as Black musical genres, as blues, jazz, soul, hip-hop, and so on.

In postulating aesthetics of Black performance, critics often consider how performance is particularly Black as well as how Black people might be particularly performative. That is, part of the use of performance prompts consideration of what Black performance *is* as well as what and how it *does*. W. E. B. Du Bois's notion of Black theater as by, about, and for the people often serves as a guide toward what performances might be assessed for such characteristics. Sketching "Black features" of performance can teeter toward reductive, essentialized thinking but has been a process of identifying what Black performance *is*, even as these attempts also acknowledge its movement and mutability. In ironic tension with pinning down identifiable characteristics of Black performance, improvisation, then, always emerges as a component of Black performance principles in reflection of this tendency toward change. Several theorists of Black performance aesthetics, including Paul Carter Harrison, Brenda Dixon Gottschild, and Thomas DeFrantz, begin with language, movement, origin and capacity, and music as foundational Black performance modes.

The unique characteristics of Black performance—that is, what it is and how it can be identified—are often attributed to not just its creators but also from whence particular features and drives derive. The theorists Paul Carter Harrison (1989) and Brenda Dixon Gottschild (1996) identify "Africanisms," retentions from a broadly African past, in Black culture and performance as foundational to Black performance aesthetics. Questions of origin and diaspora lead to discussions of influences, the process of transmission, retention, and change of cultural forms over space and time. Likewise, questions of aesthetics insist on considerations of history and exchange as well as innovation and change in performance forms.

Harrison argues that Black aesthetics in the New World are primarily African based. Dogon, Akan, and Yoruba systems of thought emerge as cultural and critical epistemologies. Such aesthetics eschew realism. Harrison in "Mother/word: Black Theater in the African Continuum: Word/Song as Method" defines "Mother/word as in fore/word or first/word or *the* word as in *truth*" (1989, xi). Roughly translated, "Nommo" is the divine power of the word. Song is the "intrinsic value of heightened language" (xix). Harrison explains that "ritual is the affective technique common to most theatrical exercises in the world" through which humans access and translate the divine (xii). The word is a "creative elixir—Nommo Force—that activates the dramatic mode (context of experience) and reveals the symbolic gesture of the Mask (characterization)" (xii). Within this dramatic mode are "references to myths, common experience and significations that define the collective universe" (xii). The mask and masking in African-based traditions are significantly different from connotations of masking at play in Western symbolic derivations of minstrelsy as a performance tradition, survival strategy, or burden of invisibility. Word/song includes polyrhythm, cyclical repetition, onomatopoeia, and call and response as a selection of its characteristics and is manifest in spoken and gesticulated communication. African dancing deities in danced religions bring the ritual impact that Harrison identifies in speech, poetry, literature, and music to dance and embodiment. Brenda Dixon Gottschild explains that gesture and choreography are a physical manifestation of Nommo with specific African impacts and priorities (1996, 11). Elucidations of Africanisms in African American performance emphasize ritual as the link between the divine and social transformation, the past and everyday realities.

Twentieth- and twenty-first-century African American performance aesthetics reveal Africanist rhythms elaborated in Black postmodernisms, such as bebop, jazz, and hip-hop finding their way into Black performance generally. Thomas DeFrantz describes the "break," a Black characteristic innovated in such forms as "an intellectual concept and aesthetic capacity accessed by performers in contemporary music, drama, and dance" (2010, 30–37). Breaking the beat is a consideration of rhythm and tempo inspired by music and time/ing. "It is where an insistent beat is interrupted by a flash of contradictory rhythmic ideas" (31). The "break" encompasses both the pause of possibility and the "unexpected, uncontrolled" moment (31). It combines the opposition of silence and chaos in sound and movement. It incorporates grounding and flow, repetition and spontaneity. It is always impending, bearing on futurity. While emphasizing the familiarity of the break owing to its ubiquity in African American forms, DeFrantz explains, "the break is also an intellectual concept deployed by artists to extend the possibilities of theatrical form" (32). He describes, "African American aesthetic practices consistently break open performative structures to imagine unprecedented possibilities" in genre, song, and sound; stage, dance, and space; word, drama, and time; body, hip-hop, and vision (32–36; quote on 32).

The term "performance" has been deployed to elucidate complex critical areas and themes in Black experience, culture, and knowledge. A brief overview reveals foundational perspectives, approaches, and controversies as well as burgeoning sites of study that emerge from such research to signal the transformations of performance in African American studies. Beverly Robinson has identified key spaces that Black performers "ritualized for survival" in the development of creative production in the West. These include the slave ship, fields and the plantation, the pulpit, and the proscenium stage (2002, 332–44). For Robinson, performance, an activity of assembled bodies, claims literal space by making use of it for Black survival. In some ways, the concept of survival understands performance as a means of resistance. When considering performance as a way of doing self, this orientation might seem particularly oppositional and positioned in relation to oppression. Ritualizing space is also a gesture of resilience toward freedom. Ritual complicates a resistance approach to Black performance in its emphasis on spirit or inner force, community, and the divine. Based in spirit practice rather than opposition or modes of protection and escape, ritual enacts a relationship between practice and transformation for the individual, community, and society. Black anthropologists helped pioneer postmodern ethnography as performance practice in the tradition of Hurston. Studies of everyday performance, social activisms, and staged performances before and with assembled audiences help animate the ready slide between selfhood, identity, community, action, and theatricality.

Harry J. Elam Jr. evaluates how Black theater and performance operate as a device in artifice and in life and what these operations do. These useful frameworks, including (1) social protest and the politics of representation, (2) exploration of gender, (3) memory and tradition, and (4) race as performance / performance

PERFORMANCE   STEPHANIE LEIGH BATISTE

of race, provide for broad identification and analysis of Black performance (2001, 5–14). Studies of performance can be understood, too, as signaling what Black performance does. E. Patrick Johnson (2003) explains how Blackness as performance accrues such materiality that both Black and non-Black performers take it up. Black performance and Blackness as performance offer extensive material for display and appropriation. Politics of appropriation lead to considerations of authenticity in manifestations of Blackness by Black and non-Black performers. Black queer studies and gender studies posit the intersectional construction and contemplation of identity and identification as performance in activating concepts of nonnecessary characteristics of sexed and sexual beings and doings. Sexuality studies and queer embodiments underscore not only the diversity of staged traditions but also the shifting character of the nature of being and performing being in critical understandings of Black life. Literature as a site and medium of performance appears in the study of its content and textual features as specific as punctuation. Punctuation reveals performativity of speech, text, and typeface in literary studies and in art. Punctuation performs in aural, oral, and visual capacities and on the page in a coextension of visual art. Stage traditions and sonic performance come together in performance forms. A theatrical jazz aesthetic describes ritual performance practices that accomplish *transformation* through a use of queerness and jazz as form. To dismantle indexical measures of Blackness where performance itself indicates authenticity, scholars attend to manifestations of sensibility and affect such as "sincerity," "trauma," or "joy" in the lived experience of Blackness. Performance has been used to center Blackness in the consideration of its own subjectivities in order to contemplate proximity to power and strategies of resistance to oppression and forces of annihilation. Focused on centering considerations of Black power and resistance in creativity and innovation in performance, Black theater, film, and public embodiments are also used to illuminate the Black radical tradition.

"Performance" allows actors and agents to remain involved in the making of their own lives and, as such, to always *be* positing meaning. The research in the interdisciplinary field proliferates too quickly to catch in brief description. And yet this seems to be the very promise of Black performance and its mutable methods and manifestations.

# 32

## Philosophy

Lewis R. Gordon

"Philosophy," conventional wisdom has it, began in Ancient Greece. A problem with that line of thinking, however, is that an accepted view is not necessarily a correct one. A moment's reflection on the word, its history, and the political circumstances leading to its Euromodern reception should occasion a long pause. "Ancient Greeks," for instance, are an invention of early modern Europe that gained much currency in the French and German Enlightenment to refer to ancient Greek-speaking peoples of the Mediterranean. Those people included northern Africans, western Asians, and southern peoples of what became later known as Europe. As the presumption is that the earliest practice of philosophy was among the ancient Athenians, the term acquired a near sacred association with Hellenic peoples. Understanding that the Hellens were but one group among other Greek-speaking peoples to have emerged in antiquity reveals the fallacy. It is as if to call English-speaking peoples of the present "English." The confusion should be evident. A product of Euromodern imagination, with a series of empires ranging from the ancient Macedonian to the Seleucidian empires laying claim to the coveted metonymic intellectual identity for posterity, Ancient Greeks stand as a supposed "miracle" from which a hitherto dark and presumably intellectually limited humanity fell sway to "civilization."

"Human beings," *homo sapiens*, have, however, been around for about two hundred thousand years, and evidence of intellectual leaps abound for at least a hundred thousand. As the species has at times faced extinction, what has secured human survival is intelligence. The idea that the species remained limited until it reached the Mediterranean is far-fetched. But more, a few thousand years of writings before those inscribed in Greek should not be ignored. If they were not the beginning, on whose ideas did ancient Greek-speaking people's reflections rest? The obvious answer is *their ancients*, and for them, as for those of us who sift through the past today, we should bear in mind that they are both not "us" and are "us." They are not us in the sense of a single line of cultural inheritance, yet they are "us" in that their achievements belong to all of us, to humanity. Thus, this reflection on philosophy from the African philosopher Antef held as much resonance for ancient Athenians as it does for readers of today:

> [The seeker of wisdom is one] whose heart is informed about these things which would be otherwise ignored, the one who is clear-sighted when he is deep into a problem, the one who is moderate in his actions, who penetrates ancient writings, whose advice is [sought] to unravel complications, who is really wise, who instructed his own heart, who stays awake at night as he looks for the right paths, who surpasses what he accomplished yesterday, who is wiser than a sage, who brought himself to wisdom, who asks for advice and sees to it that he is asked advice.
> (Inscription of Antef, Twelfth Dynasty, KMT / Ancient Egypt, 1991–1782 BCE)

More than a millennium before the emergence of the pre-Socratic philosophers (sixth century BCE), Antef's reflections offer no doubt about the existence of early philosophical thought. Even more, his reference to other "ancient" writings offers additional intellectual resources that, given the conceptual framework of "upper" KMT (Greek name: Egypt) being southward in his context, lead us into a world in which the night offered the beauty and wonder from the stars and the journey of human reflection. As the architect, philosopher, and physician Imhotep pondered seven hundred years earlier, the night sky in Antef's time also stimulated awe and reflection, as it could for those of us today who embrace such an opportunity.

Though the word "philosophy" is often translated as "the love of wisdom"; it represents an important meeting of language and worlds, as the Greek word *philia* (fondness or devotional love) was conjoined with the transformed word *sophia* (wisdom), which emerged from the MdwNtr (language of KMT) word *sebayit* (wise teachings). The related word *seba* (to teach or to be wise) was transformed through the Greek tendency to transform the MdwNtr *b* to *ph* or, in English, *f*. The intellectual meeting of worlds that met in every other respects was not new, and what should be noticeable is that throughout such meetings, reflections on what such intellectual work was about immediately followed. Antef, after all, was reflecting both on philosophy and on the philosopher. Later on, in the *Symposium* (ca. 385–370 BC), Plato (actual name Aristokles) similarly reflected on the love of wisdom and the difficulty of loving its lover. Thus, the origins of philosophy on the continent in which humanity evolved versus the one that subsequently dominated much of the globe are not as distant as many scholars of their subsequent intellectual histories lead most people to believe. Beyond that south-to-north movement, there were, as well, many others in which human beings, as thinking creatures, produced ideas while they migrated in every direction. Wherever human beings were afforded sufficient time for reflection, ideas on organization and the makeup of reality followed.

Philosophy, then, should be separated into the plethora of human efforts to understand our relationship to reality, which includes each other, and the subsequent *professionalizing* of that task into the academically formalized discipline housed in universities today. This distinction offers additional challenges, since it is possible for the latter to become so focused that it ceases to offer intellectual contributions beyond the demonstration of skill. The former thus always speaks to humanity, whereas the latter only at times does so, and not always intentionally.

What philosophers do is also a complicated and fluid matter. Some proponents regard its activity as a battle for truth. In that version, one "wins" through "knocking down" one's "opponents," through demonstrating the "weakness" of their arguments. A problem with that approach, however, is that it is possible to win arguments, become hegemonic, and yet be wrong in the sense of adhering to what is false. Another model of philosophy holds metaphors of midwifery, communication, collaboration, collective curiosity—in short, working together to appreciate, hear, see, and understand, and at times, even discover, what we often fail to engage or comprehend. In this version, philosophy is not only a communicative practice but also a social enterprise of expanding human intellectual potential. In this sense, philosophy is humanity reaching beyond itself. It is no accident, for instance, that many of its metaphors, from antiquity to recent times, are about the human struggle to escape the prison of ignorance.

The focus of philosophy in different parts of the world over the ages varied according to the priorities of where it was practiced. Among ancient East Africans, for instance, astronomy, architecture, and medicine offered paths to philosophical reflection, and the complicated negotiation of power among increasingly dense populations of peoples occasioned much reflection on laws, balance, truth, and justice. In KMT, the concept of *Ma'at* addressed such themes. Among the Greek-speaking peoples, *dikaiosuné* was similar. In Asia, similar concerns about learning, order, rule, and respect emerged, especially in Ruism, most known today as Confucianism. A trend of perfecting or at least improving marked these developments, and questions flowed over the ages as human beings struggled with concerns of eternity and change, appearance and reality, right and wrong, to a point of generating questions that, despite the various preferences across philosophical groups and individual philosophers, amount to familiar concerns with matters ranging from nature and the natural to the knowable and the possible. Questions about what must be, what exists, for what human beings should aspire, the meaning and possibility of freedom, proper, correct, or justified forms of reasoning, the reach and conditions of knowledge, the good life, whether reality has a purpose or purposes, the best organization of power, and the value of all things, among many more, connect philosophers across time and cultural divides. These questions generate various "fields" in which thinkers address them under the now specialized terms of metaphysics, ontology, ethics, logic, transcendentalism, epistemology, aesthetics, political philosophy, axiology, and approaches such as phenomenology, existentialism, vitalism, pragmatism, and hermeneutics. Drawing on and extending beyond these are also constellations of ideas and challenges under rubrics of philosophical anthropology, philosophy of culture, philosophy of history, Africana or African diasporic philosophy, feminism, decolonial philosophy, and philosophy of liberation. These are not exhaustive, but they give a sense of the fecundity of philosophical expression.

There has been and unfortunately continues to be, however, the use of such reflections also for rationalizations and evasions of human responsibility not only to each other but also to other aspects of reality. Philosophy, thus, also historically struggled with, as we see from the beginning of this entry, its own integrity. Euromodern colonialism, for instance, stimulated lines of ethnophilosophical movements often disguised to themselves simply as "universal" and "primary." Thus, European Continental rationalism and Anglophone empiricism led paths to what are today known as Anglo-analytical philosophy and (European) Continental philosophy. African and Asian philosophies orient themselves in professional philosophy in relation to these, and First Nations of many kinds among colonized nations stand in relation to these hegemonic organizations of philosophical identity. Additionally, Euromodern interpretations of the history of philosophy have led to a false presupposition of neat divides, as Peter J. Park demonstrates in his *Africa, Asia, and the History of Philosophy: Racism in the Formation of the Philosophical Canon* (2013), between religious and theological thought on the one hand and secular naturalistic philosophy on the other. Despite secular disavowals of conceptual and normative commitments from Christian, Jewish, and Islamic resources, many normative presuppositions of these "world religions" could be found in what has become known as "Western" philosophical thought. Similar influences on contemporary philosophical work across the global south can be found from traditions such as Akan or Yoruba in Africa or Hinduism, Buddhism, or Daoism in Asia or Aztec or Mayan in Central America. Last, but not exhaustively, universality and primary or first questions made epistemology take the stage in Euromodern philosophy as first philosophy. Much of what is called Anglo-analytical philosophy and Eurocontinental philosophy rest on this presupposition, though there has been no shortage of internal critics. A crucial point of convergence, however, is that while debates emerged over whether epistemology, ethics, or metaphysics should stand as first or *fundamental* philosophy, the people whose humanity was challenged in Euromodernity were not afforded the luxury of thinking through which was ultimately prevalent—since, as many learned, each philosophical road led to another. Instead, a historical question of humanity came to the fore: in an age of challenged membership in the human world, philosophical anthropology proved inevitable.

Germane to this volume of keywords in African American studies, there are philosophical questions of "application" and endemic concerns. The former simply applies philosophical presuppositions to the study of African Americans. The latter, however, questions the applicability of such presuppositions. The first presumes the universality of Euromodern philosophy. The second raises concerns of metaphilosophical critique; it places philosophy, in any form, under critical scrutiny. African Americans, after all, are also black people, and the history of ideas and science offers no short supply of scandalous rationalizations of their degradation. History has also shown that black people, as philosophers and social scientists from the Haitian Anténor Firmin (2000) to the African American W. E. B. Du Bois and many others have argued, do not always fit into many disciplinary norms except as "problems." In short, their "fit" is paradoxically one of not fitting. A theodicean form of reasoning about application emerges, in which a discipline is presumed intrinsically complete and valid, which means failure to fit or, perhaps more accurately, "behave" is an expression of the subject's infelicity. Something "must be," in a word, "wrong" with such people.

W. E. B. Du Bois observed, in *The Souls of Black Folk* (1903), doubled levels of experience and research in such circumstances. Phenomenologically, there is double-consciousness: the realization of how black people are perceived and the lived reality of black consciousness. Where the system of knowledge, the philosophical presuppositions, is questioned, a movement of realized contradictions results in a dialectical expansion of knowledge. This dialectical movement, of examining the contradictions inherent in *making people into problems at epistemological, sociological, and political levels*, is a core insight of the kind of philosophy that took a path from black philosophy to African American philosophy to Africana philosophy. This kind of philosophy takes three fundamental questions posed by black people's relation to Euromodernity seriously: (1) What does it mean to be human? (2) What is freedom? (3) How are justificatory practices justifiable in light of the historical and continued challenges to reason posed by colonialism, enslavement, and racism not only as material and political projects but also as intellectual enterprises? The third question stimulated a unique branch of inquiry, as it raised the question of whether material impositions entail epistemic ones. Put differently, what could be done of reason when colonialism produced colonial forms? This led to a crisis of reason. Working backward, each question is symbiotically linked to the other, for dehumanization entails studying humanization; fighting against enslavement demands study of freedom; and the kinds of reasoning involved in all three, including offering a critique of reason itself, bring them together.

Africana philosophy has a rich history of debates on the questions of being human, free, and reasoning outlined here. The Martinican revolutionary psychiatrist and philosopher Frantz Fanon, in *Black Skin, White Masks* (1967), was among those who formulated the philosophical plight for Black philosophers (capitalized because thinking for him was a matter of agency and committed struggle, which transformed racial objects into human subjects): where even reason is made unreasonable, the challenge for African American philosophers (and by extension all in the African diaspora and those designated "black") is to reason with unreasonable reason *reasonably*. This strange formulation brings to the fore ironically a relationship with philosophy beyond Euromodernity in a connection with the ancient Antef and, as well, to descendants whom none of us today will ever know.

This concluding reflection brings forth an additional element of philosophical concern. The movements from double-consciousness to a dialectical relationship with the Euromodern world pose the following. Euromodernity produced a special form of alienation through the transformation of whole groups of people into categories of "native," "enslaved," "colonized," and "black." Such people suffer a unique form of melancholia (bereavement from separation), as they are indigenous to a world that rejects them by virtue of making them into problems. Their "home" is, unfortunately, a homeless one. Realization of that problem as a function of Euromodernity is also a form of transcending it, which entails two considerations. The first is that the particularizing of Euromodernity raises the question of other *modernities*. The question of what it means to be modern shifts, then, to a question of time and the future. "Primitive," after all, means belonging to the past. Once posed as having a future, African American philosophical reflection also becomes an expression of Afromodernity. This means, then, the possibility of agency in history and responsibility for a future whose specificities are open. The struggle with reason, then, becomes a form of reason beyond reason as presently conceived, and in turn, it leads to metaphilosophical reflection of African American and Africana philosophy as the paradox of philosophy being willing to transcend itself. This effort is, in effect, a call for the decolonization of philosophy, which means, then, that a critical consequence is one against philosophical parochialism (false claims of universality) and a demand for ongoing, universalizing philosophical practices in which ideas connect across disciplines, fields, and peoples without collapsing into delusions of completeness.

Philosophy, understood in this way, is also, then, despite protest throughout the ages, an expression, among others, of humanity's search, at the level of ideas about our relationship with reality, for a home to which one does not return but instead for which one searches and, along the way, builds.

**PHILOSOPHY** LEWIS R. GORDON

# 33

## Poetics

Meta DuEwa Jones

"Poetics" refers to the practice and philosophy of poetry and its history. Poetics, broadly conceived, includes poetry, oratory, elocution, art, narrative, music, and performative visual and verbal power. As Aristotle avowed, poetics involves rhetoric, aesthetics, and ethics. A poetics is, implicitly or not, a politics; it functions strategically and socially. A theory of poetics, at core, involves presentation and representation (Halliwell 1998). Both formalist and formally innovative poetics evoke the human, natural, and supernatural world. In African American studies specifically, poetry and poetics have described and decried the inhumane conditions of chattel slavery.

The origin story of poetics in African American literary history includes slavery; it also exceeds it. Human bondage is the silt, though not the sum, of many African Americans' lived experience historically. As Langston Hughes noted in his survey of more than "200 Years of American Negro Poetry," "poets and versifiers of African descent have been publishing poetry on American shores since the year 1746 when a slave woman named Lucy Terry penned a rhymed description of an Indian attack on the town of Deerfield, Massachusetts" ([1966] 1997, 90). Terry's poem "Bars Fight" was passed down orally for decades (Proper 1992). Her oratory features what I have identified as *rituals of recital* central to Black expressive modes of virtuosic storytelling that mark "poetics" as a cornerstone within the tradition (Meta Jones 2011). The unethical experience of enslavement was the immediate and arguably most influential backdrop of the earliest known African rhetoricians and versifiers in the Americas. The enslavement of African people indelibly stains the fabric of America's mythic history of its democracy. Viewing "poetics" as a keyword, one can see why the fact of this historical phenomenon, the fight against unjust labor exploitation and racialized dehumanization, and the force of its contemporary legacy would endure in the lyrics of versifiers across centuries.

For more than three hundred years, Phillis Wheatley has been a key name. Comprehending "poetics" in African American studies demands delineating her comprehensive influence. Her life story and her literary script have often served as an origin narrative for African American literary history and popular culture. This is so despite Terry's aforementioned inaugural contributions and notwithstanding Jupiter Hammon's publication of foundational poetry broadsides more than a decade before Wheatley's *Poems on Various Subjects, Religious and Moral* became the first *bound* volume by an African-*transplanted*-American to appear in print in 1773 (Wheatley 2001). A first edition of the book is showcased in the National Museum of African American History and Culture, and a photograph of its frontispiece is featured in the museum's accompanying souvenir book (Smithsonian 2016). Wheatley was, like the poet Terence she invokes in "To Macenas," an "African by birth"; she was among those bondspersons whose "equal genius" was invoked in abolitionist debates ([1773] 1989, 49). Her poetry has been the source for lively debates concerning whether its elegiac form and content subtly challenged racism and the ideology behind slavery (Foster 1993). Wheatley, for many poets and scholars, was the compass rose. She is the compass star.

*Compass rose, where does your floral finger point?* The petals point [to] where the flower flourishes, toward freedom. Robert Hayden's ode to Frederick Douglass frames freedom as "this beautiful / and terrible thing, needful to man as air" (Hayden [1966] 2013, 62). *Compass star, why must you steer Black poets' verses toward the vessels of transatlantic terror, ships harboring human cargo?* The star steers the reader, lighting a path through the dark past of slavery into its present legacy. This legacy underscores the biographer Arnold Rampersad's claim that "being black in America often complicates and even threatens the role of the poetry and the practice of poetry" (2006, xix). Or, as June Jordan, one of contemporary Black poetry's "North Stars," has phrased it, "the difficult miracle of Black poetry in America: we persist, published or not and loved or unloved. . . . Like Wheatley, we have persisted for freedom" (2002a, 185). The Compass Star and the North Star point toward "slavery" and "freedom" as key terms in poetics and in the conceptual constellation of African American studies.

Keywords are core words; they are code words. As Toni Morrison wrote in her treatise *Playing in the Dark*, "the formation of the nation necessitated coded language and purposeful restriction to deal with the racial disingenuousness and moral frailty at its heart, so too did the literature" (1992, 6). These codes have been considered essential to deciphering or explaining cultural mores and moves (Gray 2005). Yet the conditions for revolt on the slave ship—and rebellion on shore as well—also necessitated the use of coded words to obfuscate, not clarify. The kind of strategic opacity that Edouard Glissant (1997) invoked for Martinique and the Caribbean serves here. Thus, for the disciplinary mandates within Black studies, keywording is a verb, in the poet Nathaniel Mackey's (1993) sense of "othering." "Poetics" in this sense is process. "Cipher" is a verb: actively subversive coding.

For Hughes, like many artists and theorists of Africana studies, the *act* of writing was subversion; it was the necessary vessel for emancipation. Hughes also wrote of George Moses Horton, who "issued *The Hope of Liberty* [1829] while still in bondage in North Carolina" ([1966] 1997, 92). Horton was the first enslaved African American writer from the South to publish a volume of poetry. He made a modest income by selling his love poems to college students and even petitioned the president at the University of North Carolina, Chapel Hill, to barter his poetry books in order to buy his freedom. His poems on love and liberty live on in contemporary songs and societies dedicated to him (Horton 1997; Red Clay Ramblers 2001). But as Hughes scathingly laments, "Horton's books never sold enough copies . . . to buy his freedom. Perhaps this was because Freedom was often the subject of his poems, and such a subject was no more pleasing to white Southerners a hundred years ago than it is today" ([1966] 1997, 49). Horton's experience starkly contrasted Wheatley's. She "was well known throughout the New England colonies for her poems"; Hughes adds that she "wrote herself to freedom" (Hughes [1966] 1997, 90). Incidentally, as Raymond Williams notes in *Keywords: A Vocabulary of Culture and Society*, the "subsequent shift from emancipation to liberation seems to mark a shift from ideas of the removal of disabilities . . . to more active ideas of winning freedom and self-determination" (1985, 34). It is apropos, then, that "literature" and "liberation" are sequential entries in Williams's annotations. It is insightful to view the front jacket of the 1985 revised edition in which the word "LIBERATION" is emblazoned in blue violet beneath Williams's full name capitalized in white. As Joanne Gabbin (1997) observed, "The cultural movement of the 1960s and 1970s," for instance, "not only changed the way African Americans thought about their political and social status as American citizens, for the poets it also planted the seeds for a truly liberated exploration of literary possibilities." If liberation marks self-determination, then the ability to name, the assertion of the authorial signature, makes this freedom—or its lack—a form of felt knowledge, felt absence.

Hughes's succinct biography of Wheatley is punctuated with the power of names, of place, of the vocabulary of slave-trading society. His scorn is subtle, his words pitched deliberately *off* key. "Born in Senegal," Hughes writes, "Wheatley *fortunately* had been purchased at the age of seven or eight by a *kindly* master and mistress who took a *fancy* to the little black girl offered for sale on the deck of the slave ship in Boston Harbor. Of course, the tiny African spoke no English, and *nobody* knew her name. So she was given her master's name, Wheatley, and her mistress, who called her Phillis, taught her to read and write" ([1966] 1997, 49, italics mine). Keywords also point to an index, a resource, an archive. Hughes draws phrases like "kindly" master and "fancy" from the archive of slavery. Advertisements aiming to recapture fugitive slaves often featured such words.

Hughes's assertions serve threefold ambitions that dovetail my own in elucidating "poetics" as a keyword: (1) he insists, as I do, that African American (poetic) history precedes and propagates American history; (2) he asserts, as I claim, that for the nation's earliest poets, the literal terrain of freedom was sought and *sometimes* secured on literary terms; and (3) he suggests, as I demonstrate, that the primary concerns voiced by Terry, Wheatley, Horton, and others in the distant past have resurfaced in the present.

Notably, Hughes's survey of Black poets deploys a nautical motif. He sights the sea voyage to New England shores. He does not speak of rivers coursing through the diaspora; he does not scale racial mountains (Hughes [1926] 1995). Instead, he crests at the crucial point of the sea crossing. He cites a Senagalese child's miraculous survival from the shipment, in captivity, on a floating dungeon across the ocean.

Somebody. Some mother. Some father. Some brother. Some sister. Some griot. So many who loved her. Some several little Black girls knew the African (from Senegal? from Gambia?) called "Phillis" in America. The precise place of her theft from kin and kind is unknown. Yet I know—and Hughes knows, too—her family and friends knew her blessed birth name and birth place. I, too, *fancy* that she might have shared (in Wolof, perhaps?), may have secreted her cherished, coded family name with fellow captive passengers aboard the schooner *Phillis*—site of her transport, scene of her trauma, and source of her renaming by John and Susanna Wheatley.

Some poets resisted this naming practice. June Jordan, in her ars poetica "The Difficult Miracle of Black Poetry in America," rhetorically ponders, "Why did they give her that name?" (2002a, 176). The name of a slaver's ship? ~~Phillis~~'s natal name is a keyword. And our inability to retrieve and remember her name is also the lock to the *Door of No Return*. ~~Phillis~~'s legacy as a poet, in life, and in literature, is "our inheritance." What she lost, we lost, and it costs us. There is not now, nor has there ever been, "free shipping." As the poet Dionne Brand notes, "Our inheritance in the Diaspora is to live in this inexplicable space. That space is the measure of our ancestor's step through the door toward the ship" (2002, 3). Jordan apprises and revises Wheatley's designation, calling her "Phillis Miracle Wheatley." She highlights her race and gender, noting, "was the second female to be published in America. And the miracle begins in Africa" (2002a, 176). It is often noted that in Greek, *poetes*, denotes a "maker, author, poet." Here, Jordan, like Hughes, emphasizes Wheatley's ancestral origins, her diasporic distances. Both remind the reader that this foundational author of the African American poetic tradition is truly an African diaspora poetess. Marvel, they say, at this miracle of maroonage. The sites of maroonage, *cimarronaje*, like the sources of poetics, are historical and cartographic. Poetics makes and marks the site of Wheatley as a part of a literal and metaphorical tradition of Black diasporic maroon communities.

Time's passage has changed the topography somewhat, yet Black writers are still, to paraphrase Ralph Ellison (1986), going to the (same) territory. Their poems and statements of poetics travel to and through the Middle Passage and traverse the "~~Free~~" State. This evokes queries pertinent to "poetics" as a quarry, as a conceptual cornerstone: Can a poetics of African American studies produce liberation? If so, how so? What kind of Black magical, miraculous freedom from fetters can be conjured by the mastery of verse letters? How do Black Bardic poets unleash what the scholar Keith Leonard (2006) has identified as their "fettered genius"?

One possible liberatory answer provided by the poet Audre Lorde is to fuse ideas with feeling, to harness the epistemic value of emotion. We "come closest to this combination in our poetry," Lorde writes, and this fusion is a "keystone for survival" (1984, 36). Keystones, key feelings, key thoughts, keywords, and key poems turn open the lock on our liberation. Lorde continues, "our feelings were not meant to survive. . . . But women have survived. As poets." Our power, she insist, springs from "our dreams that point the way to freedom . . . through our poems." "Poetry is not a luxury," then, but the lever for liberation (ibid.).

Lorde's words are wrung from the long line of historical and contemporary poets who have crafted a poetics that turns toward the fight, or flight, for freedom. As we have witnessed, that battle entails a literal fight to read and write during the antebellum period. It also entails a politically motivated flight toward literary and aesthetic freedom grounded in some of the sociocultural dicta of the Black Arts Movement (BAM) or both coursing through and soaring beyond any imposed proscriptions on the African American writer's imaginative life and work, characterized by poetry of the "Third Renaissance" or New Black Renaissance and Post-Black aesthetics

deeply indebted to BAM-era innovations (Gabbin 1997; Crawford 2017).

This variety indicates that the experience of (*European*) slavery or colonialism should not serve as the only origin narrative for the engaged presence of African-descended peoples in the Americas, as Ivan Van Sertima ([1976] 2003) asserted more than four decades ago. Nevertheless, poets and scholars such as Major Jackson and Evie Shockley have observed a millennial turn toward "historical poems by African Americans" with "a noticeable increase" in poetry collections "treating the era, the institution, the condition of slavery" (Shockley 2011, 792). Moreover, these poets represent a range of aesthetics from formalist sonnets to more formally innovative, experimental approaches to poetic language. Evie Shockley cites several poetry collections, including Fred D'Aguiar's *Bloodlines* (2015), Thylias Moss's *Slave Moth* (2006), Vievee Francis's *Blue-Tail Fly* (2006), Camille Dungy's *Suck on the Marrow* (2010), Douglass Kearney's "Swimchant for Nigger Mer-folk (An Aquaboogie Set in Lapis)" (2009), and NourbeSe Philip's *Zong!* (2008). I would add to this genre poetic treatments of the Amistad case evident in *American Sublime* by Elizabeth Alexander (2005) and *Ardency: A Chronicle of the Amistad Rebels* by Kevin Young (2012), and Kwame Dawes's Requiem (1996), a collection of ekphrastic poems based on the visual artist's Tom Feeling's Middle Passage, is also notable. I would like to turn to a recent collection by the poet Drea Brown, *Dear Girl, a Reckoning*, for example, that includes "sonnets" that "conjure" and rememory Phillis Wheatley as well as concrete poems that ask and answer "questions after [her transit] aboard a 'cross-section of the schooner phillis'" (2015, 29). Slave ships such as the schooner *Phillis* were spaces of horror, and yet, as Brown writes, "reader this is my hope that in voyage across / Churning waters in the filth and forgotten self there were moments of warmth / and benevolence" (29). This hope, this imaginative leap across the sea in rememory, is the province of artists and of poets especially. Therein lies poetry's power as a portal to African American literary and cultural history. This is what Roman Jakobson (1987) noted as "poeticity"—the presence of the poetic function.

And this poetic function is present in the realm of literary tradition as well as in music and art. In fact, the most pervasive influence in which poetics is heard, read, and experienced contemporarily is not in book form but through sound waves, sound bites, and social and visual media. Hip-hop culture is a cipher of oceanic proportions, crossing currents and frequencies of lingua, rhythm, and sound—the very currency of poetics and a lyric passport to global communities. The riffs and remembrances of poets reveal that "slavery," "slaveholding shores," and "ships" are loaded terms. The ship and the sea are queer spaces. As Omise'eke Tinsley has persuasively avowed, "Wateriness is metaphor, and history too. The brown-skinned, fluid-bodied experiences now called blackness and queerness surfaced in intercontinental, maritime contacts hundreds of years ago: in the seventeenth century, in the Atlantic Ocean" (2008, 191). So, too, is the omnifarious and fluid tradition of "poetics" in the African diaspora. I conclude, then, with one of the more prominent contemporary hip-hop emcees, the poet Kendrick Lamar. In his single "HiiiPower" (2011), Lamar concludes each of the song's three verses by riffing on the slave ship and the art of the lyricist as composer, as architect, engaged in an art as ancient and enduring as Kemet's pyramids. In the concluding couplet of the first verse, Lamar asserts, "I be off the slave ship, / Building pyramids, writing my own hieroglyphs." In the second, he commands, "So get up off that slave ship, / Build your own pyramids, write your own hieroglyphs," and in the third verse, he insists, "'Cause we been off them slave ships, / Got our own pyramids, write our own hieroglyphs." Kendrick Lamar's movement from the lyric *I* (be off that slave ship) to the imperative (and implied) *you* (get up off that slave ship) and to the final collective and reflective *we* (been off them slave ships) demonstrates the spirit of rebellion that Black artists move with.

This movement is *not* made from the subjugated position of poet-as-slave or poet-as-property. Rather, beneath the Black banner on which "poetics" as a keyword is figuratively stitched are phrases that capture the honored position of poetry in African American literary history: the poet-as-rebel, poet-as-word-warrior, poet-as-word-welder, engaged in making poems as word-weaponry, poems as a word-world, poems as a Black world (Baraka 1991). This represents the practice of poetry as a form of *black visionary alchemy* through which Black poets continue to sharpen the sickle of their imaginations, cutting a swath through the thicket of physical, mental, and spiritual enslavement: "None but ourselves can free the mind. Mind is your only ruler, sovereign" (Garvey [1937] 1990, 791). "Sovereignty," too, is a signifying keyword.

Such sovereignty signals a poetics of independence that seeks more than citizenship in an African, an African American, or a Black nation. Instead, Black poets trouble the very waters in which the hyphenated citizenry called "African-America" has been set afloat—as the watershed pervasive critical acclaim of Claudia Rankine's long prose poem *Citizen: An American Lyric* indicates (2014).

Leaping from a poetry of enslavement at the beginning of the essay, through a quest for a poetics of liberation, to a poetics of hip-hop underscores the point that all these are forms of "HiiiPower" poetry and poetics. Authors and artists alike can harness this *power* when we remember in the beginning was the word. And the word was life. And the word was lyric. And the lyric was poetry. And the poem was a song in the key of life. And key to life.

# 34

## Police

Bryan Wagner

The term "police" derives from *polis*, a Greek word meaning "city-state." In its original meaning, "police" refers to the state's responsibility to protect public welfare. "Police" does not officially appear in the English language until the mid-eighteenth century, when it is adapted from French, and it is not used colloquially to refer to the civil institution tasked with enforcing laws and detecting crime ("the police") until the nineteenth century.

The word "police" does not appear in the U.S. Constitution, but the concept was discussed in contemporary writings on the function of government. In these writings, it was argued that the state's police powers were analogous to the individual's natural right to self-defense. When individuals were attacked, they had the right to defend themselves, and when society was attacked, it had the same right to self-defense by whatever means. Police powers were necessary to preserve the peace of society. Without them, there was no way for society to defend itself against imminent threats to public health and safety (Dubber 2005).

In federal and state courts, these discretionary powers were justified by imagining threat scenarios that required immediate preventive action. In some cases, these threats were objects, whether rickety buildings or ticking time bombs. In others, they were dangerous persons, such as vagrants or fugitive slaves. In *Prigg v. Pennsylvania* (1842), for example, Justice Joseph Story cites the fugitive slave as an exemplary object for the police power. According to Story, the immediate threat posed by fugitive slaves was beyond dispute. Because their very existence was sufficient to disturb the peace of society, fugitive slaves could stand not only as a specific target for policing but also as an axiomatic example that demonstrated the necessity of police as a fundamental principle of governance.

The threat posed by the recalcitrant or runaway slave was important to the development of modern police departments in the United States. This fact has not always been recognized. It is still sometimes argued that modern police forces appeared first in the 1840s and 1850s in cities on the northeastern seaboard, such as Boston and New York. This argument ignores the fact that southern cities such as Charleston and New Orleans had similarly equipped police forces as early as the 1780s. In these southern police forces, officers wore uniforms. They were paid salaries rather than fees. They were armed with swords and guns, and they were authorized to use these weapons in the course of duty. The first modern police forces in the United States, in other words, were not established for the general maintenance of the public peace in rapidly industrializing cities. Rather, they were designed for a more specific purpose: the restraint of urban slave populations.

This genealogy changes our sense of the institutional history of police departments in the United States, and it forces us to rethink how we understand "police" as a legal principle. Police institutions in the slave states had to be justified in some way. Arguments had to be made for the police, and these arguments, more often than not, asserted the practical necessity of police by referring to the general threat posed by the slave population. In New Orleans in the 1830s, for example, there was a campaign to disarm the police. It was argued that having armed police on the street was not a prerequisite for modernization but instead a remnant of colonial barbarism. The police replied by publicizing the threats to public safety posed by disobedient slaves in the city and fugitive slaves in the swamp. If you take the guns away from the police, they argued, who will defend you against the rebel slaves who are the natural enemies of society? Police authority in the United States was staked from the start on the mortal threat posed by the slave (Wagner 2009, 58–115).

After emancipation, police powers were crucial to the state's effort to extract labor from ex-slaves. Misdemeanor statutes against vagrancy required that persons unable to prove their gainful employment were subject to a fine. If vagrants lacked the resources to pay the fine, they were forced to work on the chain gang. This arrangement allowed police officers and magistrates to act as de facto labor agents for the state. Like statutes concerned with fugitive slaves, vagrancy was cited by jurists as a self-evidently legitimate occasion for the exercise of police power. The danger posed by vagrants was considered sufficient to justify preventive measures even when no crime was committed. Legal protections, including the new constitutional considerations of due process and equal protection, were irrelevant in cases where summary arrests were warranted in this way.

The police power is also the legal principle under which racial segregation was legislated in neighborhoods, schools, and semipublic conveyances such as buses and trains. It was decided in *Plessy v. Ferguson* (1896), for example, that racial segregation was a legitimate "exercise of [the] police power" (163 U.S. 537, 544). In response to the claim that segregation laws would allow application of arbitrary rules—forcing railways, for instance, to have separate cars for people with different hair colors—the Supreme Court cautioned that "every exercise of the police power must be reasonable, and extend only to such laws as are enacted in good faith for the promotion of the public good" (*id.* at 550). Racial

segregation statutes met this standard according to the Court's definition of public necessity. Under the police power, such laws were legitimate, as their aim was to protect the peace by promoting "the public good."

Vagrancy and segregation statutes are only two examples of the ways in which officers on the street were given summary discretion under the police power. At the turn of the twentieth century, Ida B. Wells-Barnett characterized this discretion specifically as a racial dispensation, noting that "policemen" remained "secure in the firm belief that they could do anything to a Negro that they wished," whether or not "the peace" had been "broken" (1900, 5–6). This structural vulnerability to police violence described by Wells-Barnett has remained a constant feature of public life in the United States. Even as vagrancy and segregation statutes were struck down in the 1960s and 1970s, federal and state courts remained committed to the police power as a bedrock principle in their jurisprudence, which meant that the concept could still be invoked as the basis for aggressive prosecution of misdemeanors. Community policing, which emphasized the flexible role of the beat patrol in maintaining the peace in urban neighborhoods, was justified as the legitimate exercise of the same authority that had previously been applied to the fugitive slave, the emancipated vagrant, the segregated passenger, and the individuals, eulogized by Wells-Barnett, who were stopped, frisked, and detained merely for standing together on the street. The lessons that Wells-Barnett drew from Robert Charles's fateful encounter with the police in 1900 remain applicable to Amadou Diallo, Oscar Grant, Michael Brown, Freddy Gray, Sandra Bland, Eric Garner, and countless others who have lost their lives in recent years.

Understanding "police" as a fundamental principle in law and as an institution in society is necessary to understanding the history of racism in the United

States—necessary but not sufficient in the sense that we also need to take into account how public consent to police institutions has come to rely on moral panics (about mugging, about narcotics) that are stoked by mass media and compounded in social science on urban pathology. Moral panic has been a central theme in the interdisciplinary cultural studies, notably in the landmark research produced in the 1960s and 1970s by the Birmingham Centre for Contemporary Cultural Studies, a research unit whose most enduring contribution is arguably the collectively authored *Policing the Crisis: Mugging, the State, and Law and Order* (Hall et al. 1978).

The research team behind *Policing the Crisis* was led by Stuart Hall, a thinker with a commitment to overcoming reductive approaches that portray law as a tool of elites, culture as an industry of mass deception, and the entire superstructure (including law and culture) as a projection of the economic mode of production. *Policing the Crisis* addresses a specific moment (or "conjuncture") in history, in this case, the moment in Great Britain in 1972–73 when police and media turned public attention to a purported epidemic of street crime. *Policing the Crisis* treats "mugging" not as a problem needing a policy solution (as statistics show there was no increase in crime) but instead as a moral panic that arose in response to a breakdown in government legitimacy after years of economic instability. In this conjuncture, Hall and his collaborators diagnose an increased reliance on violence to manage the class struggle, both directly, through police and prisons, and indirectly, through the consolidation of an authoritarian consensus that bolsters support for government as necessary defense against the alleged threat posed by outsiders. In *Policing the Crisis*, the outsiders in question are predominantly black immigrants from former colonies represented in the communications media by a racial archetype (the "mugger") imported from the United States.

Hall and his collaborators take an approach sometimes known as "labeling theory," which emphasizes the state's role in defining what counts as crime and who counts as a criminal. This is an approach with strong precedents in critical criminology, extending back to the research of Ida B. Wells-Barnett and W. E. B. Du Bois, two black scholars whose foundational contributions are frequently ignored. According to labeling theory, criminal sanctions have purposes and effects that are broadly symbolic. Criminal sanctions are concerned not only with the identification, arrest, prosecution, and punishment of individual offenders but also with the manipulation of symbolic boundaries between types of people. Recent books by historians including Khalil Muhammad (2011), Kali Gross (2006), and Sarah Haley (2016) have shown how criminal sanctions have been exploited in this symbolic capacity by lawmakers intent on reproducing the caste system associated with slavery. One reason why criminal law was indispensable to this effort was that it offered a means of racial control that could be reconciled with the demand for equal protection. On paper, laws against petty theft and vagrancy were colorblind. Their work, however, was to disguise rather than to eliminate race in law. By giving police unlimited discretion to arrest and police courts unlimited discretion to determine standards of evidence and guidelines for sentencing, criminal law authorized state functionaries to ascribe legal status and implicitly racial status. Without explicitly invoking the fact of race, criminal law could reproduce racial distinctions as an outcome of enforcement.

Scholars in black studies continue to disagree about how to characterize the relationship between slavery and crime. As scholars including Angela Davis (2003) and Michelle Alexander (2012) have argued, crime now stands as a proxy for race in contexts where it is no longer permissible to treat race as an independent variable.

In the United States, it is now less acceptable than it once was to discriminate based on race, but this does not mean that racism has disappeared. On the contrary, what it means is that the language in which racism is expressed has changed, and there is apparently nothing that means more in the new language of racism than crime. Whereas Alexander emphasizes the continuity between slavery and its aftermath, between segregation and mass incarceration, other scholars, including Ruth Wilson Gilmore (2007) and Dan Berger (2014), have questioned whether it is useful to describe the criminal justice system primarily in terms of its continuity with slavery. From the convict lease system to mass incarceration, it is essential to comprehend the ways in which policing is implicated in structural adjustments that have dictated how labor is extracted and capital is invested in response to changing circumstances.

# 35

## Popular
Rebecca Wanzo

The term "popular" is a tendentious term defined by both audience and content. A popular cultural production is generally understood as appealing to a large group of people or as designed to do so, with the mass appeal suggesting—to some people—that the popular is of lesser quality or inferior.

Part of what can make the popular "lesser" is its association with identity-based entertainment. "High" culture is problematically but frequently associated with the universal, while the popular is often seen as targeting groups such as women, children, or the working class. Ironically, the association with an identity group has also made popular texts interesting to many scholars, who see the texts as offering a possibility for subjected or minority groups to voice perspectives not found in mainstream culture. But whether these representations actually speak to the experiences and identities of these groups is a constant source of debate. In the influential 1992 essay "What Is the 'Black' in Black Popular Culture?," Stuart Hall calls attention to the fact that black popular culture is a profoundly contradictory and contested category. Given the heterogeneous and hybrid cultures of black people in the diaspora, no singular and essential blackness exists, and yet people still believe in and police boundaries over what "real" blackness can be. Locating what some people might term the "authentic" in the popular has also been challenging because capitalism shapes the conditions for mass cultural productions to spread and popular culture has traditionally been deeply intertwined with a market that often compromises the vision of artists and over-determines what circulates. While there have always been underground, local, and resistant strands, people often struggle to find, defend, or embrace a black voice entangled with commercialism that has played an indelible role in defining it. The foundational works in black popular culture typically address these tensions. Donald Bogle's *Toms, Coons, Mulattoes, Mammies, and Bucks: An Interpretative History of Blacks in American Film* (1973) acknowledges the stereotypical constraints under which so many celebrated black actors and actresses have crafted their performances in Hollywood. Tricia Rose's study of hip-hop, *Black Noise: Rap Music and Black Culture in Contemporary America* (1994), as well as many other studies of this most exported of black genres, explores how emcees negotiate tensions between capitalism and black life. Despite capitalism's often inhibiting influence on creative expression, many scholars and consumers nevertheless recognize what Mark Anthony Neal has referred to as an "aesthetic center" in black popular culture, a center that takes up a number of issues but may also be an ever-moving target (2002, 2).

Because it is hard to put a finger on the thing that can mark black popular culture as black, Hall's most profound intervention into how people often talk about black popular culture is to ask, What if we understand popular culture *not* as the "arena where we find who we really are" and "the truth of our experience"? What if instead we recognize that it is "profoundly mythic" and "a theater of popular fantasies" where "we discover and play with the identifications of ourselves, where we are imagined, where we are represented, not only to the audiences out there who do not get the message, but to ourselves for the very first time"? While Hall argues that "popular culture always has as its base in the experiences, the pleasures, the memories, the traditions of the people," his recognition of the mythic aspect of popular culture highlights how it functions as an expression of desire and fantasy (1992, 113). Thus, "real" black life may be less the essence of what black popular culture always is and more of a subsidiary. What unites African American popular cultural productions is not a demonstration of who African Americans—a heterogeneous group—"really are" but an expression of what diverse groupings of African Americans desire and resist in relationship to black identity and community, a desire that often involves struggles over black expressive culture and placing less phantasmagoric representations of blackness into the U.S. public sphere.

The black body has been both a bogeyman and an ideal vessel for expressions of white pleasure and pathos in popular culture. From minstrelsy to what Susan Douglas (2010) has identified as the vicarious pleasures of black female sassiness on television for white women, black vernacular and performance styles have been sites for white performers to play with freedom. The black subject is also a mechanism for expressions of heroism—either to save other whites from an imagined black menace or to transform the world of subjected blacks. The Ku Klux Klan saves white womanhood from black rapists in *The Birth of a Nation*; white teachers and white heroes save subjected African Americans who apparently have no heroes in their own communities in countless novels, films, and television shows. While these kinds of texts are rarely considered examples of what African American popular culture *is*, part of what African American popular culture has historically *done* is resist these representations and provide part of the foundation for what we understand as aesthetically American.

Popular culture is often described as important to understanding identity. One reason is that the most common denotation of the "popular" is that it is a cultural production that is liked by many people, and these people may often share identity characteristics. But this can be complicated by something we categorize as popular but that very few people seem to like. Hollywood film flops and failed television shows can fit this category—few people watch them, but they are still "popular" cultural productions. The second most common aspect of the definition is about genre, as some genres are created to appeal to the masses. According to this definition, even if not widely consumed, action films, romance novels, and talk shows would all fit into the category of the popular because these genres are understood as popular forms. Both the content and the means of production mark it as popular. Something could also be "popular" in one period—Shakespeare being one of the most famous examples—and then become understood as high culture over time (Levine 1990). And finally, one connotation of the term is that popular is *of* the people, sometimes produced by "the people" or at the very least substantively linked to the concerns of audiences, particularly consumers who are working class. These different notions of the popular overlap and can also be somewhat contradictory. One of the major sources of conflict in scholarship about the popular concerns a tension between the idea that media produced by what Theodor Adorno and Max Horkheimer (2002) have termed the "culture industry" replicates ideology through repetitive, standardized pleasures and serves as distraction from politics, and the possibility that subversive politics can nonetheless emerge in popular forms.

This tension between believing in the possibility of resistance and the assertion that ideology is simply maintained by popular forms runs through many discussions of black popular culture. These theoretical frameworks often hinge on an "aesthetic center" of blackness. Discussions of African American dance and music have sometimes been marked by constructions of black ability that suggest the performances emerge from something inherent to black people or some homogeneous black experience. Such discussions of tradition sometimes limit what counts as black aesthetic production. Tradition is nonetheless an important part of what counts as black popular culture, as long as it is not overly narrow. Black identity and culture in the diaspora have also been defined by a specifically oppositional subjectivity. Theorists of blackness, such as W. E. B. Du Bois, Aimé Césaire, and Frantz Fanon, have suggested that blackness is defined by and through whiteness and that the concept of whiteness developed by defining itself against indigenous groups and people of Asian and African descent (Du Bois 1903; Césaire [1972] 2000; Fanon 1952; M. Wright 2004). Notions of black popular culture inflected by a notion of blackness as foundationally oppositional thus will discuss the ways in which the aesthetic of a cultural production stands in contrast to white aesthetics or will demonstrate a self-conscious, "oppositional gaze" as a response to historical representations of black people (hooks 1992; M. Wright 2004). Other theories of black diasporic culture focus on the fact that "blackness" outside of Africa is ineradicably, as Paul Gilroy (1993) has argued, hybrid. As the documentary filmmaker Marlon Riggs memorably framed it, "black is" *and* "black ain't." Blackness has some kind of presence that is linked to memory, intersubjectivity, and material histories of inequality and dehumanization, but it cannot and should not be overly confined as a concept. But not only racist projects attempt to essentialize blackness—antiracist projects often attempt to limit or construct black identity hierarchies and can also be injurious and exclusionary. Claiming certain kinds of blackness as "real," "authentic," "traditional," or "respectable" results in this same logic being marked onto "black" popular cultural productions. But that desire for a clear and coherent blackness is clearly one of the mythic aspects of black popular culture to which black cultural producers often gesture in generative ways.

The definition of African American popular culture may seem, then, too broad, containing nothing at all. Given the diversity of African American experience, is there anything that would clearly fall outside of black popular culture if an African American creates it, even if it does not appeal to many other African Americans? The African American author Frank Yerby wrote historical romances with white protagonists, the most famous being *The Foxes of Harrow* (1946), the first novel by an African American to receive a Hollywood film adaptation. Are his books part of black popular culture since he was intentionally resisting the black protest tradition in black letters (Jarrett 2006)? Or, as some scholars have argued, do we see him challenging race relations and constructions of whiteness in his narratives (V. Watson 2011)? Many African Americans have had an interest in kung fu and taken a lot of pleasure in kung fu films. Is this interest an example of cultural appropriation, an example of cultural exchange, or a part of African American popular culture? Or is it all three? Blues is rooted in the African American tradition, but the regional origins of blues make it an important part of the country music tradition. Is the blues only an African American cultural production, or is it an important part of white rural culture as well? Jazz was also born of the African American music tradition and now has a predominantly white audience in the United States. The genre would rarely be categorized as "popular" music today. Is jazz music still black popular culture? Hip-hop performers have often referenced the Brian De Palma film *Scarface*, demonstrating how the mob film has spoken to the experiences of urban African American men who also took pleasure in the expression of masculinity in the film. Can we consider the film part of black popular culture?

These examples demonstrate the hybridity of African American cultural touchstones. African Americans might claim many cultural productions as speaking to their identities, but it is hard to imagine defining popular culture in the United States without including cultural production by African Americans. Asserting that something can be part of African American popular culture when African Americans are neither producers nor central to the content risks making the idea so expansive that it loses an already limited coherence as a concept. But by the same token, African Americans may be central to a cultural production—as subjects or aesthetically inspiring it—without it being African American popular culture. Racist representations in a variety of genres of visual and material culture may speak to the desires and fantasies of white audiences about black people, which is why representations of African Americans have been foundational to the development of so many forms of popular culture in the United States. Minstrelsy is a performance form that focuses on African Americans, but it was, as Eric Lott (1993) explains, a cultural formation shaped by the white working class. Much of the music that the "father of American music" Stephen Foster is best known for employs the black vernacular and was linked to the minstrel stage. African American performers and musical traditions shaped rock 'n' roll. The first successful modern musical—blending a serious plot with musical performance—was *Show Boat* (1927), which has as its emotional core the story of a tragic mulatta. The first dramatized radio show with continuing characters was the tremendously popular *Amos 'n' Andy*, derived from minstrel shows and initially starring two white men playing the two African American title characters. The first full-length film synchronizing speech and image was *The Jazz Singer* (1927), depicting Al Jolson singing "Mammy" in blackface. D. W. Griffith's *Birth of a Nation*, which transformed storytelling in American cinema, is filled with historical inaccuracies that romanticize the rise of the Ku Klux Klan after the Civil War and depict African Americans as rapists and coons unfit for citizenship. These representations demonstrate how central African American history, performance, and vernacular have been to American popular culture more broadly. To return to Hall, (white) American heroes and ideal and "innovative" performers are often shaped by their relationship to and distance from racialized others, particularly black subjects.

And yet a consequence of this very long history of stereotype and degradation in American popular culture is that talented African American performers have often been forced to play a limited set of roles to be employed. The gifted singer and comedian Bert Williams had to put on blackface as a black man, but despite the requirement that he conform to the logic of racist humor, real pathos and his comic gifts sometimes transcended the stereotypical frame.

Black performers would struggle to escape the legacy of stereotype, and the question of whether they are simply embodying stereotype would continue. Blaxploitation, a film genre that developed in the 1970s and responded to the politics and aesthetics of the Black Power movement, was, on the one hand, a profound intervention into representations of blackness, privileging a black aesthetic and narratives describing black urban life. On the other hand, it also—as a genre of exploitation—trafficked as much in black racial stereotypes as it did in fantasies of black empowerment. While Melvin van Peebles produced and financed *Sweet Sweetback Baadasssss Song* (an aesthetically radical 1971 film that nonetheless includes a number of stereotypes), white filmmakers produced most Blaxploitation films. Many members of black audiences nevertheless embraced the performers as epitomizing black pleasures. African American popular culture is often a complex site of identification and pleasure, and uplift and positive representation is not, despite what some people may wish, always the point of the works.

African American popular culture is thus fundamentally a site of contestation and negotiation over African American aesthetics and performance practices. To limit any definition to black creation and consumption would be to ignore the ways in which African American culture is embedded in almost all the traditions of popular cultural production in the United States. At the same time, African American agency is also at the center of what African American popular culture is and how it circulates. The sociopolitical dreams and nightmares of African Americans, as creators or consumers, as objects of fear or desire, ignored or recuperated, should be at the *center* of any cultural production that we count as part of African American culture.

# 36

## Post-Race

Roopali Mukherjee

By most accounts, the term "post-race" entered the U.S. popular lexicon in 2008 over the course of raucous electoral campaigns that ended with the election of the first African American to the U.S. presidency. Circulating with enthusiasm in news commentaries, via viral circuits of social media, and within the performative repertoires of the campaigns themselves, the 2008 election took shape as "trailblazing" and "historic" (Herbert 2008). Barack Obama's unprecedented victory promised "an affirmation of American ideals and a celebration of American circumstances, . . . a particularly American achievement" (Wallace-Wells 2006) and, as the filmmaker Spike Lee put it, cleaved time itself, from "B.B., Before Barack to A.B., After Barack" (quoted in Colapinto 2008). On November 4, 2008, in the giddy euphoria of election-night celebrations, a jubilant black voter from California proclaimed, "Color has no meaning, and Obama has proved it." The *Atlantic*'s Twitter feed, likewise, summed things up, paraphrasing a white voter who observed, "Glad the battle btwn black & white, slave & slave owner finally over."

Circulating with immense affective power, post-race articulates inchoate aspirations and needs, powerfully enshrining certain interpretations of social experience as credible and authoritative. As the philosopher Michel Foucault would remind us, the discursive power of the term lies in its special potency to say what counts as true, even as its hold over the imaginary requires constant reinforcement and reassurance. As grim evidence of the persistence of race as an axis of savage structural inequality coheres counterknowledges of post-race as farce—elaborate, extravagant, improbable—the term remained open to the lash of scorn and ridicule, little more than a cruel joke for many people. Likewise, triumphant proclamations of the end of race accompanied equally triumphant Tea Party and birther claims, which stoked the cultural logics of white racial grievance and strident renewals of anti-immigrant, Islamophobic, and antiblack racist license. Alongside mass mobilizations in support of Deferred Action for Childhood Arrivals (DACA) policies and the Black Lives Matter movement and opposing state violence in antiterror and border detention camps, the affective appeal of post-race tracks pitched struggles over interpreting, organizing, and ordering social reality.

Key to these struggles, post-race embeds and eases the ongoing march of the neoliberalization of race, working to shore up a whole bundle of beliefs—the naturalness of the market, the primacy of the competitive individual, the superiority of the private over the public, and so on. Enrolling whole populations materially and imaginatively into financialized and marketized views of the world, post-race separates "self-made" heroes/heroines from "state-made" villains, shoring up resonant mythologies of national character and progress. Rendering black grievance an anachronism, as little more than tedious investments in long-ago crimes and fetishizing a victimhood that no longer exists, post-race works with fresh vigor to censure twin bad habits of state dependency and racial stridency. Its semiotic and mythic schema substantiating new modes of "racism without race, racism gone private, racism without the categories to name it as such" (Goldberg 2009, 23), the keyword draws numbers of people to the common sense that makes race disappear, but whiteness persists.

If the epistemic logics of post-race, always on the move, consolidate rather than muddle (and are, themselves, consolidated rather than muddled by) the power and permeation of neoliberal ideas, the emergence of post-racialism in the politico-cultural context of Obama's 2008 victory smooths over decades of struggle that cohered and roiled another powerful keyword—"colorblindness"—whose ideological and discursive histories, likewise, hold clues to the particular allure and appeal of post-race. Premised centrally on strategic erasures within which the white norm and silent operations of white privilege do not disappear but, rather, become submerged within racial consciousness, colorblindness turns on the technical fiction of nonrecognition, in which individuals are asked not to see race. Shaping successively prominent versions of postwar official antiracisms in the U.S.—from racial liberalism (in the mid-1940s to the 1960s) to liberal multiculturalism (from the 1980s to the 1990s) to neoliberal multiculturalism (in the 2000s)—colorblindness enjoyed significant purchase, working to incorporate a comprehensive program of racial democracy that limited official antiracist discourses to colorblind denials of racial privilege as well as stigma and that cordoned off the settlement of racial conflicts to liberal political terrain. Conceding to some of the demands of antiracist movements, the racial formations of colorblindness served two crucial ends, both integral to postwar U.S. governmentality: they repackaged the ideological structures of centuries-old white supremacy away from earlier modes of intransigent, violent, and overt racisms, and at the same time, they contained, adapted, and absorbed more progressive demands for antiracist justice and reform.

Within global contexts of massive economic restructuring that transformed the U.S. economy starting in the 1970s and immigration and intermarriage trends that projected a "browning" of U.S. demographics and a concomitant statistical decline in the white majority, it did not take long for the colorblind paradigm to shift shape from a progressive demand to a reactionary one. Consolidating a potent and visceral politics of white male backlash against legal and social gains hard won by the civil rights, feminist, and gay liberation movements, the patrons of colorblindness, recruited from the ranks of besieged white masculinities, transformed the colorblind paradigm by the 1990s in the service of devastating assaults against redistributive programs such as affirmative action, social welfare, and immigrant rights. As the divisive bent of these campaigns strained credulity by claiming as their own the language and legacies of the black civil rights movement, they entangled the racial projects of colorblindness with the transparent racial-subordination agendas of the radical Right, injuring the brand for moderate-to-liberal voters (Cho 2009). A new concept such as post-race would effectively rearticulate the antiracist projects of colorblindness but without so much of its retro-regressive baggage. Crucially, post-race would reach with greater effectiveness key constituencies of youth and moderate-to-liberal voters whom the tainted brand of colorblindness had turned off and away.

Against colorblind prescriptions of noticing but not considering, of seeing and then sublimating, race and its indexical categories, the 2008 embrace of post-race crystallized a range of ameliorative and integrative shifts that were already in motion. The invention, in the 2000 U.S. Census, of a new "multiracial" category and its proliferations of new mixed-race demographic constituencies, celebrations of new ethnically ambiguous identities within the U.S. mediascape, together with the advent of "mosaic marketing," which targets consumers across, rather than along, ethnoracial lines, and new attitudes emanating out of youth cultures where racial differences survive as "no big deal," little more than hip lifestyle choices—each worked to rearticulate Americanness in post-racial terms while delinking racism from material histories of race (and gender) and reinforcing key dimensions of U.S. nationalist ideology. These popular cultural fronts of post-race perform crucial disciplinary work, easing the recognition of some racial differences while disavowing others and conferring social privileges on some racial subjects (the white liberal, the multicultural American, the fully assimilable black, the racial entrepreneur) while stigmatizing others (the born-again racist, the overly race conscious, the racial grievant, the terrorist, the illegal). Echoing across powerful repertoires of popular and public culture and with real political and material consequences, these adjustments in the privilege/stigma divide reenvision the domain of racism, shifting the categories to name it as such and the vocabularies by which to claim its injury.

Shoring up a number of flagging ends of racial neoliberalism, the antiracist projects of post-race, thus, clear paths to rolling back hard-won legal protections, including notable antidiscrimination protocols enshrined in the Civil Rights Act of 1964 and the Voting Rights Act of 1965, as both necessary and fair precisely for the advancement of racial aspirations and the reconciliation of racial conflicts. As the discourse of post-race, likewise, opens up black and other nonwhite advocacy and movement organizations to ideological attacks as anachronistic, unnecessary, and irrelevant, it justifies renewed scrutiny on African American and other ethnic studies programs, policing intellectuals and intellectual projects in line with the post-racial privilege/stigma divide. Rewarding curricular endeavors that meet post-racial norms of diversity and inclusion while penalizing those that do not with budget cuts, tenure denials, and program closings, post-race clears ground for containing, adapting, and redirecting the promise of progressive antiracisms—not on racial but on thoroughly rational grounds.

As properly neoliberalized racial subjects, nonwhites and whites alike, emerge as bearers of national progress and catharsis, the unwilling, the unruly, and the resistive, in contrast, can be corralled as those who can, and must, be cut off from distributions of security, belonging, and social standing. Likewise, the coding and biopolitical management of human beings into financialized regimes of social value, the abandonment of vast surplus populations of late capital, ill suited to or unmotivated by the nostrums of neoliberalism, the recognition of some populations as those willing to get over, move on, and forget "the very vocabulary necessary to . . . make a case [or] a claim" (Goldberg 2009, 21)—each of these is authorized and normalized by the discursive labors of post-race. Indeed, as a keyword, the organizing potency of post-race, the conditions of its possibility as well as the quality of its draw, engages a much longer project of containment, adaptation, and absorption geared to two essential ends: the authorization of antiracisms that render capitalism neutral to race rather than being structured by it and the obliteration of alternative and more democratic projects for racial equality and freedom as laughable, odd, impossible.

# 37

## Race

Trica Keaton

What is race? Over time and space, many people have asked that very question. However, there is no universal definition or universally agreed-on response to this query, largely because the concept of race, born out of Europe and disseminated across the globe, is a human invention.

"The term *race*," argue the sociologist Karen Fields and the historian Barbara Fields (2012, 16) "stands for the conception or the doctrine that nature produced humankind in distinct groups, each defined by inborn traits that its members share and that differentiate them from the members of other distinct groups of the same kind but of unequal rank." How race articulates through our "mental terrain" and infiltrates our belief system results from what these scholars refer to as "racecraft," meaning "a kind of fingerprint evidence that *racism* has been on the scene" (18, 19). The anthropologist Jemima Pierre (2012, xii) locates "racecraft" in the structures of "European empire making" and defines it in her study of race and blackness in Ghana as "the design and enactment, practice, and politics of race making." In this way, race is not a matter of real and/or ascribed difference but one of artifice, currency, hierarchy, and inevitable insurgent counternarratives in ongoing struggles for human and self-recognition.

Today, there is a general consensus that race is a social construct or, more simply put, man-made. This understanding radically discredits the notion of race as something biological and thus indicative of racial purity, an entity born of nature and located in our DNA. Even so, as the famous proposition by William I. and Dorothy Swain Thomas reminds us, "If [people] define situations to be real, they are real in their consequences" (1928, 572), an observation confirmed by the prevailing beliefs in biological inferiority that the theorem's namesake and his scholarly contemporaries also espoused during their time and/or evaded in everyday life (A. Reed 1997; Steinberg 2007; Morris 2015). Race and racism are not mere social constructs but political, lived, and at times deadly experiences that play a fundamental and intersectional role in the everyday because they are deeply ingrained in our social institutions, ranging from family to education to economics to law (Crenshaw 1991; Essed 1991; Collins 1998). According to the philosopher Charles Mills (1998, 49–50), "race has not been an arbitrary social category . . . or an innocent designation, as in a horizontal system, but has functioned as a real marker . . . of privilege and subordination in a vertical system" in which race and racism lie at the core of the social contract. Still, the recognition and knowledge that race is socially constructed does not tell us what race means, of what it is constructed, nor does it solve the race problem. As the anthropologist Audrey Smedley has written, it only means that we have reached conceptual clarity of race as "a social/cultural reality that exists in a realm independent of biological or genetic variations" (2007, 1).

From a sociohistorical perspective, race can be regarded as a social category that descends from nineteenth-century scientific racism, or race as biology, and its claims of biological determinism. The evolutionary biologist Joseph L. Graves Jr. (2015, 25) explains biological determinism as "the notion that there is a simple relationship between inherent (biological/genetic) features of human beings and their position in society." On this idea, the causes of disadvantage or conversely advantage are not located in our social institutions but rather in our so-called races, in other words, in our blood or more precisely in our genes. Per this logic, race is biology, and biology is destiny from which there is no escape. Although multiple sciences substantiate that race is not a meaningful genetic or biological concept, this knowledge has not eliminated racial essentialism, racialization of categories, and the reification of race in genetic research, particularly for the purposes of population labeling. Certain biomedical research and for-profit industries find common interests in this labeling and "classification standardization"—that is, "the alignment of genetics classification with the racial classifications of powerful institutions" (Panofsky and Bliss 2017, 62). This standardization is integral, for instance, not only to race-specific pharmaceuticals but also to the billion-dollar industry of genetic ancestry testing that harbors and at times fosters essentialist assumptions about race (Duster [1990] 2003; D. Roberts 2011; Kahn 2012; Nelson 2016). The sociologists Aaron Panofsky and Catherine Bliss (2017, 61) expose an often-overlooked dimension to these issues: "the ambiguous and flexible ways that geneticists classify human populations and differences. . . . Geneticists are typically embarrassed that they have considerable difficulty articulating coherent definitions of race or racial classification, even though both are deployed in their research." These findings are not at variance with the fact that race is a social construct. Indeed, they ultimately reinforce that very point by demonstrating that human manipulation maps "race" onto human diversity, not natural forces.

More importantly, what science and opportunity have unequivocally shown is that race is not indicative of intelligence, political and moral status, musical aptitude, athleticism, or other complex abilities, as scientific racism dictates. Social movements aimed at advancing opportunities and the inclusion of marginalized and racialized groups have broken glass ceilings in nearly every profession in ways that further belie and delegitimate beliefs in racial inferiority and superiority. This is not to assert, however, that there is no biological impact or damage to groups socially defined as "races." Scholars and medical professionals have long documented correlations between health disparities due to environmental conditions, such as the deliberate placing of hazardous-waste sites in proximity to already-segregated, low-income, "minority" neighborhoods, or lead in the water supply, or the stressors of racism and their impact on infant mortality rates—all of which result from human intervention.

As the theorist Roderick A. Ferguson (2007, 191) has written, "The study of race incorporates a set of wide-ranging analyses of freedom and power. The scope of those analyses has much to do with the broad application of racial difference to academic and popular notions of epistemology, community, identity, and the body . . . [as well as] economic and political formations." For example, those power formations obscure how human beings have arbitrarily selected which traits carry social significance when fashioning categories that define a specific group. Category formation in the hands of Johann Friedrich Blumenbach, a German Enlightenment thinker, anatomist, and naturalist, illustrates well the pure randomness of race-making through his "naming" white people "Caucasian." On the basis of his personal assessment that people of the Caucasus region, situated at the border of Europe and Asia, were the most beautiful in the world and the cradle of humanity, Blumenbach established a category of whiteness that endures to this day (Gould 1994; N. Painter 2010).

Race may have originated as a European folk idea about human differences, traceable to the "Age of Discovery" during the fifteenth century, but by the eighteenth century, the idea had crystalized into a pseudoscientific categorical fact. Derived from high-stakes philosophical discourses about differences between humans and those who were ultimately written out of humanity, these explanations informed a number of academic fields that perpetuated race-making, among them anthropology, geography, medicine, sociology, and theology (Eze 1997; Bernasconi 2001; Ferguson 2004). Critical medievalists, such as Geraldine Heng (2011), reject this canonical periodization on the basis of multiple sources, dating from the thirteenth century, that appear to frustrate narrowly etched race chronologies. Similar to the political scientist Cedric Robinson ([1983] 2000), Heng found that that there is compelling evidence of "racial thinking, racial law, racial formation, and racialized behaviors and phenomena in medieval Europe before the emergence of a recognizable vocabulary of race" (2011, 268). These ideas also found fertile ground in Christian theology's contribution to the modern racial imagination, enshrined in interpretations of the curse on Ham, the putative father of Black Africa, with heritable servitude. The sociologist David Goldenberg's (2003) exegetical study of the uses of this allegory to rationalize racial slavery shows, however, the absence of referential antiblackness in this story, which has been ironically passed down over thousands of years to justify the enslavement of racialized black bodies throughout the Atlantic world (Gomez 2005; Diouf 2014; R. Johnson 2016). Still, as Toni Morrison (1992, 49) judiciously recognizes, there is "a long history on the meaning of color" that signified "not simply that [a] slave population had a distinctive color; it was that this color 'meant' something," something antithetical to that against which it was defined and thereby made to matter: whiteness. Color is not race, but it serves often as its surrogate, and, as with race, it is no more biologically predictive of who we are or will be than are ear or shoe size.

Framed this way, it is insufficient to say that race is socially constructed or to advocate, as do color/race-blind adherents, the purging or effacement of the idea with the expectation and/or hope that doing so will mitigate or nullify the effects of the concept's protracted and destructive career in the world. Race has a material life whose definition has never been fixed, precisely because it is a product of human perception that dominant groups have wielded to preserve their position of dominance. As the cases of Nazi Germany, racial passing, and Rwanda show, people must be taught or compelled to see race when it is not discernable through selected racialized markers in a society (i.e., skin color, features, body type, hair texture, language, clothing, names, identity cards, or zip codes), again the stuff of racial categorization. Nonetheless, racial meaning and causality are created in their absence, as the theorist Michelle Wright elucidates similarly in her analysis of the phenomenology of blackness, a blackness ascribed, assumed, and/or performed by a variety of diasporic bodies, some of which are not always apprehended as black. "Blackness," she argues, "operates as a construct (implicitly or explicitly defined as a shared set of physical and behavioral characteristics) and . . . phenomenological[ly] (imagined through individual perceptions in various ways depending on the context)" (2015, 4). The social and legal principle of the "one-drop rule," white supremacy's definition of blackness, exemplifies well her point, as it asserts that African ancestry, real or imagined, defines a person as black, thus inferior.

That race is so historically entrenched in a society begs several questions: Is it possible or even desirable to negotiate, become "liberated" from, or transcend race without recourse to the "master's tools," chief among them being the term and concept of race themselves? What, if anything, is redemptive about race? What of its life-saving effects: communities, solidarities, pride, pleasure, traditions, and the arts that evolved in response to its imposition, its distortions, and a complicity with it that obtains without explicit demand (W. Du Bois 1897a, 1903, [1935] 1998; Woodson 1933; Fanon [1967] 2008; Appiah 1992; L. Gordon 1999; Gilroy 2000; Outlaw 2014)? The violence of race is not often recognized institutionally, neither is it one-directional, as the decolonial theorist Aimé Césaire ([1972] 2000) makes plain: the dehumanizer becomes dehumanized in that very process and thereby amputated from all humanity in order to rationalize and justify that violence. Race, then, is not destiny, but it can often feel that way.

The fact that race is invented suggests strongly that it can be whatever people define it to be. However, the concept, its deployment, its persistence, and its ultimate purpose—racial rule for capitalist gain—are intimately linked to politics and power that rely on coercion (i.e., violence, threats, and pressure) and consent for their existence. In the logic of Antonio Gramsci, "hegemony operates by including its subjects [and] incorporating its opposition," argues the sociologists Michael Omi and Howard Winant (1994, 68; cf. Feagin and Elias 2012). To accomplish this end, "the ruling groups must elaborate and maintain a popular system of ideas and practices—through education, the media, religion, folk wisdom, etc." (Omi and Winant 1994, 67). It is through this inculcated knowledge that society's consent occurs so that the dominant group's ways of thinking and being in the world appear natural, reasonable, indeed in society's collective interest, despite resistance and at times because of it.

A common, salient illustration from my research in metropolitan France concerns the international practice of repetitive identity checks or stop-and-frisks performed by "ethnically" diverse law enforcers, which include large, frequently black security guards in places of commerce. In a climate of "normalcy," these individuals, imbued with the authority of the state, profile and stop youth racialized as black or Arab not for what they have done but for what they are *perceived to be*, particularly in public space, where their already-demonized bodies are deemed incongruous with the norm. As a demonstration of that authority, they are routinely harassed in their neighborhoods, located in segregated areas where relations with the police are little more than relations of force. Should they resist or self-defend, even as a reflex reaction to a policing aggression or attack, an already-humiliating situation quickly escalates to detainment, physical violence, or death by a militarized police force against "suitable enemies," long racialized as delinquents, terrorist in the making, or/and an immigrant threat (Keaton 2006, 2013). It is not surprising that movements such as Black Lives Matter are both local and global and firmly within worldwide traditions of antiracism struggles for human and civil rights (K. Taylor 2016). Meanwhile, media-savvy, though solutionless, politicians and social analysts (from the left and the right) respond to race problems by denying their existence or resorting to proxy issues, such as immigration and cultural pathology. In so doing, they deflect attention from racism and racial discrimination, intersected by socioeconomic precarity, for which they have no viable answers in a supposed post-race and post-truth era. Scapegoating marginalized groups for their marginalization remains, then, a tried and tested mechanism to exculpate that same society (i.e., people and their institutions) for having structured race-based and intersectional exclusions as both desired and acceptable.

Everything old becomes new again, as revivals of explicit authoritarian white nationalism and supremacy well illustrate, particularly during high-stakes elections. In the language of the sociologist Eduardo Bonilla-Silva (2001, 6), who captures the global implications of these issues beyond the site of his research in the U.S., "present-day victim-blamers, as their older cousins, believe (1) that government interventions on behalf of minorities is a waste of time and money," that is, against white interests and dominance, irrespective of class and gender, "and (2) that racial and class-based stratification is an irrelevant factor in understanding black/white inequality." This latter point also renders inconsequential, if not invisible, inequality suffered by other racialized groups in societies whose extreme racial outer limits continue to be constituted in terms of variations on whiteness and anything-but-blackness. When framed by racial hegemony, practices such as mass incarceration and deportation enjoy public approval when scripted as crime and apprehended as a matter of individuals' moral or cultural deficiencies and/or a threat to dominate groups (Elias 1965; Mamdani 2002; A. Davis 2003; Wacquant 2009; Michelle Alexander 2012; Camp and Heatherton 2016; DuVernay 2016). By a sleight of hand, historically situated and systemic state-driven racial dynamics are erased, dynamics in play since enslavement through colonialism through Jim Crow and apartheid systems to this day. What is more, whether race-making nation-states and those who are ensnared in their orbit are race conscious with a long-standing history of deploying racial categories, as in Canada, the U.S., or the United Kingdom, or race blind in that states reject or retreat from a concept of race and thereby ban racial categories, the social outcomes are the same. Racial inequality and racial violence abound because race, even when unnamed or misrecognized, continues to play a critical role in how those societies are organized and how people are accordingly mis/treated. To take, however, the position that those who bore the stigmata of race exercised no agency is not only to err but also to adopt the perspective of a racist. Oft-overlooked everyday forms of resistance and revolts were central to race rebellions that make legible and visible civil rights battles waged on the ground (Kelley 1994; Kendi 2016).

What, then, is race? Paradoxically, race is everything and nothing at the same time but ultimately whatever a society has made it to mean. One thing is certain, as the theorist Hortense Spillers (2003, 378) writes, race, "unnatural and preponderant in its grotesque mandates," has no scientific basis. Yet, through its protean registers, race is always insisting violently that a racialized world is a natural one, the way it was meant to be. Nothing could be further from the truth.

# 38

## Reconstruction

David Roediger

"Reconstruction" is traditionally used to name the period of contestation over political power in the U.S. South from the Civil War until 1877. The word carries substance and power but not quite enough of those to express the dramas experienced by slaves experiencing self-emancipation or the insights of African Americanists studying that drama. In developing counternarratives of the coming of freedom and the dashing of hopes, freedpeople and scholars have changed this keyword in order to make its meaning more precise. In the 1860s, those who lived through the period often preferred "jubilee" to capture the possibilities of freedom and its immediate aftermath. W. E. B. Du Bois rewrote the past as one centering on "Black Reconstruction," in an epic 1935 study designed to change the whole story of the period. Du Bois's challenges to the extant white-supremacist scholarship eventually won a fragile place in the mainstream wisdom regarding Reconstruction, but its impact on scholars of African American life has been profound, especially as its conclusions have more recently been extended and supported by Barbara Fields (1985), Gerald Jaynes (1986), Julie Saville (1994), Thavolia Glymph (2008), and others.

The first profound interpreters of emancipation and of the promise and perils of early Reconstruction were the freedpeople themselves. They quickly sang,

No more auction block for me, no more, no more (× 3)
Many thousand gone.

Such lines deeply mixed an oppressive past and exhilarating present. The many thousand gone evoked both the million-plus slaves sold away from loved ones domestically and the millions who had died in chains. The evoking of those dead suggested the need for public policy worthy of the ancestors. A later verse intoned, "No more peck of corn," bringing into the frame postemancipation crises of health and hunger and the future need to sustain Black communities in the absence of rations from masters. Meanwhile the other great anthem to emancipation, "Oh, Freedom," emphasized Black direct action as the existential heart of its narrative:

Oh freedom, oh freedom, oh freedom over me
And before I'd be a slave I'll be buried in my grave
And go home to my Lord and be free (Ballad of America, n.d.)

The word "jubilee" enabled freedpeople to reflect on both the marvelous present and the future that they desired. While "Reconstruction" could be heard as implying simply rebuilding or reanimating state governments even before African American rights had been secured, "jubilee" bespoke a total transformation that had partially unfolded and that logically needed to proceed. Borrowing from a Bible often kept from slaves, the emancipated turned to Leviticus for an Old Testament endorsement of freeing slaves but also of redistributing land. The word made sacred the logic of reparations for slavery through the securing of "40 acres and a mule" by Black families. Its use persisted into the postwar campaigns to carve up the estates of masters in order to create the means for future pecks of corn to be secured. Extraordinarily brave ex-slave testimony before 1871 congressional hearings on Ku Klux Klan violence also gave future historians the opportunity to write a rounded history of Reconstruction.

Du Bois, born during Reconstruction, began writing on the period decades before *Black Reconstruction* appeared. In so doing, he joined a group of African Americans challenging the almost unrelieved hostility to postwar experiments in democracy and in African American civil rights. At the time, the brightest lights of Hollywood (the film *The Birth of a Nation*) and the highest rungs of academia (the "Dunning school" of Reconstruction history) conspired to discredit all such experiments, making African American freedom more unimaginable in the present as well. Carter G. Woodson's *Journal of Negro History* kept an alternative vision alive, especially in publishing the important work on South Carolina and Virginia by A. A. Taylor during the 1920s. Taylor's *The Negro in South Carolina during the Reconstruction* (1924) studies whiteness and terror—*The Birth of a Nation* had made the Ku Klux Klan its collective hero—in ways that much anticipate Du Bois's masterpiece of a decade later, as did his emphases on public education.

*Black Reconstruction* itself changed everything. Du Bois wrote in alternating currents of elegant restraint, claiming "Truth" as his desideratum, and boiling prose that built in each chapter to a concluding poem. In his closing provocation, "The Propaganda of History," he patiently charted the errors of fact and the dismissal of important sources by the leading mainstream authorities on Reconstruction. His still-sharper indictment was that the white supremacists missed the "magnificent drama" of Black Reconstruction and ignored a "tragedy that beggared the Greek" ([1935] 1998, 727). Du Bois calculated the extent of the tragedy sternly but in a way that allowed for something of the momentous achievement of emancipation. His burden was to show movement "back toward slavery" without presuming that slavery and the Jim Crow system to come were the same.

Du Bois's study offered a perfect example of what St. Clair Drake has called "vindicationist" history, showing the positive achievements of the maligned Reconstruction governments in which African Americans participated and the white terror necessary to defeat those efforts toward democracy (Drake 1987, 7–10). Most importantly, it made the "general strike of the slaves" the moving force in changing a War to Preserve Slavery, with North and South contesting only the terms of such preservation, into a world-historical freedom struggle (W. Du Bois [1935] 1998, 55). Du Bois included in that general strike both the hundreds of thousands who left slavery during the war and those who stayed and challenged masters' and mistresses' authority.

*Black Reconstruction* insisted methodologically on several approaches that have continued to transform our understanding of the Reconstruction period and of a longer run of U.S. history. The book began with chapters on "the Black worker" and "the white worker" and their pre–Civil War trajectories. These paired chapters signaled seminal contributions to Black Marxism made by the whole book, which began with the category of labor but refused to pretend that the working class had any precise meaning without a consideration of race. As he had since 1910, Du Bois regarded the absence of land reform and meaningful economic aid from the Freedman's Bureau as material facts helping to doom the exercise of the political freedoms that were legislated during Reconstruction.

Du Bois's material on the white worker constituted the first serious study of that racialized class position by a U.S. historian. Later in the book, he introduced the much-cited idea that the loyalty of poor whites to white supremacy rested in part on their receiving a "public and psychological wage" based on the color of their skin. In his subtitle, Du Bois dated the period of Black Reconstruction as stretching from 1860 to 1880, and elsewhere he offered the periodization 1850 to 1880 for the Civil War and Reconstruction. It was therefore necessary to study slavery and freedom together.

Needless to say, the politics, the fierceness, and the willingness to credit fully African American testimony of *Black Reconstruction* placed it far outside academic respectability, a situation exacerbated after World War II by Du Bois's persecution as a Communist and later by his actually becoming one. The book's excellence, its controversial nature, and its author's importance, as Herbert Aptheker's introduction to a 1976 reprint of *Black Reconstruction* makes clear, made it impossible to ignore, though possible to marginalize. However, even positive reviews tended to suspect Du Bois's passion. *Time* magazine's review featured his photograph over the caption "AX-GRINDER" (Lewis 2000, 365).

The increasing acknowledgment of elements of Du Bois's insights undoubtedly owed more to Rosa Parks than to any academic historian. For a time, 1950s and '60s Black Freedom Movement activity, sometimes called a "Second Reconstruction," saliently raised the Reconstruction history of federal protection of civil rights in the South. Du Bois's insistence that Black political participation did not lead to disastrous results received enough acceptance that when the great African American historian John Hope Franklin defended such ideas in *Reconstruction after the Civil War* (1961), his arguments could be seen as sober ones. However, Franklin took note of *Black Reconstruction* only briefly, registering awareness of its "Marxist bias" (229).

As Black nationalist and Marxist currents within the Black Power movement increasingly raised questions of land and economic rights, the fuller agenda of jubilee and of Du Bois gained a hearing. Within African American studies, *Black Reconstruction* was studied as a canonical work. Within the New Left, its insights gave rise to a Ted Allen and Noel Ignatin's (1967) theorization of a "white blindspot" among workers and even among radicals. The mainstream of the historical profession also shifted. Indeed, by the time Thomas Holt revisited the Reconstruction of South Carolina in *Black over White* (1979), he regarded Du Bois as simply a leading voice to be challenged, criticizing *Black Reconstruction* for not going still further with class analysis by exploring intraracial social divisions.

For a time, radical African Americanists even made great headway in fleshing out and winning acceptance for the Du Boisian idea that self-emancipation was the central dynamic of the U.S. Civil War. The leading voice in this instance belonged to the historian Barbara Fields, whose insights were supported by the very impressive work documenting emancipation and early Reconstruction done by the Freedmen and Southern Society Project. Fields's "Who Freed the Slaves?" (1990) and her interventions regarding self-emancipation in the Ken Burns television miniseries *The Civil War* that same year more than answered the traditional view that Lincoln freed the slaves. In 1995, the eminent Civil War historian James McPherson, likewise writing under the title "Who Freed the Slaves?," cast his views as those of an underdog, holding that the "self-emancipation thesis" decidedly and unfortunately held among professional historians. Such a view proved fragile. By 2000, when the Black historian and journalist Lerone Bennett's *Forced into Glory: Abraham Lincoln's White Dream* appeared, McPherson was back in command of the narrative, ridiculing the book in the *New York Times* in a review appearing under the title "Lincoln the Devil."

Ironically, the triumph of one important dimension of Du Bois's argument may well have contributed to the decline in influence of his central insight on self-emancipation. That is, the 1988 appearance of Eric Foner's *Reconstruction: America's Unfinished Revolution, 1863–1877* began with an homage to Du Bois and with assent to Du Bois's view that "with perplexed and laggard steps the United States government followed in the footsteps of the black slave" ([1935] 1998, 81; cf. Foner 1988, 4). However, Foner, beginning as he did in 1863, could hardly treat the transformative impact of the general strike of the slaves. His general agreement with the sympathetic treatment by Du Bois of Radical Republican efforts toward reform marks Foner's *Reconstruction* as seeming to be the equally weighty but more fully documented successor to *Black Reconstruction*. Such a view is not wrong, but it is partial and misses the importance of self-emancipation and the significant differences between the two approaches.

However, in other ways, the Black radical tradition stretching from jubilee through Du Bois and beyond has also matured and deepened. The study of slavery and freedom in the same work has come to enrich much scholarship, including Fields's *Slavery and Freedom on the Middle Ground* (1985). From Gerald David Jaynes's *Branches without Roots: Genesis of the Black Working Class in the American South, 1862–1882* (1986) and Julie Saville's *The Work of Reconstruction: From Slave to Wage Laborer in South Carolina, 1860–1870* (1994), we know in far greater detail what underpinned the desire of freedpeople for land and of capital to keep them from acquiring it. As suggestive as Du Bois's accounts of the general strike of the slaves remain, multiple impacts of their withdrawal of labor on the Confederacy are nowhere better understood than in Armstead Robinson's *Bitter Fruits of Bondage: The Demise of Slavery and the Collapse of the Confederacy, 1861–1865* (2005).

The most certain index of the ability of African American studies to reanimate the magnificent drama of Black Reconstruction lies in the ability to enter new areas not broached by Du Bois's masterwork, which has perhaps both inspired and limited new work, given the long shadow it casts. In this sense and others, the most exciting work within and extending African American studies of Reconstruction is Thavolia Glymph's *Out of the House of Bondage: The Transformation of the Plantation Household* (2008). No modern study so captures the coexistence of promise and tragedy. No work more firmly underlines that to know about Reconstruction, we need to know about slavery. Moreover, Glymph subtly conveys the less obvious point that how enslaved people made their ways through emancipation ought also to make us rethink the history of slavery. Most importantly, Glymph illuminates a set of intersections, of race, labor, and gender, that eluded Du Bois and shows how deeply those mattered on both sides of the color line.

# 39

## Refugee

### Régine Michelle Jean-Charles

In a *Washington Post* article commemorating the one-year anniversary of the death of Michael Brown, the immigration lawyer and professor of law Raha Jorjani (2015) argues that African Americans be considered refugees. She explains, "Black people in the United States face such racial violence that they could qualify as refugees if they didn't live there." Identifying racial injustice and violence as a human rights issue, she goes on to write, "The United States claims to be a country that protects refugees, not produces them; a country that chastises nations with poor human rights records. But what of our own human rights record, which shows how far we still have to go in eradicating racial injustice and violence?" Jorjani's question is a compelling point of entry for a discussion on the meaning of the term "refugee" in the context of African American studies.

At the most basic level, a refugee leaves his or her home in search of a safer place. To understand the relevance of the term in this field, it is important to acknowledge that people of African descent were forced out of their native land to be enslaved in a country that was and would continue to be hostile to their existence. If a refugee is someone forced to leave one's country to escape war, persecution, and violence, then what do you call someone who is forced to leave one's country in order to enter the war-like conditions of slavery? Given the realities of black life under siege in the United States, it seems as though too often for people of African descent, it is far from a place a refuge.

The example of displaced people in the aftermath of Hurricane Katrina in 2005 is emblematic of the term's fraught application to African Americans. For these citizens, refugee status was conferred on them because of their race and not because of national belonging. Americans were suddenly labeled refugees as they fled rising floodwaters in New Orleans. Here "refugee" was a misnomer because from a legal standpoint, citizens are not refugees; they are internally displaced. Likewise, in the aftermath of the 2010 earthquake in Haiti, the tent cities that sprang up across Port-au-Prince became known as refugee camps, until activists began urging people to use the term "internally displaced." What these examples share is that race and class caused these subjects to be labeled as refugee regardless of the status of their citizenship. With Katrina, it was the mostly black and often poor people forced to leave after the levees broke; after the earthquake in Port-au-Prince, it was the black and poor of Haiti who had no recourse in the aftermath of that disaster. Another telling example of how the term "refugee" is raced and classed is in comparisons of the United States' policies toward people leaving the Caribbean by boat. Here again, race plays a critical role in determining who is and is not viewed as a refugee, and blackness has the ability to determine one's refugee status.

Refugee status has become one of the ultimate signs of alterity. It functions as shorthand for "other": Outsider. Not from here. One who does not belong. Different from an immigrant or an economic migrant, "refugee" connotes the abject. The term "refugee" is supposed to denote a legal status linked to a human rights imperative but instead has become a marker, a sign, even a condition that brands one's existence. The category of refugee helps us to think through normativity, alterity, belonging, nonbelonging, visibility, and invisibility. Nowhere is this movement between these poles more evident than in the popular images of refugees, whose bodies and deaths are routinely put on spectacular display in the mass media. As April Shemak has argued, "both the refugee seeking political asylum and the undocumented transnational laborer seeking economic refuge function as a new incarnation of the native informant who occupies some of the most contested spaces of articulation" (2011, 4). In this contested space of articulation, refugees rarely speak for themselves, although their bodies are omnipresent signs of loss and crisis.

The Bureau of Refugees, Freedmen, and Abandoned Lands offers one of the earliest uses of the term in the specific context of African American studies. Established in 1865, what was known more commonly as the Freedmen's Bureau was created to facilitate the transition from enslavement to freedom. Despite the fact that the Freedmen's Bureau resulted in the creation of historically black colleges and universities (HBCUs), it was largely unsuccessful and problematic. As W. E. B. Du Bois expressed in 1903, "the large legacy of the Freedmen's Bureau [is] the work it did not do because it could not" (40), which is to say that the institution was destined for failure because the end of chattel slavery never resulted in true freedom or the extension of the full rights of citizenship for people of African descent in the U.S. Thus, the first application of the word "refugee" to African Americans reminds us that the term is intended to denote nonbelonging. Pamela Reed (2007) draws a line from the creation of the Freedmen's Bureau to the treatment of African Americans by FEMA after Hurricane Katrina, pointing out that use of the word "refugee" is a historical reference. That history is one in which refugees are discounted, mistreated, and silenced.

But one realm in which refugee voices are audible is in sonic cultures. Two examples come to mind: the 1990s rap group the Fugees and the twenty-first-century rapper K'naan. The Somali-born rapper K'naan opens his debut album, *The Dusty Foot Philosopher* (2005), with an ode to water, titled "Wash It Down." Accompanied by only the sounds of drums beating and water splashing, he repeats, "My people drum on water, drink on water, live on water, and die for water." The song captures the fraught dynamics of global movements in the age of globalization, because of which an element as basic as water means life or death in one country, while it is wastefully poured out in another. The song title has a double meaning because "Wash It Down" introduces the entire album—a carefully crafted refugee narrative that is not meant to be easy to swallow. K'naan's album is a testimony of displacement in the twenty-first century that covers topics such as childhood ended due to war, posttraumatic stress disorder, fleeing from the violence of war, the crisis of global poverty, water shortages, and more. Yet through his playful tone and style, K'naan, "one of the most prominent spokesmen for the figure of the political refugee in popular culture" (Sobral 2013, 23), demonstrates that examining the term "refugee" means not only exploring themes such as loss, war, tragedy, and persecution but also acknowledging the innovation, productivity, and philosophy generated by displaced people. In the popular sonic imagination, an earlier well-known use of the term comes from the rap group the Fugees, mostly of Haitian origin, who excised the "re-" from the word. That innovation, the quirky-sounding shortened version of the word, was a reclamation of a term that had been used to marginalize Haitians and others seeking to make their homes in the United States after fleeing their countries of origin. The choice of "refugee" over "immigrant" suggested that the members of the group were not coming to the United States by choice but because of the circumstances in their country.

Two of the most common tropes of refugee narratives are tragedy and victimization, both of which have a dehumanizing effect; but refugee artists are uniquely positioned to complicate the dominant perspective on what it means to be a refugee. Warsan Shire's poem "Home" (2011) can serve as a final example for how artists enhance and nuance perspectives on the meaning of refugee. As Shire articulates the painful circumstances that force one to become a refugee, each verse confronts the pain and desperation in graphic and lyrical language: "No one leaves home / unless / home is the mouth of a shark / you only run for the border / when you see / the whole city running as well . . . / you only leave home / when home won't let you stay." Shire's poem "Home" is a plea for people to shift their perception of refugees from what their present condition is to what led to that condition: "you have to understand / no one puts their children in a boat / unless the water is safer than the land." By juxtaposing what refugees leave behind (physical and sexual violence, uncertainty, hunger) with what they endure on their journeys, and when they arrive in hostile locations, Shire reminds readers that becoming a refugee is never trite. Likewise, the use of the term in African American studies reveals its lengthy and complicated history.

# 40

## Religion

LeRhonda S. Manigault-Bryant

"Religion" has been used within African American studies to identify the sacred rituals, symbols, traditions, and worldviews to which black folks adhere and to distinguish them from the ordinary, informal, and nonsacred principles that structure black life. Inherent in the etymology of "religion" and its subsequent genealogy is its connection to formal, identifiable traditions. The word "religion" immediately invokes an organized system on which sacred beliefs are placed and subsequent behaviors are enacted. Within African American studies, this includes, most prominently, Christianity and, less popularly, Islam, Judaism, Buddhism, African traditional religions (ATRs) such as Yoruba, Santería, and Candomblé, and African-derived religions (ADRs) and folk traditions such as voodoo, conjure, and hoodoo.

It is impossible to understate the conceptual significance of religion—the effervescent, ethereal, and expressive faiths—to the experiences of African Americans. After all, whether called "African American religion" or, as interchangeably deployed here, "black religion," the psychic, soulful expressions of black folks have influenced key moments of American history. The experience of the Middle Passage cultivated burgeoning spiritual identities and practices for blacks in America (and in the black Atlantic world), shaped by the trauma of forced bondage, honed by the demands of the plantocracy, and refined beyond institutional enslavement. Hush harbors housed the sacred diasporic cosmologies that were transported during the transatlantic slave trade and morphed into the unique expressions of spirituality exemplified in the emergence of Negro spirituals. The features of black religious expression that emerged in those clandestine spaces of "slave religion" have yet to be fully uncovered (Raboteau 1978). They are the foundations of what has become *African American* religion.

Central to the civil rights movement, for example, were the music and sounds—including the call-and-response style—that emerged from the hush harbors of North America. Black religious groups and organizations aided black Americans through tumultuous eras—abolitionism, Reconstruction, and Jim Crow among them—and helped usher in the broadest institutional and legal applications of equality for African Americans. Some of the most *visible* figures within African American history—Frederick Douglass, Martin Luther King Jr., Malcolm X, Jarena Lee, Maria Stewart, "Gullah" Jack Pritchard, Septima Clark, Clara Muhammad, Marcus Garvey, Nat Turner, Fannie Lou Hamer, and others—emerged from black churches, temples, mosques, and spiritual movements. Even as the "great leader" model is not the most effective or accurate means of understanding black religious, political, social, historical, and cultural change (E. Edwards 2012), it is notable that there is no single space, sole tradition, or particular locale that produced these leaders.

This is a fairly straightforward conceptual framing of religion, and yet, as it is common to black experience and black expression, this claim to meaning is not without its irony. At the root of the connotation of "religion" in its Latin (*religare*) and Old French (*religio*) origins is the assumption of bondage, where one binds oneself to—or is bound by—a sense of obligation, intimacy (i.e., bond), or reverence to a holy other. Considering those faiths that the enslaved held onto during the Middle Passage, then, gives us a new way of interpreting the meaning of a double bind, for as they were being subjugated, they wrestled with holding onto the beliefs that would allow their survival. This active wrestling between bond and bondage, agency and submission, is too an instrumental part of African American religion and has resulted in a shift of how the term "religion" has been used over time. Put another way, the keyword "religion" reflects the intimate struggles that black folks face as they strive to loosen the strongholds of imposed bondage while acquiescing to the agency inherent in choosing their own gods. Hence, various idioms including "faith," "belief," and most recently, "spirituality," have been appropriated in place of the religion. Yet they largely convey the same thing, even as the terms all point toward the idea that what black folk believe in is no longer exclusively or predominantly tied to formal traditions or practices. Rather, these concepts all tap into a sacred undercurrent, so to speak—of how African Americans structure their lives and actions around what they deem holy, irrefutable, and sacred. In essence, "religion" for African Americans has always been, as William D. Hart describes, "a conceptual tool, a historically and discursively informed way of categorizing a heterogeneous ensemble of cultural practices in the Black Atlantic world" (2006, 476).

Mapping the contoured meanings of religion for blacks in the United States thus poses a distinct challenge, as one result of enslavement was an active dismantling of ATRs, ADRs, and folk religion. Christianity, a religion of "the masters," took its own roots in black life, which resulted in a perception of its becoming synonymous with black religion. From the earliest iterations, literature on black religion has been focused on its Protestant, Christian expressions. One need only turn to the famed sociologist W. E. B. Du Bois's 1903 articulation of African American religion in *The Souls of Black*

*Folks* or, a century later, the incomparable sociological work presented by C. Eric Lincoln and Lawrence Mamiya (1990) to see how the creation of seven mainline Protestant denominations between the late eighteenth and early nineteenth centuries left a remarkable impression on the formation of black religion in America. It was within these denominations that the largest numbers of enslaved, formerly enslaved, and free blacks publicly participated and that documented accounts of African American religious expression were most readily made.

Even as history has revealed that the complexities of black religiosity are not—and have never been—*just* Christian, the impact of Christianity on African American religion is quite significant. The visibility, centrality, and predominance of black Protestantism within historical presentations have resulted in the treatment of black religion as synonymous with the formation of the black (Christian) church. This move, which William Hart (2008) calls the "Standard Narrative of Black Religion as the Black Church," has diminished the robust and dynamic features of black religion that do not fall within the confines of Christianity. Hart has provided a more comprehensive way of thinking about the "Three Rival Narratives of Black Religion" that disrupt popular reductions of black religion to the black church. To Hart, black religion is as much the typical notion of the black (Protestant, Christian) church as it is the "souls of black folks," or an existential phenomenology shaped by racial identity and the condition of antiblack racism. Black religion, to Hart, is also *relegare*, meaning "ancestor piety," in which one celebrates the names of *all* ancestors, including those "who invoke the gods of Africa, . . . who invoke other gods, . . . who invoke no gods at all, who are indifferent to the gods, or curse the gods" (2006, 490).

Hart's inclusive treatment of black religion in America should not be viewed as a counternarrative.

Historically, the Christianizing thread is in fact disingenuous to the origins of black religion in America. When one examines the earliest iterations of what has become African American religion, it is evident that blacks spent nearly two centuries on the shores of North America before Christianity took root. Instrumental, then, to any understanding of black religion is the notion of religious syncretism, the merging of distinct (or conflicting) practices, rituals, and traditions into a single system of belief. Inherent to the idea of religious syncretism is the fusing of multiple religions. African American religion is, at its core, the blending of traditions created from practices, rituals, and cosmologies that originate from places throughout the black Atlantic. Inherently, then, the plurality of African American religions has necessitated multidisciplinary and interdisciplinary approaches to their examination.

A small number of early works on black religion disrupted the Christocentric narrative of black religion, including especially Arthur Fauset's *Black Gods of the Metropolis* (1944) and Lincoln's *The Black Muslims in America* (1961). In the tradition of those forebears, contemporary scholarship in the field has increasingly (and rightly) moved further away from the overwhelmingly Christocentric focus that has dominated popular notions of black religiosity and has focused more readily on the syncretic aspects of African American religion. Works such as Yvonne Chireau's *Black Magic: Religion and the African American Conjuring Tradition* (2006); Tracey Hucks's *Yoruba Traditions and African American Religion Nationalism* (2012); Jacob Dorman's *Chosen People: The Rise of American Black Israelite Religions* (2013); Manigault-Bryant's *Talking to the Dead: Religion, Music, and Lived Memory among Gullah/Geechee Women* (2014), and Eddie Glaude's *African American Religion: A Very Short Introduction* (2014) are indicative of this shift. Judith Weisenfeld's (2017) recent exploration of religio-racial formation among black participants in the Moorish Science Temple, the Nation of Islam, Father Divine's Peace Mission Movement, and Ethiopian Hebrew sects takes the fluid intersections of religion and race as the framing traditions for which to consider and imagine the vast diversity of black religious expression in the United States. As a collective, these works suggest that any routine reflection on black religion must begin with the knowledge that African American religion is as diverse in its expression as it is vast in its appropriation.

The increase of more syncretic approaches to understanding African American religion is not the only development that has altered our understanding of black religion. A more explicit focus on gender has also expanded notions of black religion beyond places where men are the preeminent religious participants and authorities. Admittedly, this is a shift in the scope of African American religion that has taken unnecessarily long to unfold. Critical analyses of black women's roles within (Christian) sacred spaces were led by the deployment of Alice Walker's (1983) terminology into the establishment of womanist theology. Jacquelyn Grant, for example, was particularly critical of the invisibility of black women within black theology in her landmark essay "Black Theology and the Black Woman" (1979) and subsequent text *White Women's Christ and Black Women's Jesus: Feminist Christology and Womanist Response* (1989). This intervention, along with Evelyn Brooks Higginbotham's (1993) extensive historical work on black women's activism within the Baptist church, led to an extensive scholarly collection on black women's religious histories that harks back to the powerful narrative of the African Methodist Episcopal church's first female preacher, Jarena Lee (b. 1783), and has continued into the present. Notably, however, black women's stories are still largely framed within the context of Christianity.

Modern communities of black folks are increasingly turning away from formalized religion. Similarly, female members of the faith (who continue to hold the largest membership within black churches) ruminate aloud, as Eddie Glaude Jr. (2010) did in his (hotly contested) public obituary, whether "the black church is dead." This suggests that engendered exposés of the confines of black religion and the question of the efficacy of Christianity for black women will continue to be a point of critical reflection.

Another important development within African American religion has been an increased focus on the black body and sexuality. This too is a more recent shift within the field, demarcated by the work of Kelly Brown Douglas (1999), Horace L. Griffin (2006), Ashon T. Crawley (2008), and Roger Sneed (2010). The limited focus on the black religious body and its engendered and sexualized manifestations is particularly intriguing considering the role that black corporeality played upon the arrival of blacks in North America. Moreover, the placement of black bodies at the lowest rung of the global racial-hierarchical ladder has meant that within religion, sacred corporeality has given way to diminishing misperceptions of the black body as deviant and hypersexual. These silences around the black body and black sexuality within religion are diminishing as increased focus on how the body facilitates communication and encounter with the sacred continues to complicate any perceived "normativity" within black religious expression.

These modern shifts in the field come from a longstanding practice of critiquing the cultural implications of black religion, laid bare in the prolific, scathing critique of black Pentecostalism in James Baldwin's classic text *Go Tell It on the Mountain* (1953) and in the less publicized folk practices made infamous by the inimitable griot Zora Neale Hurston in *The Sanctified Church*

(1981) and *Tell My Horse: Voodoo Life in Haiti and Jamaica* (1990). Black women and gay-, lesbian-, queer-, and transgender-identified bodies have radically altered our perceptions of the spaces in which black sacred altars are erected. The emergence of womanism and queer and sexuality studies have simultaneously transformed what we now know or think of as African American religion.

To fully understand the connotation of religion within African American studies, then, is not to explore the *what* or *who* of black religion but to revel in the *why*. Even as it is important to understand *what* African Americans believe and *who* has contributed to that understanding, knowledge of which religious traditions black folks adhere to and whether they are Christian, Jewish, African, nationalistic, folk, and so on is less meaningful to religion's place as a keyword. Rather, it is more consequential to comprehend *why* religion matters in the most rudimentary sense, which is expressly connected to the wrestling between narratives of bondage and narratives of freedom and the black believing bodies that struggle with the agency of choice in a world that frequently deems it as "other."

African American religion has always been shaped by its people, geographies, and contexts. In the mid-nineteenth century, the spiritual desires of black people demanded the creation and cultivation of their own spaces, which became black churches, mosques, temples, and sacred sanctuaries. This current moment is no different, and the emergence of the #BlackLivesMatter movement is a modern example of the dialectical interplay between American political and social environments and black religion. The movement formally began in 2012, in response to the controversial, racially polarizing case in Sanford, Florida, where George Zimmerman shot and killed Trayvon Martin, an unarmed black teenager. The outcry and protest surrounding Martin's death and Zimmerman's subsequent acquittal certainly stand in the black activist tradition of Ida B. Wells and are reminiscent of the Student Nonviolent Coordinating Committee (SNCC) and the Southern Christian Leadership Conference (SCLC) of the 1960s. What distinguishes the #BlackLivesMatter movement from others is the current context in which it has emerged. Social media, digital technologies, and hashtag activism have immediately placed it within a global, diasporic conversation. That one of the founders and leaders of the movement—Patrisse Cullors—is the embodiment of black religious syncretism as a self-identified queer polyamorous practitioner of the Yoruban divination tradition called Ifá further differentiates this moment and this movement from its historical antecedents (Farrag 2015).

#BlackLivesMatter exemplifies the permeability of the term "religion" within African American studies to mean more than just formal tradition or adherence to a neatly outlined system of belief. Even as it is designated as a "political movement," its sacred undercurrents are palpable via its leadership and its calls for black agency and the removal of the contemporary forms of political, structural, and social bondage that threaten to deem black lives irrelevant. The #BlackLivesMatter movement reminds us that the killing of unarmed black bodies is not exceptional or unique. Rather, the movement confirms more names to be added to a disturbing litany of lynchings, murders, and deaths of black women, men, and children, including Jordan Davis, Eric Garner, Rekia Boyd, Yvette Smith, Tamir Rice, Michelle Vash Payne, Sam DuBose, Aiyana Jones, the Charleston Nine, and Sandra Bland. #BlackLivesMatter further affirms that the spilling of black blood on American soil is more normative than not, and black religion has always had to grapple with—and respond to—that reality. *This is the why.* Even when black religious organizations have not formally responded to these deaths, it is within sacred spaces that the grieving families and loved ones are comforted, that communities are rallied to action, and that the bodies of the dead are ceremoniously laid to rest. Black religion, in all of its variants, contours, traditions, cosmologies, and histories, forces us to grapple with what it means to believe in *anything* within a country that frequently leaves its black citizens questioning the meaning of their lives.

Black religion is as much the heart-wrenching angst communicated in the Negro spiritual "Nobody Knows the Trouble I See" as it is the visual representation of the *Baptism of Sue Mae* by the South Carolinian artist Jonathan Green (1986). Black religion is as much the sacred significance communicated in hip-hop culture (Miller and Pinn 2014) as it is the creation of a protest sign by Daniel José Camacho (2015), influenced by black liberation theology and resulting in the trending hashtag #JamesConeWasRight. Black religion is deeply historical yet simultaneously influenced by its current contexts. Black religion is Christianity, Islam, Judaism, Pan-Africanism, agnosticism, atheism, humanism, conjure, folklore, call-and-response, musical, oral, aural, visual, activism, protest, soul, death, life, and eternity. To acknowledge the significance of black religion means that one accepts that there has always been an active wrestling with the meaning of religion in black life and that experiences of spirituality, faith, and ritualized expression among African Americans are as diverse, broad, and purposeful in their scope as they are in their function. Taking religion seriously means recognizing that any consideration of social identities, social movements, history, and cultural production that has impacted African Americans likely has had black religiosity or spirituality at its core. In sum, the complexities of African American religion and spirituality are as vast and diverse as are the millions of black folks who contribute to its formation—past, present, and future.

# 41

## Riot

Charles W. McKinney Jr.

An exploration of the keyword "riot" reveals a phenomenon that grapples with the nexus of race, class, violence, space, power, and resistance. Attempts to define "riot" are often overtaken by efforts to scapegoat people at the center of a given confrontation. Frequently, the dominant question bandied about by popular media after a riot is "why are they destroying their own communities?" This question typifies much of the fuzzy thinking related to defining a riot—a focus on the reactions of aggrieved communities, rather than the dynamics that provide the backdrop for the disruption itself. An analysis of the term points the way toward a clearer definition, one grounded in historical context and responsive to new theoretical interventions.

Riots in the early twentieth century were defined largely by white-on-black violence that occurred in the wake of significant shifts in American society (Abu Lughod 2012). Regrettably, much of the scholarship produced during this period revealed an inability to grapple with the centrality of race. Buttressed by a naked commitment to white supremacy, sociology and criminology reinforced the intellectual underpinnings of black inferiority laid by biology, history, and anthropology. As such, explanations of racial conflict and riot assumed a rudimentary analysis based on simple cause and effect: a precipitating physical conflict between a black assailant and white victim triggered larger, widespread acts of violence, resulting in a racial conflagration ultimately quelled by law enforcement. This scholarship left little to the imagination when it came to identifying the causes of riots: black criminality and a degenerate, violence-prone culture that devalued life (Muhammad 2011; N. Painter 2010; L. Baker 1998).

The long-held notion of predatory black sexuality also served as a centerpiece of this literature. Just as the trope of the black sexualized beast fueled justification for lynching early in the twentieth century, rumors of black sexual impropriety also fueled riots (Wells-Barnett [1892] 1996, 1917). In Atlanta in 1906, rumors of the sexual assault of white women at the hands of black men, published in local newspapers, fanned the flames of violence that erupted into the Atlanta Riot. Over two days in September, somewhere between ten and one hundred black people lost their lives. Mobs of whites beat black women and men who were pulled from trolley cars or walking down the street. A mob also attempted to burn down black-owned homes surrounding the Atlanta University Center. The governor called in the state militia to quell the violence. After the *Tulsa Tribune* published an article with the headline, "Nab Negro for Attacking Girl in an Elevator," a white mob attacked the Greenwood District, also known as "the black Wall Street." In just over fifteen hours, the mob laid waste to thirty-five city blocks, burning 191 businesses and over twelve hundred homes. The riot left over ten thousand people homeless. Conflicting reports generated after the riot made an accurate count of fatalities impossible (Cecelski and Tyson 1998; Driskell 2014; Capeci and Knight 1996; Brophy 2002).

Black theorists and journalists constructed counternarratives that rendered the cause and impact of riots with a complexity the topic deserved. After the East St. Louis riot in 1917, W. E. B. Du Bois brought a sociologist's eye to the conflagration that left between forty and two hundred people dead. Du Bois, writing in the *Crisis*, explained the motivation of the violence:

tension in response to heavy black migration into the city spurred by labor shortages during the First World War. Black workers, initially used as strikebreakers, maintained their positions after a strike, angering white workers unaccustomed to working alongside blacks. Du Bois and others showed that riots were often the violent manifestation of a group of factors: social tensions arising from a contraction of employment opportunities and an increasingly interracial pool of labor; migration of African Americans into racially homogeneous spaces; and, perhaps most importantly, the persistent antiblack animus woven into the fabric of American life (W. Du Bois 1917, 1920).

The pioneering journalist and antilynching crusader Ida B. Wells-Barnett conducted extensive interviews with riot survivors. These interviews—rendered in her searing prose—laid bare the casual, endemic nature of antiblack violence. While white men were the primary perpetrators of violence, white women also participated by chasing, beating, and stabbing black women during the riot. National Guard troops—deployed as peacekeepers—frequently joined in the violence by attacking black citizens (Wells-Barnett 1917). Additionally, Du Bois discovered documents produced by white union officials threatening violence against black workers in the days *before* the riot. For both Du Bois and Wells-Barnett, violence perpetrated against blacks *during* the riot was inseparable from threats of violence *before* the riot. The historian Charles Lumpkins calls the violence in East St. Louis "an American pogrom, ethnic cleansing, in which officials directed the organized physical destruction of a racially defined community" (2008, 8). This assertion is borne out when considering the major demographic shifts that riot-torn cities endured early in the century. East St. Louis, Chicago, and Tulsa all experienced a dramatic increase in their African American populations. From 1910 to 1920, Chicago's black population swelled from ten thousand to one hundred thousand. Between 1910 and 1917, East St. Louis's black population increased from six to thirteen thousand. This growth occurred alongside long-established ethnic enclaves in each city, pitting older neighborhoods against new immigrants in a battle over spatial boundaries (Olzak and Shanahan 1996). This work done after East St. Louis and other riots challenged contemporary thinking on the role of *space* and *violence* in riots and centered the intentional deployment of violence in the pursuit of social control and containment.

By the 1940s, social scientists developed wider theoretical analyses to define the contours of a riot. Building on the work of Wells-Barnett, Du Bois, and others, scholars contended with the central place of white supremacy in the formation of riots. Any continued reluctance to do so was significantly eroded by two major events that cast an unwelcome light onto racial practices in the United States: the Nazi regime's virulent racial ideology and Gunnar Myrdal's massive study, *An American Dilemma*, which placed white supremacy at the heart of a national conversation about race relations in the United States. Myrdal's work, in particular, illuminated the increased tension in American society between black folks' rapidly rising expectations of full equality and the persistent presence of white supremacy (Myrdal [1944] 1995; Clayton 1996).

Riots that occurred during the Black Freedom Struggle in the 1950s and 1960s reflected both a changed terrain for African Americans and new iterations of older tensions and conflicts. In the wake of slow, unsteady improvement in the quality of black life, riots remained as sharp points of conflict and confrontation in American society. They also increasingly found their genesis in the opposition between authorities dedicated to the racial status quo and black folks who increasingly sought greater freedom. Earlier scholarship on riots drew a distinction between those that occurred in the early part of the 1960s (Birmingham, Selma) and those that racked the nation later in the decade (Los Angeles, Detroit, Newark). This was in large part because the scholarship on the Black Freedom Struggle carved out a distinction between the early period of racial violence (during the integrationist, direct-action phase of the movement) and the latter period, defined by the limits of nonviolent engagement and the rise of Black Power as an ideology and organizing tactic.

As scholars, theorists, and writers made sense of the violence that washed over the country, they began to understand riots as violent revelations that lay bare the systemic inequalities that dogged marginalized people. Over time, the events that triggered riots—police shootings, civil disobedience, and so on—became understood as complements to broader dynamics that framed the initial encounter. Heightened levels of tension in cities, expectations of change, and generations of structural racism and its attendant abuse all merged to produce conditions rife for riots across the nation. The U.S. experienced over forty riots in 1966. In the first nine months of 1967, 164 riots and racial disorders scorched the land, killing over eighty people and injuring two thousand. In Detroit, city officials called in fifteen thousand law enforcement officers to quell rioters. Fires set in the inner city consumed fourteen square miles of residential area, leaving five thousand people homeless. By the end of the decade, violent outbursts occurred in three hundred cities across the nation. "If one were to survey the country," wrote the political scientist Robert Brisbane, "it would have been difficult not to conclude that blacks in America were in open rebellion" (1974, 162; see also Marable 2007).

Riots in Detroit and Los Angeles originated in the residential segregation and economic dislocation that afflicted black communities. In Los Angeles, Cold War politics stifled a movement dedicated to expanding housing options for people of color and desegregation of municipal employment. This containment of an emergent movement laid the groundwork for the city's toxic environment in 1965, one that did not dramatically improve for a critical mass of the population three decades later (Horne 1997). In Detroit, urban poverty and racial inequality emanated from the confluence of housing and workplace discrimination exacerbated by the Second World War. After the war, deindustrialization and inadequate financing for black would-be homeowners set the ground for riots in that city (Sugrue 2014). When police lieutenant Thomas Gilligan shot and killed James Powell, a fifteen-year-old black student in Manhattan in July 1964, the incident highlighted the myriad factors that worked to create violent confrontation. Shifting residential patterns, urban renewal, and the utilization of public housing created a context of *increased* racial interaction, an interaction that became tenser as the boundaries that separated African American, Puerto Rican, and white enclaves shifted. Gilligan's murder of Powell—and the deteriorating economic, social, and racial environment that accompanied it—set off the Harlem Riot and revealed various fault lines within the city (Abu Lughod 2012).

The Kerner Commission report, issued in response to the riots that swept across the nation in the 1960s, confirmed the structural causes of racial unrest. For the commission, "white racism" lay at the heart of the country's racial chasm and imperiled the future of the nation. Pervasive discrimination, black in-migration and white flight, and the systemic persistence of the ghetto mixed with the "frustrated hopes" of black folk to create an environment suited for riots. These conclusions stood in bold relief to the "culture of poverty" analysis, which gained renewed vigor during the 1960s. Touted by scholars and politicians alike, the "culture of

poverty" thesis suggested that the primary cause of riots stemmed from the cultural deficiencies of the people who took to the streets. While conceding the challenges of structural racism and classism, emerging poverty theorists claimed that the deterioration of communities—and families—were primary factors in the triggering of riots. Daniel Patrick Moynihan's *The Negro Family: The Case for National Action* typified this type of thinking (U.S. National Advisory Commission 1968; Moynihan 1965).

As an interdisciplinary enterprise, African American studies is positioned to explicate the dynamic relationship between systems, structures, and collective responses to state-sanctioned oppression. Scholars in the field brought these analytical gifts to bear in an effort to make sense of the violent interactions that have taken place in the past three decades—and to clarify the state's role in those confrontations. During this period, conflicts across the country came to be characterized as examples of *antiauthority violence*—aggression targeted at authorities whose actions frequently intensified riot conditions (Abu Lughod 2012). From the larger sociocultural and economic contexts to the triggering event to the dissemination of the "official report" and beyond, state action plays an indispensable role in the creation of riots. This insight has motivated scholars to shift the language of these violent occurrences from "riot" to "rebellion" in an effort to bring greater clarity to the collective response to systemic oppression. With this nuanced view, the contours of the rebellion that erupted in Los Angeles in 1992 are more clearly rendered by understanding that the murder of Latasha Harlins—and the subsequent acquittal of her killer, a Korean store owner, almost a year before the Rodney King verdict—angered and alienated black communities in Los Angeles and strained relations between blacks and Koreans. The rebellion cannot be understood as a simple reaction to a single botched case. Rather, it was a response to systemic judicial malpractice, ethnic conflict, racial inequality, and the institutional inability of the state to punish individuals for the beating and killing of black people (Stevenson 2015; M. Neal 2016).

After a police officer murdered Michael Brown in Ferguson, Missouri, in August 2014, a rebellion erupted that both convulsed the city and galvanized a national response. The decision to leave Brown's lifeless, uncovered body in the street harked back to the spectacle lynching of a previous century. After law enforcement authorities shattered Freddy Gray's spine while in police custody in Baltimore in 2015, protests quickly escalated into riots. In both cities, the crowds that gathered to talk and express their collective discontent were met with authorities that emphasized *force strategies* instead of *diplomatic strategies* to contend with citizens in their respective towns (Useem 1997). These are the types of choices that have deleterious effects with regard to citizens' responses. As in years past, scholars and federal investigators revealed deep-seated racial disparities that laid the foundation for the social, economic, and political context in which these communities experienced the deaths of Brown and Gray. The violations of the law that officials in Ferguson engaged in were particularly egregious. The Justice Department report on Ferguson "revealed a pattern or practice of unlawful conduct within the Ferguson Police Department that violates the First, Fourth, and Fourteenth Amendments to the United States Constitution, and federal statutory law" (U.S. Department of Justice 2015, 1).

African American studies remains in the forefront of crafting new theoretical venues through which to understand the complicated, multivalent processes at the heart of riots. In addition to asking the questions related to traditional points of inquiry, scholars in the field are expanding the boundaries of this volatile concept. How do we distinguish between a "riot" and a "rebellion"? What are the *sonic* responses to these types of disruptions? What other sorts of media are being deployed to capture the intricacies of a riot? What are the intersections between spectacle, violence, and trauma? What are the long-term implications of the (reinvigorated) surveillance of black people? Deploying social media (Facebook, Twitter, etc.), how have black digital humanities scholars complicated (or disturbed) the once-linear process of reporting, visual consumption, analysis, and response? An exploration of "riots" will continue to yield provocative insights about the phenomenon and the society that generates them.

However, for all the new, critical theoretical excavation, the work of our intellectual ancestors remains instructive. A century ago, Ida B. Wells-Barnett crafted a brilliant analysis of the East St. Louis riot. She concluded that a foundational racial animus buttressed an unequal legal system, undermined effective law enforcement, cemented economic inequality, sanctified segregation, facilitated racial violence, and debased every aspect of civil society. These observations reverberate through the ages down to now. Her report is both timely and timeless in that the core of her analysis—penned one hundred years ago—could have been written in the wake of events in Ferguson, Baltimore, Baton Rouge, and the next American city where a riot (or rebellion) will regrettably occur.

# 42

## Rock

Daphne A. Brooks

Rock remains in a hard place as long as historians and critics alienate the form from its racially, regional, gendered, and queer roots. No popular music genre's name encapsulates its own social and cultural complexities so accurately and so succinctly. Both a verb and a noun, the doubleness of the term evokes the kinds of problems that Amiri Baraka famously outlined in relation to swing, that early-twentieth-century pop sensation innovated, in part, by black horn ensembles that staked out daring and insistent improvisational action with one another and set the tempo for a new modern rhythm and sonic velocity (L. Jones 1963). Just as Baraka traced the reification of swing resulting from the culture industry's successful efforts to reengineer it and steer it into the hands of white big-band leaders and their orchestras, so too might some critics contend that rock represents the calcification of a once vibrant, mobile, euphorically adventurous black expressive form. This line of argument suggests that once one takes the "roll" out of the equation, this music that first emerged on the Chitlin' Circuit and in subcultural black nightclubs in postwar America before traveling across the radio waves and into white youth culture would ultimately change. It would harden in sound, fortify its somewhat porous cultural boundaries, and also alter its aesthetic range, its performative vision, its pantheon of celebrated artists, and its presumptive fan base.

Historically, we know many of these points to be true inasmuch as the story of rock and roll's African

American legendary pioneers—Chuck Berry, Little Richard, Ruth Brown, Etta James, and others—is a fraught one in which 1950s and early '60s young black entertainers took big, nothing-to-lose risks on stage each night. They forged boisterous sounds and moves that evoked the volatility and possibilities of Great Migration life and culture but watched as their music circulated to wider audiences back and forth across the Atlantic world and into the hands of mid-'60s "British Invasion" bands. These subsequent artists covered their music to wild popularity and eventually carried it with their American counterparts into early-1970s arenas, where it was fully anointed "rock" and where it, likewise, became white(r), more corporate, resolutely male, and putatively straighter. But the contributions of the boundary-crossing early black architects of this music cannot be overstated, and their long-standing marginalization in the pop cultural imaginary is a crucial point to grasp when defining the keyword that is "rock."

Until the revisionist activism of artist collectives such as the Black Rock Coalition in the 1980s (discussed later), hegemonic, canon-building rock music criticism had, for instance, diminished the importance of Berry, hailing him as a kind of quaint elder statesman of the music rather than consistently conveying his lasting impact as a visionary guitar player, savvy songsmith, and magnetic performer who fused together the country and rhythm-and-blues genres into high-energy music that encapsulated the desires of New Frontier teenagers, that burgeoning marketing demographic born out of American empire's mid-twentieth-century prosperity. Critics such as Greg Tate (2017) have referred to Berry as "the double helix of rock & roll," and his genius mixing of the tropes of speed, sex, and commodity culture in classics such as "Johnny B. Goode" and "Maybellene" remain the bedrock of contemporary popular music culture. Little Richard, too, radicalized and forever changed the terms by which pop entertainers performed the erotic for mass audiences, and yet he has spent the majority of his post-1950s breakthrough moment demanding that he receive due credit for having pushed this revolutionary form into the territory of the spectacularly ecstatic and ribald. He "grabbed on to the very moment the [sex] drive took over" in popular music, as Ann Powers argues, "and rode it right into his fans' flailing arms" (2017, 129). He was, as Tavia Nyong'o (2014) observes, one who turned his restless freakishness into expansive sociality. Both Little Richard (born Richard Wayne Penniman) and Chuck Berry were men of movement—action like the kind that Baraka and, before him, Zora Neale Hurston ([1934] 1984) had theorized as central to African American expressive life pushing hard against the limits of Jim Crow culture. Each sped up the tempo and converted the affective energy of wanderlust blues into pleasure-seeking mischief and aspirational thrills. It was music that both emerged out of and responded to the shifting tides of midcentury racial capitalism and the volatile conditions of modernity.

The director Darnell Martin's 2008 film *Cadillac Records* effectively encapsulates a number of these tensions as it traces the rise of Chess Records, founded in 1950 by the white Jewish entrepreneur Leonard Chess and his brother Phil and hailed for its remarkable array of foundational blues musicians—Muddy Waters, Little Walter, Willie Dixon, Bo Diddley, Howlin' Wolf, John Lee Hooker, Buddy Guy—as well as for promoting the early careers of crossover (and out of the blues market) rebels such as Berry (played by Mos Def), who appears midway through the film as a shrewd trickster figure sly enough to face off with white venue managers, claiming, "I can be whoever you want me to be in this fine establishment." Martin's film vividly considers the extent to which questions of manhood, property, and class mobilization undergird rock and roll's origins. Cadillac

Records follows the Polish immigrant Leonard (Adrian Brody) as he pursues a means to shoring up the socioeconomic value of his own inchoate white patriarchy by reaping the fruits of black musicians' artistic labor ("Someday, my wife's gonna drive a Cadillac!"), and it, likewise, explores the complex social and cultural ambitions of the African American artists who produce the Chess Records capital. The film shapes this narrative of masculinist desire, material wealth, and aesthetic production through its focus on the relationship between Leonard and Muddy Waters (Jeffrey Wright). The escalating tensions between these two striving men suggest the extent to which black and white constructions of masculinity in this era were mutually constitutive of each other. Leonard depends on Muddy's performance of sonic and histrionically conceived black masculinity (on hits such as "I Can't Be Satisfied" and "Got My Mojo Working," songs, it is worth noting, that went on to influence rock's first generation of performers, particularly from across the pond) to instantiate his ascendant white manhood. Muddy is dependent on Leonard for both the technological and economic means to produce and distribute his Afromodernist, electric-blues masculinity, which, in turn, provides him with the funds to purchase fancy cars for himself as well as his wife. All of the men in the film are thus driven by an axiom voiced by the narrator, Willie Dixon (Cedric the Entertainer), which asserts that if "you get enough money to cover you, . . . you ain't no Jew boy no more. You ain't no colored boy either. Just green."

But in the era of Jim Crow segregation and what the anthropologist and pop music studies scholar Maureen Mahon refers to as the period characterized by "the racialized political economy of the recording industry" (2005, 146), the Chess brothers' company clearly held the upper hand and often, like their industry peers, took songwriting credits, which enriched them and their fellow industry executives while leaving black recording artists under- or wholly uncompensated for their work. Even the term "rock and roll" has racial capitalism at its core. Attributed to the Cleveland disc jockey Alan Freed, who spun the work of these new artists in the early '50s, it is a term that Freed used in lieu of "race music" so as to market the records to white young listeners who found the blues to be too foreign and taboo. (Some historians note, too, that use of this formulation can be traced back much earlier to the blues, jazz, and gospel eras.) That Martin's film enlists Dixon's character to narrate is a provocative salvo and a kind of symbolic reparations in its own right since this enormously influential bassist and songwriter was one of the central creative forces at the Chess label. Dixon was yet another builder and shaker in early rock and roll whose songs were covered by the white "rock" stars of the 1960s and '70s: Bob Dylan, Cream, Led Zeppelin, the Rolling Stones. He and Ruth Brown went on to lead the movement in the 1970s and '80s to secure copyrights and royalties for pioneering artists like themselves who suffered egregious financial exploitation for significant portions of their careers.

"Rock" is thus a term that is deeply entangled with race, class, sexuality, and the history of men jockeying for social space, audibility, visibility, and cold, hard cash. But from its very beginnings, it was also always a zone where young as well as more seasoned women artists boldly experimented with voice, instrumentality, and showmanship in ways that fundamentally set the music on course to becoming the most popular music genre of the twentieth century. The sanctified singer and steel guitarist Sister Rosetta Tharpe, for instance, dropped a monster hit in 1944, "Strange Things Happening Every Day," which anticipated the inherent swing and playfulness of rock and roll, and the men who came after her brashly lifted her jubilant stage charisma (Wald 2008). Along similar lines, in spite of the fact that Willie Mae

"Big Mama" Thornton appears most often as a historical footnote to Elvis, the woman who recorded Lieber and Stoller's rhythm-and-blues stomper "Hound Dog" in 1952, four years before Presley, innovated a style of vocality that resonates throughout rock's canon. The propulsion and potency of Thornton's signature performances, as the queer theorist Jack Halberstam (2007) has shown, reveals an insurgent style of female masculinity that helped to establish rock and roll's transgressive gender politics. Chess Records' most high-profile female artist, Etta James, was an even more self-consciously disruptive and experimental force in this regard. Originally hailing from the West Coast, James drew on the cultural hybridities of her Bay Area adolescence, her affinity for gut-bucket blues, burgeoning teen rhythm and blues, subcultural nightlife fashion and spectacle, and the vocal virtuosity of queer gospel choir mentors to concoct a kind of charged, aesthetic eccentricity that forecast the modern rock star profile. The daughter of an African American migrant mother who took up prostitution and an absent white father, believed to be the pool legend Minnesota Fats, James has characterized her life and career as fast and furious, as having great difficulty (James and Ritz 2003). And it was her generation, the one that came of age in those heady years of the second Reconstruction, in and around *Brown v. the Board of Education* in '54, the Montgomery Bus Boycott in '55, and the March on Washington in '63, that primarily set in play this music of interracial encounter and new world possibility.

James's rock and roll sister-peer on Atlantic Records, Ruth Brown (so successful at that label that it came to be known as "the House that Ruth Built"), summed up the audacious promise of this moment when she recounted those rugged touring days out on the road and gigging under the pressures of white supremacy. In an interview with the Rock and Roll Hall of Fame, Brown reflects on how this music, "this early R&B" (what she, like Little Richard, claims to stand for "really black" music), "this beat was being picked up by everybody":

> I mean it was danceable, . . . and that's what happened in those days. When we went to the south we played dances where people could enjoy each other. . . . We played facilities where there was a division between the races because at that time it was a no-no to even rub shoulders. It was permissible to dance. . . . If there were not two partitions down the floor there was a rope, . . . a long rope . . . like a clothesline, and on one side it would say 'white' and on one side it would say 'colored.' Don't come across that rope. That was what they intended to have happen. That was not always the case. Because I'm a living witness to how many times those ropes fell down. (Rock Hall, n.d.)

Young women such as Brown and others thunderously brought the ropes down, but by the mid- to late 1960s, walls were replacing them instead. By then, superstar Liverpool lads who had cycled off the concert tour circuit for good were instead immersing themselves in massively experimental studio efforts (the *Sgt. Pepper's Lonely Hearts Club Band* album by the Beatles was released in 1967) that steered away from overtly black American influences and toward Eastern and symphonic sounds, and the especially fetishistic Rolling Stones were, at decade's end, forging ahead with recording albums that continued to champion the sonic blackness of the form in spirit but that also walked a tightrope between paying homage to their heroes and falling into pure racial and cultural mimicry. Guitarist Keith Richards knew his Waters and Diddley licks, and front man Mick Jagger could emulate the longing in Howlin' Wolf's "How Many More Days" and "Little Red Rooster," but their recordings and performances, along with that of their fellow white male musicians—which ran the gamut from deeply inventive to simply ersatz—ultimately eclipsed the work of the black veterans who had gotten the party started. Increasingly, as Mahon and others have shown, the black presence in "rock" could now be found most often in the background, voiced by powerhouse female vocalists such as the fiercely commanding vocalist Merry Clayton, who supplied one of the most famous backup solos in the history of the music on the Stones' 1969 hit "Gimme Shelter" (Mahon 2005). That she was asked by Jagger to belt out the song's most infamous lines, "Rape! Murder! / It's just a shot away" ("It'd be wonderful if a woman could sing this part I'd written about rape and murder," muses Jagger, recalling the origins of how he approached Clayton, in the film *20 Feet from Stardom*: "We'd love to have a woman sing this part! . . . It was kind of a raunchy part."), underscores how racialized and gendered bodies have historically operated as repositories of eroticized mayhem and sexual violence in rock culture (Nelville 2013).

The discursive arm of the music took shape in tandem with these changes and rapidly reinstantiated these kinds of tropes and divisions. Founded in 1967, *Rolling Stone* magazine set to building a taste canon that further whitewashed and masculinized the music, showcasing the criticism of colorful, "Gonzo" journalists such as Lester Bangs and lionizing the heavy sounds of bands such as Led Zeppelin, which became notorious for its flagrant appropriations of material by blues musicians such as Memphis Minnie ("When the Levee Breaks"). In this period of rock's peak ascendance and cultural domination, few artists of color broke through the wall. But singular figures such as Tina Turner and Jimi Hendrix were pivotal not only because of their pathbreaking artistry but also because of the ways that they sustained and redeployed blackness's radicalism in the context of the rock world. A Nutbush, Tennessee, native turned St. Louis migrant, Turner navigated myriad forms of patriarchal and masculinist power in her personal and professional life while nonetheless forging ahead in developing a kind of aggressively controlled movement onstage that recuperated and yet again reimagined the frenetic, embodied energy central to rock and roll's origins. Turner's storehouse of kinetic power, endurance, choreographic discipline, and spectacle in her stage performances recalled key elements of iconic black female dancers who broke through to the global pop mainstream, such as Josephine Baker and Eartha Kitt. Yet she also innovated a distinct kind of dance that shimmied and go-go-ed and reverberated with the plugged-in volume of the newly foregrounded electric guitar in the world of late '60s and early '70s pop. Hers was a kind of movement that physically embodied the history of black diasporic aesthetic radicalism as it perpetually oscillates between the threat of subjugation and the thrill of insistent escape and release. Hendrix, too, as cultural critics such as Paul Gilroy have shown, was an artist who brilliantly transduced black resistance into unmatched instrumental rock and roll virtuosity and exploration that "reach[ed] for and conjur[ed] up not just the future but a more philosophically coherent 'not-yet'" that "unsettled his contemporaries" (2004, 112–25). Hendrix's cosmic utopianism, his "Afrocyberdelia," as Gilroy refers to it, worked in the service of antiwar, Black Freedom Struggle world making that upset rock's racial hierarchies during a remarkable career cut short by premature death.

Hendrix's visionary contributions arguably quickened the pace of rock's avant-gardism, particularly if one considers the fast-evolving queerness of the form, which took a different shape in the early '70s from that of its pioneers' stylings as the glam rock of David Bowie and his fellow gender-fluid Brit and downtown New York comrades gained traction. Bowie's interplanetary and often Brechtian questioning of gender and sexual identity formations reactivated rock's playfully theatrical roots, which his idol, Little Richard, had inspired in him. And artists such as the glam-funk, black feminist supergroup Labelle and the Jamaican dancehall-punk and New Wave queen Grace Jones followed suit as the decade unfolded and in spite of the aggressive homophobia, racism, and sexism that fueled rock's antidisco movement as well as punk's dark underbelly, which the feminist critic Ellen Willis has incisively described as that genre's penchant for the "antihuman" and "antiwoman" (Hoby 2014).

Three decades after the rise of rock and roll, a cadre of New York–based African American artists who had grown up in the wake of both the civil rights and Black Power movements, attended integrated schools, and came of age listening to rock as well as soul came together to form the Black Rock Coalition (BRC), an organization committed to reappropriating the music and supporting black artists dedicated to righting the historical record and dismantling the established hagiography of the genre (Mahon 2004). It was activism set to the sounds of the BRC's most famous band, Living Colour, which would remind audiences that "Elvis is dead," and it gained subcultural momentum in the mid- to late '80s as Prince, the icon who both drew on and wholly reinvented the aesthetics and styles of rock and roll's past, was emerging as a global phenomenon. Prince's music sounded then as well as now like the antidote to antiblackness. At his most radical moments, he was generating an anthem for a new human—what the black feminist philosopher Sylvia Wynter might refer to as a different expression of being human (Wynter and McKittrick 2015). As he chanted out the prophetic call for "reproduction of a new breed, leaders, stand up,

ROCK  DAPHNE A. BROOKS

organize" on more than one occasion, he reminded pop culture of rock's black radical potential (Prince 1981, 2001).

Like Prince, his twenty-first-century protégées—black feminists such as Beyoncé and the Afropunk freedom fighter Janelle Monáe—know that rock was and will forever be a black thing. It is all the more absurd, then, that the former artist's work in 2016 was the subject of heated debates—both before and after her Grammy nomination—as to whether hers was music that "belonged" in the best rock performance category that year. As the *New York Times'* Rob Tannenbaum (2017) reported, "about 70 members of the Rock Sorting Committee met" during nominations season "to discuss, among other topics, whether 'Don't Hurt Yourself' is a rock song. Beyoncé wrote, produced and recorded the song with Jack White, and they used a Led Zeppelin sample. 'We played it for the group,'" Record Academy senior vice president Bill Freimuth declared. "There wasn't all that much discussion. Everybody said, 'That's a rock song.'" Tagging the blues archivist and alternative-rock guitar hero Jack White as her accomplice, Beyoncé, the world's biggest (rock) star, had moved to her own beat like Chuck and Richard and Tina and those venturesome swing men from way back in the day. She had also raided the purloined goods in Zeppelin guitarist Jimmy Page and company's vaults, laying claim to, sampling, and radically repurposing the song that that supergroup had infamously lifted from Memphis "When the Levee Breaks" Minnie. By returning it to the black masses for the post-Katrina age, she had taken the genre simultaneously way back to its rough and gritty, classic blues woman's roots and also forward into the rock and roll future, which is (once again) female.

# 43

## Science
### Daylanne K. English

It is tempting to understand the keyword "science" as fundamentally and strictly an enemy of African American people. And there is no doubt that natural sciences and social sciences in the West have historically helped to construct and reinforce a racial hierarchy: a seemingly data-driven white supremacy built on the presupposed inferiority of nonwhite, particularly black, people. Yet science and critical-historical approaches to science can also serve to dismantle white supremacy, to eliminate race as a viable scientific category, and to affirm the resilience and power of African American intellection, culture, and activism. Especially in the past two decades, science, understood in the contexts of the *arts* and *popular culture*, points us to the most significant political, academic, political, and cultural African American movement since the Harlem Renaissance and the Black Arts Movement: Afrofuturism.

The etymology of the word "science" provides clues as to its ongoing power both to oppress and to liberate. Early modern use of the term "science" signified broadly that which was taught in universities or could be learned by study, without the specific disciplinary connotations that the term now possesses. Although this usage is archaic, science still carries with it a whiff of true knowledge. Current preoccupation with STEM (science, technology, engineering, and math) fields in the administration and regulation of higher education—along with recent trends toward quantitative methods and cognitive and neuroscience studies in the humanities—suggests that, regardless of home discipline, many people in the academy view "science" as the epitome of fact-based, verifiable knowledge—that is, truth. This is *not* to say that such approaches do not produce valuable research but rather that the objectivity associated with scientific study, over and against the apparently more subjective methods of humanistic study, continues to hold a great deal of seductive power.

Science's *method* produces its most seductive claim to truth. The scientific method governs the natural sciences (meaning those disciplines that study the phenomena of the physical universe, including biology, chemistry, and physics) as well as quantitative approaches to the social sciences (meaning those disciplines that study human behavior and social relationships, including psychology, anthropology, and sociology). The scientific method, formulated via the cumulative work of a number of seventeenth-century European philosophers, including René Descartes and especially Francis Bacon, entails systematic observation and experimentation that are initiated by a hypothesis tested via the collection and analysis of data. Testable, quantitative, and objective: these are the primary characteristics associated with the scientific method.

Such a method sounds quite promising for the furthering of our knowledge of the universe, including its humans and its physical phenomena. Of course, the scientific method works, often just as promised, to advance our accurate understanding of the world. Sometimes it has done so in the face of fierce and dangerous opposition. As Stephen Jay Gould succinctly puts it, "the earth really does revolve about the sun" (1996, 54). However, as the rise of scientific racism in Europe and the United States in the late eighteenth century demonstrates, value-free application of the scientific method cannot be guaranteed. As it turns out, quantities can be "mismeasured," to use Gould's apt term, and the

scientific method, like any method, can fail to deliver either objective results or plausible theories. Any study that begins with a hypothesis regarding race or racial difference is always already on shaky ground because it starts from the (faulty) premise that racial difference exists at all, given the widely acknowledged fact that race is a fiction (Keita and Kittles 1997; Templeton 1998; Long and Kittles 2009; Sussmann 2014; Gannon 2016). Perhaps the most infamous of contemporary studies to do so, the best-selling *The Bell Curve*, argued for intelligence differences among ethnic groups using empirical data (Herrnstein and Murray 1994). Studies such as *The Bell Curve* undermine our understanding of human inequality as a product of human-created, rather than biologically determined, forms of social organization. There is a long history in Europe and the United States of such interested (read: racist) science, extending from the foundation of the nation on up to today.

In *Notes on the State of Virginia* (1781), Thomas Jefferson described his plan for the colonization of freed black people to some other land in an anticipated postemancipation era. Along with his fear of black retribution, black-white racial differences that he believed to be "fixed in nature" stood as his primary reason for this colonization scheme ([1781] 1984, 264). Jefferson concluded that these, for him essential, racial differences, not "their condition of life," produced what he perceived to be the "inferiority" of black people (267). A number of race scientists in the nineteenth century furthered a Jeffersonian project of scientifically proving white supremacy. Count Joseph Arthur de Gobineau's four-volume *Essay on the Inequality of Races* (1853–55) was especially influential. Gobineau relied on data and ideas from earlier racial science, particularly the 1839 and 1849 craniometrical studies (measuring skulls to determine intelligence) of the Philadelphia physician Samuel Morton and the polygenetic (multiple genetic origins for the various human races) theories of the Swiss natural scientist Louis Agassiz, published in 1850. Gobineau concluded, just as Jefferson had, that there are "permanent and ineradicable differences" by race and that "dark races are the lowest on the scale" (1915, 125, 205). Complementing the racial science of the period was what we might term a science of class, in which criminality was systematically linked with certain families, classes, or types, via sociological studies such as *The Jukes: A Study in Crime, Pauperism, Disease, and Heredity* (Dugdale [1877] 1910) and Cesare Lombroso's *Criminal Man* (1876), a work that showcased Lombroso's ideas about atavism and race, as in as his declaration that "criminals resemble savages and the colored races" ([1876] 2006, 91).

In the late nineteenth and early twentieth centuries, these hierarchies of race and class merged with nationalist discourse and nascent understandings of human genetics to produce eugenics, the science of breeding better human beings. "Eugenics," a word derived from Greek and meaning "wellborn," was coined in 1883 by Francis Galton, a natural scientist and cousin to Charles Darwin. Eugenics reached a peak in the U.S. during the 1920s, with intelligence testing, immigration restrictions, compulsory sterilization of the "feebleminded," and other social policies all responding to perceived overbreeding by the American dysgenic (i.e., the badly born). Popular culture, too, was influenced by eugenics, as in fitter family contests at state fairs and prize baby contests sponsored by some NAACP chapters. As suggested by this last example, eugenics, despite its origins in racist and classist science, found expression across the political spectrum and across racial lines. W. E. B. Du Bois, for example, argued in 1922 that the "Negro has not been breeding for an object" and therefore must start to "train and breed for efficiency, for beauty" (1922, 152–53).

Although Du Bois held intraracial eugenic ideas (at least for a time), he was a steadfast opponent of white supremacy and racist science. As he declared in his "Manifesto of the Second Pan-African Congress" in 1921, in a direct challenge to Jefferson's and Gobineau's brand of science, "No one denies great differences of gift, capacity and attainment among individuals of all races, but the voice of science, religion and practical politics is one in denying the God-appointed existence of super-races, or of races naturally an inevitably and eternally inferior" (5). And after the 1930s, quite alert to the ways that biological determinism masks injustice, Du Bois distanced himself from eugenics, telling the story of his rebuttal to a white eugenicist in his 1940 autobiography, *Dusk of Dawn*: "To be sure, good seed proves itself in the flower and the fruit, but the failure of seed to sprout is no proof that it is not good. It may be proof of the absence of manure—or its excessive presence" ([1940] 2014, 660).

Du Bois was certainly not alone in his resistance to eugenics and science-based white supremacy; there is a long and distinguished history of challenges to such racist science. African American women writers such as Nella Larsen ([1928] 1986) and Angelina Weld Grimké ([1916] 1998) rejected both white supremacy and any project to breed better human beings (English 2004). During the same period, the anthropologist Franz Boas worked to dismantle the racist and anti-Semitic discourses of primitivism within his field, influencing a generation of anthropologists, including Margaret Mead, Claude Lévi-Strauss, and Zora Neale Hurston. Hurston collaborated with Boas to disprove prior, racist craniometrical studies by measuring heads in Harlem over the course of two years, as Langston Hughes famously described in his autobiography, *The Big Sea* ([1940] 1993, 236).

Of course, science can be racist even when race is not its explicit object of study. In the landmark book

*Medical Apartheid* (2006), Harriet Washington thoroughly documents the long history of unethical American medical experimentation on the black *body*, from Jefferson's testing of a smallpox vaccine on slaves to surgical gynecological experimentation on enslaved black women, to the infamous Tuskegee experiment that involved withholding treatment from poor black men with syphilis, and to recent experimentation on prisoners of color. And it was only with the publication of the science writer Rebecca Skloot's 2010 bestselling book *The Immortal Life of Henrietta Lacks* that the worldwide laboratory use, across fifty years, of cervical cancer cells harvested from a poor black woman, in the absence of any form of patient or family consent, became widely known. Henrietta Lacks's cells were, and continue to be, used for an immense range of (often profitable) histological, immune, and genetic studies.

In spite of the racially specific effects of these recent scientific pursuits, none of them depends on race as a category; however, explicit studies of race and racial difference, along with racially differential public health policies, persist too. For instance, although explicitly eugenic practices may have been on the wane in the United States after the 1930s and the rise of Nazi Germany, less overt but no less eugenic practices continued. Welfare and birth-control policies, differential access to fertility treatment, and insurance practices regarding reproductive health: all can work to promote births among some while discouraging births among others. As a result, sterilization practices between the 1960s and the present have been the most common topic among contemporary scholars who study the ongoing power of racist science and public policy in the United States—for example, Dorothy Roberts in her influential book *Killing the Black Body* (1997). More recently, Roberts has sounded the alarm about a reemergence of genetic

studies of race, cautioning us not to let science reinvent race. As she puts it, in the twenty-first century, a newly "emerging genetic understanding of race . . . focuses attention on molecular differences while obscuring the impact of racism in our society," in what she terms a "new biopolitics of race" (2011, x, xii). And yet African American people themselves are not immune from the allure of sure knowledge that studies of DNA promise. For many, DNA analysis enables a process of identity formation.

Uniquely among contemporary people in the United States, African Americans whose family histories contain enslavement face seemingly insurmountable difficulties in tracing their genealogies. In Alondra Nelson's words, DNA testing seems to be "a cutting-edge answer . . . to a central enigma of African America—a remedy that seemed ripped from the pages of a sci-fi novel" (2016, xi). The popular PBS television show *Finding Your Roots* taps into this drive to know one's own origins, with segments that culminate in DNA blood testing to determine an individual's genetic origins, by precise percentages, in particular regions and populations. Although Nelson points out the contingency and the highly variable nature of the scientific "truth" in such cases, she also understands that African American "root-seekers" are not necessarily looking for an absolutely accurate genetic account but rather something more like a "serviceable account of the past" (2016, 79). They are using science to add a piece to the puzzle of a larger individual, family, and community picture.

But it may not be in the realm of the gene or genetic science that the greatest revisionary and visionary power of science lies for contemporary African American culture but in the realm of the imagination and of humanistic study. For example, Afrofuturism, a flourishing contemporary movement of African American,

**SCIENCE**   DAYLANNE K. ENGLISH

African, and black diasporic writers, artists, musicians, and theorists, "hypothesizes" the *centrality* of African American subjects. It comprises cultural production and scholarly thought—literature, visual art, photography, film, multimedia art, performance art, music, and theory—that imagine and represent greater justice and a freer expression of black subjectivity in alternative times or realities. It offers speculation about a world wherein black people are normative subjects rather than objects of study, often engaging technoculture and the discourses and tropes of science and science fiction to do so.

Samuel Delany has remarked on science fiction's power to critically examine contemporary social formations; it is in the business of representing a "significant distortion of the present," thus enabling a critique of that present (1984, 177). Or, as Fredric Jameson puts it, science fiction's "multiple mock futures" can refashion "our own present into the determinate past of something yet to come," permitting us see "the present as history" (1982, 152). Just so, Afrofuturists reimagine and re-create black experiences, bodies, and identities in other times and realities at least in part in order to critique and supplant *current* racial, social, and economic orders. This is true of Octavia Butler's multiple series of science-fiction novels centered on heroic black woman protagonists and of Janelle Monáe's rebel android alter ego from the year 2719 (O. Butler 1993, 1998; Monáe 2010). The multimedia breadth of Afrofuturism as an artistic/cultural movement finds its analog in current interdisciplinary scholarly work in African American and black diaspora studies that encompasses the humanities and the sciences; see Michelle M. Wright's book *Physics of Blackness* (2015) for an example.

In the end, although "science" may not have morphed precisely into a consistent "friend" within black studies, it does carry new potentialities as a progressive force. Science fiction and Afrofuturism, radical interdisciplinarity in African American and black diaspora studies, black feminist approaches across the natural and social sciences as well as the arts: all are among the aesthetic and critical formations and activisms that will reform science itself.

# 44

## Segregation

David Canton

Many Americans believe segregation was only a southern issue and not an American problem. As a result, when one hears the term "segregation," one thinks of lynching, voter disfranchisement, and separate water fountains, the Jim Crow South. Prior to the passing of the 1964 Civil Rights Act and 1965 Voting Rights Act, the majority of scholarship and the term "segregation" connoted de facto or legalized segregation, and civil rights activists fought to eliminate de facto segregation. From 1909 to 1965, the National Association for the Advancement of Colored People (NAACP) had won numerous court cases that challenged de facto segregation in the South.

The civil rights movement fought to end de facto segregation in the South; but de jure segregation had a long history in the North. According to the historian C. Vann Woodward, "Jim Crow . . . was born in the North and reached an advanced age before moving South in force" (1966, 17). African Americans in the North had the right to vote, but as a racial minority, it was not powerful enough to eradicate de facto segregation. Davison M. Douglass contends that civil rights activists in northern cities fought to eliminate "a dual school system" in the North (2005, 7). During the past two decades, civil rights scholars such as Thomas Sugrue, in *Sweet Land of Liberty: The Forgotten Struggle for Civil Rights in the North* (2008), examine the civil rights struggle against segregated housing and schools in northern cities. In contemporary society, segregation connotes African Americans living in predominantly black neighborhoods and attending predominantly underfunded public schools.

After Reconstruction, the South implemented a legalized system of segregation: Jim Crow. Starting in 1889 in Florida to 1908 in Georgia, southern states passed laws such as grandfather clauses, which required freedpeople's grandfather to have voted so that they could vote, disfranchising thousands of black voters. In addition to political disfranchisement, southern states created segregation laws on streetcars, railroads, and schools to keep the races separate. In 1896, the U.S. Supreme Court ruled in the *Plessy v. Ferguson* decision that "separate but equal" was constitutional. Due to the larger number of free blacks, southern whites developed legalized segregation to ensure white political power. Blacks in the North remained a minority, and because northern whites did not feel as threatened by black political and economic power, de facto segregation was the rule.

Segregation forced African Americans to develop their own institutions. During the nineteenth century, African Americans built churches, schools, and mutual-aid societies to educate and provide financial assistance to members of the community. They also developed national organizations such as the Black Convention Movement and their own newspapers such Ida B. Wells's *Memphis Free Speech*. The historian Darlene Clark Hine states between 1890 and 1950, black professionals had developed their own professional organizations such as the National Medical Association (1895) and the National Bar Association (NBA; 1925). These "parallel institutions . . . nurtured positive self images, sharpen skills, and demonstrate expertise" (Hine 2003, 1280) and provided the foundation for the civil rights movement. Segregation allowed black professionals and laypersons opportunities to strategize, empower, and develop their own cultural legacies. From the eighteenth century to the present, African Americans have created and maintained their own professional and social organizations.

Segregation emerged as a major issue among black leaders. The majority of African American social organizations were black, but they were fighting to end segregation. In January 1934, W. E. B. Du Bois, wrote what many black leaders believed a controversial editorial in the *Crisis* titled "Segregation." Du Bois wrote, "the opposition to segregation is an opposition to discrimination" (20). This summarized the legal struggle to end segregation. However, three months later, in another editorial in the *Crisis*, titled "Separation and Self-Respect," Du Bois stated that the legal or nonlegal separation of humanity requires "internal self-organization for self-respect and self-defense" (85). At the end of the essay, Du Bois writes about the founding of the African Methodist Episcopal church in Philadelphia. These black leaders desired their own black space, while some blacks remained in a segregated white church. Du Bois states, "No matter which solution seems to you wisest," the "only answer" was "internal self-organization" (85). Segregation forced blacks to work with one another to combat segregation and improve their communities. Black lawyers and black activists were in the forefront to end legal segregation. Legalized segregation violated the Fourteenth Amendment, but by the late '40s, this southern strategy had received national attention and resources, while local attorneys in the North had battled housing segregation, in spite of the U.S. Supreme Court decision in *Shelley v. Kraemer* (1948), which declared restrictive covenants unconstitutional.

During the past few years, there have been a number of golden anniversary milestones of events from the civil rights / Black Power era, such as of the Selma march and the founding of the Black Panther Party. The civil rights / Black Power era has eradicated all forms of overt and legalized segregation. However, in 2017, when one talks about segregation, one is usually referring to African Americans in housing and education. In fact, according to the *Atlanta Black Star*, eight of the ten most segregated cities in the Untied States are located in the North (ABS Contributor 2014). Housing segregation impacts the amount of funds and quality of education that a community receives. Teacher of the year Nathan Bowling (2016) argues, "Much of white and wealthy America is perfectly happy with segregated schools and inequity in funding." Segregation is the norm in American public education because it is related to housing. In spite of the 1954 *Brown* decision, housing segregation has left 90 percent of white students attending predominantly white schools and the majority of students of color attending schools with a majority of students of color.

Similar to the nineteenth century, many white Americans contend that black people "naturally" desire to live with each other and that all Americans have the right to live where they choose because discrimination in housing is illegal. In spite of civil rights legislation, segregation continues to create two separate and unequal societies.

# 45

## Sexuality

Marlon M. Bailey and L. H. Stallings

"Sexuality," the word and concept, emerges out of discourses that have produced both problematic and useful ways to understand black sexuality in all its complexities, contradictions, and expansiveness. In its most common understanding, sexuality is the quality of being sexual or possessing sex; it is understood as what one does in terms of sex acts and practices and who one is, often (inadequately) defined as heterosexual, homosexual, or bisexual (Burgett 2007). Sexuality can be best understood, conceptually, as a category that entails desire, pleasure, practice, and more that interact with each other in complicated and often contradictory ways. Sexuality has also been used to denote sex assignment or male-versus-female differences, largely on the basis of genital and secondary sex characteristics and reproductive functions. It is a concept that has been applicable to the social organization and formation of human and nonhumans alike.

In a December 2012 essay in the *Chronicle Review* of the *Chronicle of Higher Education*, titled "Who's Afraid of Black Sexuality?," the writer Stacey Patton suggests that for a long time, scholars, including black scholars, have avoided mentioning the word "sex," let alone discussing it openly. Patton goes on to say that black sex was particularly fraught because it invoked too many taboos: stereotypes and caricatures of "black Hottentots" with freakish feminine proportions; asexual mammies or lascivious Jezebels; and hypersexual black men lusting after white women. This has been compounded by the painful history of slavery, rape, and lynching and the panoply of ways in which black bodies have been subjected to and victimized by brutal forms of sexual violence and abuse by both state and nonstate actors in the U.S. Further, Patton explains in her essay that, conversely, in recent years, some black scholars from a number of disciplines have begun to "break the silence" and conspicuously engage issues around sexuality confronting black communities. This engagement is not just focused on the violence, oppression, and trauma; rather, these scholars examine and highlight eroticism, sexual desire, pleasure, and practice, including nonnormative sexual subjects and community formations. A summit on doctoral programs held at Northwestern University in 2012, titled "A Beautiful Struggle: Transformative Black Studies in Shifting Political Landscapes," inspired Patton's essay. This event sparked a spirited discussion about sexuality studies that marks a pivotal turn in the contemporary discourse on sexuality in the field of African American studies and black communities.

The etymology of "sexuality" is derived from the postclassical Latin *sexualitas*. But the etymology reveals nothing of the history of sexuality, which appears to be just as discursively homogeneous as its linguistic foundations. As documented by the French theorist Michel Foucault's (1978) three-volume treatise on the history of sexuality, sexuality has been constructed by various institutions over the past two centuries: medical and scientific, judicial, religious, military, and economic. One of the most fecund aspects of Foucault's work is his contention that sexuality is produced out of discourse whereby sexual acts become associated with actual human beings. Hence, the "sodomite" becoming the "homosexual" is a modern phenomenon (Foucault 1978). But, while Foucault also highlights the double impetus of power and pleasure embedded in Western constructs of sexuality, the genealogies he relies on are derived from Western regimes of knowledge. For black people, however, the formation of sexuality does not rest solely on a foundation of Greco/Roman/European histories of sexuality, the "objectivity" of the sciences, or Christian dogma. African Americans may have assimilated into such histories, but when resistance to a universal experience of sexuality has been waged, black people relied on the culture, language, and representations produced in their own communities to correct the gaps and errors produced by *a* history of sexuality. According to the ever-changing B.E.D. (Black English Dictionary), there are multiple terms that connote sexuality, all of them heterogeneous and requiring more context rather than a linear symmetrical history.

In addition, research on sexuality has compelled African American studies to redefine and expand its premise as an intellectual field foundationally situated as a linear, unilateral project based on the biological and sociological constructs of race and racialization. In many ways, African American studies remains somewhat ambivalent about sexuality, specifically because the discourses surrounding it cannot be separated from colonial and imperialist legacies. And although African Americans live at the intersections of race, class, and sexuality, ironically, scholarship on black sexuality in African American studies has developed on two contentious and disparate terrains that intend to define, control, and represent discourses on black sexuality in the field and in black culture and politics. Drawing from black feminist and queer theories, some sexuality scholars examine the historical forms of racialized sexual oppression of black people and how black sexual minorities are oppressed within and excluded from black sociocultural institutions. Yet this productive scholarship on sexuality has been suppressed and marginalized in African American studies due, in part, to an overcompensatory response to racist/white-supremacist renderings of black people as sexually deviant. Too often, on this side of the epistemological struggle, an essentialist, race-based, cisgendered, and heterosexist discourse of black sexuality dominates.

However, with the black political scientist Cathy J. Cohen's (2004) notion of "deviance as resistance," it seems that the most generative scholarship on black sexuality that is also critical and contextual has been produced by and from studies of minoritized communities and cultures: those black sexual dissidents who are oppressed within or excluded from black communities. Through their ongoing contestation, the work of these mostly black queer scholars constitutes Foucault's notion of an "insurrection of subjugated knowledges" (1980, 81) in African American studies that uncovers deviant sexual practices and advances an expansive approach to studying black sexuality within its already-situated contexts of race, gender, and class. It is this movement in black sexuality studies—in academic, cultural, and sociopolitical realms—that is most productive and promising toward understanding and capturing the meaning and role of sex and sexuality in the lives of everyday black people.

Historically, from the very beginning of Western Manifest Destiny, sexuality determined one's moral foundation, while morality determined one's humanity. Thus, any analysis of sexuality in African American studies must begin with a discussion of freedom and liberation. For better or worse, sexuality in African American studies has consistently been used to determine the depth and nature of black ontologies. It is, like race, a measure of how one's humanity is defined. Concepts of self-determination within the Black Power movement might be heralded as the significant intervention for rethinking black sexuality, moving away from white theories of hypersexual pathology, trauma, and abuse. Robert Staples's (1971) and Alvin Poussaint's

(*Phil Donahue Show* 1980) early social science work was quite simply about challenging these pathologies. For example, the pioneering sociologist Staples once asked a significant question about sexuality and black America in a 1974 issue of *Ebony* magazine, one that still haunts black people across the globe today: Has the sexual revolution bypassed blacks? Staples may have been comparing the lack of a visible civil rights movement centered on sexuality or sexual identity to white America's historical sexual revolution, but the truth is more complicated since sexuality, including the study of it, entails a revolution, rebellion, and decolonization that would be illegible in white histories of sexuality and sexual revolution. Since black people across the globe continue to live under white supremacy, African Americans' sexual revolution is an ongoing process that does not begin or end with the 1960s. However, what does happen in the late 1960s is a stream of thought that invokes debate about eroticism and sexuality in discourses other than science, medicine, and history.

Unlike any other keyword, "sexuality" demands both rational and affective modalities to circumvent the imperatives imposed by Western empire. The poet and playwright Ntozake Shange asks, "So how do we speak of our desires for each other to each other in a language where our relationships to our bodies and desires lack dignity as well as nuance?" (1992, xx). Shange's question eloquently sums up sexuality, its conflicts, its possibilities, and its origins in African American studies. It also implicates art and culture as important to evolving discourses on black sexuality.

In African American communities, the genealogy of sexuality has been theorized and engaged through the critical/rational as well as the imaginative and affective. This has meant that the most generative sites for understanding sexuality have come from black feminist theories and African American literary traditions.

In each of these sites, the topics of slavery, colonialism, and imperialism have been deliberately taken up as essential to sexuality, and they have done so in a manner that sexology and Eurocentric theories of sexuality have not commented on.

As the remnants of chattel slavery, scientific racism, and eugenics continued to impact African American life, sexuality continued to be an issue, especially in novels by nineteenth-century black women writers, such as Frances Ellen Watkins Harper in *Iola Leroy, or, Shadows Uplifted* ([1892] 1988), Pauline Hopkins in *Contending Forces* ([1899] 1969), and Harriet Jacobs in *Incidents in the Life of a Slave Girl* ([1861] 1988). By fictionalizing sexual topics such as chaste and virginal womanhood, rape, miscegenation, and passing, these texts, alongside conduct manuals written by black ministers and preachers, captured the unaired tensions surrounding the sexual trauma of black women during chattel slavery and white anxiety about black masculinity and hypersexuality in freedom. Male writers such as W. E. B. Du Bois (1920) contributed other theories, resulting in an early archive of black culture and history linking sexual inquiries with a moral agenda to rescue black women's virtue from the clutches of white men and black men's masculinity from white ideologies of deviance.

Later, Richard Wright's *Native Son* (1940), Ralph Ellison's *Invisible Man* ([1947] 1995), John A. Williams's *The Man Who Cried I Am* (1967), Toni Morrison's *The Bluest Eye* ([1970] 2007), and Gayl Jones's *Corregidora* ([1975] 1986) and *Eva's Man* ([1976] 1987) provided daring perspectives on race and gender, observing sexuality as a distinct category that could shift critical conversations about race and black humanity. James Baldwin's *Giovanni's Room* ([1956] 2001) and *Another Country* ([1962] 1993) eventually broached questions of sexual identity to move beyond concerns about proper heterosexuality and productive black families. The 1970s ushered in a new era of critical inquiries and excavation of black sexuality in which critics read not only for race but for gender and sexuality as well. It is no coincidence that the recovery of out-of-print nineteenth-century slave narratives and novels coincided with the Black Women Writers Renaissance and the women's representations of sexuality in their work. Likewise, the social and political discourse of an emasculating matriarch, fueled, in part, by the Moynihan Report (1965), bolstered more work on black sexuality from Robert Staples, who authored *The Black Woman in America: Sex, Marriage, Family* (1973). This book, as well as others, built on the critical tradition left by Du Bois's early questions that linked black liberation with black women's bodies. In this way, it became impossible for any critical analysis to separate gender from sexuality in studies of black sexuality.

Such was the case with the recovery of black women's literary traditions, which sought to correct and collectively engage the discourses of black sexual pathology. During the 1980s, critics such as Hazel Carby (1987), Barbara Christian (1980), Darlene Clark Hine (1989), and Sander Gilman (1985) provided necessary interventions into African American studies by creating a field of inquiry around representation of black women's sexuality. At the same time, the theories of someone such as Hortense Spillers (1987) invoked a diasporic and gender-neutral subject out of African American literary representations of sexuality, such as in Ralph Ellison's *Invisible Man*. Audre Lorde (1984) revised notions of eroticism, elevated sexual difference, and prioritized black feminism. Likewise, Cheryl Clarke began theorizing the failure of a black political sphere to transform its homophobic stance, saying of twentieth-century black politics, "We have expended much energy trying to debunk the racist mythology which says our sexuality is depraved. Unfortunately, many of us have overcompensated and assimilated to the Puritan value that sex is

for procreation, occurs only between men and women, and is only valid within the confines of heterosexual marriage" (1983, 192). Clarke's words were necessary because just as African American studies was moving from a political and activist endeavor to an intellectual enterprise, productive examinations of sexuality were being stymied by conservative gender politics.

Analyses of sexuality in African American studies were also spurred on by the emergence of Afrocentric thought on sexuality. Molefi Asante (1980) and Frances Cress Welsing (1991) put forth essentialist arguments on African sexuality, suggesting that all nonheterosexual forms of sexuality were European cultural importations. Each posited that such categories were themselves the result of white supremacy and terrorism. Major lines of inquiry no longer simply asked whether black people were virtuous and chaste enough to obtain and retain citizenship but whether black hyperheterosexuality and homosexuality were a result of white terror during slavery and Jim Crow. However, anthropologists and historians of the African diaspora, such as James Sweet (1996), Lorand Matory (2005), and Gloria Wekker (2006), provided compelling arguments that alternative sexualities, including homosexuality, have always existed in African cultures, both traditional and modern. Diverse sexualities in Africa predate colonization.

At the beginning of the twenty-first century, black queer studies began to broaden perspectives beyond cisgender heterosexuality and to provide alternative analyses of black sexuality. For example, the "Black Queer Studies in New Millennium" conference (2000) and the collection based on the conference proceedings, *Black Queer Studies* (Johnson and Henderson 2005), ushered in significant interventions in African American studies by emphasizing black queer cultural formations and the queer of color scholars who study them. In what the critics Jennifer Devere Brody and Dwight McBride

(2000) metaphorically denote as "plum nelly," black queer studies located itself in between two fields, queer studies and African American studies, so as to begin the transdisciplinary critique of plumbing or questioning African American studies' avoidance of sexuality and queer studies' avoidance of race. In the questioning of sexuality, queer of color critique insists that African American studies be a site to deconstruct previous sexuality studies and queer theories that make no mention of race and ethnicity. Both African American studies and queer studies changed the questions being asked and the objects of study to answer the questions. Rather than relying on religion and biological sciences, African American studies began to generate theories beyond deracinated histories and discourses of sexuality, specifically interrogating concepts of racialized sexuality.

For example, Abdul Jan Mohammed (1992) develops a theory of racialized sexuality through an analysis of the fictive discourses of Richard Wright. Siobhan Somerville (2000) also uses African American literature and culture to "queer the colorline." The cultural theorist Roderick Ferguson uses canonical texts in African American literature to critique sociological examinations of black sexuality to create his queer of color critique, stating, "The specific history of African Americans' constitution as the objects of racial and sexual knowledge through canonical sociology has produced modes of deployment that cohere with and diverge from those outlined by Foucault" (2004, 72). Elsewhere, Ferguson warns us not to ask, "How can we make sexuality the *object* of African American studies"; instead, we should ask, "In what ways has the racialized, classed, and gendered discourse known as sexuality dispersed itself to constitute this particular discipline or interdiscipline?" (2005, 87). In the majority of his work, Ferguson notes that sexuality is the critical product of interventions made by women of color feminisms. Nevertheless,

as debates about black lesbianism and sex wars demonstrated, women of color feminism had inadvertently erected barriers about proper objects and subjects that queer theory would push against.

Despite the work done by many scholars within black queer studies, too much of African American studies still views sexuality as a minor concern: racial identity and solidarity politics take precedent over sexual identity politics. Therefore, in the first quarter of the twenty-first century, radical studies of sexuality have necessarily become about further resistance to legacies of morality and respectability politics. These strategies entail using improper objects of study to intervene in both queer studies and African American studies. Picking up from where feminists such as Cheryl Clarke left off in her criticism of African American political agendas, Cathy Cohen has consistently advised African American studies to sharpen its knowledge and politics around improper objects and deviance to avoid the fallacy of previous generations. More specifically, Cohen suggests that the repetition of deviant practices by multiple individuals and the creation of new identities and communities can lead to an emerging politics of deviance as resistance (2004, 27). In addition to Cohen's ideas about deviance, Robert Reid-Pharr has also contested queer theory's and queer studies' conservative editorial mandates of language, stating that he has "continued . . . to be amazed by the implication that, even though utilizing a queer apparatus implied a commitment to bringing new topics into polite academic discourse, it did not obligate one to call into question the necessity of the polite, civil, gentlemanly nature of that discourse" (2001, 101). Here Reid-Pharr highlights both the possibilities and limits of black queer theoretical and sociopolitical interventions.

Yet, as noted earlier, often marginalized people and communities and the transgressive practices that they undertake provide a useful perspective for defining and

SEXUALITY   MARLON M. BAILEY AND L. H. STALLINGS

redefining sexuality in general and black sexuality in particular, so as to push beyond the confines of academic discourse. As contemporary scholars refuse to ignore the lives and culture of nontraditional families, sex workers, transgender artists and activists, and queer folk alike, they remind us that black sexuality is lived, just as it is examined and talked about. An ongoing critical dialogic relationship is required, particularly during these times when the stakes are high in the struggle over black sexual knowledge and when the sexual domain continues to be a means through which epistemological, and literal, violence, oppression, and exclusion are inflicted on black people. Likewise, however, this meditation of the keyword and the discursive terrain out of which it emerges highlights the potential for sexuality to be a space of freedom to explore and experience agency and pleasure and to achieve at least a modicum of autonomy and bliss.

# 46

## Slavery

Sowande' M. Mustakeem

"Slavery" describes the condition of a person or people in permanent servitude, dating back to practices of human bondage that began during ancient times. These practices have taken different forms in the evolutionary sprawl of societies from small kingdoms through the vast reach of European imperialism. Primarily due to geographic proximity, throughout most of world history, people have been enslaved by others who have been "racially" (in our modern sense) identical. It was not until the early modern history (sixteenth and seventeenth centuries) that slavery assumed a racialized dimension, as the expansion of European empires accelerated with the Atlantic slave trade. New constructions of national, ethnic, and racial difference emerged as the concept of "race" developed as a crucial teleological justification for the enslavement of millions of Africans and their forced migration to the Americas. This point stresses the need for a substantive grasp of slavery and its central relationship within African American studies.

As part of the British Empire, American settler colonists embraced slavery as a normative part of society. Through America's independence and industrial rise, slavery was fundamental to the nation's legal, social, religious, economic, and cultural development. Inasmuch as slavery was woven into the fabric of the United States, no people's existence had been as inexorably shaped by it as African Americans. It is, therefore, no surprise that slavery is critical to the evolution and understanding of

African American studies. As a discipline, African American studies emerged out of sociopolitical struggles that demanded more than intellectual inclusion at colleges and universities. The field also offered a long-term vision of building a discipline with essential points of intellectual inquiry with important frameworks for the study of the black experience. Although scholarly writing on slavery did not begin with the founding of African American studies, its role remains the central diasporic foundation from and through which all other critical aspects of African American studies have been built over time.

While some of the oldest literature explored in African American studies includes autobiographies from formerly enslaved people, such as Frederick Douglass (1845) and Harriet Jacobs (1861), it was in 1896 that W. E. B Du Bois published the first African American scholarly monograph on the slave trade, *The Suppression of the African Slave Trade* (1896), based on his doctoral dissertation at Harvard. The book stood as the dominant narrative showing intellectual depth and grasp of the ending of a commercial enterprise founded on the buying and selling of black bodies. It proved especially instructive for many scholars, setting into motion the wheels of intellectual engagement through the exploration of slavery's many contours and scholarly debates on its critical themes. Du Bois's book framed the intellectual tone of inquiry, by exploring slavery's economic motives as a crucial basis for the racialized exploitation of African people. In the opening years of the twentieth century, these explorations of the past served dual purposes: (1) such discourses were critical in confronting and surviving the blatant racism in everyday life, and (2) their formulation allowed African Americans to develop an autonomous voice, value, and most of all, respect for the archival productions of black historical narratives. This work, of course, reflected all too well the racial politics of intellectual history in the United States, which was often dismissive, if not hostile, to black assertions of humanity. Few white historians of slavery were as well known as Ulrich B. Phillips, most widely remembered for his 1918 publication *American Negro Slavery*. In his treatise, Phillips offered a deeply paternalistic view of the United States' "peculiar" institution, arguing that black people were not only happy as slaves but civilized by slavery. Slavery was, Phillips argued, a benign institution that transformed African savages into docile servants for whites. His work affirmed widespread perceptions of white racial superiority, while also stressing the glaring need for epistemic challenges that would disrupt ahistorical, racist, and myopic narratives of the black past.

While many white historians were less moved by Du Bois's view of slavery and the economic consequences of the U.S. slave-trading enterprise, his pioneering interpretations forged several shifts in the writing of slavery and the slave trade among other African American intellectuals. These heroic efforts to engage black history as a professional enterprise were led most diligently by Carter G. Woodson, who worked toward archiving black history and creating an intellectual space for the community to ensure a future for black historical and cultural studies. This was realized most profoundly through Woodson's establishment of the Association for the Study of Negro Life and History (ASNLH, 1915) and the *Journal of Negro History*. Such empowering and institutionalizing efforts were deeply aligned with progressive and collective racial uplift endorsed by many black leaders of the early twentieth century. As a result, research-based rigorous productions of collective history, centering on slavery, emerged during this period. These included early works by Harvey Wish (1964), Raymond and Alice Bauer (1942), Herbert Aptheker (1943), Darold Wax (1967), and Lorenzo Green (1944), among many others, who published books as well as scholarly articles in the *Journal of Negro History* (Dagbovie 2007, 2017).

As African American leaders battled slavery's many legacies, including codified forms of oppression and violence, a classic 1933 text by the Brazilian scholar Gilberto Freye, *The Masters and the Slaves*, set yet another hostile racial tone for the study of plantation slavery. Many U.S. scholars were forced to refute the work, while attending to the distinct similarities and differences between U.S. and Brazilian forms of slavery (Wish 1937; Bauer and Bauer 1942; Wax 1967; L. Green 1944; H. Aptheker 1943). The more macro-global approach to uncovering slaving commerce expanded onward with Eric Williams's 1944 book *Capitalism and Slavery*, centering on the commercial rise of industries and wealth tied to the exploitation of enslaved bodies. This book in many ways signaled the end of a period and a scholarly shift that still focused deeply on the economic ramifications of capitalistic endeavors through slavery and its inhumanity to black others.

In the postwar period, the foci of slavery were ever shifting, and slave-trade scholarship soon delved into deeper economics and sophisticated data sets to uncover a slaving past at sea full of unimaginable horrors. Kenneth Stampp's *The Peculiar Institution: Slavery in the Ante-bellum South* (1956) and Stanley Elkins's *Slavery: A Problem in American Institutional and Intellectual Life* (1959) were two classic texts of the era. And while historian John Blassingame ([1972] 1979) rejected Elkins's thesis that slavery reduced many slaves into a "Sambo" or infantile state, Stampp's and Elkins's works gave slavery scholars an intellectual contrast to the mid-twentieth-century U.S. still grappling with realizing freedom and democracy.

Plantation slavery scholarship continued through the civil rights movement and Black Power eras as scholar-activists from many disciplines made important contributions to the histories through new questions of the archives and fragmented sources. Such revived engagement in slavery's racialized past expanded access to black history for many people—not only in the collegiate world but also among the black masses. This was most evinced through wide circulation of *Jet* and *Ebony* magazines, which often educated those who were unable to be in the university's halls of learning. The San Francisco State College conference of 1968 made hopeful an actively vibrant future of black studies. Simultaneously, there were shifts in scholarly methods across the country and worldwide, signaling new directions of the study of race and slavery. Increasingly, scholars shifted the gaze to the experiences of enslaved people, researching and writing to expand the humanization of those who were most dehumanized by enslavement.

Winthrop Jordan's 1968 seminal text *White over Black: American Attitudes towards the Negro, 1550–1812* was published the same year that black studies came into most tangible being, providing an important historical treatise on the foundational ideas around the history of race in the United States. The following year, another book with critical acclaim was published: *The Atlantic Slave Trade: A Census*, by Philip Curtin. It introduced a newer method of assessing the number of enslaved Africans through a more scientific evaluation. Even more critical to the future of slave-trade scholarship was Curtin's significantly lower numerical estimation of slavery's toll, which was revised downward to ten million from Du Bois's early estimation of fifteen million. This estimation, in turn, became the basis of scholarly debate for many people across the globe in history, political science, economics, and many other fields, which reflected the then-current influence of the rise of cliometrics.

While numbers were sensationalized by a multitude of scholars attempting to get closest to slavery's full body count on ships and plantations, there remained a greater emphasis on religion, race, African culture, resistance, and the racial legacies of sickness and mortality in the world of slavery. Scholarship on the everyday life of slavery expanded through the impactful works of Eugene Genovese (1974), Todd Savitt (1976), Gerda Lerner (1972), and William D. Piersen (1977).

To be sure, the decade of the 1960s was framed by major epistemic upheavals. Amid the protests in pursuit of justice and peace, a key text on the transatlantic slave trade came with Daniel Mannix and Malcolm Cowley's 1962 *Black Cargoes*. Three years later, Daniel Patrick Moynihan infamously penned his 1965 report *The Negro Family: The Case for National Action* and, consequently, precipitated vigorous debates about the role of black women, from slavery onward, as matriarchal figures in black families. Politically driven, the report spilled over into the production of scholarship on black women and their many histories. Theretofore, there was an acute lack of scholarship centered on black women, let alone focused on their traumas in bondage. This fundamental shift to examine the role of gender in slavery began to gain traction in African American studies in the 1970s.

Angela Davis in 1971 wrote her critically acclaimed article "Reflections on the Black Woman's Role in the Community of Slaves," which placed black women in the lexicon of memory and critical meaning of slavery for the first time, showing the myriad roles forced on them across conditions of enslavement. Although the article was written while Davis was infamously incarcerated, it served as a critical influential moment for a future of scholarship fully attentive to the range of black women and their diverse experiences in bondage. Subsequently, African American studies and history scholars such as Darlene Clark Hine (1986), Deborah Gray White ([1985] 1999), and Nell Painter (1997) emerged as some of the most prominent scholars to explore gender and its complications more seriously.

The 1980s saw a rise in narratives of slavery based on resistance, death in slavery, and the ever-explosive writing on quantity and the slave trade. Vincent Harding's classic text poetically tracing the flow of slavery and beyond, *There Is a River*, was published in 1981. The study of black women—in slavery and freedom—continued to expand, even in fictional literature. Mildred D. Taylor's novel *Roll of Thunder Hear My Cry*, published in 1976, and Octavia Butler's classic science-fiction novel *Kindred*, published in 1979, reimagined slavery in nuanced ways. Though works of fiction, these new approaches resonated with scholars of slavery in African American studies. For example, the exploration of slavery with historical nonfiction found fascinating complementary use with Toni Morrison's novel *Beloved* (1987). In fact, some of these novels on slavery became required reading in U.S. schools.

The 1990s represented a monumental turning point and an expansion of scholarship on slavery. With increased attention to various forms of racial inequities, bias, and abuses, there emerged a growing emphasis on black history and culture, which complemented the more visible expression of black political activism. Therefore, alongside Paula Giddings (1984), Saidiya Hartman (1997), David Barry Gaspar (1993), and Michael Gomez (1998), the study of slavery grew exponentially from historians and literary scholars. Additionally, many people also learned from notable public historians such as John Henrik Clarke (Bourne 1996), along with black psychologists, especially Na'im Akbar (1996). These popular scholars made connections between the contemporary conditions of people who have struggled through the psychological and cultural intergenerational legacies of enslavement. Various debates and theories invigorated the field. One theme that has continued to generate considerable discussion in African American studies is the agentic nature of enslaved people. To what degree did enslaved Africans exert agency and resistance and cultivate and sustain identities separate from those imposed on them by their enslavers?

One leading voice in this debate is sociologist Orlando Patterson (1982), who has argued that slavery is a form of "social death," where the enslaved are rendered so powerless that they have no control of their own most basic human needs, including the ability to defend oneself from sexual assault or other forms of physical and mental abuse. Even the instinctive will to protect one's child is denied those who are in bondage. Their very identity has been shaped by the condition of slavery, erasing the critical features that make humans socially engaged within communities and societies. A person's worth as chattel is akin to the worth of an inanimate object or an animal. Other scholars, particularly historians, have disagreed with the notion of absolute social death for the enslaved. Sterling Stuckey (1987), Michael Gomez (1998), and other historians have explored African cultural retention as surreptitious forms of resistance, while Manisha Sinha (2016), Tera Hunter (2017), Erica Armstrong Dunbar (2017), and Richard J. M. Blackett (2018) have explored the curious ways that enslaved people have resisted via escape, sabotage, and rebellion, sometimes with black and white abolitionist collusion. Black people, enslaved or not, as these historians detail, managed to forge a strong cultural identity as partial respite from the horrors of their condition. They maintained and affirmed their sense of humanity, down to the impulses to create art, worship, and build communities—even in the state of slavery. Moreover, these communities became the foundation for the free African American social world that coalesced in the aftermath of the Civil War and end of slavery in 1865.

The public gaze on history and its transmission continues to circulate beyond historians and other scholars toward musical artists, filmmakers, and visual artists such as Kara Walker, whose work depicts silhouettes and shadows of people embroiled in various slave-based settings. These artists are forging, albeit basic, understandings of African American studies, blackness, black history, and most of all the meanings, limits, relevance, and reinterpretations of a distant and not-too-distant past through their art. Various scholars have explored these works, evincing the continued expansion of how slavery is discursively studied, understood, interrogated, and positioned in the field (Mustakeem 2016).

# 47

## Soul

Emily J. Lordi

"For those who don't understand / Soul, there is this word, / you never will" (B. Simmons [1967] 2007, 308). The parting blow of Barbara Simmons's 1967 poem "Soul" typified black artists' discussions of soul in the Black Power era. Yet even as writers and artists insisted that "soul" could not be defined, their discussions of it consistently outlined a hermeneutics of black experience that recuperated suffering into the worldly badge of soul. So whereas the term had evoked a deep spiritual-racial consciousness at least since W. E. B. Du Bois's theorization in *The Souls of Black Folk* (1903), it was in the late 1960s that "soul" acquired keyword status, emerging as a name for the social and aesthetic grace wrought from racialized pressure. In an era of conservative reentrenchment and spectacular antiblack violence, debates about soul helped to mark black cultural production as the desired yet inappropriable result of oppression while organizing a community's redefinition—from "Negro" to "black," civil rights to Black Power—around the concept of resilience.

While many commentators have described soul as black essence (see Moten 1999, 171–74; Gilroy 1998, 250–52), it is more fruitfully understood as what Robin D. G. Kelley calls "a discourse" through which black Americans reimagined the contours of their community in the late 1960s (1998, 25). Kelley writes, "The concept of soul was an assertion that there are 'black ways' of doing things, even if those ways are contested and the boundaries around what is 'black' are fluid.

How it manifests itself and how it shifts is less important than the fact that the boundaries exist in the first place" (26). In other words, soul did not signify a "repository of racial consciousness" so much as it became a means of what Toni Cade Bambara might have called "gathering-us-in" (Van Deburg 1992, 205; Bambara 1981, xxix). Monique Guillory and Richard C. Green's anthology *Soul: Black Power, Politics, and Pleasure* (1998), which offers the most extensive theorization of the concept to date, stresses the word's multiplicity of meanings. But I would stress that, despite its capaciousness, the discourse of soul did encourage a specific and historically grounded vision of black struggle and survival. If the black aesthetic was a theory of black art making meant to establish criteria for the just evaluation of black artists' work, soul was a theory of life designed to fortify one's sense of belonging to a uniquely resilient and capacious black collective.

Before soul was consolidated as a musical genre or a cultural style, it was most often described as a quality associated with African American music. In a pioneering 1961 article about the new subgenre of "soul-jazz," the *Ebony* writer and editor Lerone Bennett claimed that soul was not so much a form of music as "the feeling with which an artist invests his creation" (112). The techniques for expressing that feeling, according to Bennett and many others, were honed in the black Baptist church. By tying black musical aesthetics to the church, which Bennett coyly described as "a never-never land from which [white musicians] are barred" (114), Bennett and other commentators framed soul as a spiritual quality that whites could not appropriate. As the term came to signify a massively popular genre of music, writers increasingly tied the "soul" of soul music not only to the church but also to the historical conditions that had made the church a segregated crucible of black expression in the first place. In the landmark 1969 book *The*

*Sound of Soul*, Phyl Garland dated soul to the arrival of the first enslaved Africans at Jamestown, arguing that, notwithstanding its popularity among whites, "soul music in all of its forms is the aesthetic property of a race of people who were brought to this country against their will and were forced to make drastic social adjustments in order to survive in a hostile environment" (vii). Such claims strategically turned black social oppression into a kind of cultural advantage, which commentators often described in spiritual terms. At a moment when it was becoming possible to describe oneself as "spiritual but not religious"—a moment when, as Amiri Baraka described it, religious concepts such as faith and transformation were "expand[ing] past religion" to "permeate the entire culture" (1987, 270)—the language of soul offered a secular redemption narrative that posited black suffering as the medium of worldly grace.

That grace was often manifest as a stylized performance of survivorship, and it had representative artists, sounds, and images: Otis Redding's sweating brow, James Brown's "hardest-working-man-in-show-business" dance moves, Aretha Franklin's labored yet astounding vocal pyrotechnics. But the discourse of soul was elastic enough to encompass countless "how I got over" stories about people's own lives. The language of soul therefore democratized and spiritualized theories of black experience that had previously been routed through the subject of the blues. While the blues had been largely associated with Langston Hughes's "low-down folks" ([1926] 1998, 55) and Baraka's (poor and working-class) "blues people," soul was something that, according to the television host Ellis Haizlip, all black people possessed, regardless of "economic or educational or social level" (quoted in Wald 2015, 64–65). The aim of Haizlip's public access show *Soul!* (1968–73) was to gather and sacralize black community—to generate, in the words of the critic Clayton Riley (1970), "a people's

sense of themselves as a reborn, spiritually awakened 20th-century tribe" (quoted in Wald 2015, 105).

Garland's and other critics' descriptions of soul as the enviable product of racial struggle have proven remarkably durable. As late as 1994, for instance, the linguist Geneva Smitherman defined soul as "the essence of life; feeling, passion, emotional depth—all of which are believed to be derived from struggle, suffering, and having participated in the Black Experience. Having risen above the suffering, the person gains *soul*" (2000, 266). For subsequent generations of intellectuals sensitive to the risks of essentialism, Smitherman's definite article ("*the* black experience") tends to catch the eye quicker than does her modifier ("the *black* experience"). Despite Kelley's insistence that soul discourse sought to validate nonwhite ways of seeing and doing things, "post-soul" discourse often associates soul itself with the policing of black authenticity. It is therefore important to discuss theories of post-soul in whose wake soul has been retroactively and reductively defined.

Although the term "post-soul" was originally used by Nelson George (2001) and Mark Anthony Neal (2002) to describe the promises and perils of post-1960s black popular culture and politics, the dominant strain of post-soul discourse takes up the more optimistic accounts advanced by Greg Tate in his 1986 *Village Voice* essay "Cult-Nats Meet Freaky-Deke" and Trey Ellis in his 1989 *Callaloo* article "The New Black Aesthetic." Both works, which hailed a new generation of black artists unfettered by Black Arts / Black Power–era strictures and free to "crossbreed aesthetic references," have been foundational to celebrations of post-soul aesthetics that link soul itself to "say it loud" machismo, compulsory heterosexism, and a narrow view of what counts as a black aesthetic (G. Tate [1986] 1992, 207). In a 2007 issue of *African American Review* devoted to post-soul aesthetics, for instance, the editor, Bertram Ashe, claims that, in contrast to the "fixed, iron-clad black aesthetic" of the 1960s, post-soul artists represent "blackness [as] constantly in flux" (615). One problem with this influential paradigm is that it overemphasizes integration as a positive turning point in the history of African American aesthetics; another is that it reframes the Black Arts and Black Power movements as primary obstacles to black expressive freedom, thereby shifting the object of critique from the repressive state onto the movements designed to defeat it.

Despite the popularity of this view, several recent studies of Black Arts and Black Power—by James Smethurst (2006), Margo Crawford and Lisa Gail Collins (2008), Aldon Nielsen (2007), Amy Ongiri (2010), Cynthia Young (2006), Darieck Scott (2010), Gayle Wald (2015), Tanisha Ford (2015), and GerShun Avilez (2016)—have, as Gayle Wald writes, challenged "prevalent assumptions about the 1960s and 1970s nationalist political culture as a homophobic and patriarchal monolith" in the interest of recovering the nuances and textures of these movements (2015, 19). These new works of scholarship encourage a new vision of soul: as a complex discourse that operated in tandem with but also independently of Black Power politics.

There are several other directions that explorations of soul music and culture might take. We might examine soul music through the feminist, queer, and homosocial performances that post-soul theory associates with a later historical moment. Whereas Francesca Royster (2013) highlights a queer post-soul aesthetic in the work of musicians such as Grace Jones and Michael Jackson, we can examine the queer aesthetics of soul music itself. We need not look far to find queer and gender-nonconforming alternatives to the archetype of "Black Macho" soul: they are in Nina Simone's deep voice, Marvin Gaye's falsetto singing, the gold chainmail suit that Isaac Hayes wears at the 1972 Wattstax concert, and

Aretha Franklin's defamiliarizing concept of "feel[ing] like" (but not necessarily *being*) a "natural woman."

While scholars such as Cynthia Young (2006) have addressed the global commitments of Black Power activists within the United States, Tsitsi Jaji (2014) and Tanisha Ford (2015) have amplified the international dimensions of soul music and style. Ford highlights a "soul style" of adornment popularized by black women singers such as Miriam Makeba, Odetta, and Nina Simone, whereas Jaji examines the 1971 film of the "Soul to Soul" concert held in Accra that year as both a representation of Pan-African unity and "a remarkable document of some of the contradictions between local, national, and transnational forms of collectivity" (2015, 189).

In addition to studying soul as a discourse of black resilience that encompasses varied expressions of gender and sexuality and that informs myriad local and international communities, we might also theorize soul literature alongside soul music. I myself have posited James Baldwin as a soul writer, for instance, just as other critics frame Ralph Ellison as a jazz writer and Gayl Jones a blues novelist; not only does Baldwin's career trajectory from child preacher to public intellectual-prophet reflect soul singers' own movements from gospel to popular music, but, according to Phyl Garland, Baldwin's *The Fire Next Time* offers "perhaps the most eloquent and concise definition of soul . . . ever to be set down on paper" (1969, 27; Lordi 2016a). Elsewhere, I suggest that Audre Lorde's "biomythography" *Zami* contains a theory of soul that resonates with Aretha Franklin's and Nina Simone's formal and thematic enactments of survivorship (Lordi 2016b). These women artists' synthesis of multiple generic modes could, moreover, be aligned with the aesthetic diversity of other soul-era writers and singers, such as Toni Morrison and Donny Hathaway. Such a cross-medial approach might also highlight shared structural devices, such as the "false endings" that are featured in soul performances as well as in literary narratives. How might those moments when a song fades out only to start up again illuminate Baldwin's *Another Country* (1962) or Morrison's *Sula* (1973), in which a main character or characters die long before the narrative concludes? To view these texts and performances through a soul paradigm is not only to add "soul aesthetics" to the roster of musical aesthetics now codified within African American literary studies (blues, jazz, hip-hop, post-soul). It is also to see how black artists working in and through the civil rights and Black Power eras translated suffering and loss into a "will to proceed" against seemingly impossible odds (Moten 1999, 174)—which was, at heart, what the discourse of soul was about.

# 48

# Transnationalism

Quito Swan

Borrowed judiciously and grappled with by a myriad of academic disciplines, "transnationalism" broadly refers to the ways in which peoples, ideas, and culture transcend the borders of nation-states and their adjacent structures in their lived experiences (Stephens 1998). "Black transnationalism" usually refers to the ways in which Black freedom struggles have related to one another beyond the boundaries of white nationhood.

African American studies and its disciplinary relatives have long been uncomfortably concerned with the overlapping questions of Black transnationalism, race, and politics (Harris [1982] 1993a; Hanchard 2004). They have historically framed "Black transcendence" by terms produced by Black movements and praxis—such as "Ethiopianism," "Black nationalism," *négritude*, the "Black international," and "Pan-Africanism"—as opposed to Black transnationalism. For example, African diaspora studies has inherently been an interdisciplinary project of Black transnational *border thinking* (Mignolo and Tlostanova 2006). It has sought to make sense of the historical, political, and cultural linkages between Black communities across the globe (Patterson and Kelley 2000). From its inception, diaspora studies was intended to be a discourse that included the Atlantic, Indian, and Pacific Oceans (Harris 1971). However, triggered by Paul Gilroy's popular *Black Atlantic* (1993), the Anglophone Atlantic has arguably been a border more difficult to breach for scholarship on Black transnationalism than has been the nation-state.

This essay illumines transnationalism through the historical, cultural, gendered, and political lens of the global Black Power movement. Traversing the thread of *Black radical imagination*, this entry methodologically transcends the walls of prose, archival memory, and historical convention (Kelley 2002; Rickford 2016).

Black Power's transnationalism began in Africa, the cradle of humanity. While the African diaspora usually refers to the dispersal of African people outside of Africa, Africa produced diasporas within the continent as well. African history began long before the construction of nation-states. African communities related to one another through a diverse set of geographical, cultural, religious, ethnic, political, gendered, linguistic, kinship, economic, ancestral, and cosmological relationships and *syncretisms*.

African people traveled the world before the idea of Europe was born. However, the creation of the modern African diaspora was largely launched by the Atlantic and Indian Ocean slave trades. Europe's enslavement, dispersal, and colonization of millions of African people and hundreds of Africa's communities, ethnic groups, states, and nations created new Black diasporas. Central to the formation of the diaspora was Africa's own challenges to these modes of genocide and the provenance of Africa's internal *transnationalisms*. Dispersed across the Americas, Africa, Europe, Asia, and Oceania, the painful process in which African people became "African" and "Black"—Garifuna, Negro, "Bush" Negro, Mulatto, Gullah, Quadroon, Seasoned, Maroon, Quilombola, Zanj, Moor, African American, Aborigine, Akátá, Jump Ups, Country, Town, Saltwater, West Indian, Habshi, Mina, Kanak, Geechee, Creole—was in itself a project of forced and intentionally resistant *Black transnationalism*.

The freedom struggles of the modern Black world were transnational and international, arguably aimed at dismantling and delegitimizing the power of white transnationalism and the violence of the *myth of white supremacy* (Martin, Wilkins, and West 2009). This *Black radical tradition* (C. Robinson [1983] 2000) included the dramatic fights against slavery across the Atlantic, Pacific, and Indian Ocean worlds, the formation of maroon communities (Mexico's Yanga, Janjira's Siddis, Jamaica's Nanny, and Iraq's Zanj), the creation of Africana culture systems (Brazil's Candomblé, Cuba's Lucumi, Trinidad's Shango Baptists, Haiti's Vodun, the Nation of Islam), the Haitian Revolution, and Melanesian resistance to *blackbirding*. Historically, the diaspora cosmologically, physically, and politically resisted the white world's transnational definitions of nation, gender, race, state, and labor. Along the way, members of the African diaspora crafted new identities through cultural and political syncretism with other African ethnic groups. Of course, all of this occurred within the context of and collective struggle for power (Gomez 1998, 2005).

In 1914 in Jamaica, Marcus and Amy Ashwood Garvey founded the Universal Negro Improvement Association, which was eventually headquartered in the Black transnational streets of Harlem, New York. Along with millions of African men and women from across the world, they built the UNIA into the world's largest Black mass movement. Under the banner of "Africa for the Africans at home and abroad," the UNIA challenged white-supremacist transnationalism across the British, German, Portuguese, Spanish, French, Dutch, American, and Australian (neo)colonial and imperial worlds (R. Martin 2012; U. Taylor 2002).

Emerging in the 1960s, the Black Power movement arguably was the most visible example of global Black transnationalism since the UNIA. *Black Power was a political Anansi.* Reminiscent of the lore of this quintessential, trickster hero of the black Americas, Black Power spread across the world in ways both predictable and unexpected. It traversed along the long-standing webs of historical Black internationalism, such as Black nationalism, Pan-Africanism, *négritude*, civil rights activism, *cimarronaje*, African diasporic liberation struggles, and Global South revolutionary praxis. From the fibers of these battle-tested forms of protest, it spun new networks of global radicalism. Like our proverbial spider— *sometimes man, sometimes spider woman*—Black Power boldly weaved a tapestry of ironic possibilities that linked the Black world sometimes through contradiction, coincidence, and intentionality in ways that require us, now, to look twice to notice. *Elegba, too, makes history.*

Black Power broke the chains of the $40 million slave who refused to tuck in her jersey. She bum-rushed boxing rings in Kinshasa through the gloves of world champions like Muhammad Ali, donned gold medals with clenched fists at Olympic games like Tommie Smith and John Carlos in Mexico City, and fashioned college basketball uniforms like Bo Ellis at Marquette that made the rage of an entire Black, fed-up generation look like "new money" (Levy-Hinte 2008; Pudi 2014). It was in the fliers denouncing racism in Australia distributed by Rasta activists at the grounds of Australia's Test Cricket team's 1973 match in Jamaica. The fliers were written by the Australian Black Power activist Bobbi Sykes while he was in Kingston helping to organize the Sixth Pan-African Congress (Sykes 1998). Black Power was as Pan-African as Howard University's 1971 Division I soccer champions (S. Lee 2016). It was in the red, black, and green wristband wiping the sweat from the brow of Viv Richards, after he sent yet another cricket ball beyond the boundary for the West Indies' 1979 Test Match championship victory against England (S. Riley 2010). *Black Power saw itself as a child of the last over, on a Fanonian mission of no return to finish the incomplete projects of Black liberation.*

Black Power was a time-traveling Pan-African sound system (Jaji 2014). It was a reggae chant, a political lament against Babylon. The Last Poet onstage, the first encore of an outdoor Nina Simone concert, a 1969 Jamaican sound system called *Kilimanjaro*. George Jackson on Steel Pulse's 1979 *Tribute to the Martyrs*. A *stepping razor* that would have walked into Rome and started a fire if only it could have gotten off the Vatican's immigration *stop list*. London Black Panther Olive Morris speaking into a megaphone—putting pure *pressure* on Brixton like Horace Ové (1976), Black Uhuru and *Rocksteady*'s Alton Ellis. Black Panthers in Trinidad's carnival, Toronto's Black Student Union boycotting Carabana 1970, Bahia's Ile Aiye, Afro-Venezuelans calling down San Juan in Curiepe. Peter Tosh giving discourses on colonialism. West Papua's Black Brothers, Melbourne's Koori Club, and Fela's Shrine. *Water Nah Get No Enemy.*

Black Power was not a gentleman *like that* but could dress like one if need be. Its *liberated threads* included *elekes*, top hats, fatigues, khufis, tams, Adidas mundials, a black beret and leather jacket, jellabiyas, sandals, dashikis, locks, jacket and tie, Skywalker's midnight Jedi suit in the lair of Jabba, Bruce Lee's ganzie in the *Fist of Fury* (Ford 2015).

Her mother wore many faces. Oshun carrying blades under her *lapa*. Nanny waging guerilla war in the mountains of Jamaica. Black Power was the Vodun blessed knife of Cécile Fatiman—at Bois Caïman, she cut the throat of a pig to launch the Haitian Revolution. As true as Truganini, she survived a gunshot to her head while fighting against Tasmania's British invaders. She guided the canoe of the five Melanesian women from the Solomon Islands, who took part in a "payback killing" for the kidnapping of their brothers by white blackbirders. *Make them think twice.* Black Power's powerful hands simultaneously loaded the rifles of Ida B. Wells, Harriet Tubman, and Yaa Asante Waa. She had the Black world looking to the east for the coming of a black queen, like Empress Taitu's checkmate of Italian imperialism at

Adwa. Black Power *was* 1896. She sat next to Ana Julia Cooper at the 1900 Pan-African Congress. She survived the 1912 massacre of Cuba's Partido Independiente de Color with Reyita. She watched Louise Langdon, the Grenadian-born mother of Malcolm X, navigate the Caribbean, Canada, and the United States under the banner of the UNIA. She built clandestine Black liberation armies with Grace Campbell and the African Blood Brotherhood. She spoke of "Internationalisme Noir" à la Martinique's Jane Nardal in 1928. She was a creased copy of the *Negro World*, nestled under the arm of Madame M. L. T. De Mena, fluent in the Black nationalism of Henrietta Vinton Davis. A brown-skinned lady smuggling food to the Mau-Mau. Amy Jacques Garvey loading a Kalashnikov. Left of Marx like Claudia Jones.

Black Power told stories that transcended time, nation, and space. She was both poet and poem. Backed against the political walls of oppression, she wrote herself into the historical consciousness of the world. An artist. Black Power liked to *conversate* and congregate in many languages, lingua, creoles, and patois. You could find her at Montreal's 1968 Congress of Black Writers, Atlanta's 1970 Congress of African Peoples, and Tanzania's Sixth Pan-African Congress (1974). She spoke through the words and the art and the photographs in the pages of Jamaica's *Abeng*, *Muhammad Speaks*, Bermuda's *Black Beret*, Australia's *Kooribana*, *Black News*, and *Smoke Signals*, *Présence Africaine*, *Black Panthers Speak*, Barbados's *Black Star*, Antigua's *Outlet*, Belize's *Amandala*, Curaçao's *Vitó*, St. Vincent's *YULIMO*, Guyana's *Ratoon*, and Trinidad's *Moko*. She pressed her own narratives through spaces such as Black Classic Press, Bogle-Ouverture Publishers, Third World Press, Panaf Books, and Kitchen Table: Women of Color Press.

Black Power was a transnational chef. Its radical recipes for Black liberation called for cups of Malcolm, bowls of Bassett's white toad, pounds of Garvey, dashes of Ida, spoons of Ataï, a piece of Guevara, Angela's anise, ground-up Rodney, Assata's sorrel, a bushel of fresh Fanon, seven scoops of Winnie Mandela, a whisk of Denis Walker, lickle bit of Cabral, basil de Biko, Empress Menen's berbere, cubes of Dessalines's bouillon, Miriam Makeba's margarine, and sprinkles of King. Lawd a mercy, even Bob Marley couldn't simmer down Black Power's pepper pot. For Leo Hannett and the Niugini Black Power Group, Black Power was the ginger, pepper, and limestuff of self-determination. As relative to Papua New Guinea as the *betel nut*, it was a pot of ital stew (Hannett 1971). It spread across the Pacific, Indian, and Atlantic Ocean worlds like *breadfruit*. With an *Ital Mix*, Black Power organically blended ingredients of the Black sufferers—the mackerel, the chicken back, the tripe and beef, the ox tail, the dumplings, the corned beef hash, the codfish and potatoes, the chitterlings, the guts and the blood pudding to make nourishing food for the soul. It fed children through the Black Panther Party's breakfast programs and slayed Bobby Socks. Hot like *scotch bonnet*, it resisted police harassment like nine London Black Panthers in Notting Hill's Mangrove Restaurant. Its meals fed Panthers across the United States, New Zealand, London, India, Trinidad, and Australia.

Black Power shot the Sheriff and the Governor. It was the bullet of Buck Burrows that cuffed the Great Dane. It wanted jobs, freedom, and revolution. It was a political and cultural transnationalist. A Young Lord, a Dalit, an American Indian. Unity and fragments. Love and hate. Nations and tribes. Not always armed but always dangerous. Sometimes blessing and sometimes curse, Black Power was all these things and much more. Like Anansi's web, it was fundamentally grounded around the principles of Black self-determination yet transnationally elastic enough to have global relevance. And this is what made the movement a serious threat to a world order of white power, capitalism, and colonialism. The phrase, once uttered by Kwame Ture in 1966 Greenwood, Mississippi, stuck to the lips of the earth's wretched.

*But what manner of axiom was this that could torch the hearts of the world's sufferers and strike fear into the minds of the benefactors of world imperialism?* The U.S., Canadian, French, Australian, British, some African, Caribbean, and South American governments saw this phrase as a two-legged insect that needed to be stamped out. Agents armed with insecticide like propaganda used *x-amount* of prisons, bribes, vacuums, spells of Gargamel, bombs dropped from police helicopters, visas, sedatives, laws, bullets, and malice to destroy this powerful Anansi.

But there was no killing what could not be killed. Black Power never licked marbles with John Crow but knew sweet Jesus real well. It was Lerone Bennett's reference to Kwame Ture as a statue of a Nubian God (1966, 26). Anpu. A lioness on the rise. A Black ninja on a poetic pilgrimage to Shaolin temple to reclaim the lost arts of a stolen but chosen people. From a Harlem wooden crate, it could begin a story in a cool Kemetic temple and end it with a Binghi drum in a tenement yard on a humid Port of Spain night. It could zoom around the world in sixty-eight days, make *jummah* on Friday, get a political prisoner to Cuba by Saturday, easily be in the front pews come Sunday, and still find time to make *ebo* at the shrine for the martyrs.

Black Power's undying love for Black people crossed the political and cultural meridians of the Black world. Its transnational critiques of capitalism, colonialism, police brutality, political prisoners, and sexism and calls for self-determination remain relative in a world full of Black and Brown criminalization, xenophobic immigration policies, mass incarceration, patriarchy, racism, and neocolonialism.

# 49

## University
Ashon Crawley

The university is a collective space of learning beyond compulsory education, a collectivity of faculty and students working together with the purpose and aim of producing and disseminating knowledge. This means that the university, with the power to produce and grant degrees, is a site of struggle and contestation precisely because it is a site of power to confer or withhold. The university is a site that makes claims about knowledge and its acquisition, knowledge and its production, knowledge and its dissemination. By the thirteenth century, this term referred to the work of scholars and faculty together to receive instruction generally. The university is a space designated for thought, in other words, but such thought is not neutral; such universality emerges through exclusion. It is an exclusion that is made possible through difference and differentiation—of gendered, raced, sexed difference—being carried in the flesh that produces a crisis of meaning for the university as a neutral zone and territory of knowledge production.

Much has been written regarding the history, emergence, sociology, and future of institutional black studies and the disruptive force such an interdiscipline has meant for the coherence of the university as a space of thought. African American studies constitutes one mode of critique that lays bare the ongoing fact of contestation, struggle, and power that is the university. These various studies illustrate the ways the university itself is a contested space, how it is not neutral, how the desired production of knowledge, how the desired gathering of resources and thought, has been intervened into by difference carried in the flesh. For example, Martha Biondi (2012) demonstrates the way black revolution, taking place in the 1960s for civil rights, was a contributing factor to protests that eventually occurred on college campuses in the United States. Such protests led to the instituting African American studies, Africana studies, black studies, and ethnic studies, with students on college campuses compelling institutions to account for the kinds of knowledges that were excluded, that were discarded, that were deemed unnecessary for thought. Fabio Rojas (2010) has also underscored the necessity of protest movements outside the confines of university spaces as the foundations from which the interdiscipline of black studies would emerge. Roderick Ferguson (2012) also adds texture to the conversation regarding the relation of black studies to the university as a space for thought, tracing the way minority difference and differentiation was used to establish disciplinary boundaries, how what is codified as minor difference became the ground from which the university—as a space of contestation and struggle over knowledge production—would produce thought. Noliwe Rooks (2006), too, traces a history of the relation between the university and the interdiscipline by highlighting the economic underpinnings of black studies at colleges and universities. By discussing the way philanthropic institutions such as the Ford Foundation share an intimate history, what we find is the way economic forces that converge to produce a space for thought can also easily be enclosed by the logics of racial capitalism, a use value of race and minority difference, such difference being an exploitable resource for the proliferation of a neoliberal project of financialization. And what work such as Rooks's demonstrates are the ways the struggle over the meaning of the university is a contestation over resource allocation, about abundance and lack.

The university is a site of struggle and contestation. This struggle and contestation often makes itself felt and known through settler-colonial logics and logistics of displacing communities of color around which universities and colleges are located, using land acquisition and real estate building projects to increase revenue and growth. Craig Wilder (2013) recounts the ways enslavement as a practice and race as a concept and construct in the United States were integral to the development of colleges and universities. And the Morrill Act of 1862 and the Morrill Act of 1890, land grant acts, erase indigeneity through the idea that land was available to be exploited for the building of institutes of higher education. This history of settler-colonial logics and logistics and antiblack racism at the heart of the project of U.S. higher education is one that the university as a concept produces, and as a term, "university" veils that settler-colonial violence and antiblack racism.

"University" describes a gathering of resources. But in our neoliberal world, such gathering is at the expense of the intensification of displacement and degradation through settler-colonial logics of land acquisition, the privatization of knowledge production and the adjunctification of faculties, the making customers of students, the financialization and profitability of research projects. In its normative function and form, then, the university exists to short circuit and extinguish black study (Harney and Moten 2013) because black study is the ongoing and unceasing variation around a theme, the performative force of the critique of Western civilization. The university, in its normative function and form, is against the flourishing of abundance.

In another register and key, we might say that constitution of the university, without grappling with its foundational forces of exclusion, is against the flourishing of black thought, of black feminist and blackqueer thriving and abundance. The line and root of the word "abundant" is tied to an overflowing quantity, a large number, more than sufficient, plentiful supply of good things. The university thrives in the antithesis to abundance, thrives in producing knowledge as a limited resource and good, a limited supply and store. The university exists by considering knowledge as a project of lack. The university is as much a place of inhabitation and dwelling for neoliberal logics of privatization and financialization as it is an idea, a concept, a way to think antisociality as the grounds for relation. The university thrives, in other words, by not being able to account for its grounding in settler-colonial and antiblack racist logics. The university is a site of struggle because it is the production of European thought as a material project of how to produce race and place as knowledge acquisition. One of the most intensely felt but not necessarily recognized aspects of Europeanization and its problem of racial, class, and gender distinction is that it attacks thought and imagination. Institutions that presume to cultivate thought and imagination, then, must be interrogated for how they produce and are produced by European modalities.

The university is a site of contestation and struggle because what is being argued over, and argued against, is epistemology itself, the method of knowing and the path to such knowability. Knowledge produced in the university is based on a European epistemology of identity and difference, a European epistemology of man, the human, the citizen, the subject, what Sylvia Wynter (2003) reminds us is the coloniality of being/power/truth/freedom. Epistemology is a theory of knowledge, a theory for thinking itself, and is a way to investigate how knowledge is produced in particular ways to think the world. To separate the world out through racial, classed, and gendered distinction is European in its line

and root. The epistemology of dividing the world into types, types that receive benefits, is a product of European thought. And blackqueer, black feminist survivance has given models and examples for how we might produce knowledge against the Europeanization of thought. Audre Lorde is one such example.

Audre Lorde, in her essay "Poetry Is Not a Luxury" (2007), through the poetic, allows us to consider how there are ways to think and produce relation to the world while also acknowledging the violence and violation that have been produced by the modern era. Poetry is not just about words on pages but is a blackqueer, black feminist project of collective, improvisational, intellectual flow, a project of collective, improvisational, intellectual unfolding. Poetry would then be capacious enough to include singing, dancing, laughing, lovemaking, which is to say capacious enough to be about flesh, black flesh, about a disruption to the modality of European thought and the institutions that ground themselves in such thinking, such as the university. The poetic flows, overflows, is abundant and, even in the tightest quarters and cramped spaces, like inhaled and exhaled breath, the poetic a sign of life, is and thus exceeds thriving. The kind of work that should be done *in* the university is one that the university—if it is to remain as it has been—can contain or hold. The kind of poetic work done in the university should make the poet inhospitable by the university. It is a kind of work that takes as its object of interrogation the university itself, the university as a space of thought that has not allowed thought in its imaginative leaps and bounds, in its imaginative blackness and queerness, to unfold unless immediately folded into neoliberal logics of diversity and multiculturalism, but not in the service of radically changing the way we inhabit the world.

The university, when yielding to the undercommon movement and force of blackness, of black study, is a space from which poetic force emerges. This, the poetic possibility of the university, is the announcement and enunciation of otherwise possibility than the normative function and form of such a place of inhabitation, such a zone of institutional politic. It would be a reckoning with the originary and ongoing violence and violation that makes the university possible. But more than a reckoning, attending to the poetic force of blackness, of blackqueer, black feminist abundance, would chart a way otherwise to inhabit the university. It would be a collective, improvisational practice, a collective, improvisational process. The study in this otherwise modality would take the university as an object of interrogation that would ask how we would inhabit thought, how we would attempt to produce knowledge, in a decolonial way that affirms the life worlds of the excluded, the life worlds of the tokenized and discarded. It would be to imagine that the university could be something other than an aspiration to universal, totalized knowledge. It would be to imagine—and then to inhabit the practice of that imagining—that "university" could denote something otherwise than an aspiration to universal, totalized knowledge.

# 50

## War

Jennifer James

African American and diasporic discussions of war reveal how authoritative white, Western theorists have oversimplified the important role of "difference" in theorizing war, whether we are thinking of war as a practice or as a metaphor for social relations. A racially and historically inflected exploration of such complications is critical to a robust consideration of the myriad meanings war has accrued within an African American and black diasporic framework.

The Prussian military strategist and former general Carl von Clausewitz famously conceptualized the structure of war in his influential treatise *On War* ([1832] 1997, 42): war is "nothing but a duel on a larger scale." As he imagines it, war is akin to a contest between two people—a "self" and an "other"—but enlarged into a conflict between multiple "selves" (the same as you) and multiple "others" (different from you but indistinct from one another). Clausewitz's representation of war as a simple dichotomy had a lasting influence on later cultural theorists' interpretations of war. Analyzing the canon of British modernist writing of World War I, Paul Fussell has argued that the compulsion to identify with a "side" during a complex war involving multiple entities produced a "persisting imaginative habit" of "gross dichotomizing" (2013, 82): "'We' are all here on this side; 'the enemy' is over there. 'We' are individuals with names and personal identities; 'he' is a mere collective entity. . . . We are normal; he is grotesque." Fussell claims that this "versus habit" became World War

I's most problematic and destructive legacy, leading the affected to perceive the larger world in antagonistic terms. We no longer live in nature, for instance; we are positioned in a struggle against it.

Later scholars have interrogated Fussell's temporality to argue that dichotomous, binaristic thinking was an already extant mind-set that made violence against the designated enemy-other possible, even desirable, particularly when that enemy-other was racialized. Examining whether war is a cause or an outcome of deleterious forms of binaristic thinking is not merely a circular debate about antecedents. Such examinations, especially those by minority scholars, are essential reevaluations of the origins, purpose, and definitions of war. If war is a means of simultaneous consolidating *and* creating an "us," black participation in U.S. warfare can be viewed as an effort to disrupt and destabilize the violent dichotomies that rendered African Americans "them" and the "other."

The Civil War provides the most evident example. While black skeptics cautioned against serving until abolition was formally declared the aim of the war, free and enslaved black men clamored to serve without the explicit promises of emancipation and citizenship rights. Frederick Douglass famously envisioned black participation in the Union army as an opportunity to "secure" "the black man's rights" ([1863] 1975, 478). African American soldiers similarly expressed hope in letters to family and friends that their "manhood" rights would be recognized. After the war, Susie King Taylor (1902), a soldier-teacher and nurse for the Thirty-Third USCT, reflected on black women's roles in the conflict to demonstrate that "loyal women" were worthy contributors to a reforming nation. All anticipated that their support for the cause of union against the Confederacy would garner black people the rewards and responsibilities of belonging in the nation on an equal footing

as their former enslavers. The support was also part of a historical pattern that began with the Revolutionary War: African Americans revising official military goals into objectives abetting black liberation.

Black people's participation in national warfare, even as they were consistently denied civic inclusion, should thus be considered a performance of black aspirations, pointing to many African Americans' decision to use war as a tool in black political struggle. The most recognized quotation from Clausewitz's treatise is helpful here: "War is . . . a continuation of policy by other means. It is not merely a political act but a real political instrument, a continuation of political intercourse" ([1832] 1997, 53). He then claims that political instrumentality is only one part of a "trinity" of warfare and is quickly subsumed to the other two, "the violence of its essence, the hate and enmity," and "the play of probability and chance." Instrumentality become "subordinate" (55).

Discussions of national warfare in the black political sphere reverse Clausewitz's theory of subordination. That is, regardless of the officially stated purpose of any given conflict, U.S. wars have become key sites for the articulation and enactment of a range of black sociopolitical desires: allegiance, mobility, dissent, liberation. In a similar manner, African Americans have turned to the language of war and warfare to conceptualize black struggle against a racialized state.

During World War II, for example, the *Pittsburgh Courier* initiated the famous "Double V" campaign after the *Courier* correspondent James Thompson penned a piece urging blacks to "adopt the Double VV for a double victory. The first V for victory over our enemies from without, the second V for victory over our enemies from within." The editor of the New York edition remarked that the "two wars were inextricably intertwined." The radical publication the *Militant* argued that blacks gained nothing from positioning Hitler as "their main enemy" while "poll taxers, lynchers and advocates of white supremacy" remained unvanquished at home (Stanton 1980, 157–58). "Hitlerism at home" became a popular phrase for American racism among blacks, collapsing the ideological distinction between "the enemy" and "us" and further dissecting the "us" into two distinct sides at war: blacks and whites.

It would be erroneous to think of these or similar examples as interjections of race into a preexisting phenomenon we call "war." The French historian Michel Foucault (2003) has convincingly demonstrated that "war," both as an idea and as a set of practices, was racial from its onset. The *OED* traces origins of the word "war" to the Late Old English "wyrre" and "werre," which originated in the Old French "werre." By the Middle Ages, there were several English variations, including "weorre," and "wore." The example the editors choose to illustrate the term, "uuerre," is from the *Anglo-Saxon Chronicles* (1140–50), a work describing the Norman conquest of the Saxons and its aftermath (*Oxford English Dictionary*, n.d.-b). Foucault emphasizes two things of note. First, while we might think of the Normans and the Saxons as civilizations, they considered themselves "races," "biological" but "historio-political," bound by linguistic, religious, and regional commonalities. This was a racial war. Second, prior to the denotative codification of "uuerre" within this particular historical and textual context, this word was merely one of many Old English terms describing conflicts of varying scales as small as a hand-to-hand fight between neighbors. The "private" wars shifted to a concentration of central consolidation of power: "The state acquired a monopoly on war . . . wars, the practices of war, and the institution of war tended to exist . . . on the outer limits of great state unites, and only as a violent relationship . . . between States" (Foucault 2003, 48).

Foucault further asserts that the nature of these state-driven racial wars against the sovereign invading or conquered "other" was transformed when those others were incorporated within state boundaries, creating heterogeneous populations. War migrated inward, culminating in an "internal colonialism" enacted in the state-sponsored regimes of biopower that aimed to control, and eventually eliminate, the inner social enemy through "purifying" (Hanssen 2000). Purifying the state was executed through expulsion and, in the most extreme instance, genocide. War was no longer solely about maintaining the integrity of external boundaries; rather, war became the very structure of the state. Hence, the title of Foucault's lectures: "Society Must Be Defended." For order to be maintained within a nation, for "peaceful coexistence" among individuals and groups, quite paradoxically, he argues, a war-like environment had to be instituted. Even more paradoxically, peaceful coexistence meant that the "inner social enemy" had to, by some means, *cease* to exist, a condition most efficiently brought about by expulsion or, in the most extreme instance, genocide. In the U.S., expulsion took many forms: "back to Africa," being disappeared into the prison system, or being excluded from the realms of civics and politics. Extermination could be effected through the imposition of poverty, forced sterilization, or intentionally poor health care; and of course, it could be effected through overt form, particularly in racially motivated murder emblemized in lynching (Jennifer James 2007).

Although Foucault turns to the Holocaust as an emblem of statist biopower—the state's control over life and death—it is necessary to consider whether black enslavement was a prior instance of this form of control. Certainly, the neologism "genocide" in the aftermath of World War II provided African Americans a lens and language through which to further examine antiblack violence in the U.S., placing quotidian black death within a larger human rights context. During the Nuremberg trials, the *Chicago Defender* published editorials defining "genocide" for its readers and asking whether the term could be productively applied to lynching. During the same period, the Civil Rights Congress produced a petition for the United Nations cataloguing antiblack violence, *We Charge Genocide: The Crime of Government against the Negro People* (1951), claiming that "Negro citizens . . . suffer from genocide as a result of the consistent, conscious, unified policies of every branch of government" (xiv).

The ascription of genocidal intentions to the assaults against black existence in the U.S. could be dismissed as mere analogy or hyperbole. The postcolonial philosopher Achille Mbembe offers a more generative frame for thinking about the relationship of black death in the diaspora to the Holocaust. Mbembe's essential essay "Necropolitics" in part grapples with Foucault's deployment of "the camp" as the fullest expression of biopower, endeavoring instead to construct a framework to account for the ongoing instrumentalization of dead and injured black bodies in Western political projects. For Mbembe, "the plantation system" was not only a "terror formation" predating the technologies of the Holocaust; it might have given rise to them (2003, 22).

The idea of African Americans being in an internal war with the U.S. racial state took on even greater urgency during the Vietnam War, as black men were disproportionately dying in an unpopular war abroad while they and their communities were subjected to technologies of violence domestically.

The literary critic Larry Neal's introduction to the groundbreaking Black Arts Movement's anthology *Black* unpacks the ways metaphors of war can be used against the marginalized. Taking aim at the "war on poverty" as a veiled attempt to berate the African American poor,

Neal heralded art as a defense: "The Black Arts Theatre stood in radical opposition to the feeble attitudes about culture of the 'War on Poverty' bureaucrats" (1968b, 32). Critics of the "war against drugs" have denounced the war framework for the way it has enabled and justified the stigmatization, criminalization, and incarceration of black Americans, who have become "the enemy" within. Neal further suggests that nationalists have the "sense" they are in an ongoing "war" with their oppressors (1968a, 646).

Neal's piece also provides the occasion to consider the relationship of two terms, "war" and "revolution." At the time he was writing, advocates of Black Power had relinquished the organizing philosophy of nonviolence for the "right of revolution." Floyd McKissick, the head of the Congress of Racial Equality, was unequivocal: "We know [the white man] will kill us if he can. . . . The right of revolution is a constitutional right, condoned by the creation of the American Revolution itself" ([1967] 2000, 460). These Black Power advocates were steeping themselves in revolutionary thinkers such as Frantz Fanon and viewed the Vietnamese National Liberation Front and others engaged in anticolonial struggles across Africa, Asia, and the Americas as exercising a parallel right.

It is important to note that calling on the American Revolution in the struggle for black rights had a long history in African American political discourse. David Walker's 1829 jeremiad, *An Appeal . . . to the Coloured Citizens of the World*, warns white Americans that if they fail to give blacks their freedom, they will reap what they have sown, and he advocates blacks to declare "war" against them if they do not: "O Americans! Americans! I call God—I call angels—I call men, to witness, that your DESTRUCTION *is at hand*, and will be speedily consummated unless you REPENT" ([1829] 1995, 43). He refers to "Hayti" as "the glory of the blacks and terror of tyrants" (21). He calculates the black population in some southern states to consider the feasibility of full-scale black rebellion.

Walker's writings also offer insight into the ways religion provided a foundation for framing war and uprising in the African American imagination. He decides that if blacks "be well equipt for war," victory would be probable, and he cautions against fear: "when that hour arrives, and you move, be not afraid or dismayed; for be you assured that Jesus Christ the King of heaven and of earth who is the God of justice and of armies, will surely go before you" (1829, 11–12). Walker has declared a holy war. Walker's justification for violence in the *Appeal* is an evident tautology: you must rise up because God commands it, and when you rise up, you will know it is his command. He closes his work declaring that whites will be humbled, quoting from Revelation and the Declaration in rapid succession, bringing natural and divine law within close ideological and syntactical proximity of each other. In *The Souls of Black Folk* (1903), the sociologist W. E. B. Du Bois suggests that the enslaved read the "blood and fire" of the Civil War within a prophetic framework that subordinated human will within an eschatological worldview: "When Emancipation finally came, it seemed to the freedman a literal Coming of the Lord. . . . What had he to do with it? Was it not the Lord's doing, and marvellous in his eyes?" (201).

Martin Luther King Jr. decried some African Americans' tendency to romanticize uprising as a destructive inclination that minimized the ramifications of violence at the same time it encouraged the black violence erupting in "ghettos" across the United States. His writing nonetheless reveals genuine ambivalence about oppressed subjects' recourse to violence under colonial rule, voicing his disapproval of anti-imperialist revolution in the mildest of terms, even characterizing it as a necessary stage of "young nations" (1967, 57). To some extent, King's attitude reflects his sense of moral proportion. King also pushed blacks to see their own struggles as bound to those of other people of color inhabiting the "world house," whether African villagers or Vietnamese peasants (57). His later sermon "Why I Am Opposed to the War in Vietnam" celebrates Third World revolt: "These are revolutionary times. All over the globe men are revolting against old systems of exploitation and oppression, and out of the wounds of a frail world, new systems of justice and equality are being born" (1967, 57).

King also dismissed religious justifications for war in expressing his dismay with those who questioned his transition into antiwar activism: "To me the relationship of this ministry to the making of peace is so obvious that I sometimes marvel at those who ask me why I am speaking against the war. . . . Have they forgotten that my ministry is in obedience to the one who loved his enemies so fully that he died for them?" (1967, 253). He endeavors to dismantle the "just war" rationale, arguing that the notion of an "unjust means to a just ends" is a prima facie contradiction perpetuated by world leaders seeking to rationalize slaughter: "Hitler contended that everything he did in Germany was for peace. . . . Every time we drop our bombs in North Vietnam . . . Johnson speaks eloquently about peace" (253).

The current wars in Afghanistan and Iraq, it seems, have yet to garner the same depth of symbolic power in African American political thought as the previous wars did. However, the concepts of "terrorism" and a "war on terror" have prompted rich discussion about the meaning of "terror" and uses of the idea. In general, groups that have used "terror" against the U.S. have drawn on three general historical justifications. Without military resources and the backing of a state, groups seeking power or political redress are "forced" to resort to "illegitimate" forms of violence as a means of destabilizing the targeted government, its apparatus, and its populace. Second, the very distinctions made in categorizing violence are false: there is no such thing as "illegitimate" violence to begin with; violence, whether the violence of "legitimate" warfare or the violence of "revolutionary" causes, has the same goal, purposes, and effects. In this way of thinking, the illegitimate/legitimate distinction is characterized as an ideological tool wielded to keep the dominated helpless and compliant, afraid to aggress against the oppressor, and in a related goal, it is intended to coalesce sentiment against the "revolutionary," thought to operate outside the laws of civilization that the rest of "us" abide by. Finally, the use of violence leveled against civilians is justified by drawing an analogy to the inevitable and "acceptable" death and injury of civilians in state warfare; moreover, these civilians, as citizens of the offending state, are claimed to necessarily support structures of domination simply by participating in a given society's operations. There are no "innocents." Public debate in the African American public square has produced rich and useful intellectual inquiry about the deployment of this concept. Is "terror" only perpetuated by peoples whom we identify as "Muslim" and who have grievances against the United States? Can, for instance, a white mass shooter with a political agenda be considered a purveyor of "domestic" terror? Can the state itself be guilty of terrorizing marginalized people within its borders? Who is imperiled if the U.S. insists that the "terror" is only practiced by brown and black people and foreign "others"?

In sum, the African American vocabulary of war is expressive of the historical condition of black people in the U.S. If it has, at times, spoken to the possibilities of racial opportunity, it has also addressed the certainty of racial risk. If, historically, some African Americans publicly touted black participation in U.S. warfare as an instrument in the struggle for inclusion, there is an attendant awareness that black participation also empowers a state that might remain hostile to black citizenship claims, indifferent to black survival, and in some cases, actively devoted to black annihilation within the U.S. and beyond (Jennifer James 2007; Mbembe 2003). During the Persian Gulf War, June Jordan published an essay about the boxer Mike Tyson, which castigated the celebratory mood surrounding that conflict and took issue with the larger role that sanctioned violence plays in creating toxic manifestations of masculine power, whether that violence takes the form of violence against another nation, the "intentional" impoverishment of black people, or in the case of Tyson, sexual assault. She reminds us that "war means you hurt somebody, or something, until there's nothing soft or sensible left" (2002b, 120). At the bottom of her considerations lies a fundamental question: whether the use of violence can ever be justified, even if it is wielded against the oppressor, or whether, as black antiwar activists have argued, the means and the ends are bound inextricably.

## Acknowledgments

While it is indeed cliché to argue that every book is a collective effort, it is certainly the case where anthologies are concerned. In grateful acknowledgment of the collective process that has yielded this volume, we wish to thank the following people. Eric Zinner has been an exemplary editor, providing support for this volume throughout our time with it. Associate editor Lisha Nadkarni and editorial assistant Dolma Ombadykow have been attentive facilitators of the project as well. We would also like to express our gratitude to the anonymous readers for their careful and detailed engagement. Our deep and heartfelt thanks must go to our brilliant and impeccable research assistant, Sarah Buckner. It is not an exaggeration to say that we can honestly divide our experience with this volume in terms of "before" and "after" her engagement with it. Most of all we wish to thank our colleagues— the contributors—whose dedication and contributions have warmed and inspired us.

# Works Cited

ABS Contributor. 2014. "Top 10 Most Segregated Cities in the U.S." *Atlanta Black Star*, 24 March. http://atlantablackstar.com.

Abu Lughod, Janet. 2012. *Race, Space, and Riots in Chicago, New York, and Los Angeles*. New York: Oxford University Press.

Achebe, Chinua. 1991. *Things Fall Apart*. New York: Fawcett Crest.

Adams, Russell. 1977. "Black Studies Perspectives." *Journal of Negro Education* 46 (2): 99–117.

Adell, Sandra. 1994. *Double-Consciousness / Double Bind: Theoretical Issues in Twentieth-Century Black Literature*. Urbana: University of Illinois Press.

Adewunmi, Bim. 2014. "Kimberlé Crenshaw on Intersectionality: 'I Wanted to Come Up with an Everyday Metaphor That Anyone Could Use.'" *New Statesman*, 2 April. www.newstatesman.com.

Adorno, Theodor W., and Max Horkheimer. 2002. *Dialectic of Enlightenment*. Translated by Edmund Jephcott. Stanford, CA: Stanford University Press.

Agassiz, Louis. 1850. "The Diversity of Origin of the Human Races." *Christian Examiner* 49:110–45.

Ahmed, Sara. 2012. *On Being Included: Racism and Diversity in Institutional Life*. Durham, NC: Duke University Press.

Akbar, Na'im. 1996. *Breaking the Chains of Psychological Slavery*. Tallahassee, FL: Mind Productions.

Alaimo, Stacey. 2010. *Bodily Natures: Science, Environment, and the Material Self*. Bloomington: Indiana University Press.

Alexander, Elizabeth. 2005. *American Sublime*. Minneapolis: Graywolf.

Alexander, Michelle. 2012. *The New Jim Crow: Mass Incarceration in the Age of Colorblindness*. New York: Free Press.

Alexander, M. Jacqui. 2005. *Pedagogies of Crossing: Meditations on Feminism, Sexual Politics, Memory and the Sacred*. Durham, NC: Duke University Press.

Alexander-Floyd, Nikol. 2012. "Disappearing Acts: Reclaiming Intersectionality in the Social Sciences in a Post Black Feminist Era." *Feminist Formations* 24 (1): 1–25.

Alim, H. Samy. 2009. "Straight Outta Compton, Straight *aus München*: GlobalLinguistic Flows, Identities, and the Politics of Languagein a Global Hip Hop Nation." In *Global Linguistic Flows: Hip Hop Cultures, Youth Identities, and the Politics of Language*, edited by H. Samy Alim, Awad Ibrahim, and Alastair Pennycook, 1–24. New York: Routledge.

Allen, Jafari. 2011. *Venceremos? The Erotics of Black Self-Making in Cuba*. Durham, NC: Duke University Press.

Allen, Robert L. 1969. *Black Awakening in Capitalist America: An Analytic History*. Garden City, NY: Doubleday.

Anderson, Benedict. (1983) 2006. *Imagined Communities: Reflections on the Origin and Spread of Nationalism*. New York: Verso.

Anderson, James D. 1988. *The Education of Blacks in the South, 1860–1915*. Chapel Hill: University of North Carolina Press.

Anderson, Margo J. 2015. *The American Census: A Social History*. 2nd ed. New Haven, CT: Yale University Press.

Andrews, Penelope. 2014. "A Champion for African Freedom: Paul Robeson and the Struggle against Apartheid." *Albany Law Review* 77 (1): 473–98.

Andrews, Steve. 2007. "Toward a Synaesthetics of Soul: W. E. B. Du Bois and the Teleology of Race." In *Re-cognizing W. E. B. Du Bois in the Twenty-First Century: Essays on W. E. B. Du Bois*, edited by Mary Keller and Chester J. Fontenot Jr., 142–85. Macon, GA: Mercer University Press.

Androutsopoulos, Jannis. 2009. "Language and the Three Spheres of Hip Hop." In *Global Linguistic Flows: Hip Hop Cultures, Youth Identities, and the Politics of Language*, edited by H. Samy Alim, Awad Ibrahim, and Alastair Pennycook, 43–63. New York: Routledge.

Appiah, Anthony. 1991. "Is the Post- in Postmodernism the Post- in Postcolonial?" *Critical Inquiry* 17 (2): 336–57.

———. 1992. *In My Father's House: Africa in the Philosophy of Culture*. New York: Oxford University Press.

Aptheker, Bettina. 1971. "The Social Functions of the Prisons in the United States." In *If They Come in the Morning: Voices of Resistance*, edited by Angela Y. Davis, 39–48. New York: Signet.

———. 1982. *Woman's Legacy: Essays on Race, Sex, and Class in American History*. Amherst: University of Massachusetts Press.

Aptheker, Herbert. 1943. *American Negro Slave Revolts*. New York: Columbia University Press.

———. 1951. *Documentary History of the Negro People*. Vol. 1. New York: Citadel.

———. 1976. Introduction to *Black Reconstruction*, by W. E. B. Du Bois, xxv–lxii. Millwood, NY: Kraus-Thomson.

Asante, Molefi Kete. 1980. *Afrocentricity: The Theory of Social Change*. Buffalo, NY Amulefi.

———. 1988. *Afrocentricity*. Rev. ed. Trenton, NJ: Africa World.

Ashcroft, Bill. 2012. "Colonialism." In *Blackwell Encyclopedias in Social Sciences: The Wiley-Blackwell Encyclopedia of Globalization*, edited by George Ritzer. Hoboken, NJ: Wiley. https://search.credoreference.com.

Ashe, Bertram. 2007. "Theorizing the Post-Soul Aesthetic: An Introduction." In "Post-Soul Aesthetic." Special issue, *African American Review* 41 (4): 609–23.

Assensoh, Akwasi B. 2000. "Conflict or Cooperation? Africans and African Americans in Multiracial America." In *Black and Multiracial Politics in America*, edited by Yvette M. Alex-Assensoh and Lawrence J. Hanks, 113–30. New York: NYU Press.

Association for the Study of African American Life and History. 2013. "The Long Movement: State of the Scholarship Roundtable." Proceedings of ninety-eighth meeting of the Association of the Study of African American Life and History, Jacksonville, FL, 5 October.

Avilez, GerShun. 2016. *Radical Aesthetics and Modern Black Nationalism*. Urbana: University of Illinois Press.

Azurara, Gomes Eannes de. 1936. *Conquest and Discoveries of Henry the Navigator: Being the Chronicles of Azurara, Portuguese Navigators & Colonizers of the Fifteenth & Sixteenth Centuries*. Translated by Bernard Miall. London: Allen and Unwin.

Bailey, Marlon. 2011. "Gender/Racial Realness: Theorizing the Gender System in Ballroom Culture." *Feminist Studies* 37 (2): 365–86.

Bair, Barbara. 2000. "Though Justice Sleeps, 1880-1900." In *To Make Our World Anew: A History of African Americans*, edited by Robin D. G. Kelley and Earl Lewis, 281–344. New York: Oxford University Press.

Baker, Ella. 1960. "Bigger than a Hamburger." *Southern Patriot*, May, 4.

Baker, Ella, and Marvel Cooke. 1935. "The Bronx Slave Market." *Crisis* 42 (November): 330–31.

Baker, Lee D. 1998. *From Savage to Negro: Anthropology and the Construction of Race, 1896-1954*. Berkeley: University of California Press.

Baldwin, Davarian. 2007. *Chicago's New Negroes: Modernity, the Great Migration and Black Urban Life*. Chapel Hill: University of North Carolina Press.

Baldwin, Davarian, and Minkah Makalani, eds. 2009. *Escape from New York: The New Negro Renaissance beyond Harlem*. Minneapolis: University of Minnesota Press.

Baldwin, James. 1953. *Go Tell It on the Mountain*. New York: New American Library.

———. (1956) 2001. *Giovanni's Room*. New York: Modern Library.

———. (1962) 1993. *Another Country*. New York: Vintage Books.

———. (1963) 1993. *The Fire Next Time*. New York: Vintage International.

———. (1972) 2007. *No Name in the Street*. New York: Vintage Books.

Balfour, Lawrie. 2011. *Democracy's Reconstruction: Thinking Politically with W. E. B. Du Bois*. New York: Oxford University Press.

Ball, Charles. 1858. *Fifty Years in Chains; or, The Life of an American Slave*. New York: Dayton and Asher.

Ballad of America. n.d. "Oh Freedom." Accessed 2017. www.balladofamerica.com.

Bambaataa, Afrika. 1984. "Unity." With James Brown. Tommy Boy / Warner Bros.

Bambara, Toni Cade, ed. 1970. *The Black Woman: An Anthology*. New York New American Library.

———. 1981. Foreword to *This Bridge Called My Back: Writings by Radical Women of Color*, edited by Cherríe Moraga and Gloria Anzaldúa, xxix–xxxii. Albany: SUNY Press.

Baptist, Edward. 2014. *The Half Has Never Been Told: Slavery and the Making of American Capitalism*. New York: Basic Books.

Baraka, Amiri. 1987. "The Phenomenon of Soul in African-American Music." In *The Music: Reflections on Jazz and Blues*, edited by Amiri Baraka and Amina Baraka, 268–76. New York: William Morrow.

———. 1991. "Black Art." In *The Leroi Jones / Amiri Baraka Reader*, edited by William J. Harris, 219–20. New York: Thunder's Mouth.

Baraka, Amiri, and Larry Neal, eds. 1968. *Black Fire: An Anthology of Afro-American Writing*. New York: Morrow.

Bardolph, Richard. 1970. *The Civil Rights Record: Black Americans and the Law, 1849-1970*. New York: Thomas Y. Crowell.

Bate, Peter, dir. 2003. *Congo: White King, Red Rubber, Black Death*. ArtMattan Films.

Baudrillard, Jean. 1988. "Simulacra and Simulations." In *Jean Baudrillard, Selected Writings*, edited by Mark Poster, 166–84. Stanford, CA: Stanford University Press.

Bauer, Raymond, and Alice Bauer. 1942. "Day to Day Resistance to Slavery." *Journal of Negro History* 27:388–419.

Bay, Mia. 2009. *To Tell the Truth Freely: The Life of Ida B. Wells*. New York: Hill and Wang.

Beale, Frances. (1970) 2010. "Double Jeopardy: To Be Black and Female." In *The Black Woman: An Anthology*, edited by Toni Cade Bambara, 109–22. New York: New American Library.

Beckert, Sven. 2014. *Empire of Cotton: A Global History*. New York: Knopf.

Bederman, Gail. 1995. *Manliness and Civilization: A Cultural History of Gender and Race in the United States, 1880–1917*. Chicago: University of Chicago Press.

Bell, Karen Cook. 2016. "Self-Emancipating Women, Civil War, and the Union Army in Southern Louisiana and Lowcountry Georgia, 1861–1865." *Journal of African American History* 101 (Winter–Spring): 1–22.

Bennett, Andy. 2000. *Popular Music and Youth Culture: Music, Identity, and Place*. Basingstoke, UK: Macmillan.

Bennett, Jane. 2010. *Vibrant Matter: A Political Ecology of Things*. Durham, NC: Duke University Press.

Bennett, Lerone. 1961. "The Soul of Soul." *Ebony*, December.

———. 1966. "Stokely Carmichael: Architect of Black Power." *Ebony*, September.

———. 1984. *Before the Mayflower: A History of Black America*. New York: Penguin Books.

———. 2000. *Forced into Glory: Abraham Lincoln's White Dream*. Chicago: Johnson.

Ben-zvi, Yael. 2017. *Native Land Talk: Indigenous and Arrivant Rights Theories*. Lebanon, NH: University Press of New England.

Berger, Dan. 2014. *Captive Nation: Black Prison Organizing in the Civil Rights Era*. Chapel Hill: University of North Carolina Press.

Berger, Dan, Mariame Kaba, and David Stein. 2017. "What Abolitionists Do." *Jacobin*, 24 August.

Bernasconi, Robert. 2001. "Who Invented the Concept of Race? Kant's Role in the Enlightenment Construction of Race." In *Race*, edited by Robert Bernasconi, 11–36. Malden, MA: Wiley-Blackwell.

Berrey, Ellen. 2015. *The Enigma of Diversity: The Language of Race and the Limits of Racial Justice*. Chicago: University of Chicago Press.

BET.com. 2015. "David Banner: White Rappers Are Getting More Lyrical—and We're Mumbling." 29 September. www.bet.com.

Bhabha, Homi K. 1994. *The Location of Culture*. New York: Routledge.

Bibb, Henry. (1849) 2001. *Life and Adventures of Henry Bibb: An American Slave*. Madison: University of Wisconsin Press.

Bierria, Alisa, Mimi Kim, and Clarissa Rojas. 2011–12. "Community Accountability: Emerging Movements to Transform Violence." *Social Justice* 37:1–11.

Biko, Steve. 2002. *I Write What I Like: Selected Writings*. Edited by Aelred Stubbs. Chicago: University of Chicago Press.

Biondi, Martha. 2012. *The Black Revolution on Campus*. Berkeley: University of California Press.

Black, Stephanie, dir. 2001. *Life and Debt*. Tuff Gong Pictures.

Blackett, Richard J. M. 2018. *The Captive's Quest for Freedom: Fugitive Slaves, the 1850 Fugitive Slave Law, and the Politics of Slavery*. New York: Cambridge University Press.

Black Lives Matter. n.d.-a. "Herstory." Accessed 2017. http://blacklivesmatter.com.

———. n.d.-b. "What We Believe." Accessed 2017. http://blacklivesmatter.com.

Blackmon, Douglas A. 2008. *Slavery by Another Name: The Reenslavement of Black People in America from the Civil War to World War II*. New York: Doubleday.

Blassingame, John W. (1972) 1979. *The Slave Community: Plantation Life in the Antebellum South*. New York: Oxford University Press.

Blight, David W. 2001. *Race and Reunion: The Civil War in American Memory*. Cambridge, MA: Harvard University Press.

Bogle, Donald. (1973) 1994. *Toms, Coons, Mammies, and Bucks: An Interpretative History of Blacks in American Films*. New York: Continuum.

Bond, Patrick. 2000. *Elite Transition: From Apartheid to Neoliberalism in South Africa*. London: Pluto.

Bonilla-Silva, Eduardo. 2001. *White Supremacy and Racism in the Post–Civil Rights Era*. Boulder, CO: Lynne Rienner.

Boogie Down Productions. 1987. "South Bronx." *Criminal Minded*. Traffic/Traffic Entertainment Group.

Borstelmann, Thomas. 2001. *The Cold War and the Color Line: American Race Relations in the Global Arena*. Cambridge, MA: Harvard University Press.

Bourne, St. Clair, dir. 1996. *John Henrik Clarke: A Great Mighty Walk*. Black Dot Media.

Bowling, Nathan. 2016. "Much of White America Is 'Perfectly Happy' with Segregated Schools, Says One Teacher of the Year." *Hechinger Report*, 1 February. http://hechingerreport.org.

Boxer, Marilyn Jacoby. 1998. *When Women Ask the Questions: Creating Women's Studies in America*. Baltimore: Johns Hopkins University Press.

Bracey, John H., Jr. 2014. "Coming from a Black Thing: Remembering the Black Arts Movement." In *SOS: Calling All Black People, a Black Arts Movement Reader*, edited by John H. Bracey Jr., Sonia Sanchez, and James Smethurst, 650–55. Amherst: University of Massachusetts Press.

Braidotti, Rosi. 2006. "Posthuman, All Too Human: Towards a New Process Ontology." *Theory, Culture & Society* 23 (7–8): 197–208.

Brand, Dionne. 2002. *A Map to the Door of No Return: Notes to Belonging*. Toronto: Vintage Canada.

Braz, Rose. 2006. "Kinder, Gentler, Gender Responsive Cages: Prison Expansion Is Not Prison Reform." *Women, Girls, & Criminal Justice*, October–November, 87–91.

Brisbane, Robert H. 1974. *Black Activism: Racial Revolution in the United States, 1954–1970*. Valley Forge, PA: Judson.

Brock, Lisa. 1996. "Questioning the Diaspora: Hegemony, Black Intellectuals and Doing International History from Below." *Issue: A Journal of Opinion* 24 (2): 9–12.

Brody, Jennifer DeVere. 2008. *Punctuation: Art, Politics, Play*. Durham, NC: Duke University Press.

Brody, Jennifer DeVere, and Dwight A. McBride. 2000. "Plum Nelly: New Essays in Black Queer Studies: Introduction." *Callaloo* 23 (1): 286–88.

Brophy, Alfred L. 2002. *Reconstructing the Dreamland: The Tulsa Race Riot of 1921, Race Reparations, and Reconciliation*. New York: Oxford University Press.

Brown, Drea. 2015. *Dear Girl, a Reckoning*. Los Angeles: Gold Line.

Brown, Elsa Barkley. 1994. "Negotiating and Transforming the Public Sphere: African American Political Life in the Transition from Slavery to Freedom." *Public Culture* 7 (1): 107–46.

Brown, Frank L. (1959) 2005. *Trumbull Park*. Lebanon, NH: Northeastern University Press.

Brown, Kimberly Juanita. 2015. *Repeating Body: Slavery's Visual Resonance in the Contemporary*. Durham, NC: Duke University Press.

Brown, Vincent. 2008. *The Reaper's Garden: Death and Power in the World of Atlantic Slavery*. Cambridge, MA: Harvard University Press.

Brown, William Wells. (1847) 1970. *The Narrative of William W. Brown, a Fugitive Slave*. New York: Johnson.

Browne, Simone. 2015. *Dark Matters: On the Surveillance of Blackness*. Durham, NC: Duke University Press Books.

*Brown v. Board of Education of Topeka, Kansas*. 1954. 347 U.S. 483.

Bruce, Dickson D., Jr. 1989. *Black American Writing from the Nadir: The Evolution of a Literary Tradition, 1877–1915*. Baton Rouge: Louisiana State University Press.

Bruyneel, Kevin. 2007. *The Third Space of Sovereignty: The Postcolonial Politics of U.S.-Indigenous Relations*. Minneapolis: University of Minnesota Press.

Buck-Morss, Susan. 2000. "Hegel and Haiti." *Critical Inquiry* 26 (4): 821–65.

Bunche, Ralph Johnson. 1992. *An African American in South Africa: The Travel Notes of Ralph J. Bunche, 28 September 1937–1 January 1938*. Edited by Robert R. Edgar. Athens: Ohio University Press.

Bundy, Colin. 1979. *The Rise and Fall of the South African Peasantry*. Berkeley: University of California Press.

Burgett, Bruce. 2007. "Sex." In *Keywords for American Cultural Studies*, edited by Bruce Burgett and Glenn Hendler, 217–20. New York: NYU Press.

Bush, Rod. 1999. *We Are Not What We Seem: Black Nationalism and Class Struggle in the American Century*. New York: NYU Press.

Bushnell, Amy Turner. 2009. "Indigenous America and the Limits of the Atlantic World, 1493 1825." In *Atlantic History: A Critical Appraisal*, edited by Jack P. Greene and Phillip D. Morgan, 191–222. New York: Oxford University Press.

Butler, Judith. 1990. *Gender Trouble: Feminism and the Subversion of Identity*. New York: Routledge.

Butler, Octavia. 1979. *Kindred*. New York: Doubleday.

———. 1993. *Parable of the Sower*. New York: Time Warner.

———. 1998. *Parable of the Talents*. New York: Time Warner.

Byrd, Jodi A. 2011. *The Transit of Empire: Indigenous Critiques of Colonialism*. Minneapolis: University of Minnesota Press.

Cahill, Cathleen D. 2011. *Federal Fathers and Mothers: A Social History of the United States Indian Service, 1869–1933*. Chapel Hill: University of North Carolina Press.

Camacho, Daniel José. 2015. "Why James H. Cone's Liberation Theology Matters More than Ever." *Religion Dispatches*, June 2. http://religiondispatches.org.

Camp, Jordan T., and Christina Heatherton, eds. 2016. *Policing the Planet: Why the Policing Crisis Led to Black Lives Matter*. London: Verso Books.

Camp, Stephanie. 2004. *Closer to Freedom: Enslaved Women and Everyday Resistance in the Plantation South*. Chapel Hill: University of North Carolina Press.

Capeci, Dominic J., Jr., and Jack C. Knight. 1996. "Reckoning with Violence: W. E. B. Du Bois and the 1906 Atlanta Race Riot." *Journal of Southern History* 62 (4): 727–66.

Carby, Hazel V. 1987. *Reconstructing Womanhood: The Emergence of the Afro-American Woman Novelist*. New York: Oxford University Press.

———. 1998. *Race Men*. Cambridge, MA: Harvard University Press.

———. 1999. *Cultures in Babylon: Black Britain and African America*. New York: Verso.

Carmichael, Stokely, and Charles Hamilton. (1967) 2003. *Black Power: The Politics of Liberation in America*. New York: Vintage.

Carrington, Ben. 2010. *Race, Sport and Politics: The Sporting Diaspora*. Los Angeles: Sage.

Carson, Clayborne. 1986. "Civil Rights Reform and the Black Freedom Struggle." In *The Civil Rights Movement in America*, edited by Charles Eagles, 19-32. Jackson: University Press of Mississippi.

Cartwright, Samuel. 1851. "Report on the Diseases and Physical Peculiarities of the Negro Race." *New Orleans Medical and Surgical Journal*, May, 691-715.

Cecelski, David, and Timothy Tyson, eds. 1998. *Democracy Betrayed: The Wilmington Race Riot of 1898 and Its Legacy*. Chapel Hill: University of North Carolina Press.

Césaire, Aimé. (1972) 2000. *Discourse on Colonialism*. Translated by Joan Pinkham. New York: Monthly Review Press. French original published in 1950 and then, in a revised edition, in 1955.

Césaire, Aimé, et al. 1956. "Discussion: 20th September, at 9 p.m.: The 1st International Congress of Negro Writers and Artists: Full Account." *Presence Africaine: Cultural Journal of the Negro World* 9:8-9.

Cha-Jua, Sundiata Keita, and Clarence Lang. 2007. "The 'Long Movement' as Vampire: Temporal and Spatial Fallacies in Recent Black Freedom Studies." *Journal of African American History* 92 (2): 265-88.

Chandler, Nahum Dimitri. 2000. "Originary Displacement." *Boundary 2* 27 (3): 249-86.

———. 2014. *X: The Problem of the Negro as a Problem for Thought*. New York: Fordham University Press.

Chang, Jeff. 2005. *Can't Stop, Won't Stop: A History of the Hip-Hop Generation*. New York: St. Martin's.

Chateauvert, Melinda. 1998. *Marching Together: Women of the Brotherhood of Sleeping Car Porters*. Urbana: University of Illinois Press.

Chibber, Vivek. 2013. *The Debate on Postcolonial Theory and the Specter of Capital*. London: Verso.

*Chicago Defender*. (1919) 1998. "Jazzing Away Prejudice." 10 May. Reprinted in *Keeping Time: Readings in Jazz History*, edited by Robert Walser, 15-16. New York: Oxford University Press. Citations refer to the reprinted edition.

Childers, Joseph, and Gary Hentzi, eds. 1995. *Columbia Dictionary of Modern Literary and Cultural Criticism*. New York: Columbia University Press.

Childs, Dennis. 2015. *Slaves of the State: Black Incarceration from the Chain Gang to the Penitentiary*. Minneapolis: University of Minnesota Press.

Chireau, Yvonne. 2006. *Black Magic: Religion and the African American Conjuring Tradition*. Berkeley: University of California Press.

Cho, Sumi. 2009. "Post-Racialism." *Iowa Law Review* 94:1589-1645.

Christian, Barbara. 1980. *Black Women Novelists: The Development of a Tradition, 1892-1976*. Westport, CT: Greenwood.

———. 1985. *Black Women Novelists and Black Feminist Literary Criticism*. New York: Pergamon.

Christie, Nils. 2000. *Crime Control as Industry: Towards Gulags, Western Style*. 3rd ed. London: Routledge.

Civil Rights Act. 1866. Ch. 31. 14 Stat. 27-30.

Civil Rights Congress (U.S.). 1970. *We Charge Genocide: The Historic Petition to the United Nations for Relief from a Crime of the United States Government against the Negro People*. New York: International.

Clarke, Cheryl. 1983. "The Failure to Transform." In *Home Girls: A Black Feminist Anthology*, edited by Barbara Smith, 190-202. New York: Kitchen Table—Women of Color Press.

Clausewitz, Carl von. (1832) 1997. *War, Politics, and Power*. Washington, DC: Regnery.

Clayton, Obie, ed. 1996. *An American Dilemma Revisited: Race Relations in a Changing World*. New York: Russell Sage Foundation.

Clifford Larson, Kate. 2004. *Bound for the Promised Land: Harriet Tubman, Portrait of an American Hero*. New York: Random House.

Clinton, Catherine. 2004. *Harriet Tubman: The Road to Freedom*. New York: Little, Brown.

Coates, Ta-Nehisi. 2014. "The Case for Reparations." *Atlantic*, June. www.theatlantic.com.

Cohen, Cathy J. 1999. *Boundaries of Blackness: AIDS and the Breakdown of Black Politics*. Chicago: University of Chicago Press.

———. 2004. "Deviance as Resistance: A New Research Agenda for the Study of Black Politics." *Du Bois Review: Social Science Research on Race* 1 (1): 27-45.

Cohen, Stanley. 2002. *Folk Devils and Moral Panics: The Creation of the Mods and Rockers*. 3rd ed. New York: Routledge.

Cohn, Bernard S. 1996. *Colonialism and Its Forms of Knowledge: The British in India*. Princeton, NJ: Princeton University Press.

Colapinto, John. 2008. "Outside Man: Spike Lee's Celluloid Struggles." *New Yorker*, 22 September, 52.

Collins, Patricia Hill. 1990. *Black Feminist Thought: Knowledge, Consciousness and the Politics of Empowerment.* New York: Hyman.

———. 1998. *Fighting Words: Black Women and the Search for Justice.* Minneapolis: University of Minnesota Press.

———. 2013. *On Intellectual Activism.* Philadelphia: Temple University Press.

Combahee River Collective. 1978. "Combahee River Collective Statement." In *Capitalist Patriarchy and the Case for Socialist Feminism,* edited by Zillah Eisenstein. New York: Monthly Review Press.

Common. 2007. "Southside." Featuring Kanye West. *Finding Forever.* Interscope.

Cone, James H. 2003. "Martin and Malcolm: Integrationism and Nationalism in African American Religious History." In *Religion and American Culture: A Reader,* 2nd ed., edited by David G. Hackett, 399–412. New York: Routledge.

Cooper, Anna J. 1998. *The Voice of Anna Julia Cooper: Including "A Voice from the South" and Other Important Essays, Papers, and Letters.* Lanham, MD: Rowman and Littlefield.

Cooper, Frederick. 2002. *Africa since 1940: The Past of the Present.* Cambridge: Cambridge University Press.

Copeland, Huey. 2013. *Bound to Appear: Art, Slavery, and the Site of Blackness in Multicultural America.* Chicago: University of Chicago Press.

Cortez, Jayne. (1969) 1997. "How Long Has Trane Been Gone." In *The Norton Anthology of African American Literature,* edited by Henry Louis Gates Jr. and Nellie McKay, 1957–59. New York: Norton.

Cott, Nancy. 1987. *The Grounding of Modern Feminism.* New Haven, CT: Yale University Press.

Cotten, Trystan T., ed. 2011. *Trans Migrations: The Bodies, Borders, and Politics of Transition.* New York: Routledge.

Cox, Aimee Meredith. 2015. *Shapeshifters: Black Girls and the Choreography of Citizenship.* Durham, NC: Duke University Press.

Craft, William. (1860) 1999. *Running a Thousand Miles for Freedom: The Escape of William and Ellen Craft.* Athens: University of Georgia Press.

Crawford, Margo Natalie. 2017. *Black Post-Blackness: The Black Arts Movement and Twenty-First-Century Aesthetics.* Urbana: University of Illinois Press.

Crawford, Margo Natalie, and Lisa Gail Collins. 2008. *New Thoughts on the Black Arts Movement.* New Brunswick, NJ: Rutgers University Press.

Crawley, Ashon T. 2008. "Circum-Religious Performance: Queer(ed) Black Bodies and the Black Church." *Theology and Sexuality* 14 (2): 201–22.

Crenshaw, Kimberlé. 1989. "Demarginalizing the Intersection of Race and Sex: A Black Feminist Critique of Antidiscrimination Doctrine, Feminist Theory and Antiracist Politics." In "Feminism in the Law: Theory, Practice and Criticism." Special issue, *University of Chicago Legal Forum,* 139–67.

———. 1991. "Mapping the Margins: Intersectionality, Identity Politics, and Violence against Women of Color." *Stanford Law Review* 43 (6): 1241–99.

Crosland, Alan, dir. 1927. *The Jazz Singer.* DVD. Warner Brothers, 2007.

Curtin, Mary Ellen. 2000. *Black Prisoners and Their World: Alabama, 1865–1900.* Charlottesville: University of Virginia Press.

Curtin, Philip. 1972. *The Atlantic Slave Trade: A Census.* Madison: University of Wisconsin Press.

Cuvier, Georges. 1817. *Extraits d'observations faites sur le cadavre d'une femme connue a Paris et a Londre sous le nom de Venus Hottentote.* Paris: Muséum national d'histoire naturelle.

Dagbovie, Pero G. 2007. "History as a Core Subject Area of African American Studies: Self-Taught and Self-Proclaimed African American Historians, 1960s–1980s." *Journal of Black Studies* 37 (5): 602–29.

———. 2017. "(Re)Introducing Foundational African American Historical Thought to a Twenty-First Century Readership." *Journal of African American History* 102 (2): 232–41.

D'Aguiar, Fred. 2015. *Bloodlines.* New York: Random House.

Dahl, Robert A. 1961. *Who Governs? Democracy and Power in an American City.* New Haven, CT: Yale University Press.

*Daily News.* 2017. "50 Cent Slams Jay-Z's '4.44' Album for Being 'Too Smart.'" 6 July. www.dailynews.com.

Dangarembga, Tsitsi. 1988. *Nervous Conditions.* London: Women's Press.

Daniel, Pete. 1990. *Shadow of Slavery: Peonage in the South, 1901–1969.* Urbana: University of Illinois Press.

Darwin, Charles. (1859) 2009. *On the Origin of Species.* Cambridge: Cambridge University Press.

Davis, Angela Y. 1971a. *If They Come in the Morning: Voices of Resistance.* New York: Third Press.

———. 1971b. "Reflections on the Black Woman's Role in the Community of Slaves." *Black Scholar* 3 (December 1971): 2–15.

———. 1972. "Reflections on the Black Woman's Role in the Community of Slaves." *Massachusetts Review* 13 (1–2): 81–100. www.jstor.org.

———. 1975. "Interview with Angela Davis." *Social Justice* 3 (Summer): 30–35.

———. 1981. *Women, Race & Class.* New York: Vintage Books.

———. 1998. "Racialized Punishment and Prison Abolition."

In *The Angela Y. Davis Reader*, edited by Joy James, 96–106. Malden, MA: Blackwell.

———. 2003. *Are Prisons Obsolete?* New York: Seven Stories.

———. 2005. *Abolition Democracy: Beyond Empire, Prisons, and Torture.* New York: Seven Stories.

Davis, Angela Y., and Elizabeth Martinez. 1994. "Coalition Building among People of Color." *Inscriptions* (Center for Cultural Studies) 7. http://ccs.ihr.ucsc.edu.

Davis, Charles T., and Henry Louis Gates, Jr., eds. 1985. *The Slave's Narrative.* New York: Oxford University Press.

Davis, F. James. 1991. *Who Is Black? One Nation's Definition.* University Park: Pennsylvania State University Press.

Davis, Mike. 1990. *City of Quartz: Excavating the Future in Los Angeles.* London: Verso.

Davis, Uri. 1987. *Israel: An Apartheid State.* London: Zed Books.

Dawes, Kwame. 1996. *Requiem: A Lament for the Dead.* London: Peepal Tree.

Dawson, Michael C. 1994. *Behind the Mule: Race and Class in African-American Politics.* Princeton, NJ: Princeton University Press.

Dearden, Lizzie. 2016. "Russia Withdraws Request for Warships to Refuel in Spanish Port of Ceuta on Way to Bomb Syria Amid Anger." *Independent*, 26 October. www.independent.co.uk.

DeFrantz, Thomas F. 2001. *Dancing Many Drums: Excavations in African American Dance.* Madison: University of Wisconsin Press.

———. 2010. "Performing the Breaks: African American Aesthetic Structures" *Theater* 40 (1): 30–37.

Delany, Samuel. 1984. *Starboard Wine: More Notes on the Language of Science Fiction.* Pleasantville, NY: Dragon.

Deloria, Philip. 2015. "American Master Narratives and the Problem of Indian Citizenship in the Gilded Age and Progressive Era." *Journal of the Gilded Age and Progressive Era* 14 (1): 3–12.

Deloria, Vine, Jr. 2003. *God Is Red: A Native View of Religion.* Golden, CO: Fulcrum.

Desai, Ashwin. 2002. *We Are the Poors: Community Struggles in Post-Apartheid South Africa.* New York: NYU Press.

Dillard, Cynthia B. 2000. "The Substance of Things Hoped For, the Evidence of Things Not Seen: Examining an Endarkened Feminist Epistemology in Educational Research and Leadership." *International Journal of Qualitative Studies in Education* 13 (6): 661–81.

Dillon, Stephen. 2012. "Possessed by Death: The Neoliberal-Carceral State, Black Feminism, and the Afterlife of Slavery." *Radical History Review* 112 (Winter 2012): 113–25.

Diouf, Sylviane. 2014. *Slavery's Exiles: The Story of the American Maroons.* New York: NYU Press.

Dirlik, Arif. 1994. "The Postcolonial Aura: Third World Criticism in the Age of Global Capitalism." *Critical Inquiry* 20 (2): 328–56.

Dorman, Jacob S. 2013. *Chosen People: The Rise of American Black Israelite Religions.* New York: Oxford University Press.

Douglas, Davison. 2005. *Jim Crow Moves North: The Battle over Northern School Segregation, 1865–1954.* Cambridge: Cambridge University Press.

Douglas, Kelly Brown. 1999. *Sexuality and the Black Church: A Womanist Perspective.* Maryknoll, NY: Orbis Books.

Douglas, Susan. 2010. *The Rise of Enlightened Sexism: How Pop Culture Took Us from Girl Power to Girls Gone Wild.* New York: Macmillan.

Douglass, Frederick. (1845) 2009. *Narrative of the Life of Frederick Douglass, an American Slave.* Cambridge, MA: Harvard University Press.

———. (1863) 1975. "Colored Men, to Arms!" In *A Documentary History of the Negro People of the United States*, vol. 1, edited by Hebert Aptheker, 477–80. New York: Carol.

Downs, Gregory P. 2011. *Declarations of Dependence: The Long Reconstruction of Popular Politics in the South, 1861–1908.* Chapel Hill: University of North Carolina Press.

Drake, St. Clair. 1987. *Black Folks Here and There: An Essay in History and Anthropology.* Los Angeles: University of California Center for Afro-American Studies.

Drake, St. Clair, and Horace R. Cayton. 1945. *Black Metropolis: A Study of Negro Life in a Northern City.* Chicago: University of Chicago Press.

Draper, Theodore, and Eric Foner. 1970. "Exchange on Black Nationalism." *New York Times Review of Books*, 3 December, 6.

*Dred Scott v. Sandford.* 1857. 60 U.S. 393.

Driskell, Jay W. 2014. *Schooling Jim Crow: The Fight for Atlanta's Booker T. Washington High School and the Roots of Black Protest Politics.* Charlottesville: University of Virginia Press.

DuBois, Ellen. 1978. *Feminism and Suffrage: The Emergence of an Independent Women's Movement in America, 1848–1869.* Ithaca, NY: Cornell University Press.

Du Bois, W. E. B. 1896. *The Suppression of the African Slave Trade to the United States of America, 1638–1870.* New York: Longmans, Green.

———. 1897a. *The Conservation of Races.* American Negro Academy Occasional Papers 2. Washington, DC: American Negro Academy.

———. 1897b. "Strivings of the Negro People." *Atlantic Monthly* 80 (August): 194–98.

———. (1899) 1996. *The Philadelphia Negro*. Pennsylvania: University of Pennsylvania Press.

———. 1903. *The Souls of Black Folk: Essays and Sketches*. Chicago: A. C. McClurg.

———. 1917. "Massacre at East St. Louis." *Crisis* 14 (September): 219–38.

———. 1920. *Darkwater: Voices from Within the Veil*. New York: Harcourt, Brace and Howe.

———. 1921. "Manifesto of the Second Pan-African Congress." *Crisis* 23 (November): 5–6.

———. 1922. "Opinion of W. E. B. Du Bois." *Crisis* 24 (August): 152–53.

———. 1934a. "Segregation." *Crisis* 41 (January): 20.

———. 1934b. "Separation and Self-Respect." *Crisis* 41 (March): 85.

———. (1935) 1998. *Black Reconstruction in America, 1860–1880*. New York: Free Press.

———. (1940) 2014. *Dusk of Dawn: An Essay toward an Autobiography of a Race Concept*. New York: Oxford University Press.

Dubber, Markus Dirk. 2005. *The Police Power: Patriarchy and the Foundations of American Government*. New York: Columbia University Press.

Dudziak, Mary L. 2000. *Cold War Civil Rights: Race and the Image of American Democracy*. Princeton, NJ: Princeton University Press.

Dugdale, Robert L. (1877) 1910. *The Jukes: A Study in Crime, Pauperism, Disease, and Heredity*. New York: Putnam.

Duggan, Lisa. 2000. *Sapphic Slashers: Sex, Violence, and American Modernity*. Durham, NC: Duke University Press.

Dunbar, Elizabeth Armstrong. 2017. *Never Caught: The Washingtons' Relentless Pursuit of Their Runaway Slave, Ona Judge*. New York: Artria.

Dungy, Camille T. 2010. *Suck on the Marrow: Poems*. Pasadena, CA: Red Hen.

Dupri, Jermaine. 2002. "Welcome to Atlanta." *So So Def: Definition of a Remix*. Columbia/Sony Music Distribution.

Dussel, Enrique. (1985) 2003. *Philosophy of Liberation*. Eugene, OR: Wipf and Stock.

Duster, Troy. (1990) 2003. *Backdoor to Eugenics*. London: Routledge.

DuVernay, Ava, dir. 2016. *13th*. Netflix.

Dworkin, Ira. 2017. *Congo Love Song: African American Culture and the Crisis of the Colonial State*. Chapel Hill: University of North Carolina Press.

———. 2018. "Radwa Ashour, African American Criticism, and the Production of Modern Arabic Literature." *Cambridge Journal of Postcolonial Literary Inquiry* 5 (1): 1–19.

Early, Gerald L, ed. 1993. *Lure and Loathing: Essays on Race,*

*Identity, and the Ambivalence of Assimilation*. New York: Penguin.

Edwards, Brent Hayes. 2001. "The Uses of Diaspora." *Social Text* 19 (1): 45–73.

———. 2003. *The Practice of Diaspora: Literature, Translation, and the Rise of Black Internationalism*. Cambridge, MA: Harvard University Press.

Edwards, Erica R. 2012. *Charisma and the Fictions of Black Leadership*. Minneapolis: University of Minnesota Press.

Edwards, Laura F. 1997. *Gendered Strife and Confusion: The Political Culture of Reconstruction*. Urbana: University of Illinois Press.

E-40. 2006. "Tell Me When To Go." *My Ghetto Report Card*. Reprise / Warner Bros. / BME.

Elam, Harry J., Jr. 2001. "The Device of Race: An Introduction." In *African American Performance and Theater History: A Critical Reader*, edited by Harry J. Elam Jr. and David Krasner, 3–16. Oxford: Oxford University Press.

Elias, Norbert. 1965. *Established and Outsiders*. London: Sage.

Elkins, Caroline, and Susan Pederson, eds. 2005. *Settler Colonialism in the Twentieth Century: Projects, Practices, Legacies*. New York: Routledge.

Elkins, Stanley. 1959. *Slavery: A Problem in American Institutional and Intellectual Life*. Chicago: University of Chicago Press.

Ellington, Duke. (1973) 1976. *Music Is My Mistress*. New York: Da Capo, 1976.

Ellis, Trey. 1989. "The New Black Aesthetic." *Callaloo* 38 (Winter): 233–43.

Ellison, Ralph. (1947) 1995. *Invisible Man*. New York: Vintage International.

———. 1986. *Going to the Territory*. New York: Random House.

———. 1995. *Shadow and Act*. New York: Quality Paperback Book Club.

English, Daylanne. 2004. "Blessed Are the Barren: Lynching, Reproduction, and the Drama of New Negro Womanhood, 1916–1930." In *Unnatural Selections: Eugenics in American Modernism and the Harlem Renaissance*, 117–40. Chapel Hill: University of North Carolina Press.

Equiano, Olaudah. (1789) 1969. *Interesting Narrative of the Life of Olaudah Equiano*. New York: Negro Universities Press.

Essed, Philomena. 1991. *Understanding Everyday Racism: An Interdisciplinary Theory*. London: Sage.

Everett, Anna. 2001. *Returning the Gaze: A Genealogy of Black Film Criticism, 1909–1949*. Durham, NC: Duke University Press.

Ewing, Adam. 2014. *The Age of Garvey: How a Jamaican Activist*

*Created a Mass Movement and Changed Global Black Politics.* Princeton, NJ: Princeton University Press.

Eze, Emmanuel Chukwudi, ed. 1997. *Race and the Enlightenment: A Reader.* Malden, MA: Blackwell.

Fanon, Frantz. 1952. *Peau noire, masques blancs.* Paris: Éditions du Seuil.

———. 1963. *The Wretched of the Earth.* Translated by Constance Farrington. New York: Grove.

———. (1967) 2008. *Black Skin, White Masks.* New York: Grove. French original published in 1952.

Farrag, Hebah H. 2015. "The Role of Spirit in the #BlackLivesMatter Movement: A Conversation with Activist and Artist Patrisse Cullors." *Religion Dispatches,* June 24. http://religiondispatches.org.

Farred, Grant. 2008. "The Unsettler." *South Atlantic Quarterly* 107 (4): 791–808.

Fauset, Arthur. 1944. *Black Gods of the Metropolis: Negro Religious Cults of the Urban North.* Philadelphia: University of Pennsylvania Press.

Feagin, Joe, and Sean Elias. 2012. "Rethinking Racial Formation Theory: A Systemic Racism Critique." *Ethnic and Racial Studies* 36 (6): 931–960.

Fergus, Devin. 2009. *Liberalism, Black Power, and the Making of American Politics, 1965–1980.* Athens: University of Georgia Press.

Ferguson, Roderick. 2004. *Aberrations in Black: Toward a Queer of Color Critique.* Minneapolis: University of Minnesota Press.

———. 2005. "Of Our Normative Strivings: African American Studies and the Histories of Sexuality." *Social Text* 84 (85): 85–100.

———. 2007. "Race." In *Keywords for American Cultural Studies,* edited by Bruce Burgett and Glenn Hendler, 191–95. New York: NYU Press.

———. 2012. *The Reorder of Things: The University and Its Pedagogies of Minority Difference.* Minneapolis: University of Minnesota Press.

Ferree, Myra Marx, and Beth B. Hess. 2000. *Controversy and Coalition: The New Feminist Movement across Three Decades of Change.* 3rd ed. New York: Routledge.

Ferree, Myra Marx, and Patricia Yancey Martin, eds. 1995. *Feminist Organizations: Harvest of the New Women's Movement.* Philadelphia: Temple University Press.

Field, Allyson Nadia. 2015. *Uplift Cinema: The Emergence of African American Film and the Possibility of Black Modernity.* Durham, NC: Duke University Press.

Fields, Barbara. 1985. *Slavery and Freedom on the Middle Ground.* New Haven, CT: Yale University Press.

———. 1990. "Who Freed the Slaves?" In *The Civil War: An Illustrated History,* by Geoffrey Ward, with Ric Burns and Ken Burns, 178–81. New York: Knopf.

Fields, Karen E., and Barbara J. Fields. 2012. *Racecraft: The Soul of Inequality in American Life.* London: Verso Books.

Finch, Aisha K. 2015. *Rethinking Slave Rebellion in Cuba: La Escalera and the Insurgencies of 1841–1844.* Chapel Hill: University of North Carolina Press.

Findlay, Eileen J. Suárez. 2000. *Imposing Decency: The Politics of Sexuality and Race in Puerto Rico, 1870-1920.* Durham, NC: Duke University Press.

Firmin, Anténor. 2000. *Equality of Human Races: A Nineteenth Century Haitian Scholar's Response to European Racialism.* Translated by Asselin Charles. New York: Garland.

Fleetwood, Nicole R. 2011. *Troubling Vision: Performance, Visuality, and Blackness.* Chicago: University of Chicago Press.

———. 2015. *On Racial Icons: Blackness and the Public Imagination.* New Brunswick, NJ: Rutgers University Press.

Floyd, Samuel A. 1995. *The Power of Black Music: Interpreting Its History from Africa to the United States.* New York: Oxford University Press.

Foner, Eric. 1988. *Reconstruction: America's Unfinished Revolution, 1863-1877.* New York: Harper and Row.

———. 1997. Introduction to *The Betrayal of the Negro: From Rutherford B. Hayes to Woodrow Wilson,* by Rayford W. Logan, xi–xvi. New York: Da Capo.

Ford, Tanisha C. 2015. *Liberated Threads: Black Women, Style, and the Global Politics of Soul.* Chapel Hill: University of North Carolina Press.

Forte, Maximillian. 2004-5. "Extinction: The Historical Trope of Anti-Indigeneity in the Caribbean." *Issues in Caribbean Amerindian Studies* 6 (4): 1–24.

Foster, Frances Smith. 1993. *Written by Herself: Literary Production by African American Women, 1746-1892.* Bloomington: Indiana University Press.

Foucault, Michel. 1977. *Discipline and Punish: The Birth of the Prison.* Translated by Alan Sheridan. New York: Vintage.

———. 1978. *The History of Sexuality: Volume One.* Translated by Robert Hurley. New York: Pantheon Books.

———. 1980. *Power/Knowledge: Selected Interviews and Other Writings, 1972/1977.* New York: Pantheon.

———. 2003. *Society Must Be Defended: Lectures at the Collège de France, 1975-76.* Edited by Mauro Bertani and Alessandro Fontana. Translated by David Macey. New York: Picador.

Francis, Megan Ming. 2014. *Civil Rights and the Making of the Modern American State.* New York: Cambridge University Press.

Francis, Vievee. 2006. *Blue-Tail Fly.* Detroit: Wayne State University Press.

Franklin, John Hope. 1961. *Reconstruction after the Civil War*. Chicago: University of Chicago Press.

———. 1986. "On the Evolution of Scholarship in Afro-American History." In *The State of Afro-American History: Past, Present, and Future*, edited by Darlene Clark Hine, 13–22. Baton Rouge: Louisiana State University Press.

Franklin, John Hope, and Loren Schweninger. 1999. *Runaway Slaves: Rebels on the Plantation*. Oxford: Oxford University Press.

Frazier, E. Franklin. 1939. *The Negro Family in the United States*. Notre Dame, IN: University of Notre Dame Press.

Freedman, Estelle B. 2013. *Redefining Rape: Sexual Violence in the Era of Suffrage and Segregation*. Cambridge, MA: Harvard University Press.

Freund, Bill. (1984) 2016. *The Development of African Society since 1800*. London: Palgrave Macmillan.

Freyre, Gilberto. (1933) 1964. *The Masters and the Slaves*. New York: Knopf.

Fuentes, Marisa. 2016. *Dispossessed Lives: Enslaved Women, Violence, and the Archive*. Philadelphia: University of Pennsylvania Press.

Fussell, Paul. 2013. *The Great War and Modern Memory*. New York: Oxford University Press.

Gabbin, Joanne. 1997. "Furious Flower: African American Poetry, an Overview." In *The Oxford Companion to African American Literature*, edited by William L. Andrews, Trudier Harris, and Frances Smith Foster. New York: Oxford University Press. www.english.illinois.edu.

Gaines, Kevin K. 1996. *Uplifting the Race: Black Leadership, Politics, and Culture in the Twentieth Century*. Chapel Hill: University of North Carolina Press.

———. 2006. *African Americans in Ghana: Black Expatriates and the Civil Rights Era*. Chapel Hill: University of North Carolina Press.

Galton, Francis. 1833. *Inquiries into Human Faculty and Its Development*. London: Macmillan.

Gandhi, Leela. 1998. *Postcolonial Theory: A Critical Introduction*. Sydney: Allen and Unwin.

Gannon, Megan. 2016. "Race Is a Social Construct, Scientists Argue." *Scientific American*, 5 February. www.scientificamerican.com.

Garland, Phyl. 1969. *The Sound of Soul*. Chicago: Regnery.

Garvey, Marcus. (1937) 1990. "Speech by Marcus Garvey." 1 October 1937. In *The Marcus Garvey and Universal Negro Improvement Association*, vol. 7, *November 1927–August 1940*, edited by Robert A. Hill, 788–94. Berkeley: University of California Press.

———. 2004. *Selected Writings and Speeches of Marcus Garvey*. New York: Dover.

Gaspar, David Barry. 1993. *Bondmen and Rebels: A Study of Master-Slave Relations in Antigua*. Durham, NC: Duke University Press.

Gaspar, David Barry, and Darlene Clark Hine, eds. 1996. *More than Chattel: Black Women and Slavery in the Americas*. Bloomington: Indiana University Press.

Gates, Henry Louis, Jr. 2007. "The Black Letters on the Sign: W. E. B. Du Bois and the Canon." In *The Oxford W. E. B. Du Bois*, 19 vols., edited by Henry Louis Gates, Jr., xi–xxiv. Oxford: Oxford University Press.

Gatewood, Willard B. 1990. *Aristocrats of Color: The Black Elite, 1880–1920*. Bloomington: Indiana University Press.

Gay, Claudine, Jennifer L. Hochschild, and Ariel White. 2014. "Americans' Belief in Linked Fate: A Wide Reach but Limited Impact." Paper originally presented at the 2010 annual meeting of the American Political Science Association. http://ssrn.com.

Gay, Claudine, and Katherine Tate. 1998. "Doubly Bound: The Impact of Gender and Race on the Politics of Black Women." *Political Psychology* 19 (1): 169–84.

Gaye, Marvin. 1973. "Inner City Blues." *Let's Get It On*. Synergy.

Gayle, Addison. 1971. *The Black Aesthetic*. Garden City, NY: Doubleday.

Gearan, Anne, and Abby Phillip. 2016. "Clinton Regrets 1996 Remark on 'Super-Predators' after Encounter with Activist." *Washington Post*, 25 February. www.washingtonpost.com.

Genovese, Eugene. 1974. *Roll, Jordan, Roll: The World the Slaves Made*. New York: Vintage.

George, Nelson. 2001. *Buppies, B-Boys, Baps, and Bohos: Notes on Post-Soul Black Culture*. New York: Da Capo.

Giddings, Paula. 1984. *When and Where I Enter*. New York: Quill William Morrow.

Gillespie, Dizzy. 1947. "Groovin' High." Savoy.

Gillespie, Dizzy, with Al Fraser. 1979. *To Be, or Not . . . to Bop*. New York: Da Capo.

Gillespie, Michael. 2016. *Film Blackness: American Cinema and the Idea of Black Film*. Durham, NC: Duke University Press.

Gilman, Sander L. 1985. "Black Bodies, White Bodies: Toward an Iconography of Female Sexuality in Late Nineteenth-Century Art, Medicine, and Literature." *Critical Inquiry* 12 (1): 204–42.

Gilmore, Glenda Elizabeth. 1996. *Gender and Jim Crow: Women and the Politics of White Supremacy in North Carolina, 1896–1920*. Chapel Hill: University of North Carolina Press.

Gilmore, Ruth Wilson. 2007. *Golden Gulag: Prisons, Surplus,*

*Crisis, and Opposition in Globalizing California.* Berkeley: University of California Press.

——. 2015. "The Worrying State of the Anti-Prison Movement." *Social Justice: A Journal of Crime, Conflict & World Order,* 23 February. www.socialjusticejournal.org.

Gilmore, Stephanie. 2008. *Feminist Coalitions: Historical Perspectives on Second-Wave Feminism in the United Sates.* Urbana: University of Illinois Press.

Gilroy, Paul. 1991. "'It's a Family Affair': Black Culture and the Trope of Kinship." In *Small Acts: Thoughts on the Politics of Black Cultures,* 192–207. London: Serpent's Tail.

——. 1993. *The Black Atlantic: Modernity and Double Consciousness.* Cambridge, MA: Harvard University Press.

——. 1998. "Question of a 'Soulful Style': Interview with Paul Gilroy." Interview by Richard C. Green and Monique Guillory. In *Soul: Black Power, Politics, and Pleasure,* edited by Monique Guillory and Richard C. Green, 250–66. New York: NYU Press.

——. 2000. *Against Race: Imagining Political Culture beyond the Color Line.* Cambridge, MA: Harvard University Press.

——. 2004. "Bold as Love? Jimi's Afrocyberdelia and the Challenge of the Not Yet." In *Rip It Up: The Black Experience in Rock 'N Roll,* edited by Kandia Crazy Horse, 25–38. New York: Palgrave.

——. 2005. *Postcolonial Melancholia.* New York: Columbia University Press.

Glare, P. G. W., ed. (1982) 2000. *Oxford Latin Dictionary.* Oxford: Oxford University Press.

Glaude, Eddie S., Jr. 2010. "The Black Church Is Dead." *Huffington Post,* 26 April. www.huffingtonpost.com.

——. 2014. *African American Religion: A Very Short Introduction.* New York: Oxford University Press.

Glenn, Evelyn Nakano. 2002. *Unequal Freedom: How Race and Gender Shaped American Citizenship and Labor.* Cambridge, MA: Harvard University Press.

Glissant, Édouard. 1997. "For Opacity." In *Poetics of Relation,* 189–94. Translated by Betsy Wing. Ann Arbor: University of Michigan Press.

Glymph, Thavolia. 2008. *Out of the House of Bondage: The Transformation of the Plantation Household.* Cambridge: Cambridge University Press.

——. 2013. "Du Bois's 'Black Reconstruction and Slave Women's War for Freedom.'" *South Atlantic Quarterly* 112 (Summer): 489–505.

Gobineau, Arthur. 1915. *The Inequality of Human Races.* Translated by Adrian Collins. London: Heinemann. Internet Archive, https://archive.org.

Goings, Kenneth W. 1994. *Mammy and Uncle Mose: Black Collectibles and American Stereotyping.* Bloomington: University of Indiana Press.

Goldberg, David Theo. 2009. *The Threat of Race: Reflections on Racial Neoliberalism.* Malden, MA: Wiley-Blackwell.

Goldenberg, David M. 2003. *The Curse of Ham: Race and Slavery in Early Judaism, Christianity, and Islam.* Princeton, NJ: Princeton University Press.

Gomez, Michael A. 1998. *Exchanging Our Country Marks: The Transformation of African Identities in the Colonial and Antebellum South.* Chapel Hill: University of North Carolina Press.

——. 2005. *Reversing Sail: A History of the African Diaspora.* Cambridge: Cambridge University Press.

Gooding-Williams, Robert. 2009. *In the Shadow of Du Bois: Afro-Modern Political Thought in America.* Cambridge, MA: Harvard University Press.

Gordon, Avery. 1997. *Ghostly Matters: Haunting and the Sociological Imagination.* Minneapolis: University of Minnesota Press.

Gordon, Lewis R. 1999. *Bad Faith and Antiblack Racism.* New York: Humanity Books.

Gore, Dayo F. 2011. *Radicalism at the Crossroads: African American Women Activists in the Cold War.* New York: NYU Press.

Gossett, Thomas F. (1963) 1989. *Race: The History of an Idea in America.* New York: Schocken Books.

Gottschild, Brenda Dixon. 1996. *Digging the Africanist Presence in American Dance.* Westport, CT: Greenwood.

——. 2003. *The Black Dancing Body: A Geography from Coon to Cool.* New York: Palgrave Macmillan.

Gould, Stephen Jay. 1994. "The Geometer of Race." *Discover* 15 (11): 65–69.

——. 1996. *The Mismeasure of Man.* New York: Norton.

Goyal, Yogita. 2010. *Romance, Diaspora, and Black Atlantic Literature.* New York: Cambridge University Press.

Gramsci, Antonio. 1971. *Selections from the Prison Notebooks of Antonio Gramsci.* Edited and translated by Quintin Hoare and Geoffrey Nowell-Smith. New York: International.

Grant, Jacquelyn. (1979) 1993. "Black Theology and the Black Woman." In *Black Theology: A Documentary History,* vol. 1, *1966–1979,* edited by James H. Cone and Gayraud S. Wilmore, 323–38. Maryknoll, NY: Orbis Books.

——. 1989. *White Women's Christ and Black Women's Jesus: Feminist Christology and Womanist Response.* Maryknoll, NY: Orbis Books.

Graves, Joseph L., Jr. 2015. "Great Is Their Sin: Biological Determinism in the Age of Genomics." *Annals of the American Academy of Political and Social Science* 661 (1): 24–50.

Gray, Herman. 1995. *Watching Race: Television and the Struggle for "Blackness."* Minneapolis: University of Minnesota Press.

———. 2005. *Cultural Moves: African Americans and the Politics of Representation*. Berkeley: University of California Press.

Green, Jonathan. 1986. *Baptism of Sue Mae*. Oil on masonite. www.jonathangreenstudios.com.

Green, Kai M., and Treva Ellison. 2014. "Keywords: Tranifest." *TSQ: Transgender Studies Quarterly* 1 (1–2): 222–25.

Green, Lorenzo. 1944. "Mutiny on the Slave Ships." *Phylon* 5:346–54.

Greer, Christina M. 2013. *Black Ethnics: Race, Immigration, and the Pursuit of the American Dream*. Oxford: Oxford University Press.

Griffin, Farah Jasmine. 2013. *Harlem Nocturne: Women Artists and Progressive Politics during World War II*. New York: Basic-Civitas Books.

Griffin, Horace L. 2006. *Their Own Receive Them Not: African American Lesbians and Gays in Black Churches*. Cleveland, OH: Pilgrim.

Grimké, Angelina Weld. (1916) 1998. "Rachel." In *Strange Fruit: Plays on Lynching by African American Women*, edited by Kathy A. Perkins and Judith L. Stephens, 27–91. Bloomington: Indiana University Press.

Gross, Ariela J. 2008. *What Blood Won't Tell: A History of Race on Trial in America*. Cambridge, MA: Harvard University Press.

Gross, Kali Nicole. 2006. *Colored Amazons: Crime, Violence, and Black Women in the City of Brotherly Love, 1880–1910*. Durham, NC: Duke University Press.

Grossman, James R. 1989. *Land of Hope: Chicago, Black Southerners, and the Great Migration*. Chicago: University of Chicago Press.

Grosz, Elizabeth. 1998. "Bodies-Cities." In *Places through the Body*, edited by Heidi J. Nast and Steve Pile, 31–38. New York: Routledge.

*Guardian*. 1960. "Marred: M. Lumumba's Offensive Speech in King's Presence." 1 July. www.theguardian.com.

Guerrero, Ed. 1993. *Framing Blackness: The African-American Image in Film*. Philadelphia: Temple University Press.

Guidotti-Hernández, Nicole M. 2011. *Unspeakable Violence: Remapping U.S. and Mexican National Imaginaries*. Durham, NC: Duke University Press.

Guillory, Monique, and Richard C. Green, eds. 1998. *Soul: Black Power, Politics, and Pleasure*. New York: NYU Press.

Gunning, Sandra. 1995. *Race, Rape, and Lynching: The Red Record of American Literature*. New York: Oxford University Press.

Guridy, Frank Andre. 2010. *Forging Diaspora: Afro-Cubans and African Americans in a World of Empire and Jim Crow*. Chapel Hill: University of North Carolina Press.

Gutman, Herbert G. 1977. *The Black Family in Slavery and Freedom, 1750–1925*. New York: Vintage.

Guy-Sheftall, Beverly, ed. 1995. *Words of Fire: An Anthology of African-American Feminist Thought*. New York: New Press.

Hahn, Stephen. 2003. *A Nation under Our Feet: Black Political Struggles in the Rural South from Slavery to the Great Migration*. Cambridge, MA: Harvard University Press.

Halberstam, Judith (Jack). 2007. "Queer Voices and Musical Genders." In *Oh Boy! Masculinities and Popular Music*, edited by Freya Jarman Ivens, 183–96. New York: Routledge.

Haley, Sarah. 2016. *No Mercy Here: Gender, Punishment, and the Making of Jim Crow Modernity*. Chapel Hill: University of North Carolina Press.

Hall, Jacquelyn Dowd. 2005. "The Long Civil Rights Movement and the Political Uses of the Past." *Journal of American History* 91 (4): 1233–63.

Hall, Stuart. 1980. "Race, Articulation and Societies Structured in Dominance." In *Sociological Theories: Race and Colonialism*, 305–45. Paris: UNESCO.

———. (1989) 1996. "New Ethnicities." In *Stuart Hall: Critical Dialogues in Cultural Studies*, edited by David Morley and Kuan-Hsing Chen, 442–51. New York: Routledge.

———. 1990. "Cultural Identity and Diaspora." In *Identity: Community, Culture, Difference*, edited by Jonathan Rutherford, 222–37. London: Lawrence and Wishart.

———. 1992. "What Is This 'Black' in Black Popular Culture?" In *Black Popular Culture*, edited by Gina Dent, 21–33. Seattle: Bay.

Hall, Stuart, Chas Critcher, Tony Jefferson, John Clarke, and Brian Roberts. 1978. *Policing the Crisis: Mugging, the State and Law and Order*. London: Macmillan.

Hallam, Henry. (1837) 1876. *Introduction to the Literature of Europe, in the Fifteenth, Sixteenth, and Seventeenth Centuries*. Vol. 1. London: John Murray.

Halliwell, Stephen. 1998. *Aristotle's Poetics*. Chicago: University of Chicago Press.

Hamer, Fannie Lou. 1964. "Jim Crow Medical Care Hit." *Memphis World*, 8 May, 8.

Hanchard, Michael. 2004. "Black Transnationalism, Africana Studies, and the 21st Century." *Journal of Black Studies* 35 (2): 139–53.

Hannett, Leo. 1971. "The Niugini Black Power Movement." In *Tertiary Students and the Politics of Papua New Guinea*, 41–51. Lae: Papua New Guinea Institute of Technology.

Hansberry, Lorraine. 1958. *A Raisin in the Sun*. New York: Vintage.

Hanssen, Beatrice. 2000. *Critique of Violence: Between Poststructuralism and Critical Theory*. New York: Routledge.

Harding, Sandra. 2009. "Standpoint Theories: Productively Controversial." *Hypatia* 24 (4): 192–200.

Harding, Vincent. 1981. *There Is a River: The Black Struggle for Freedom in America*. New York: Houghton Mifflin Harcourt.

Harney, Stefano, and Fred Moten. 2013. *The Undercommons: Fugitive Planning and Black Study*. London: Minor Compositions.

Harper, Frances Ellen Watkins. (1892) 1988. *Iola Leroy, or, Shadows Uplifted*. New York: Oxford University Press.

Harper, Phillip Brian. 1996. *Are We Not Men? Masculine Anxiety and the Problem of African-American Identity*. New York: Oxford University Press.

Harris, Joseph. 1971. *The African Presence in Asia: Consequences of the East African Slave Trade*. Evanston: Northwestern University Press.

———, ed. (1982) 1993a. *Global Dimensions of the African Diaspora*. Washington, DC: Howard University Press.

———. (1982) 1993b. *Introduction to Global Dimensions of the African Diaspora*, edited by Joseph E. Harris, 3–14. Washington, DC: Howard University Press.

Harrison, Paul Carter. 1989. *In the Shadow of the Great White Way: Images from the Black Theatre*. New York: Thunder's Mouth.

Hart, William D. 2006. "Three Rival Narratives of Black Religion." In *A Companion to African-American Studies*, edited by Lewis R. Gordon and Jane Anna Gordon, 476–93. Malden, MA: Blackwell.

———. 2008. *Black Religion: Malcolm X, Julius Lester, and Jan Willis*. London: Palgrave Macmillan.

Hartman, Saidiya. 1996. "Seduction and the Ruses of Power." *Callaloo* 19 (2): 537–60.

———. 1997. *Scenes of Subjection: Terror, Slavery, and Self-Making in Nineteenth-Century America*. New York: Oxford University Press.

———. 2002. "The Time of Slavery." *South Atlantic Quarterly* 101 (Fall): 757–77.

———. 2007. *Lose Your Mother: A Journey along the Atlantic Slave Route*. New York: Farrar, Straus and Giroux.

———. 2016. "The Belly of the World: A Note on Black Women's Labors." *Souls: A Critical Journal of Black Politics, Culture, and Society* 18 (January–March): 166–73.

Hayden, Robert. (1966) 2013. "Frederick Douglass." In *Collected Poems*, edited by Frederick Glaysher, 62. New York: Liveright.

Hegel, Georg W. F. (1837) 1899. *The Philosophy of History*. Translated by John Sibree. New York: Colonial.

Heinze, Denise. 1993. *The Dilemma of "Double-Consciousness": Toni Morrison's Novels*. Athens: University of Georgia Press.

Henderson, Mae Gwendolyn. (1993) 2000. "Speaking in Tongues: Dialogics, Dialectics, and the Black Woman Writer's Literary Tradition." In *African American Literary Theory: A Reader*, edited by Winston Napier, 348–68. New York: NYU Press.

Hendricks, Wanda. 2013. *Fannie Barrier Williams: Crossing Borders of Region and Race*. Urbana: University of Illinois Press.

Heng, Geraldine. 2011. "The Invention of Race in the European Middle Ages I & 2: Race Studies, Modernity, and the Middle Ages." *Literature Compass* 8 (5): 258–74.

Henwood, Doug. 2000. "Profiteering in the Hemisphere." *NACLA Report on the Americas* 34 (3): 49–59.

Herbert, Bob. 2008. "The Obama Phenomenon." *New York Times*, 5 January, A15.

Herrnstein, Richard J., and Charles Murray. 1994. *The Bell Curve: Intelligence and Class Structure in American Life*. New York: Free Press.

Herzing, Rachel. 2015. "'Tweaking Armageddon': The Potential and Limits of Conditions of Confinement Campaigns." *Social Justice* 41:190–96.

Hicks, Cheryl. 2010. *Talk with You like a Woman: African American Women: Justice, and Reform in New York, 1890–1935*. Chapel Hill: University of North Carolina Press.

Higginbotham, A. Leon, Jr. 1980. *In the Matter of Color: Race and the American Legal Process: The Colonial Period*. New York: Oxford University Press.

Higginbotham, Evelyn Brooks. 1993. *Righteous Discontent: The Women's Movement in the Black Baptist Church*. Cambridge, MA: Harvard University Press.

Higginson, John. 2014. *Collective Violence and the Agrarian Origins of South African Apartheid, 1900–1948*. New York: Cambridge University Press.

Hill, Edwin C., Jr. 2013. *Black Soundscapes White Stages: The Meaning of Francophone Sound in the Black Atlantic*. Baltimore: Johns Hopkins University Press.

Hill, Myrna. 1971. "Feminism and Black Nationalism." *Militant*, 2 April.

Hine, Darlene Clark. 1986. "Lifting the Veil, Shattering the Silence: Black Women's History in Slavery and Freedom." In *The State of Afro-American History: Past, Present, and Future*, edited by Darlene Clark Hine, 224–49. Baton Rouge: Louisiana State University Press.

———. 1989. "Rape and the Inner Lives of Black Women in the Middle West: Preliminary Thoughts on the Culture of Dissemblance." *Signs: Journal of Women in Culture and Society* 14 (4): 912–20.

———. 1994. *Hine Sight: Black Women and the Re-construction of American History*. Brooklyn, NY: Carlson.

———. 2003. "Black Professionals and Race Consciousness: Origins of the Civil Rights Movement, 1890–1950." *Journal of American History* 89:1279–94.

Hoby, Hermione. 2014. "Ellen Willis Rock On." *Times Literary Supplement*, 13 August. www.the-tls.co.uk.

Hochschild, Adam. 1998. *King Leopold's Ghost: A Story of Greed, Terror, and Heroism in Colonial Africa*. New York: Houghton Mifflin.

Holt, Thomas C. 1979. *Black over White: Negro Political Leadership in South Carolina during Reconstruction*. Urbana: University of Illinois Press.

hooks, bell. 1992. *Black Looks: Race and Representation*. Boston: South End.

———. 2015. *Yearning: Race, Gender, and Cultural Politics*. New York: Routledge.

Hopkins, Pauline E. (1899) 1969. *Contending Forces: A Romance Illustrative of Negro Life North and South*. Miami, FL: Mnemo.

Horne, Gerald. 1997. *Fire This Time: The Watts Uprising and the 1960s*. New York: Da Capo.

———. 2014. *The Counter-revolution of 1776: Slave Resistance and the Origins of the United States of America*. New York: NYU Press.

Horton, George Moses. 1997. *The Black Bard of North Carolina: George Moses Horton and His Poetry*. Edited by Joan R. Sherman. Chapel Hill: University of North Carolina Press.

Hucks, Tracey E. 2012. *Yoruba Traditions and African American Religion Nationalism*. Albuquerque: University of New Mexico Press.

Hughes, Langston. (1926) 1995. "The Negro Speaks of Rivers." In *The Collected Poems of Langston Hughes*, edited by Arnold Rampersad, 23. New York: Vintage Books.

———. (1926) 1998. "The Negro Artist and the Racial Mountain." *Nation*, 23 June, 692–93. Reprinted in *Keeping Time: Readings in Jazz History*, edited by Robert Walser, 55–57. New York: Oxford University Press. Citations refer to the reprinted edition.

———. (1931) 1995. "House in the World" (formerly "White Shadows"). In *The Collected Poems of Langston Hughes*, edited by Arnold Rampersad, 138. New York: Vintage Classics.

———. (1940) 1959. "Notes on Commercial Theater." In *Selected Poems*, 190. New York: Knopf.

———. (1940) 1993. *The Big Sea: An Autobiography*. New York: Farrar, Straus and Giroux.

———. (1966) 1997. "200 Years of American Negro Poetry." *Transition* 75/76:90–96.

Hull, Gloria T., Patricia Bell-Scott, and Barbara Smith, eds. 1982. *All the Women Are White, All the Blacks Are Men, but Some of Us Are Brave: Black Women's Studies*. New York: Feminist Press.

Hunter, Tera. 1997. *To 'Joy My Freedom: Southern Black Women's Lives and Labors after the Civil War*. Cambridge, MA: Harvard University Press.

———. 2017. *Bound in Wedlock: Slave and Free Black Marriage in the Nineteenth Century*. Cambridge, MA: Harvard University Press.

Hurston, Zora Neale. (1928) 2004. "How It Feels to Be Colored Me." In *The Norton Anthology of African American Literature*, 2nd ed., edited by Henry Louis Gates Jr. and Nellie Y. McKay, 1030–33. New York: Norton.

———. (1934) 1984. "Characteristics of Negro Expression." In *Negro: An Anthology*, edited by Nancy Cunard and Hugh Ford, 39–61. New York: Frederick Unger.

———. (1934) 2008. *Jonah's Gourd Vine: A Novel*. New York: Harper Perennial Modern Classics.

———. (1935) 2008. *Of Mules and Men*. New York: Harper Perennial.

———. (1937) 1990. *Their Eyes Were Watching God*. New York: Perennial Library.

———. (1942) 1971. *Dust Tracks on a Road: An Autobiography*. Philadelphia: Lippincott.

———. 1981. *The Sanctified Church*. Berkeley, CA: Turtle Island.

———. 1990. *Tell My Horse: Voodoo and Life in Haiti and Jamaica*. New York: Perennial.

Ibrahim, Habiba. 2012. *Troubling the Family: The Promise of Personhood and the Rise of Multiracialism*. Minneapolis: University of Minnesota Press.

Ignatin, Noel. 1967. "White Blindspot." In *Understanding and Fighting White Supremacy*, edited by Noel Ignatin and Ted Allen. Chicago: Sojourner Truth Organization. www.sojournertruth.net.

Incite!/Critical Resistance. 2014. "Statement on Gender and the Prison Industrial Complex." In "Interchange: The History of Capitalism." *Journal of American History* 101 (September): 503–36.

Inikori, Joseph E. 1983. *Forced Migration: The Impact of the Export Slave Trade on African Societies*. New York: Holmes and Meier.

———. 2002. *Africans and the Industrial Revolution in England: A Study in International Trade and Economic Development*. Cambridge: Cambridge University Press.

Iton, Richard. 2008. *In Search of the Black Fantastic: Politics and*

*Popular Culture in the Post–Civil Rights Era*. Oxford: Oxford University Press.

Ivy, Nicole. 2016. "Bodies of Work: A Meditation on Medical Imaginaries and Enslaved Women." *Souls: A Critical Journal of Black Politics, Culture, and Society* 18 (1): 11–31.

Jackson, George. 1972. *Blood in My Eye*. New York: Random House.

Jackson, Shona N. 2012. *Creole Indigeneity: Between Myth and Nation in the Caribbean*. Minneapolis: University of Minnesota Press.

Jacobs, Harriet A. (1861) 1988. *Incidents in the Life of a Slave Girl*. New York: Oxford University Press.

Jacobs, Margaret D. 2009. *White Mothers to a Dark Race: Settler Colonialism, Maternalism, and the Removal of Indigenous Children in the American West and Australia*. Lincoln: University of Nebraska Press.

Jacobson, Matthew Frye. 1998. *Whiteness of a Different Color: European Immigrants and the Alchemy of Race*. Cambridge, MA: Harvard University Press.

Jacoby, Karl. 2008. *Shadows at Dawn: A Borderlands Massacre and the Violence of History*. New York: Penguin.

Jaji, Tsitsi. 2014. *Africa in Stereo: Modernism, Music, and Pan-African Solidarity*. Oxford: Oxford University Press.

Jakobson, Roman. 1987. "What Is Poetry?" In *Language in Literature*, 368–78. Cambridge, MA: Harvard University Press.

James, C. L. R. 1938. *The Black Jacobins*. New York: Dial.

James, Etta, and David Ritz. 2003. *Rage to Survive: The Etta James Story*. New York: Da Capo.

James, Jennifer C. 2007. *Freedom Bought with Blood: African American War Literature from the Civil War to World War II*. Chapel Hill: University of North Carolina Press.

——. 2012. "Blessed Are the Warmakers: Martin Luther King, Vietnam, and the Black Prophetic Tradition." In *Fighting Words and Images: Representing War across the Disciplines*, edited by Stephan Jaeger, Elena V. Baraban, and Adam Muller, 165–84. Toronto: University of Toronto Press.

James, Joy. 2005. *New Abolitionists: (Neo)Slave Narratives and Contemporary Prison Writings*. Albany: SUNY Press.

James, Winston. 1998. *Holding Aloft the Banner of Ethiopia: Caribbean Radicalism in Early Twentieth-Century America*. London: Verso.

Jameson, Fredric. 1982. "Progress versus Utopia: Or, Can We Imagine the Future?" *Science Fiction Studies* 9 (2): 147–58.

Jarrett, Gene Andrew. 2006. "'For Endless Generations': Myth, Dynasty, and Frank Yerby's *The Foxes of Harrow*." *Southern Literary Journal* 39 (1): 54–70.

Jaynes, Gerald David. 1986. *Branches without Roots: Genesis of the Black Working Class in the American South, 1862–1882*. New York: Oxford University Press.

Jay-Z. 1998. "Hard Knock Life (Ghetto Anthem)." Roc-A-Fella Records.

——. 2009. "Empire State of Mind." *The Blueprint 3*. Virgin EMI.

Jefferson, Thomas. (1781) 1984. *Notes on the State of Virginia*. In *Writings*, 123–325. New York: Library of America.

Jenkins, Candice M. 2007. *Private Lives, Proper Relations: Regulating Black Intimacy*. Minneapolis: University of Minnesota Press.

Johnson, E. Patrick. 2003. *Appropriating Blackness: Performance and the Politics of Authenticity*. Durham, NC: Duke University Press.

Johnson, E. Patrick, and Mae Henderson, eds. 2005. *Black Queer Studies: A Critical Anthology*. Durham, NC: Duke University Press.

Johnson, James Weldon. (1912) 1995. *The Autobiography of an Ex-Colored Man*. New York: Dover.

——. (1930) 1972. *Black Manhattan*. New York: Atheneum.

Johnson, Rashauna. 2016. *Slavery's Metropolis: Unfree Labor in New Orleans during the Age of Revolutions*. New York: Cambridge University Press.

Johnson, Walter. 2013. *River of Dark Dreams: Slavery and Empire in the Cotton Kingdom*. Cambridge, MA: Harvard University Press.

Jones, Gayl. (1975) 1986. *Corregidora*. Boston: Beacon.

——. (1976) 1987. *Eva's Man*. Boston: Beacon.

Jones, Jacqueline. 1985. *Labor of Love, Labor of Sorrow: Black Women, Work and the Family, from Slavery to the Present*. New York: Basic Books.

Jones, Jo, and William D. Mosher. 2013. *Fathers' Involvement with Their Children: United States, 2006–2010*. National Health Statistics Reports 71. Centers for Disease Control and Prevention, Department of Health and Human Services. www.cdc.gov.

Jones, Kellie. 2011. *Now Dig This! Art and Black Los Angeles, 1960–1980*. New York: Presetel.

Jones, LeRoi. 1963. *Blues People: Negro Music in White America*. New York: William Morrow.

——. 1967. *Black Music*. New York: William Morrow.

Jones, Martha S. 2007. *All Bound Up Together: The Woman Question in African American Public Culture, 1830–1900*. Chapel Hill: University of North Carolina Press.

Jones, Meta DuEwa. 2011. *The Muse Is Music: Jazz Poetry from the Harlem Renaissance to Spoken Word*. Urbana: University of Illinois Press.

Jordan, June. 1981. "Black Studies: Bringing Back the Person."

In *Civil Wars: Observations from the Front Lines of America*, 45–55. New York: Simon and Schuster.

———. 1985. *On Call: Political Essays.* Boston: South End.

———. 2002a. "The Difficult Miracle of Black Poetry in America." In *Some of Us Did Not Die: New and Selected Essays of June Jordan*, 174–86. New York: Basic.

———. 2002b. "Requiem for the Champ." In *Some of Us Did Not Die: New and Selected Essays of June Jordan*, 120–24. New York: Basic.

Jordan, Winthrop. 1968. *White over Black: American Attitudes towards the Negro, 1550–1812.* University of North Carolina Press.

Jorjani, Raha. 2015. "Could Black People in the U.S. Qualify as Refugees?" *Washington Post*, 14 August. www.washingtonpost.com.

Judy, Ronald. 1991. "Kant and the Negro." *Surfaces* 1 (8): 1–70.

Kaba, Mariame. 2015. "Summer Heat." *New Inquiry*, 8 June.

Kahn, Jonathan. 2012. *Race in a Bottle: The Story of BiDil and Racialized Medicine in a Post-Genomic Age.* New York: Columbia University Press.

Kale, Madhavi. 1998. *Fragments of Empire: Capital, Slavery, and Indian Indentured Labor Migration to the British Caribbean.* Philadelphia: University of Pennsylvania Press.

Kandaswamy, Priya. 2016. "Centering Prison Abolition in Women's, Gender, and Sexuality Studies." *Scholar and the Feminist Online* 13 (2). http://sfonline.barnard.edu.

Kangam Squad. 2013. *Hip Hopology.* Soulfood Edutainment.

Kauanui, J. Kēhaulani. 2016. "A Structure, Not an Event: Settler Colonialism and Enduring Indigeneity." *Lateral: Journal of the Cultural Studies Association* 5 (1). http://csalateral.org.

Kauanui, J. Kēhaulani, and Patrick Wolfe. 2012. "Settler Colonialism Then and Now: A Conversation between J. Kēhaulani Kauanui and Patrick Wolfe." *Politica & Societá* 1 (2): 235–58.

Kazanjian, David. 2014. "Colonial." In *Keywords in American Cultural Studies*, 2nd ed., edited by Bruce Burgett and Glenn Hendler, 48–52. New York: NYU Press.

Kearney, Douglas. 2009. "Swimchant for Nigger Mer-folk (An Aquaboogie Set in Lapis)." In *The Black Automaton*, 62–63. Albany, NY: Fence Books.

Keaton, Trica. 2006. *Muslim Girls and the Other France: Race, Identity Politics, and Social Exclusion.* Bloomington: Indiana University Press.

———. 2013. "Racial Profiling and the 'French Exception.'" *French Cultural Studies* 24 (2): 231–42.

Keita, S. O. Y., and Rick A. Kittles. 1997. "The Persistence of Racial Thinking and the Myth of Racial Divergence." *American Anthropologist* 99 (1997): 534–44.

Kelley, Robin D. G. (1990) 2015. *Hammer and Hoe: Alabama Communists during the Great Depression.* Chapel Hill: University of North Carolina Press.

———. 1994. *Race Rebels: Culture, Politics, and the Black Working Class.* New York: Free Press.

———. 1998. *Yo' Mama's Disfunktional! Fighting the Culture Wars in Urban America.* Boston: Beacon.

———. 2002. *Freedom Dreams: The Black Radical Imagination.* Boston: Beacon.

———. 2012. *Africa Speaks, American Answers: Modern Jazz in Revolutionary Times.* Cambridge, MA: Harvard University Press.

Kelly, Erin, and Frank Dobbin. 1998. "How Affirmative Action Became Diversity Management: Employer Response to Anti-discrimination Law, 1961–1996." *American Behavioral Scientist* 41 (7): 960–84.

Kendi, Ibram X. 2012. *The Black Campus Movement: Black Students and the Racial Reconstitution of Higher Education, 1965–1972.* New York: Palgrave Macmillan.

———. 2016. *Stamped from the Beginning: The Definitive History of Racist Ideas in America.* New York: Nation Books.

Kim, Mimi. 2011–12. "Moving beyond Critique: Creative Interventions and Reconstructions of Community Accountability." *Social Justice* 37 (2011–12): 14–35.

Kincaid, Jamaica. 1988. *A Small Place.* New York: Plume.

King, Martin Luther, Jr. (1965) 1991. "Next Stop: The North." In *A Testament of Hope: The Essential Writings and Speeches of Martin Luther King, Jr.*, edited by and James M. Washington, 189–94. San Francisco: HarperSanFrancisco.

———. 1967. *Where Do We Go from Here: Chaos or Community?* New York: Beacon.

Kitwana, Bakari. 2002. *The Hip-Hop Generation: Young Blacks and the Crisis in African-American Culture.* New York: BasicCivitas Books.

Kletzing, H. F., and W. H. Crogman. 1898. *Progress of a Race, or, The Remarkable Advancement of the Colored American.* Rev. ed. Atlanta: J. L. Nichols.

K'naan. 2005. *The Dusty Foot Philosopher.* BMG Music.

Knight, Franklin W. 1990. *The Caribbean: The Genesis of Fragmented Nationalism.* New York: Oxford University Press.

Kohler-Hausmann, Julilly. 2017. *Getting Tough: Welfare and Imprisonment in 1970s America.* Princeton, NJ: Princeton University Press.

Kohn, Margaret. 2014. "Colonialism." In *The Stanford Encyclopedia of Philosophy*, edited by Edward N. Zalta. http://plato.stanford.edu.

Kornbluh, Felicia. 2007. *Battle for Welfare Rights: Politics and Poverty in Modern America.* Philadelphia: University of Pennsylvania Press.

Kraditor, Aileen. 1981. *The Ideas of the Woman Suffrage Movement, 1890–1920*. New York: Norton.

Kramer, Paul. 2015. "Imperial Openings: Civilization, Exemption, and the Geopolitics of Mobility in the History of Chinese Exclusion." *Journal of the Gilded Age and Progressive Era* 14 (3): 317–47.

Krasner, David. 2002. *A Beautiful Pageant: African American Theatre, Drama and Performance in the Harlem Renaissance, 1910–1927*. New York: Palgrave Macmillan.

Krenn, Michael. 2006. *The Color of Empire: Race and American Foreign Relations*. Washington, DC: Potomac Books.

KRS-One. 2007. *Hip Hop Lives*. Marley Marl.

———. 2009. *The Gospel of Hip-Hop: The First Instrument*. Brooklyn, NY: powerHouse Books.

Kunzel, Regina. 2008. *Criminal Intimacy: Prison and the Uneven History of Modern American Sexuality*. Chicago: University of Chicago Press.

Ladner, Joyce, ed. (1973) 1998. *The Death of White Sociology: Essays on Race and Culture*. Baltimore: Black Classic.

Laguerre, Michel. 1998. *Diasporic Citizenship: Haitian Americans in Transnational America*. New York: Palgrave Macmillan.

Lamar, Kendrick. 2011. "HiiiPower." Top Dawg.

Lapsansky-Werner, and Margaret Hope Bacon. 2005. *Benjamin Coates and the Colonization Movement in America, 1848–1880*. University Park: Pennsylvania State University Press.

Larsen, Nella. (1928) 1986. *Quicksand*. In *"Quicksand" and "Passing,"* edited by Deborah E. McDowell, 1–142. New Brunswick, NJ: Rutgers University Press.

———. (1929) 1986. *Passing*. In *"Quicksand" and "Passing,"* edited by Deborah E. McDowell, 143–243. New Brunswick, NJ: Rutgers University Press.

Lawson, Steven. 2004. *To Secure These Rights: The Report of Harry S. Truman's Committee on Civil Rights*. New York: Bedford / St. Martin's.

Lee, Erika. 2003. *At America's Gates: Chinese Immigration during the Exclusion Era, 1882–1943*. Chapel Hill: University of North Carolina Press.

Lee, Rachel. 2000. "Notes from the (Non)Field: Teaching and Theorizing Women of Color." *Meridians* 1 (1): 85–109.

Lee, Spike, dir. 2016. *Redemption Song*. ESPN Films.

Lefebvre, Henri. 2006. *Writings on Cities*. Malden, MA: Blackwell.

LeFlouria, Talitha L. 2015. *Chained in Silence: Black Women and Convict Labor in the New South*. Chapel Hill: University of North Carolina Press.

Lemons, J. Stanley. 1977. "Black Stereotypes as Reflected in Popular Culture, 1880–1920." *American Quarterly* 29 (1): 102–16.

Leonard, Keith D. 2006. *Fettered Genius: The African American Bardic Poet from Slaver to Civil Rights*. Charlottesville: University of Virginia Press.

Leong, Karen J. 2001. "'A Distinct and Antagonistic Race': Constructions of Chinese Manhood in the Exclusionist Debates, 1869–1878." In *Across the Great Divide: Centuries of Manhood in the American West*, edited by Matthew Basso, Laura McCall, and Dee Garceau, 131–48. New York: Routledge.

Lerner, Gerda. 1972. *Black Women in White America: A Documentary History*. New York: Vintage Books.

Lernoux, Penny. 1980. *Cry of the People: United States Involvement in the Rise of Fascism, Torture, and Murder and the Persecution of the Catholic Church in Latin America*. New York: Doubleday.

Levine, Lawrence. 1990. *Highbrow/Lowbrow: The Emergence of Cultural Hierarchy in America*. Cambridge, MA: Harvard University Press.

Levy-Hinte, Jeff, dir. 2008. *Soul Power*. Antidote Films.

Lewis, David Levering. 1994. *W. E. B. Du Bois: Biography of a Race, 1868–1919*. New York: Holt.

———. 2000. *W. E. B. Du Bois: The Fight for Equality and the American Century, 1919–1963*. New York: Holt.

Lew-Williams, Beth. 2014. "Before Restriction Became Exclusion: America's Experiment in Diplomatic Immigration Control." *Pacific Historical Review* 83 (1): 24–56.

Library of Congress, with David Levering Lewis and Deborah Willis. 2003. *A Small Nation of People: W. E. B. Du Bois and African American Portraits of Progress*. New York: Amistad.

Lichtenstein, Alex. 1996. *Twice the Work of Free Labor: The Political Economy of Convict Labor in the New South*. New York: Verso.

Lien, Pei-Te, Margaret Conway, and Janelle Wong. 2004. *The Politics of Asian Americans: Diversity and Community*. New York: Routledge.

Lightfoot, Natasha. 2015. *Troubling Freedom: Antigua and the Aftermath of British Emancipation*. Durham, NC: Duke University Press.

Lincoln, C. Eric. 1961. *The Black Muslims in America*. Boston: Beacon.

Lincoln, C. Eric, and Lawrence H. Mamiya. 1990. *The Black Church in the African American Experience*. Durham, NC: Duke University Press.

Linebaugh, Peter, and Marcus Rediker. 2000. *The Many-Headed Hydra: Sailors, Slaves, Commoners, and the Hidden History of the Revolutionary Atlantic*. Boston: Beacon.

Linnaei, Caroli. 1758. *Systema naturae per regna tria naturae :secundum classes, ordines, genera, species, cum characteribus, differentiis, synonymis, locis*. Stockholm: Impensis Direct.

Litwack, Leon F. 1998. *Trouble in Mind: Black Southerners in the Age of Jim Crow*. New York: Knopf.

Livermon, Xavier. 2018. "It's about Time: Kwaito and the Performance of Freedom." Unpublished ms.

Logan, Rayford. (1954) 1965. *The Negro in American Life and Thought: The Nadir, 1877–1901*. Republished as *The Betrayal of the Negro: From Rutherford B. Hayes to Woodrow Wilson*. New York: Collier. Citations refer to the republished edition.

Lombroso, Cesare. (1876) 2006. *Criminal Man*. Durham, NC: Duke University Press.

Lombroso, Cesare, and Guillaume Ferrero. 1893. *La donna delinquente: La prostituta e la donna normale*. Turin: Fratelli Bocca.

Long, Edward. 1774. *History of Jamaica*. Vol. 2. London: T. Lowndes.

Long, Jeffrey C., and Rick A. Kittles. 2009. "Human Genetic Diversity and the Nonexistence of Biological Races." *Human Biology* 81 (5–6): 777–98.

Loomba, Ania. (1998) 2005. *Colonialism/Postcolonialism*. New York: Routledge.

Lorde, Audre. 1984. *Sister Outsider: Essays and Speeches*. Trumansburg, NY: Crossing.

———. 2007. "Poetry Is Not a Luxury." In *Sister Outsider: Essays and Speeches*, 36–39. Berkeley, CA: Crossing.

Lordi, Emily J. 2016a. "James Baldwin and the Sound of Soul." *CR: The New Centennial Review* 16 (2): 31–45.

———. 2016b. "Souls Intact: The Soul Performances of Audre Lorde, Nina Simone, and Aretha Franklin." *Women & Performance* 26 (3): 55–71.

Lott, Eric. 1993. *Love and Theft: Blackface Minstrelsy and the American Working Class*. Oxford: Oxford University Press.

*Loving v. Virginia*. 1967. 388 U.S. 1.

Loyd, Jenna, Matt Mitchelson, and Andrew Burridge, eds. 2012. *Beyond Walls and Cages: Prisons, Borders, and Global Crisis*. Athens: University of Georgia Press.

Lubiano, Wahneema. 1996a. "'But Compared to What?': Reading Realism, Representation, and Essentialism in School Daze, Do the Right Thing, and the Spike Lee Discourse." In *Representing Black Men*, edited by Marcellus Blount and George P. Cunningham, 173–204. New York: Routledge.

———. 1996b. "Mapping the Interstices between Afro-American Cultural Discourse and Cultural Studies: A Prolegomenon." *Callaloo* 19 (1): 67–77.

Lugones, Maria. 2003. *Pilgrimages/Peregrinajes: Theorizing Coalition against Multiple Oppressions*. Lanham, MD: Rowman and Littlefield.

Lui, Mary Ting-Ying. 2005. *The Chinatown Trunk Mystery: Murder, Miscegenation, and Other Dangerous Encounters in Turn-of-the-Century New York City*. Princeton, NJ: Princeton University Press.

Lumpkins, Charles. 2008. *American Pogrom: The East St. Louis Race Riot and Black Politics*. Athens: Ohio University Press.

Mackey, Nathaniel. 1993. *Discrepant Engagement: Dissonance, Cross-Culturality, and Experimental Writing*. Tuscaloosa: University of Alabama Press.

MacLean, Nancy. 2000. "The Leo Frank Case Reconsidered: Gender and Sexual Politics in the Making of Reactionary Populism." In *Jumpin' Jim Crow: Southern Politics from Civil War to Civil Rights*, edited by Jane Dailey, Glenda Elizabeth Gilmore, and Bryant Simon, 183–218. Princeton, NJ: Princeton University Press.

Magness, Phillip W., and Sebastian N. Page. 2011. *Colonization after Emancipation: Lincoln and the Movement for Black Resettlement*. Columbia: University of Missouri Press.

Mahon, Maureen. 2004. *The Right to Rock: The Black Rock Coalition and the Cultural Politics of Race*. Durham, NC: Duke University Press.

———. 2005. "Rock." In *African American Music: An Introduction*, edited by Mellonee V. Burnim and Portia K. Maultsby, 558–84. New York: Routledge.

Majors, Monroe Alphus. 1893. *Noted Negro Women: Their Triumphs and Activities*. Jackson, TN: M. V. Lynk.

Makalani, Minkah. 2011. *In the Cause of Freedom: Radical Black Internationalism from Harlem to London, 1917–1939*. Chapel Hill: University of North Carolina Press.

Malcolm X. (1964) 1994. "The Ballot or the Bullet." In *Malcolm X Speaks: Select Speeches and Statements*, edited by George Breitman, 23–44. New York: Grove.

Mamdani, Mahmood. 1996. *Citizen and Subject: Contemporary Africa and the Legacy of Late Colonialism*. Princeton, NJ: Princeton University Press.

———. 2001. "Beyond Settler and Native as Political Identities: Overcoming the Political Legacy of Colonialism." *Comparative Studies in Society and History* 43 (4): 651–64.

———. 2002. *When Victims Become Killers: Colonialism, Nativism, and the Genocide in Rwanda*. Princeton, NJ: Princeton University Press.

Mancini, Matthew. 1996. *One Dies, Get Another: Convict Leasing in the American South, 1866–1928*. Columbia: University of South Carolina Press.

Mangcu, Xolela. 2012. *Biko: A Biography*. London: I .B. Taurus.

Manigault-Bryant, LeRhonda S. 2014. *Talking to the Dead: Religion, Music, and Lived Memory among Gullah/Geechee Women*. Durham, NC: Duke University Press.

Mannix, Daniel P., and Malcolm Cowley. 1962. *Black Cargoes: A History of the Atlantic Slave Trade, 1518-1865*. New York: Penguin Books.

Marable, Manning. 1984. *Race, Reform, and Rebellion: The Second Reconstruction in Black America, 1945-1982*. Jackson: University Press of Mississippi.

———. 2007. *Race, Reform and Rebellion: The Second Reconstruction and Beyond in Black America, 1945-2006*. Jackson: University Press of Mississippi.

Marley, Bob. 1979. "Africa Unite." *Survival*. Island / Tuff Gong.

Marriott, David. 2000. *On Black Men*. New York: Columbia University Press.

———. 2011. "Inventions of Existence: Sylvia Wynter, Frantz Fanon, Sociogeny, and 'the Damned.'" *Centennial Review* 11 (3): 45-89.

Martin, Darnell, dir. 2008. *Cadillac Records*. Sony Pictures.

Martin, Randy. 2011. "From the Race War to the War on Terror." In *Beyond Biopolitics: Essays on the Governance of Life and Death*, edited by Patricia Ticineto and Craig Willse, 258-74. Durham, NC: Duke University Press.

———. 2012. "Bailout." In *Impasses of the Post-Global: Theory in the Era of Climate Change*, vol. 2, edited by Henry Sussman, 232-50. Ann Arbor, MI: Open Humanities Press.

Martin, William, Fanon Che Wilkins, and Michael West, eds. 2009. *From Toussaint to Tupac: The Black International since the Age of Revolution*. Chapel Hill: University of North Carolina Press.

Marx, Anthony W. 1998. *Making Race and Nation: A Comparison of South Africa, the United States, and Brazil*. Cambridge: Cambridge University Press.

Marx, Karl. 1853. "The British Rule in India." *New York Daily Tribune*, 25 June. www.marxists.org.

Massood, Paula. 2003. *Black City Cinema: African American Urban Experiences in Film*. Philadelphia: Temple University Press.

Masur, Kate. 2010. *An Example for All the Land: Emancipation and the Struggle over Equality in Washington, D.C.* Chapel Hill: University of North Carolina Press.

Materson, Lisa G. 2009. *For the Freedom of Her Race: Black Women and Electoral Politics in Illinois, 1877-1932*. Chapel Hill: University of North Carolina Press.

Matory, James Lorand. 2005. *Sex and the Empire That Is No More: Gender and the Politics of Metaphor in Oyo Yoruba Religion*. New York: Berghahn Books.

Mbembe, Achille. 2001. *On the Postcolony*. Berkeley: University of California Press.

———. 2003. "Necropolitics." *Public Culture* 15 (1): 11-40.

McAdam, Doug. 1982. *Political Process and the Development of Black Insurgency, 1930-1970*. Chicago: University of Chicago Press.

McCaskill, Barbara, and Caroline Gebhard, eds. 2006. *Postbellum, Pre-Harlem: African American Literature and Culture, 1877-1919*. New York: NYU Press.

McClintock, Anne. 1992. "The Angel of Progress: Pitfalls on the Term 'Postcolonialism.'" *Social Text* 31 (32): 84-98.

———. 1995. *Imperial Leather: Race, Gender and Sexuality in the Colonial Contest*. New York: Routledge.

McCurry, Stephanie. 2010. *Confederate Reckoning: Power and Politics in the Civil War South*. Cambridge, MA: Harvard University Press.

McDonald, CeCe. 2015. Foreword to *Captive Genders: Trans Embodiment and the Prison Industrial Complex*, 2nd ed., edited by Eric A. Stanley and Nat Smith, 1-4. Oakland, CA: AK.

McDonald, CeCe, and Omise'eke Natasha Tinsley. 2017. "'Go beyond Our Natural Selves': The Prison Letters of CeCe McDonald." *TSQ: Transgender Studies Quarterly* 4 (2): 243-65.

McDowell, Deborah. 1989. "Reading Family Matters." In *Changing Our Own Words*, edited by Cheryl A. Wall, 75-97. New Brunswick, NJ: Rutgers University Press.

McGerr, Michael. 2003. *A Fierce Discontent: The Rise and Fall of the Progressive Movement in America*. New York: Oxford University Press.

McKissick, Floyd. (1967) 2000. "CORE Endorses Black Power." In *Let Nobody Turn Us Around: Voices of Resistance, Reform and Renewal*, edited by Manning Marable and Leith Mullings, 458-60. New York: Rowman and Littlefield.

McKittrick, Katherine. 2006. *Demonic Grounds: Black Women and the Cartographies of Struggle*. Minneapolis: University of Minnesota Press.

———. 2015. *Sylvia Wynter: On Being Human as Praxis*. Durham, NC: Duke University Press.

McKittrick, Katherine, and Clyde Woods. 2007. *Black Geographies and the Politics of Place*. Boston: South End.

McMillan, Uri G. 2015. *Embodied Avatars: Genealogies of Black Feminist Art and Performance*. New York: NYU Press.

McPherson, James. 1995. "Who Freed the Slaves?" *Proceedings of the American Philosophical Society* 139 (1): 1-10.

———. 2000. "Lincoln the Devil." *New York Times*, 22 August.

Meeropol, Abel (pseud. Lewis Allan). 1939. "Strange Fruit." Edward B. Marks Music Company.

Meier, August. 1963. *Negro Thought in America, 1880-1915*. Ann Arbor: University of Michigan Press.

Meiners, Erica. 2007. *Right to Be Hostile: Schools, Prisons, and the Making of Public Enemies*. New York: Routledge.

———. 2016. *For the Children: Protecting Innocence in a Carceral State*. Minneapolis: University of Minnesota Press.

Melamed, Jodi. 2011. *Represent and Destroy: Rationalizing Violence in the New Racial Capitalism*. Minneapolis: University of Minnesota Press.

———. 2014. "Diversity." In *Keywords for American Cultural Studies*, 2nd ed., edited by Bruce Burgett and Glenn Hendler, 84–88. New York: NYU Press.

Mercer, Kobena. 1994. *Welcome to the Jungle: New Positions in Black Cultural Studies*. New York: Routledge.

Michaels, Walter Benn. 1997. "Autobiography of an Ex-White Man: Why Race Is Not a Social Construction." *Transition* 73:122–43.

———. 2006. *The Trouble with Diversity: How We Learned to Love Identity and Ignore Inequality*. New York: Holt.

Mignolo, W. D., and Tlostanova, M. V. 2006. "Theorizing from the Borders: Shifting to Geo- and Body-Politics of Knowledge." *European Journal of Social Theory* 9 (2): 205–21.

Miller, Arthur H., Patricia Gurin, Gerald Gurin, and Oksana Malanchuk. 1981. "Group Consciousness and Political Participation." *American Journal of Political Science* 25 (3): 494–511.

Miller, Monica R., and Anthony B. Pinn, eds. 2014. *The Hip Hop and Religion Reader*. New York: Routledge.

Mills, Charles W. 1998. *Blackness Visible: Essays on Philosophy and Race*. Ithaca, NY: Cornell University Press.

Mills, Quincy T. 2013. *Cutting along the Color Line: Black Barbers and Barber Shops in America*. Philadelphia: University of Pennsylvania Press.

Millward, Jessica. 2015. *Finding Charity's Folk: Enslaved and Free Black Women in Maryland*. Athens: University of Georgia Press.

Mishra, Vijay, and Bob Hodge. 2005. "What Was Postcolonialism?" *New Literary History* 36 (3): 375–402.

Mitchell, Michele. 2004. *Righteous Propagation: African Americans and the Politics of Racial Destiny after Reconstruction*. Chapel Hill: University of North Carolina Press.

Mitchell, Pablo. 2005. *Coyote Nation: Sexuality, Race, and Conquest in Modernizing New Mexico, 1880–1920*. Chicago: University of Chicago Press.

Mitchell, Tony. 2001. *Global Noise: Rap and Hip-Hop outside the USA*. Middletown, CT: Wesleyan University Press.

Mocombe, Paul C. 2008. *The Soul-less Souls of Black Folk: A Sociological Reconsideration of Black Consciousness as Du Boisian Double-Consciousness*. Lanham, MD: University Press of America.

Mogul, Joey, Andrea Ritchie, and Kay Whitlock. 2011. *Queer (In)Justice: The Criminalization of LGBT People in the United States*. Boston: Beacon.

Mohammed, Abdul Jan. 1992. "Sexuality on/of the Racial Border." In *Discourses of Sexuality: From Aristotle to AIDS*, edited by Domna C. Stanton, 94–117. Institute for the Humanities; Ratio. Ann Arbor: University of Michigan.

Mohanty, Chandra Talpade. 1984. "Under Western Eyes: Feminist Scholarship and Colonial Discourses." *Boundary 2* 12–13 (3): 333–58.

Molina, Natalia. 2006. *Fit to Be Citizens? Public Health and Race in Los Angeles, 1879–1939*. Berkeley: University of California Press.

Monáe, Janelle. 2010. *The ArchAndroid*. Bad Boy Records.

Moore, Mignon. 2011. *Invisible Families: Gay Identities, Relationships, and Motherhood among Black Women*. Berkeley: University of California Press.

*Moore et al. v. Dempsey*. 1923. 261 U.S. 86.

Moraga, Cherríe. (1983) 2000. *Loving in the War Years: Lo Que Nunca Pasó por Sus Labios*. Boston: South End.

Moraga, Cherríe, and Gloria Anzaldúa. 2015. *This Bridge Called My Back: Writings by Radical Women of Color*. 4th ed. Albany: SUNY Press.

Moran, Rachel F. 2001. *Interracial Romance: The Regulation of Race and Romance*. Chicago: University of Chicago Press.

Morgan, Jennifer L. 2004. *Laboring Women: Reproduction and Gender in New World Slavery*. Philadelphia: University of Pennsylvania Press.

Morris, Aldon. 2015. *The Scholar Denied: W. E. B. Du Bois and the Birth of Modern Sociology*. Berkeley: University of California Press.

Morrison, Toni. (1970) 2007. *The Bluest Eye*. New York: Vintage International.

———. (1973) 2004. *Sula*. New York: Vintage International.

———. 1987. *Beloved*. New York: Knopf.

———. 1992a. *Playing in the Dark: Whiteness and the Literary Imagination*. Cambridge, MA: Harvard University Press.

———, ed. 1992b. *Race-ing Justice, En-gendering Power: Essays on Anita Hill, Clarence Thomas, and the Construction of Social Reality*. New York: Pantheon.

Morrison, Toni, and Claudia Brodsky Lacour, eds. 1997. *Birth of a Nation'hood: Gaze, Script, and Spectacle in the O. J. Simpson Case*. New York: Pantheon.

Morton, Patricia. 1991. *Disfigured Images: The Historical Assault on Afro-American Women*. Westport, CT: Greenwood.

Morton, Samuel G. 1839. *Crania Americana; or, A Comparative View of the Skulls of Various Aboriginal Nations of North and South America*. Philadelphia: John Pennington.

Moses, Wilson Jeremiah. 1978. *The Golden Age of Black Nationalism, 1850–1925.* Camden, CT: Archon Books.

Moss, Thylias. 2006. *Slave Moth: A Narrative in Verse.* New York: Persea Books.

Moten, Fred. 1999. "Review of *Scenes of Subjection: Terror, Slavery, and Self-Making in Nineteenth-Century America,* by Saidiya Hartman, and *Soul: Black Power, Politics, and Pleasure,* edited by Monique Guillory and Richard C. Green." *TDR: The Drama Review* 41 (4): 169–75.

———. 2003. *In the Break: The Aesthetics of the Black Radical Tradition.* Minneapolis: University of Minnesota Press.

Moten, Fred, and Stefano Harney. 2004. "The University and the Undercommons: Seven Theses." *Social Text* 22 (2 79): 101–15.

Moynihan, Daniel P. 1965. *The Negro Family: The Case for National Action.* Washington, DC: Office of Policy Planning and Research, U.S. Department of Labor.

Mudimbe, Valentine Y. 1988. *The Invention of Africa: Gnosis, Philosophy, and the Order of Knowledge.* Bloomington: Indianan University Press.

Muhammad, Khalil Gibran. 2011. *The Condemnation of Blackness: Race, Crime, and the Making of Modern Urban America.* Cambridge, MA: Harvard University Press.

Mumford, Kevin. 1997. *Interzones: Black/White Sex Districts in Chicago and New York in the Early Twentieth Century.* New York: Columbia University Press.

Mumford, Lewis. (1937) 2011. "What Is a City." In *The City Reader,* 5th ed., edited by Richard T. LeGates and Frederic Stout, 91–95. New York: Routledge.

Murray, Albert. 1976. *Stomping the Blues.* New York: McGraw-Hill.

Murray, Pauli. 1987. *Pauli Murray: The Autobiography of a Black Activist, Feminist, Lawyer, Priest, and Poet.* Knoxville: University of Tennessee Press.

Mustakeem, Sowande' M. 2016. *Slavery at Sea: Terror, Sex, and Sickness in the Middle Passage.* Urbana: University of Illinois Press.

Myrdal, Gunnar. (1944) 1995. *An American Dilemma: The Negro Problem and Modern Democracy.* New York: Transaction.

Nadasen, Premilla. 2005. *Welfare Warriors: The Welfare Rights Movement in the United States.* New York: Routledge.

Nardal, Jane. 1928. "Internationalisme Noir." *La Dépêche Africaine,* 15 February.

Nash, Jennifer. 2008. "Rethinking Intersectionality." *Feminist Review* 89:1–15.

———. 2017. "Intersectionality and Its Discontents." *American Quarterly* 69 (1): 117–29.

Naylor, Gloria. 1982. *The Women of Brewster Place.* New York: Penguin.

N'COBRA (National Coalition of Blacks for Reparations in America). 2004. Home page. Accessed 1 January 2018. http://ncobra.org.

Neal, Larry. 1968a. "And Shine Swam On." In *Black Fire: An Anthology of Afro-American Writing,* edited by Amiri Baraka and Larry Neal, 637–56. New York: Morrow.

———. 1968b. "The Black Arts Movement." *Drama Review: TDR* 12 (4): 28–39.

Neal, Mark Anthony. 2002. *Soul Babies: Black Popular Culture and the Post-Soul Aesthetic.* New York: Routledge.

———. 2016. "A Fallen Black Girl: Remembering Latasha Harlins." *New Black Man (in Exile),* 17 March. www.newblackmaninexile.net.

Nellis, Eric. 2013. *Shaping the New World: African Slavery in the Americas, 1500–1888.* Toronto: University of Toronto Press.

Nelson, Alondra. 2016. *The Social Life of DNA: Race, Reparations, and Reconciliation after the Genome.* Boston: Beacon.

Nesbitt, Francis Njubi. 2004. *Race for Sanctions: African Americans against Apartheid, 1946–1994.* Bloomington: Indiana University Press.

Neville, Morgan, dir. 2013. *20 Feet from Stardom.* Gil Friesen Productions.

Newfield, Christopher. 2008. *Unmaking the Public University: The Forty-Year Assault on the Middle Class.* Cambridge, MA: Harvard University Press.

Newman, Louise Michele. 1999. *White Women's Rights: The Racial Origins of Feminism in the United States.* New York: Oxford University Press.

Nielsen, Aldon Lynn. 1997. *Black Chant: Languages of African American Postmodernism.* Cambridge: Cambridge University Press.

———. 2007. "Foreword: Preliminary Postings from a Neo-Soul." *African American Review* 41 (4): 601–8.

Nobles, Melissa. 2000. *Shades of Citizenship: Race and the Census in Modern Politics.* Stanford, CA: Stanford University Press.

Northup, Solomon. (1853) 2012. *Twelve Years a Slave.* New York: Penguin Books.

Nunnally, Shayla C. 2010. "Linking Blackness or Ethnic Othering? African Americans' Diasporic Linked Fate with West Indian and African Peoples in the U.S." *Du Bois Review* 7 (2): 335–55.

N.W.A. 1988. "Straight Outta Compton." *Straight Outta Compton.* CD. Priority Records.

Nwankwo, Ifeoma. 2005. *Black Cosmopolitanism: Racial Consciousness and Transnational Identity in the Nineteenth-Century Americas*. Philadelphia: University of Pennsylvania Press.

Nyong'o, Tavia. 2014. *Rip It Up: Excess and Ecstasy in Little Richard's Sound*. Durham, NC: Duke University Press.

*Obergefell v. Hodges*. 2015. 576 U.S. __.

Ocen, Priscilla. 2012. "Punishing Pregnancy: Race, Incarceration, and the Shackling of Pregnant Prisoners." *California Law Review* 100:1239–311.

Odendaal, Andre. 1984. *Vukani Bantu! The Beginnings of Black Protest Politics in South Africa to 1912*. Cape Town: D. Philip.

Ogbar, Jeffrey. 2007. *Hip-Hop Revolution: The Culture and Politics of Rap*. Lawrence: University Press of Kansas.

OHCHR (Office of the High Commissioner on Human Rights, United Nations). n.d. "Latin America and Caribbean Region." Accessed 2016. www.ohchr.org.

Okihiro, Gary. 2016. *Third World Studies: Theorizing Liberation*. Durham, NC: Duke University Press.

Olzak, Susan, and Suzanne Shanahan. 1996. "Deprivation and Race Riots: An Extension of Spillerman's Analysis." *Social Forces* 74 (3): 931–61.

Omi, Michael, and Howard Winant. 1994. *Racial Formation in the United States from the 1960s to the 1990s*. London: Routledge.

Omoniyi, Tope. 2009. "'So I Choose to Do Am Naija Style': Hip Hop, Language, and Postcolonial Identities." In *Global Linguistic Flows: Hip Hop Cultures, Youth Identities, and the Politics of Language*, edited by H. Samy Alim, Awad Ibrahim, and Alastair Pennycook, 113–38. New York: Routledge.

Ongiri, Amy Abugo. 2010. *Spectacular Blackness: The Cultural Politics of the Black Power Movement and the Search for a Black Aesthetic*. Charlottesville: University of Virginia Press.

Orleck, Annelise. 2005. *Storming Caesars Palace: How Black Mothers Fought Their Own War on Poverty*. Boston: Beacon.

Outlaw, Lucius T., Jr. 2014. "If Not Races, Then What? Toward a Revised Understanding of Bio-Social Groupings." *Graduate Faculty Philosophy Journal* 35 (1–2): 275–96.

Ové, Horace, dir. 1976. *Pressure*. Crawford Films.

Owens, Emily. 2017. "Promises: Sexual Labor between Slavery and Freedom." *Louisiana History* 58 (2): 179–216.

*Oxford English Dictionary*. n.d.-a. s.v. "Colonialism, n." Accessed 19 October 2016. www.oed.com.ezproxy.library.tamu.edu.

———. n.d.-b. s.v. "War, n. 1." Accessed 3 May 2018. www.oed.com.

*Oxford Universal Dictionary on Historical Principles*. 1955. s.v. "Nadir." 3rd ed. Oxford, UK: Clarendon.

Pagden, Anthony. 1982. *The Fall of Natural Man: The American Indian and the Origins of Comparative Ethnology*. New York: Cambridge University Press.

Page, Enoch, and Matt Richardson. 2010. "On the Fear of Small Numbers: A Twenty-First-Century Prolegomenon of the U.S. Black Transgender Experience." In *Black Sexualities: Probing Powers, Passions, Practices, and Policies*, edited by Juan Battle and Sandra Barnes, 57–81. New Brunswick, NJ: Rutgers University Press.

Painter, Nell. 1997. *Sojourner Truth: A Life, a Symbol*. New York: Norton.

———. 2002. *Southern History across the Color Line*. Chapel Hill: University of North Carolina Press.

———. 2010. *The History of White People*. New York: Norton.

Palmer, Colin A. 2000. "Defining and Studying the Modern African Diaspora." *Journal of Negro History* 85 (1–2): 27–32.

Palmisano, Joseph M. 2001. "Colonialism." In *World of Sociology*, edited by Joseph M. Palmisano. Farmington, MI: Gale. https://search.credoreference.com.

Panofsky, Aaron, and Catherine Bliss. 2017. "Ambiguity and Scientific Authority Population Classification in Genomic Science." *American Sociological Review* 82 (1): 59–87.

Park, Peter K. J. 2013. *Africa, Asia, and the History of Philosophy: Racism in the Formation of the Philosophical Canon, 1780–1830*. Albany: SUNY Press.

Parker, Charlie. 1957. "Thriving on a Riff." Savoy.

Pascoe, Peggy. 2009. *What Comes Naturally: Miscegenation Law and the Making of Race in America*. New York: Oxford University Press.

Patillo-McCoy, Mary. 1999. *Black Picket Fences: Privilege and Peril among the Black Middle Class*. Chicago: University of Chicago Press.

Patterson, Orlando. 1982. *Slavery and Social Death: A Comparative Study*. Cambridge, MA: Harvard University Press.

———.1991. *Freedom in the Making of Western Culture*. New York: Basic Books.

Patterson, Tiffany Ruby, and Robin D. G. Kelley. 2000. "Unfinished Migrations: Reflections on the African Diaspora and the Making of the Modern World." Special issue on the Diaspora, *African Studies Review* 43 (1): 11–45.

Patton, Stacey. 2012. "Who's Afraid of Black Sexuality?" *Chronicle of Higher Education*, 3 December.

Peña, Devon G. 1997. *The Terror of the Machine: Technology, Work, Gender, and Ecology on the U.S.-Mexico Border*. Austin: University of Texas Press.

Pennycook, Alastair, and Tony Mitchell. 2009. "Hip Hop as Dusty Foot Philosophy: Engaging Locality." In *Global Linguistic Flows: Hip Hop Cultures, Youth Identities, and the*

*Politics of Language*, edited by H. Samy Alim, Awad Ibrahim, and Alastair Pennycook, 25–42. New York: Routledge.

Perkinson, Robert. 2010. *Texas Tough: The Rise of America's Prison Regime*. New York: Metropolitan Books.

Perry, Imani. 2004. *Prophets of the Hood: Politics and Poetics in Hip Hop*. Durham, NC: Duke University Press.

Petry, Anne. 1946. *The Street*. New York: Houghton Mifflin.

*Phil Donahue Show*. 1980. "Alvin Poussaint Talks about the Macho Myth Adopted by Black Men and the Frequent Resentment of Black Women." 5 January.

Philip, NourbeSe. 2008. *Zong!* Toronto: Mercury.

Phillips, Ulrich B. 1918. *American Negro Slavery: A Survey of the Supply, Employment and Control of Negro Labor as Determined by the Plantation Régime*. New York: D. Appleton.

Pierre, Jemima. 2012. *The Predicament of Blackness: Postcolonial Ghana and the Politics of Race*. Chicago: University of Chicago Press.

Pierson, William D. 1977. "White Cannibals, Black Martyrs: Fear, Depression, and Religious Faith as Causes of Suicide among Slaves." *Journal of Negro History* 62:147–59.

*Plessy v. Ferguson*. 1896. 163 U.S. 537.

Poulson-Bryant, Scott. 2005. *Hung: A Meditation on the Measure of Black Men in America*. New York: Doubleday.

Powers, Ann. 2017. *Good Booty: Love and Sex, Black and White, Body and Soul in American Music*. New York: Dey Street Books.

Prather, H. Leon, Sr. 1998. "We Have Taken a City: A Centennial Essay." In *Democracy Betrayed: The Wilmington Race Riot of 1898 and Its Legacy*, edited by David S. Cecelski and Timothy B. Tyson, 15–41. Chapel Hill: University of North Carolina Press.

PREAP (Prison Research Education Action Project). (1976) 2005. *Instead of Prisons: A Handbook for Abolitionists*. Oakland, CA: Critical Resistance.

*Prigg v. Pennsylvania*. 1842. 41 U.S. 539.

Prince. 1980. "Uptown." *Dirty Mind*. Rhino / Warner Bros.

———. 1981. "Sexuality." *Controversy*. Warner Bros. Records.

———. 2001. "Rainbow Children." *Rainbow Children*. NPG Records.

Prince, Mary. (1831) 1987. *The History of Mary Prince: A West Indian Slave, Related by Herself*. London: Pandora.

Proper, David R. 1992. "Lucy Terry Prince: 'Singer of History.'" *Contributions in Black Studies* 9:187–214.

Puar, Jasbir. 2013. "I'd Rather Be a Cyborg than a Goddess: Becoming Intersectional in Assemblage Theory." *Philosophia* 2 (1): 49–66.

Public Enemy. 2012. "Get Up Stand Up." *Most of My Heroes Still Don't Appear on No Stamp*. Enemy Records.

Pudi, Danny, dir. 2014. *Untucked*. ESPN Films.

Puryear, Bennet. 1877. *The Public School in Its Relations to the Negro*. Richmond, VA: Clemmett and Jones.

Quarles, Benjamin. 1970. *Black Abolitionists*. New York: Oxford University Press.

Raboteau, Albert J. 1978. *Slave Religion: The "Invisible Institution" in the Antebellum South*. New York: Oxford University Press.

Rafael, Vicente L. 1993. "White Love: Surveillance and Nationalist Resistance in the U.S. Colonization of the Philippines." In *Cultures of United States Imperialism*, edited by Donald E. Pease and Amy Kaplan, 185–218. Durham, NC: Duke University Press.

Rampersad, Arnold. 2006. Introduction to *The Oxford Anthology of African-American Poetry*, edited by Arnold Rampersad, xix–xxix. Oxford: Oxford University Press.

Rankine, Claudia. 2014. *Citizen: An American Lyric*. Minneapolis: Graywolf.

Rawls, Anne Warfield. 2000. "'Race' as an Interaction Order Phenomenon: W. E. B. Du Bois's 'Double-Consciousness' Thesis Revisited." *Sociological Theory* 18 (2): 241–74.

Ray, Carina E. 2015. *Crossing the Color Line: Race, Sex, and the Contested Politics of Colonialism in Ghana*. Athens: Ohio University Press.

Reagon, Bernice Johnson. 2000. "Coalition Politics: Turning the Century." In *Homegirls: A Black Feminist Anthology*, edited by Barbara Smith, 343–56. New Brunswick, NJ: Rutgers University Press.

Red Clay Ramblers. 2001. "My Name Is Moses." *Yonder*. Red Clay Ramblers.

Rediker, Marcus. 2007. *The Slave Ship: A Human History*. New York: Penguin Books.

Redmond, Shana L. 2014. *Anthem: Social Movements and the Sound of Solidarity in the African Diaspora*. New York: NYU Press.

Reed, Adolph L. 1979. "Black Particularity Reconsidered." *Telos* 39:71–93.

———. 1997. *W. E. B. Du Bois and American Political Thought: Fabianism and the Color-Line*. New York: Oxford University Press.

Reed, Pamela. 2007. "From the Freedmen's Bureau to FEMA: A Post-Katrina Historical, Journalistic, and Literary Analysis." *Journal of Black Studies* 37 (4): 557–67.

*Regents of the University of California v. Bakke*. 1978. 438 U.S. 265.

Reid-Pharr, Robert. 2001. *Black Gay Man: Essays*. New York: NYU Press.

Reséndez, Andrés. 2016. *The Other Slavery: The Uncovered Story of Indian Enslavement in America.* Boston: Houghton Mifflin Harcourt.

Richardson, Matt, and Leisa Meyer. 2011. Preface to "Race and Transgender Studies: A Special Issue." *Feminist Studies* 37 (2): 247–53.

Richardson, Riché. 2007. *Black Masculinity and the U.S. South: From Uncle Tom to Gangsta.* Athens: University of Georgia Press.

Richie, Beth E. 1996. *Compelled to Crime: The Gender Entrapment of Battered, Black Women.* New York: Routledge.

———. 2012. *Arrested Justice: Black Women, Violence, and America's Prison Nation.* New York: NYU Press.

Rickford, Russell. 2016. *We Are an African People: Independent Education, Black Power, and the Radical Imagination.* Oxford: Oxford University Press.

Rifkin, Mark. 2009. *Manifesting America: The Imperial Construction of U.S. National Space.* New York: Oxford University Press.

Riggs, Marlon, dir. 1994. *Black Is . . . Black Ain't.* Docurama.

Riley, Clayton. 1970. "That New Black Magic." Review of *Soul! New York Times*, 17 May.

Riley, Stevan, dir. 2010. *Fire in Babylon.* New Video Group.

Roane, J. T. 2017. "Plotting the Black Commons: Landscapes of Death and Fugitivity around the Chesapeake." Unpublished ms. in author's possession.

Roberson, Ed. 1970. *When Thy King Is a Boy: Poems.* Pittsburgh: University of Pittsburgh Press.

Roberts, Dorothy. 1997. *Killing the Black Body: Race, Reproduction, and the Meaning of Liberty.* New York: Pantheon Books.

———. 2011. *Fatal Invention: How Science, Politics, and Big Business Re-create Race in the Twenty-First Century.* New York: New Press.

———. 2012. "Prison, Foster Care, and the Systemic Punishment of Black Mothers." *UCLA Law Review* 59 (August): 1474–1500.

Roberts, Neil. 2015. *Freedom as Marronage.* Chicago: University of Chicago Press.

Robinson, Armstead L. 2005. *Bitter Fruits of Bondage: The Demise of Slavery and the Collapse of the Confederacy, 1861–1865.* Charlottesville: University of Virginia Press.

Robinson, Beverly. 2002. "The Sense of Self in Ritualizing New Performance Spaces for Survival." In *Black Theatre: Ritual Performance in the African Diaspora*, edited by Paul Carter Harrison, Victor Leo Walker, and Gus Edwards, 332–44. Philadelphia: Temple University Press.

Robinson, Cedric J. (1983) 2000. *Black Marxism: The Making of the Black Radical Tradition.* Chapel Hill: University of North Carolina Press.

———. 2007. *Forgeries of Memory and Meaning: Blacks and the Regimes of Race in American Theater and Film before World War II.* Chapel Hill: University of North Carolina Press.

Robinson, Dean. 2001. *Black Nationalism in American Politics and Thought.* Cambridge: Cambridge University Press.

Robinson, William I. 1992. *A Faustian Bargain: U.S. Intervention in the Nicaraguan Elections and American Foreign Policy in the Post–Cold War Era.* Boulder, CO: Westview.

Rock Hall. n.d. "Digital Classroom: Ruth Brown, 'Mama, He Treats Your Daughter Mean.'" Accessed 2017. www.rockhall.com.

Rodney, Walter. (1972) 1981. *How Europe Underdeveloped Africa.* Washington, DC: Howard University Press.

Rodríguez, Dylan. 2006. *Forced Passages: Imprisoned Radical Intellectuals and the U.S. Prison Regime.* Minneapolis: University of Minnesota Press.

———. 2007. "Forced Passages." In *Warfare in the American Homeland: Policing and Prison in a Penal Democracy*, edited by Joy James, 35–57. Durham, NC: Duke University Press.

———. 2009. "The Political Logic of the Non-profit Industrial Complex." In *The Revolution Will Not Be Funded*, edited by INCITE! Women of Color Against Violence, 21–40. Boston: South End.

———. 2015. *The Illiteracy of "Mass Incarceration": Racial Terror and the Insurgent Poetics of Evisceration.* Durham, NC: Duke University Press.

Roediger, David R. 2014. *Seizing Freedom: Slave Emancipation and Liberty for All.* New York: Verso.

Rogers, Ibram. 2012. *The Black Campus Movement: Black Students and the Racial Reconstitution of Higher Education, 1965–1972.* New York: Palgrave.

Rogers, Joel A. (1925) 1977. "Jazz at Home." In *The New Negro*, edited by Alain Locke, 99–224. New York: Atheneum.

Rogers, Reuel R. 2006. *Afro-Caribbean Immigrants and the Politics of Incorporation: Ethnicity, Exception, or Exit.* Cambridge: Cambridge University Press.

Rojas, Fabio. 2010. *From Black Power to Black Studies: How a Radical Social Movement Became an Academic Discipline.* Baltimore: Johns Hopkins University Press.

Rooks, Noliwe M. 2006. *White Money / Black Power: The Surprising History of African American Studies and the Crisis of Race in Higher Education.* Boston: Beacon.

Root, Maria P. P., ed. 1992. *Racial Mixed People in America.* Newbury Park, CA: Sage.

———, ed. 1996. *The Multiracial Experience: Racial Borders as the New Frontier.* Thousand Oaks, CA: Sage.

Rose, Tricia. 1994. *Black Noise: Rap Music and Black Culture in Contemporary America.* Hanover, NH: Wesleyan University Press.

Rosen, Hannah. 2009. *Terror in the Heart of Freedom: Citizenship, Sexual Violence, and the Meaning of Race in the Postemancipation South*. Chapel Hill: University of North Carolina Press.

Ross, Luana. 1998. *Inventing the Savage: the Social Construction of Native American Criminality*. Austin: University of Texas Press.

Ross, Marlon. 2004. *Manning the Race: Reforming Black Men in the Jim Crow Era*. New York: NYU Press.

Roth, Benita. 2004. *Separate Roads to Feminism: Black, Chicana, and White Feminist Movements in America's Second Wave*. Cambridge: Cambridge University Press.

Rothman, Adam. 2004. "The Domestication of the Slave Trade in the United States." In *The Chattel Principle: Internal Slave Trades in the Americas*, edited by Walter Johnson, 32–54. New Haven, CT: Yale University Press.

Royster, Francesca T. 2013. *Sounding like a No-No: Queer Sounds and Eccentric Acts in the Post-Soul Era*. Ann Arbor: University of Michigan Press.

Royster, Jacqueline Jones. 1996. Introduction to *Southern Horrors and Other Writings: The Anti-lynching Campaign of Ida B. Wells, 1892–1900*, edited by Jacqueline Jones Royster, 1–46. New York: Bedford / St. Martin's.

Russell-Wood, A. J. R. 1978. "Iberian Expansion and the Issue of Black Slavery: Changing Portuguese Attitudes, 1440–1770." *American Historical Review* 83 (1): 16–42.

———. 1995. "Before Columbus: Portugal's African Prelude to the Middle Passage and Contribution to Discourse on Race and Slavery." In *Race, Discourse, and the Origins of the America: A New World Views*, edited by Vera Lawrence Hyatt and Rex Nettleford, 134–68. Washington, DC: Smithsonian Institution Press.

Rustin, Bayard. 1965. "From Protest to Politics: The Future of the Civil Rights Movement." *Commentary* 39 (2): 25–31.

Ryan, William J. 1971. *Blaming the Victim*. New York: Pantheon.

Said, Edward W. 1979. *Orientalism*. New York: Vintage Books.

Sajnani, Damon. 2013. "Troubling the Trope of 'Rapper as Modern Griot.'" *Journal of Pan-African Studies* 6 (3): 156–80.

———. 2014. "Rapping in the Light: American Africanism and Rap Minstrelsy." *Souls: A Critical Journal of Black Politics, Culture and Society* 16 (3–4): 303–29.

———. 2015. "Remembering Monarchy, Forgetting Coloniality: The Elision of Race in Canadian Monarchy Abolition Debates." *Canadian Ethnic Studies* 47 (2): 137–63.

Salaam, Kalamu ya. 1972. "Food for Thought." In *New Black Voices*, edited by Abraham Chapman, 378–79. New York: Mentor.

Sanchez, Gabriel, and Natalie Masuoka. 2010. "Brown-Utility Heuristic? The Presence and Contributing Factors of Latino Linked Fate." *Hispanic Journal of Behavioral Sciences* 32:519–31.

Sarkar, Mela. 2008. "'Ousqu'on chill à soir?': Pratiques multilingues comme stratégies identitaires dans la communauté hip-hop montréalaise." *Diversité Urbaine* (Numéro thématique: Plurilinguisme et identités au Canada): 27–44.

Saunders, A. D. de C. M. 1982. *A Social History of Black Slaves and Freedom in Portugal, 1441–1555*. Cambridge: Cambridge University Press.

Saville, Julie. 1994. *The Work of Reconstruction: From Slave to Wage Laborer in South Carolina, 1860–1870*. Cambridge: Cambridge University Press.

Savitt, Todd. 1976. *Medicine and Slavery: The Diseases and Health Care of Blacks in Antebellum Virginia*. Urbana: University of Illinois Press.

Schechner, Richard. 2002. *Performance Studies: An Introduction*. New York: Routledge.

Schept, Judah. 2015. *Progressive Punishment: Job Loss, Jail Growth, and the Neoliberal Logic of Carceral Expansion*. New York: NYU Press.

Schmidt, Elizabeth. 2013. *Foreign Intervention in Africa: From the Cold War to the War on Terror*. New York: Cambridge University Press.

Schwalm, Leslie. 1997. *A Hard Fight for We: Women's Transition from Slavery to Freedom in South Carolina*. Urbana: University of Illinois Press.

———. 2009. *Emancipation's Diaspora: Race and Reconstruction in the Upper Midwest*. Chapel Hill: University of North Carolina Press.

Scott, Darieck. 2010. *Extravagant Abjection: Blackness, Power, and Sexuality in the African American Literary Imagination*. New York: NYU Press.

Scott, David. 1991. "That Event, This Memory: Notes on the Anthropology of African Diasporas in the New World." *Diaspora: A Journal of Transnational Studies* 1 (3): 261–84.

———. 2000. "The Re-enchantment of Humanism: An Interview with Sylvia Wynter." *Small Axe: A Caribbean Journal of Criticism* 8 (September): 119–207.

———. 2004. *Conscripts of Modernity: The Tragedy of Colonial Enlightenment*. Durham, NC: Duke University Press.

Scruton, Roger. (1981) 1995. *A Short History of Modern Philosophy: From Descartes to Wittgenstein*. New York: Routledge.

Sebastiani, Silvia. 2013. *The Scottish Enlightenment: Race, Gender, and the Limits of Progress*. London: Palgrave Macmillan.

Sexton, Danny. 2008. "Lifting the Veil: Revision and Double-Consciousness in Rita Dove's *The Darker Face of the Earth*." *Callaloo* 31 (3): 777–87.

Sexton, Jared. 2008. *Amalgamation Schemes: Antiblackness and the Critique of Multiracialism*. Minneapolis: University of Minnesota Press.

Shabazz, Rashad. 2015. *Spatializing Blackness: Architectures of Confinement and Black Masculinity in Chicago*. Urbana: University of Illinois Press.

Shah, Nayan. 2001. *Contagious Divides: Epidemics and Race in San Francisco's Chinatown*. Berkeley: University of California Press.

Shakur, Assata. (1987) 2001. *Assata: An Autobiography*. Chicago: Lawrence Hill Books, 2001.

Shakur, Tupac. 1996. "California Love." Featuring Dr. Dre and Roger Troutman. *All Eyez On Me*. Death Row Records.

Shange, Ntozake. 1975. *For Colored Girls Who Have Considered Suicide / When the Rainbow Is Enuf*. New York: Scribner.

———. 1992. "Fore/Play." In *Erotique Noire: Black Erotica*, edited by Miriam DeCosta-Willis, Reginald Martin, and Roseann P. Bell, xix–xx. New York: Doubleday.

Sharpe, Christina. 2010. *Monstrous Intimacies: Making Post-Slavery Subjects*. Durham, NC: Duke University Press.

———. 2014. "Black Studies: In the Wake." *Black Scholar* 44 (2): 59–69.

———. 2016. *In the Wake: On Blackness and Being*. Durham, NC: Duke University Press.

Shelby, Tommie. 2005. *We Who Are Dark: The Philosophical Foundations of Black Solidarity*. Cambridge, MA: Harvard University Press.

*Shelley v. Kraemer*. 1948. 334 U.S. 1.

Shemak, April. 2011. *Asylum Speakers: Caribbean Refugees and Testimonial Discourse*. New York: Fordham University Press.

Shepperson, George. 1962. "Pan-Africanism and 'Pan African-ism': Some Historical Notes." *Phylon* 23 (4): 346–58.

Shingles, Richard D. 1981. "Black Group Consciousness and Political Participation: The Missing Link." *American Political Science Review* 75 (1): 76–91.

Shire, Warsan. 2011. "Home." In *Teaching My Mother How to Give Birth*. London: Flipped Eye.

Shockley, Evie. 2011. "Going Overboard: African American Poetic Innovation and the Middle Passage." *Contemporary Literature* 52 (4): 791–817.

Shohat, Ella. 1992. "Notes on the 'Post-colonial.'" *Social Text* 31–32:99–113.

Silva, Denise Ferreira da. 2007. *Toward a Global Idea of Race*. Minneapolis: University of Minnesota Press.

Simien, Evelyn M. 2005. "Race, Gender, and Linked Fate." *Journal of Black Studies* 35 (5): 529–50.

———. 2006. *Black Feminist Voices in Politics*. New York: SUNY Press.

Simmons, Barbara. (1967) 2007. "Soul." In *Black Fire: An Anthology of Afro-American Writing*, edited by Amiri Baraka and Larry Neal, 304–8. Baltimore: Black Classic.

Simmons, William J. 1887. *Men of Mark: Eminent, Progressive, and Rising*. Cleveland, OH: Geo. M. Rewell.

Singh, Chaitram. 1988. *Guyana: Politics in a Plantation Society*. New York: Praeger.

Sinha, Manisha. 2016. *The Slave's Cause: A History of Abolition*. New Haven, CT: Yale University Press.

Skloot, Rebecca. 2010. *The Immortal Life of Henrietta Lacks*. New York: Random House.

Smallwood, Stephanie E. 2007. *Saltwater Slavery: A Middle Passage from Africa to American Diaspora*. Cambridge, MA: Harvard University Press.

Smedley, Audrey. 2007. "The History of the Idea of Race . . . and Why It Matters." Paper presented at the "Race, Human Variation and Disease: Consensus and Frontiers" conference, 14–17 March, Warrenton, VA. www.understandingrace.org.

Smethurst, James. 2006. *The Black Arts Movement: Literary Nationalism in the 1960s and 1970s*. Chapel Hill: University of North Carolina Press.

Smith, Barbara, ed. 1983. *Home Girls: A Black Feminist Anthology*. New York: Kitchen Table—Women of Color Press.

———. 2000. Introduction to *Home Girls: A Black Feminist Anthology*, xxi–lviii. New Brunswick, NJ: Rutgers University Press.

Smith, Candis Watts. 2014. *Black Mosaic: The Politics of Black Pan-ethnic Diversity*. New York: NYU Press.

Smith, Linda Tuhiwai. 1999. *Decolonizing Methodologies: Research and Indigenous Peoples*. London: Zed Books.

Smith, Shawn Michelle. 1999. *American Archives: Gender, Race, and Class in Visual Culture*. Princeton, NJ: Princeton University Press.

———. 2004. *Photography on the Color Line: W. E. B. Du Bois, Race, and Visual Culture*. Durham, NC: Duke University Press.

Smith, Valerie. 1998. *Not Just Race, Not Just Gender: Black Feminist Readings*. New York: Routledge.

Smitherman, Geneva. 2000. *Black Talk: Words and Phrase from the Hood to the Amen Corner*. Boston: Houghton Mifflin.

Smithsonian. 2016. *The National Museum of African American History and Culture: A Souvenir Book*. Washington, DC: Smithsonian Books.

Sneed, Roger A. 2010. *Representations of Homosexuality: Black Liberation Theology and Cultural Criticism*. New York: Palgrave Macmillan.

Snorton, C. Riley. 2017. *Black on Both Sides: A Racial History of Trans-Identity*. Minneapolis: University of Minnesota.

Snorton, C. Riley, and Jin Haritaworn. 2013. "Trans Necropolitics." In *The Transgender Studies Reader*, vol. 2, edited by Aren Aizura and Susan Stryker, 66–76. New York: Routledge.

Sobral, Ana. 2013. "The Survivor's Odyssey: K'naan's The Dusty Foot Philosopher as Modern Epic." *African American Review* 46 (1): 21–36.

Sohi, Seema. 2011. "Race, Surveillance, and Indian Anticolonialism in the Transnational Western U.S.-Canadian Borderlands." *Journal of American History* 98 (2): 420–36.

Sojoyner, Damien M. 2016. *First Strike: Educational Enclosures in Black Los Angeles*. Minneapolis: University of Minnesota Press.

Sollors, Werner. 1997. *Neither Black nor White yet Both: Thematic Explorations of Interracial Literature*. New York: Oxford University Press.

Somerville, Siobhan B. 2000. *Queering the Color Line: Race and the Invention of Homosexuality in American Culture*. Durham, NC: Duke University Press.

Soyinka, Wole. 2012. *Of Africa*. New Haven, CT: Yale University Press.

Spade, Dean. 2013. "Intersectional Resistance and Law Reform." *Signs: Journal of Women in Culture and Society* 38 (4): 1031–55.

Spade, Dean, Eric Stanley, and Queer Injustice. 2012. "Queering Prison Abolition, Now?" *American Quarterly* 61 (March): 115–27.

Spillers, Hortense J. 1987. "Mama's Baby, Papa's Maybe: An American Grammar Book." *Diacritics* 17 (2): 64–81. www.jstor.org.

———. 2003. *Black, White and in Color: Essays on American Literature and Culture*. Chicago: University of Chicago Press.

Spivak, Gayatri C. 1999. *A Critique of Postcolonial Reason: Toward a History of the Vanishing Present*. Cambridge, MA: Harvard University Press.

Springer, Kimberly. 2005. *Living for the Revolution: Black Feminist Organizations, 1968–1980*. Durham, NC: Duke University Press.

Stack, Carol. 1974. *All Our Kin*. New York: Basic Books.

Stampp, Kenneth. 1956. *The Peculiar Institution: Slavery in the Ante-bellum South*. New York: Vintage Books.

Stanard, Matthew G. 2011. *Selling the Congo: A History of European Pro-Empire Propaganda and the Making of Belgian Imperialism*. Lincoln: University of Nebraska Press.

Stanley, Amy Dru. 1998. *From Bondage to Contract: Wage Labor, Marriage, and the Market in the Age of Slave Emancipation*. Cambridge: Cambridge University Press.

Stanley, Eric A., and Nat Smith. 2015. *Captive Genders: Trans Embodiment and the Prison Industrial Complex*. 2nd ed. Oakland, CA: AK.

Stanton, Fred, ed. 1980. *Fighting Racism in World War II*. New York: Pathfinder.

Staples, Robert. 1971. *The Black Family: Essays and Studies*. Belmont, CA: Wadsworth.

———. 1973. *The Black Woman in America: Sex, Marriage, and the Family*. Chicago: NelHall.

———. 1974. "Has the Sexual Revolution Bypassed Blacks?" *Ebony*, 29 April, 111–14.

———. 1979. "The Myth of the Black Macho: A Response to Angry Black Feminists." *Black Scholar* 10 (6–7): 24–33. www.jstor.org.

Stasiulis, Daiva, and Nira Yuval-Davis, eds. 1995. *Understanding Settler Societies: Articulations of Gender, Race, Ethnicity and Class*. London: Sage.

Steel Pulse. 1979. *Tribute to the Martyrs*. Island Records.

Steinberg, Stephen. 2007. *Race Relations: A Critique*. Stanford, CA: Stanford University Press.

Stephens, Michelle. 1998. "Black Transnationalism and the Politics of National Identity: West Indian Intellectuals in Harlem in the Age of War and Revolution." *American Quarterly* 50 (3): 592–608.

———. 2005. *Black Empire: The Masculine Global Imaginary of Caribbean Intellectuals in the United States, 1914–1962*. Durham, NC: Duke University Press.

Stevenson, Brenda. 2015. *The Contested Murder of Latasha Harlins: Justice, Gender, and the Origins of the LA Riots*. New York: Oxford University Press.

Stewart, Jacqueline Najuma. 2005. *Migrating to the Movies: Cinema and Black Urban Modernity*. Berkeley: University of California Press.

Stuckey, Sterling. 1987. *Slave Culture: Nationalist Theory and the Foundations of Black America*. New York: Oxford University Press.

Sudbury (Oparah), Julia. 2005. *Global Lockdown: Race, Gender, and the Prison-Industrial Complex*. New York: Routledge.

Sugarhill Gang. 1979. "Rapper's Delight." *Sugarhill Gang*. Sylvia Robinson.

Sugrue, Thomas. 2008. *Sweet Land of Liberty: The Forgotten Struggle for Civil Rights in the North*. New York: Random House.

———. 2014. *The Origins of the Urban Crisis: Race and Inequality in Postwar Detroit*. Princeton, NJ: Princeton University Press.

Summers, Martin. 2004. *Manliness and Its Discontents: The Black Middle Class and the Transformation of Masculinity, 1900–1930*. Chapel Hill: University of North Carolina Press.

Sussmann, Robert Wald. 2014. "There Is No Such Thing as Race." *Newsweek*, 11 November. www.newsweek.com.

Sweet, James H. 1996. "Male Homosexuality and Spiritism in the African Diaspora: The Legacies of a Link." *Journal of the History of Sexuality* 7 (2): 184–202.

Sykes, Bobbi. 1998. *Snake Dancing*. Sydney: Allen and Unwin.

Taketani, Etsuko. 2014. *The Black Pacific Narrative: Geographic Imaginings of Race and Empire between the World Wars*. Hanover, NH: Dartmouth University Press.

Tannenbaum, Rob. 2017. "How Best Rock Performance Became One of the Grammys' Weirdest Races." *New York Times*, 6 February. www.nytimes.com.

Tasch, Barbara. 2015. "The 23 Poorest Countries in the World." *Business Insider*, 13 July. www.businessinsider.com.

Tate, Claudia. 1992. *Domestic Allegories of Political Desire: The Black Heroine's Text at the Turn of the Century*. New York: Oxford University Press.

Tate, Greg. (1986) 1992. "Cult-Nats Meet Freaky-Deke: The Return of the Black Aesthetic." In *Flyboy in the Buttermilk: Essays on Contemporary America*, edited by Greg Tate, 198–209. New York: Simon and Schuster.

———. 2017. "Chuck Berry: The Double-Helix of Rock & Roll." *Village Voice*, 22 March. www.villagevoice.com.

Tate, Katherine. 1993. *From Protest to Politics: The New Black Voters in American Elections*. New York: Russell Sage Foundation.

Taylor, A. A. 1924. *The Negro in South Carolina during the Reconstruction*. Washington, DC: Association for the Study of Negro Life and History.

Taylor, Keeanga-Yamahtta. 2016. *From #BlackLivesMatter to Black Liberation*. Chicago: Haymarket Books.

———, ed. 2017. *How We Get Free: Black Feminism and the Combahee River Collective*. Chicago: Haymarket Books.

Taylor, Mildred D. 1976. *Roll of Thunder Hear My Cry*. New York: Penguin Books.

Taylor, Susie King. 1902. *Reminiscences of My Life in Camp with the 33rd United States Colored Troops Late 1st S.C. Volunteers*. Boston: Published by the Author.

Taylor, Ula Yvette. 2002. *The Veiled Garvey: The Life and Times of Amy Jacques Garvey*. Chapel Hill: University of North Carolina Press.

Templeton, Alan. 1998. "Human Races: A Genetic and Evolutionary Perspective." *American Anthropologist* 100:632–50.

Terborg-Penn, Rosalyn. 1998. *African American Women in the Struggle for the Vote, 1850–1920*. Bloomington: Indiana University Press.

Theoharis, Jeanne, and Komozi Woodard, eds. 2003. *Freedom North: Black Freedom Struggles outside the South*. New York: Palgrave Macmillan.

Thomas, Deborah A. 2011. *Exceptional Violence: Embodied Citizenship in Transnational Jamaica*. Durham, NC: Duke University Press.

Thomas, William I., and Dorothy Swain Thomas. 1928. *The Child in America: Behavior Problems and Programs*. New York: Knopf.

Thuma, Emily. 2015. "Lessons in Self-Defense: Gender Violence, Racial Criminalization and Anticarceral Feminism." *WSQ: Women's Studies Quarterly* 43 (Fall–Winter): 52–71.

Tillmon, Johnnie. 1972. "Welfare Is a Women's Issue." *Ms.* 1:1113–16.

Tinsley, Omise'eke Natasha. 2008. "Black Atlantic, Queer Atlantic: Queer Imaginings of the Middle Passage." *GLQ: A Journal of Lesbian and Gay Studies* 14 (2–3): 191–215.

———. 2010. *Thiefing Sugar: Eroticism between Women in Caribbean Literature*. Durham, NC: Duke University Press.

Tocqueville, Alexis de. 1841. *Democracy in America*. Translated by Harry Reeve. 4th ed. New York: Langley.

Truth, Sojourner. (1850) 1993. *Narrative of Sojourner Truth*. New York: Vintage Books.

Tucker, Mark. 1995. *The Duke Ellington Reader*. New York: Oxford University Press.

Ture, Kwame (formerly Stokely Carmichael), and Charles V. Hamilton. 2011. *Black Power: Politics of Liberation in America*. New York: Knopf Doubleday.

Turvey, Brent W. 2002. "A History of Criminal Profiling." In *Criminal Profiling: An Introduction to Behavioral Evidence Analysis*, edited by Brent Turvey, 1–20. New York: Academic.

Tushnet, Mark. 1987. *The NAACP's Legal Strategy against Segregated Education, 1925–1950*. Chapel Hill: University of North Carolina Press.

———. 1996. *Making Civil Rights Law: Thurgood Marshall and the Supreme Court, 1936–1961*. New York: Oxford University Press.

U.S. Bureau of Indian Affairs. n.d. Home page. Accessed 1 January 2018. www.bia.gov.

U.S. Census Bureau. 2010a. "Dynamics of Economic Well-Being: Spells of Unemployment, 2004–2007." *Current Population Reports*, July. www.census.gov.

———. 2010b. *Income, Poverty, and Health Coverage in the United States: 2009*. September. www.census.gov.

———. 2011. "The Black Population: 2010." *2010 Census Briefs*, September. www.census.gov.

U.S. Department of Justice. 2015. *Department of Justice Report Regarding the Criminal Investigation into the Shooting Death of Michael Brown by Ferguson, Missouri Police Officer Darren Wilson*. Washington, DC: U.S. Government Printing Office.

Useem, Bert. 1997. "The State and Collective Disorders: The Los Angeles Riot/Protest of April, 1992." *Social Forces* 76 (2): 357–77.

U.S. Government Accountability Office. 2007. *African American Children in Foster Care: Additional HHS Assistance Needed to Help States Reduce the Proportion in Care.* 11 July. www.gao.gov.

U.S. National Advisory Commission on Civil Disorders. 1968. *Report of the National Advisory Commission on Civil Disorders.* Washington, DC: U.S. Government Printing Office.

Van Deburg, William L. 1992. *New Day in Babylon: The Black Power Movement and American Culture, 1965–1975.* Chicago: University of Chicago Press.

Van Peebles, Melvin, dir. 1971. *Sweet Sweetback's Baadasssss Song.* DVD. Xenon Pictures, 2002.

Van Sertima, Ivan. (1976) 2003. *They Came before Columbus: The African Presence in Ancient America.* Reprint. New York: Random House.

Vasquez, Xavier. 1993. "The North American Free Trade Agreement and Environmental Racism." *Harvard International Law Journal* 34 (2): 357–79.

Veracini, Lorenzo. 2015. *The Settler Colonial Present.* New York: Palgrave Macmillan.

Vernon, Grenville. (1919) 2014. "That Mysterious Jazz." *New York Tribune,* 30 March, sec. 4, p. 5. Reprinted in *Keeping Time: Readings in Jazz History,* edited by Robert Walser, 10–12. New York: Oxford University Press. Citations refer to the reprinted edition.

Vinson, Robert Trent. 2012. *The Americans Are Coming! Dreams of African American Liberation in Segregationist South Africa.* Athens: Ohio University Press.

Vizenor, Gerald. 1999. *Manifest Manners: Narratives on Postindian Survivance.* Lincoln: University of Nebraska Press.

Von Eschen, Penny M. 1997. *Race against Empire: Black Americans and Anticolonialism, 1937–1957.* Ithaca, NY: Cornell University Press.

Wacquant, Loïc. 2009. *Prisons of Poverty.* Minneapolis: University of Minnesota Press.

Wagner, Bryan. 2009. *Disturbing the Peace: Black Culture and the Police Power after Slavery.* Cambridge, MA: Harvard University Press.

Wald, Gayle. 2000. *Crossing the Line: Racial Passing in Twentieth-Century U.S. Literature and Culture.* Durham, NC: Duke University Press.

———. 2008. *Shout, Sister, Shout! The Untold Story of Rock-and-Roll Trailblazer Sister Rosetta Tharpe.* Boston: Beacon.

———. 2015. *It's Been Beautiful: Soul! and Black Power Television.* Durham, NC: Duke University Press.

Walker, Alice. 1982. *The Color Purple.* Boston: Houghton Mifflin Harcourt.

———. 1983. *In Search of Our Mother's Gardens: Womanist Prose.* Orlando, FL: Harcourt Books.

Walker, Cherryl. 2008. *Landmarked: Land Claims and Land Restitution in South Africa.* Johannesburg: Jacana Media.

Walker, David. (1829) 1995. *David Walker's Appeal, in Four Articles; Together with a Preamble, to the Coloured Citizens of the World, but in Particular, and Very Expressly, to Those of the United States of America.* Edited by Sean Wilentz. New York: Hill and Wang.

Wall, Cheryl. 1995. *Women of the Harlem Renaissance.* Bloomington: Indiana University Press.

Wallace, Julia R., and Kai M. Green. 2013. "Tranifest: Queer Futures." *GLQ: A Journal of Lesbian and Gay Studies* 19 (4): 568–69.

Wallace, Michele. 1979. *Black Macho and the Myth of the Superwoman.* New York: Dial.

———. 1990. "Variations on Negation and the Heresy of Black Feminist Creativity." In *Reading Black, Reading Feminist: A Critical Anthology,* edited by Henry Louis Gates Jr., 52–67. New York: Meridian.

Wallace-Wells, Benjamin. 2006. "Is America Too Racist for Barack? Too Sexist for Hillary?" *Washington Post,* 12 November, B01.

Ward, Prothero, and Leathes. 1912. "The Colonization of Africa, 1870–1910." In *The Cambridge Modern History Atlas.* New York: Macmillan. http://etc.usf.edu.

Warren, Wendy. 2016. *New England Bound: Slavery and Colonization in Early America.* New York: Liveright.

Washington, Harriet A. 2006. *Medical Apartheid: The Dark History of Medical Experimentation on Black Americans from Colonial Times to the Present.* New York: Doubleday.

Washington, Margaret. n.d. "Rachel Weeping for Her Children: Black Women and the Abolition of Slavery." *History Now: Journal of the Gilder Lehrman Institute.* Accessed 14 May 2018. http://oa.gilderlehrman.org.

Washington, Mary Helen, ed. 1975. *Black-Eyed Susans: Classic Stories by and about Black Women.* Garden City, NY: Anchor Books.

———, ed. 1980. *Midnight Birds: Stories by Contemporary Black Women Writers.* Garden City, NY: Anchor Books.

Wa Thiong'o, Ngugi. 1986. *Decolonising the Mind: The Politics of Language in African Literature.* London: James Currey / Heinemann.

Watkins-Owens, Irma. 1996. *Blood Relations: Caribbean Immigrants and the Harlem Community, 1900–1930.* Bloomington: Indiana University Press.

Watson, Veronica. 2011. "Demythologizing Whiteness in Frank Yerby's The Foxes of Harrow." *Journal of Ethnic American Literature* 1:90–110.

Wax, Darold. 1967. "The Demand for Slave Labor in Colonial Pennsylvania." *Pennsylvania History* 34:331–45.

Weaver, Jace. 2014. *The Red Atlantic: American Indigenes and the Making of the Modern World, 1000–1927*. Chapel Hill: University of North Carolina Press.

Wekker, Gloria. 2006. *The Politics of Passion: Women's Sexual Culture in the Afro-Surinamese Diaspora*. New York: Columbia University Press.

Weinbaum, Alys. 2013. "W. E. B. Du Bois's Black Reconstruction and Black Feminism's 'Propaganda of History.'" *South Atlantic Quarterly* 112 (Summer): 437–63.

Weisenfeld, Judith. 2017. *A New World A-Coming: Black Religion and Racial Identity during the Great Migration*. New York: NYU Press.

Wells-Barnett, Ida B. (1892) 1996. *Southern Horrors and Other Writings: The Anti-Lynching Campaign of Ida B. Wells, 1892–1900*. Boston: Bedford / St. Martin's.

———. (1892) 2002. *On Lynchings*. Amherst, NY: Humanity Books.

———. 1900. *Mob Rule in New Orleans: Robert Charles and His Fight to Death, the Story of His Life, Burning Human Beings Alive, Other Lynching Statistics*. Chicago: Ida B. Wells-Barnett.

———. 1917. *The East St. Louis Massacre: The Greatest Outrage of the Century*. Chicago: Negro Fellowship Herald Press.

———. 1970. *Crusade for Justice: The Autobiography of Ida B. Wells*. Edited by Alfreda M. Duster. Chicago: University of Chicago Press.

Welsing, Frances Cress. 1991. *The Isis (Yssis) Papers*. Chicago: Third World.

Wheatley, Phyllis. (1773) 1989. *Poems on Various Subjects, Religious and Moral*. In *The Poems of Phyllis Wheatley*, rev. ed., edited by Julian D. Mason Jr., 41–112. Chapel Hill: University of North Carolina Press.

———. 2001. *Complete Writings*. Edited by Vincent Carretta. New York: Penguin Books.

White, Deborah Gray. (1985) 1999. *Ar'n't I a Woman? Female Slaves in the Plantation South*. New York: Norton.

White, E. Francis. 2001. *Dark Continent of Our Bodies: Black Feminism and the Politics of Respectability*. Philadelphia: Temple University Press.

Whites, LeAnn. 1995. *The Civil War as a Crisis in Gender: Augusta, Georgia, 1860–1890*. Athens: University of Georgia Press.

Wiebe, Robert H. 1967. *The Search for Order, 1877–1920*. New York: Hill and Wang.

Wiegman, Robyn. 1995. *American Anatomies: Theorizing Race and Gender*. Durham, NC: Duke University Press.

Wilder, Craig Steven. 2013. *Ebony and Ivy: Race, Slavery, and the Troubled History of America's Universities*. New York: Bloomsbury.

Williams, Eric. (1944) 2014. *Capitalism and Slavery*. Chapel Hill: University of North Carolina Press.

Williams, Erica Lorraine. 2013. *Sex Tourism in Bahia: Ambiguous Entanglements*. Urbana: University of Illinois Press.

Williams, Heather Andrea. 2005. *Self-Taught: African American Education in Slavery and Freedom*. Chapel Hill: University of North Carolina Press.

Williams, John A. 1967. *The Man Who Cried I Am: A Novel*. Boston: Little, Brown.

Williams, Kim M. 2006. *Mark One or More: Civil Rights in Multiracial America*. Ann Arbor: University of Michigan Press.

Williams, Raymond. 1983. *Keywords: A Vocabulary of Culture and Society*. New York: Oxford University Press.

———. 1985. *Keywords: A Vocabulary of Culture and Society*. Rev. ed. New York: Oxford University Press.

Williams, Robert A., Jr. 1990. *The American Indian in Western Legal Thought: The Discourses of Conquest*. New York: Oxford University Press.

Willis, Ellen. 2011. "Beginning to See the Light." In *Out of the Vinyl Deeps: Ellen Willis on Rock Music*, edited by Nona Willis Aronowitz, 148–56. Minneapolis: University of Minnesota Press.

Willoughby-Herard, Tiffany. 2016. "Abolition and Kinship." *Abolition Journal*, 24 May. https://abolitionjournal.org.

Wilson, Charles Erwin. 1947. *To Secure These Rights: The Report of the President's Committee on Civil Rights*. New York: Simon and Schuster.

Wilson, Olly. 1983. "Black Music as an Art Form." *Black Music Research Journal* 3:1–22.

Wilson, William Julius. 1980. *The Declining Significance of Race: Blacks and Changing American Institutions*. Chicago: University of Chicago Press.

Winn, Maisha T. 2011. *Girl Time: Literacy, Justice, and School-to-Prison Pipeline*. New York: Teachers College Press.

Wish, Harvey. 1937. "American Slave Insurrections before 1861." *Journal of Negro History* 22 (3): 299–320.

———, ed. 1964. *Slavery in the South: First-hand Accounts of the Ante-bellum American Southland*. New York: Farrar, Straus.

Wolfe, Patrick. 1999. *Settler Colonialism and the Transformation of Anthropology: The Politics and Poetics of an Ethnographic Event*. London: Cassell.

———. 2006. "Settler Colonialism and the Elimination of the Native." *Journal of Genocide Research* 8 (4): 387–409.

Wolfers, Justin, David Leonhardt, and Kevin Quealy. 2015. "1.5 Missing Black Men." *New York Times*, 20 April. www.nytimes.com.

Wonder, Stevie. 1973. "Living for the City." Motown.

Woods, Clyde. 2000. *Development Arrested: The Blues and Plantation Power in the Mississippi Delta*. London: Verso.

Woodson, Carter G. 1933. *The Miseducation of the Negro*. Washington, DC: Associated.

Woodward, C. Vann. 1966. *The Strange Career of Jim Crow*. New York: Oxford University Press.

World Bank. n.d. "GDP." Accessed 1 January 2018. http://data.worldbank.org.

Wright, Michelle. 2004. *Becoming Black: Creating Identity in the African Diaspora*. Durham, NC: Duke University Press.

———. 2015. *Physics of Blackness: Beyond the Middle Passage Epistemology*. Minneapolis: University of Minnesota Press.

Wright, Richard. 1940. *Native Son*. New York: Harper Perennial.

Wun, Connie. 2016. "Angered: Black and Non-Black Girls of Color at the Intersections of Violence and School Discipline in the United States." *Race, Ethnicity and Education*, 1–15. DOI: 10.1080/13613324.2016.1248829.

Wynter, Sylvia. 1990. "Afterword: Beyond Miranda's Meanings: Un/silencing the 'Demonic Ground' of Caliban's 'Woman.'" In *Out of the Kumbla: Caribbean Women and Literature*, edited by Carol Boyce Davies and Elaine Savory Fido, 355–72. Trenton, NJ: Africa World.

———. 1991. "Columbus and the Poetics of the Propter Nos." *Annals of Scholarship* 8 (2): 251–86.

———. 1995. "1492: A New World View." In *Race, Discourse, and the Origins of the America: A New World Views*, edited by Vera Lawrence Hyatt and Rex Nettleford, 5–57. Washington, DC: Smithsonian Institution Press.

———. 2003. "Unsettling the Coloniality of Being/Power/Truth/Freedom: Towards the Human, after Man, Its Overrepresentation—An Argument." *CR: The New Centennial Review* 3 (3): 257–337.

Wynter, Sylvia, and Katherine McKittrick. 2015. "Unparalleled Catastrophe for Our Species? Or, To Give Humanness a Different Future: Conversations." In *On Being Human as Praxis*, edited by Katherine McKittrick, 9–89. Durham, NC: Duke University Press.

Yellin, Jean Fagan. 1989. *Women and Sisters: The Antislavery Feminists in American Culture*. New Haven, CT: Yale University Press.

Yerby, Frank. 1946. *The Foxes of Harrow*. New York: Dial.

Young, Cynthia. 2006. *Soul Power: Culture Radicalism, and the Making of a U.S. Third World Left*. Durham, NC: Duke University Press.

Young, Kevin. 2012. *Ardency: A Chronicle of the Amistad Rebels*. New York: Knopf.

Young, Robert J. C. 1995. *Colonial Desire: Hybridity in Theory, Culture and Race*. London: Routledge.

Yuval-Davis, Nira. 2011. *The Politics of Belonging: Intersectional Contestations*. London: Sage.

Zack, Naomi. 1993. *Race and Mixed Race*. Philadelphia: Temple University Press.

———. 1995. *American Mixed Race: The Culture of Microdiversity*. Lanham, MD: Rowman and Littlefield.

Zackodnik, Teresa C. 2011. *Press, Platform, Pulpit: Black Feminist Politics in the Era of Reform*. Knoxville: University of Tennessee Press.

# About the Contributors

Marlon M. Bailey is Associate Professor of Women and Gender Studies in the School of Social Transformation at Arizona State University, Tempe. He is the author of *Butch Queens Up in Pumps: Gender, Performance, and Ballroom Culture in Detroit* (2013), which received the Alan Bray Memorial Book Prize by the GL/Q Caucus from the Modern Language Association in 2014.

Stephanie Leigh Batiste is Associate Professor of Black Studies and English at the University of California at Santa Barbara. She is the author of *Darkening Mirrors: Imperial Representation in Depression-Era African American Performance* (2012).

Daphne A. Brooks is Professor of African American Studies and Theater Studies at Yale University. She is the author of two books, *Bodies in Dissent: Spectacular Performances of Race and Freedom, 1850–1910* (2006), and *Jeff Buckley's Grace* (2005).

Jayna Brown is Professor of Media Studies at Pratt Institute. She is the author of *Babylon Girls: Black Women Performers and the Shaping of the Modern* (2008) and *Black Utopias: Speculative Life and the Music of Other Worlds* (forthcoming).

David Canton is Associate Professor of History and Director of the Africana Studies Program at Connecticut College. He is the author *Raymond Pace Alexander: A New Negro Lawyer Fights for Civil Rights in Philadelphia* (2010).

Erin D. Chapman is Associate Professor of History at George Washington University. She is the author of *Prove It on Me: New Negroes, Sex, and Popular Culture in the 1920s* (2012).

Ashon Crawley is Assistant Professor of Religious Studies and African American and African Studies at the University of Virginia. He is the author of *Blackpentecostal Breath: The Aesthetics of Possibility* (2016).

Erica R. Edwards is Associate Professor of English at Rutgers University, New Brunswick. She is an expert in African American literature and culture and the author of *Charisma and the Fictions of Black Leadership* (2012).

Daylanne K. English is Professor of English at Macalester College. She is the author of *Unnatural Selections: Eugenics in American Modernism and the Harlem Renaissance* (2004) and *Each Hour Redeem: Time and Justice in African American Literature* (2013).

Roderick A. Ferguson is a faculty member in the Department of African American Studies and the Gender and Women's Studies Program at the University of Illinois at Chicago. He is the author of *One-Dimensional Queer* (2018), *We Demand: The University and Student Protests* (2017), *The Reorder of Things: The University and Its Pedagogies of Minority Difference* (2012), and *Aberrations in Black: Toward a Queer of Color*

*Critique* (2004) and coeditor with Grace Hong of *Strange Affinities: The Gender and Sexual Politics of Comparative Racialization* (2011).

Michael Boyce Gillespie is Associate Professor of Film at City College of New York, CUNY. He is the author of *Film Blackness: American Cinema and the Idea of Black Film* (2016).

Lewis R. Gordon is Professor of Philosophy at UCONN-Storrs, Honorary President and Core Professor at the Global Center for Advanced Studies, and Honorary Professor at the Unit of the Humanities at Rhodes University (UHURU), South Africa. He is the author of many books, including *An Introduction to Africana Philosophy* (2008) and, more recently, *What Fanon Said* (2015).

Sarah Haley is Associate Professor of African American Studies and Gender Studies at the University of California, Los Angeles. She is the author of *No Mercy Here: Gender, Punishment, and the Making of Jim Crow Modernity* (2016).

Allyson Hobbs is Associate Professor of American History and Director of African and African American Studies at Stanford University. She is the author of *A Chosen Exile: A History of Racial Passing in American Life* (2014), which won the Frederick Jackson Turner Award and the Lawrence W. Levine Award presented by the Organization of American Historians.

Habiba Ibrahim is Associate Professor of English at the University of Washington. She is the author of *Troubling the Family: The Promise of Personhood and the Rise of Multiracialism* (2012).

Shona N. Jackson is Associate Professor of English at Texas A&M University. She is the author of *Creole Indigeneity: Between Myth and Nation in the Caribbean* (2012).

Tsitsi Jaji is Associate Professor of English and African & African American Studies at Duke University. She is the author of *Africa in Stereo: Modernism, Music, and Pan-African Solidarity* (2014) and two volumes of poetry, *Beating the Graves* (2017) and *Carnaval* (2014).

Jennifer James is Associate Professor of English and Director of Africana Studies at the George Washington University and author of *A Freedom Bought with Blood: African American War Literature, the Civil War–World War II* (2007).

Régine Michelle Jean-Charles is Associate Professor of Romance Languages and Literatures and African and African Diaspora Studies at Boston College. She is the author of *Conflict Bodies: The Politics of Rape Representation in the Francophone Imaginary* (2014).

Hasan Kwame Jeffries is Associate Professor of History at The Ohio State University. He is the author of *Bloody Lowndes: Civil Rights and Black Power in Alabama's Black Belt* (2009).

Candice M. Jenkins is Associate Professor of English at the University of Illinois at Urbana-Champaign. She is the author of *Private Lives, Proper Relations: Regulating Black Intimacy* (2007), which received the William Sanders Scarborough Prize presented by the Modern Language Association.

Meta DuEwa Jones is Associate Professor in the Department of English at University of North Carolina at Chapel Hill. She is the author of *The Muse Is Music: Jazz Poetry from the Harlem Renaissance to the Spoken Word* (2011), which received honorable mention for the William Sanders Scarborough Prize presented by the Modern Language Association.

Trica Keaton is Associate Professor of African Diaspora Studies at Dartmouth College. She is the author of *Muslim Girls and the Other France* (2006) and coeditor of *Black Europe and the African Diaspora* (2009, with Tyler Stovall) and *Black France / France Noire: The History and Politics of Blackness* (2015, with Darlene Clark Hine and Stephen Small).

Xavier Livermon is Assistant Professor of African and African Diaspora Studies at the University of Texas at Austin. He is author of *Performing Freedom: Kwaito and the Politics of Sound in Post-Apartheid South Africa* (forthcoming).

Emily J. Lordi is Associate Professor of English at the University of Massachusetts, Amherst, and the author of two books: *Black Resonance: Iconic Women Singers and African American Literature* (2013) and *Donny Hathaway Live* (2016).

LeRhonda S. Manigault-Bryant is Associate Professor of Africana Studies at Williams College. She is the author of *Talking to the Dead: Religion, Music, and Lived Memory among Gullah/Geechee Women* (2014) and coauthor of *Womanist and Black Feminist Responses to Tyler Perry's Productions* (2014, with Tamura A. Lomax and Carol B. Duncan).

Charles W. McKinney Jr. is the Neville Frierson Bryan Chair of Africana Studies and Associate Professor of History at Rhodes College. His most recent book

(coedited with Aram Goudsouzian) is *An Unseen Light: Black Struggles for Freedom in Memphis, Tennessee* (2018).

Quincy T. Mills is Associate Professor of History and Director of Africana Studies at Vassar College. He is the author of *Cutting along the Color Line: Black Barbers and Barber Shops in America* (2013).

Michele Mitchell is Associate Professor of History at New York University. Her most recent book (coedited with Naoko Shibusawa and Stephan F. Miescher) is *Gender, Imperialism, and Global Exchanges* (2015).

Nick Mitchell is Assistant Professor of Humanities at the University of California at Santa Cruz and is at work on a manuscript titled "Disciplinary Matters: Black Studies, Women's Studies, and the Neoliberal University."

Fred Moten is Professor of Performance Studies at New York University. His most recent book is *Black and Blur* (2017).

Roopali Mukherjee is Associate Professor of Media Studies at the City University of New York, Queens College. She is the author of *The Racial Order of Things: Cultural Imaginaries of the Post-Soul Era* (2006) and coeditor of *Race Post-Race: Culture, Critique and the Color Line* (forthcoming).

Sowande' M. Mustakeem is Associate Professor of History and African American Studies at Washington University in St. Louis. She is the author of *Slavery at Sea: Terror, Sex, and Sickness in the Middle Passage* (2016).

Shayla C. Nunnally is Associate Professor of Political Science and Africana Studies Institute at the University of Connecticut. She is the author of *Trust in Black*

*America: Race, Discrimination, and Politics* (NYU Press, 2012).

Jeffrey O. G. Ogbar is Professor of History and Founding Director of the Center for the Study of Popular Music at the University of Connecticut. He is the editor or author of multiple books, including *Black Power: Radical Politics and African American Identity* (2004) and *Hip-Hop Revolution: The Culture and Politics of Rap* (2007).

Samantha Pinto is Associate Professor of English and African American Studies at Georgetown University. She is the author of *Difficult Diasporas: The Transnational Feminist Aesthetic of the Black Atlantic* (NYU Press, 2013), which received the 2013 William Sanders Scarborough Prize from the Modern Language Association.

Eric Porter is Professor of History and History of Consciousness at the University of California at Santa Cruz. His most recent book, coauthored with the photographer Lewis Watts, is *New Orleans Suite: Music and Culture in Transition* (2013).

Reiland Rabaka is Professor of African, African American, and Caribbean Studies in the Department of Ethnic Studies at the University of Colorado, Boulder. He is the author of more than a dozen books, most recently *The Negritude Movement: W. E. B. Du Bois, Leon Damas, Aime Cesaire, Leopold Senghor, Frantz Fanon, and the Evolution of an Insurgent Idea* (2015).

Shana L. Redmond is Associate Professor of Musicology and African American Studies at UCLA. She is the author of *Anthem: Social Movements and the Sound of Solidarity in the African Diaspora* (NYU Press, 2014) and the forthcoming *Everything Man: The Form and Function of Paul Robeson*.

Dylan Rodríguez is Professor at the University of California, Riverside, and the author of two books: *Forced Passages: Imprisoned Radical Intellectuals and the U.S. Prison Regime* (2006) and *Suspended Apocalypse: White Supremacy, Genocide, and the Filipino Condition* (2009).

David Roediger is Foundation Distinguished Professor of American Studies at the University of Kansas. His recent work includes *Class, Race, and Marxism* (2017) and, with Elizabeth Esch, *The Production of Difference* (2012).

Damon Chandru Sajnani is Assistant Professor of African Cultural Studies at the University of Wisconsin–Madison. He is working on a book titled "The African HipHop Movement: Youth Culture and Democracy in Senegal."

Rashad Shabazz is Associate Professor of Justice and Social Inquiry at Arizona State University. He is the author of *Spatializing Blackness: Architectures of Confinement and Black Masculinity in Chicago* (2015).

James Smethurst is Professor of Afro-American Studies at the University of Massachusetts, Amherst. His most recent book is titled *From Reconstruction to Renaissance: Turn-of-Century African American Literature and the Invention of U.S. Modernism* (forthcoming).

C. Riley Snorton is Associate Professor of Africana Studies and Feminist, Gender, and Sexuality Studies at Cornell University. He is the author of *Black on Both Sides: A Racial History of Trans Identity* (2017) and *Nobody Is Supposed to Know: Black Sexuality on the Down Low* (2014).

Damien M. Sojoyner is Assistant Professor of Anthropology at the University of California, Irvine. He is the author of *First Strike: Educational Enclosures of Black Los Angeles* (2016).

L. H. Stallings is Professor of Women's Studies at the University of Maryland–College Park. She is the author of *Mutha Is Half a Word! Intersections of Folklore, Vernacular, Myth, and Queerness in Black Female Culture* (2007) and *Funk the Erotic: Transaesthetics and Black Sexual Cultures* (2015).

Quito Swan is Professor of African Diaspora History at Howard University. He is the author of *Black Power in Bermuda: The Struggle for Decolonization* (2010).

Lisa B. Thompson is Associate Professor of African and African Diaspora Studies at the University of Texas at Austin. Thomson is the author of *Beyond the Black Lady: Sexuality and the New African American Middle Class* (2012).

Bryan Wagner is Associate Professor of English at the University of California, Berkeley. His books include *Disturbing the Peace: Black Culture and the Police Power after Slavery* (2009) and *The Tar Baby: A Global History* (2017).

Rebecca Wanzo is Associate Professor of Women, Gender, and Sexuality Studies at Washington University in St. Louis. She is the author of *The Suffering Will Not Be Televised: African American Women and Sentimental Political Storytelling* (2009) and various essays in the fields of popular culture, African American literature, critical race theory, and feminist media studies.

Fanon Che Wilkins is Associate Professor of American Studies at Doshisha University. He is the coeditor, with Michael O. West and William G. Martin, of *From*

*Toussaint to Tupac: The Black International since the Age of Revolution* (2009).

Yohuru Williams is Professor of History and Dean and McQuinn Distinguished Chair of the College of Arts and Sciences at the University of St. Thomas in Minnesota. He is the author, coauthor, and editor of numerous books including *Rethinking the Black Freedom Movement* (2016) and *The Black Panthers: Portraits from an Unfinished Revolution* (2016).

Michelle M. Wright is the Augustus Baldwin Longstreet Professor of English at Emory University. She is the author of *Becoming Black: Creating Identity in the African Diaspora* (2004) and *Physics of Blackness: Beyond the Middle Passage Epistemology* (2015).